Exploring Picard's

Exploring Picard's Galaxy

Essays on
Star Trek: The Next Generation

Edited by PETER W. LEE

McFarland & Company, Inc., Publishers
Jefferson, North Carolina

ISBN (print) 978-1-4766-6661-7
ISBN (ebook) 978-1-4766-3096-0

LIBRARY OF CONGRESS CATALOGUING-IN-PUBLICATION DATA

BRITISH LIBRARY CATALOGUING DATA ARE AVAILABLE

Front cover images © 2018 iStock

Printed in the United States of America

*McFarland & Company, Inc., Publishers
Box 611, Jefferson, North Carolina 28640
www.mcfarlandpub.com*

For James and Theresa Lee,
who inaugurated my trek through science fiction

Table of Contents

Introduction: Pushing the Boundaries of the Final Frontier   1

**Part I—Building a Galaxy: Structural Foundations
in Interstellar Government**

Engage! Captain Picard, Federationism and U.S. Foreign Policy
in the Emerging Post–Cold War World   7
ALEX BURSTON-CHOROWICZ

An Impossible Standard: Dangerous Knowledge, Moral Progress
and the Prime Directive   23
LARRY A. GRANT

Policing Loyalty: Comparing the Tal Shiar and the FBI's COINTELPRO   43
ANH T. TRAN

"You will be assimilated": Multicultural Utopianism in the 24th Century   60
MEHDI ACHOUCHE

Material Agency: The Limits of Technostructure in the 24th Century   74
JUSTIN REAM *and* ALEXANDER LEE

Part II—Gender and Identity Constructions

Perfect Society and Flawless Human Beings: The Biopolitics of Genetic
Enhancement, Cloning and Disability in the 24th Century   91
SIMON LEDDER, JENS KOLATA *and* OONAGH HAYES

The Borg: The Antithesis of Lieutenant Commander Data   118
OLAF MEUTHER

"It's Kirk vs. Picard!": Changing Notions of Heroism from the 1960s
to the 1990s   134
KATHARINA THALMANN

The Queerness of Villainy in the 24th Century   150
BRUCE E. DRUSHEL

Going Where No Woman Had Gone Before: Women's Roles
on the *Enterprise-D* as Reflective of Women's Changing Roles
in the American Labor Force   166
   ERIN C. CALLAHAN

I Sensed It: Deanna Troi's Cognitively Restructured *Trek* and the Futurism
of *The Next Generation*   179
   JOUL SMITH

Out of Order: Tasha Yar's Downfall in the Age of Reagan   198
   PETER W. LEE

Part III—Cultural Textures
in Twenty-Fourth Century Living

Klingon Kung Fu: Martial Arts in Future History   211
   JARED MIRACLE

Listening to the 24th Century: Music and Musicians Heard Throughout
the Voyages of the *Enterprise-D* (and Some of the *Enterprise-E*) 223
   TOM ZLABINGER

The Future Past: Reflections on the Role of History   237
   ALEXANDER SIMMETH

About the Contributors   249
Index   251

Introduction:
Pushing the Boundaries
of the Final Frontier

I would hate to think our imagination is so slender
that there aren't other possibilities to think about.
—Gene Roddenberry, 1987 (Nemecek 2)

According to William Shatner, Gene Roddenberry initially resisted the idea of a next generation.

Roddenberry was not the only one who had doubts about a revamped *Star Trek*. In 1986, many critics, both within the industry and among the legion of Trekkies, rejected the notion of casting aside the then 20-year history of the future. The new show would fail, some asserted, or remain the butt of jokes (Koenig n.p.; Robb 135). The studios—and the fans—had shot down a previous proposal, that of movie producer Harve Bennett's plan to produce cadet-oriented projects, on multiple occasions (Shatner and Kreski 270–276). The fan-based loyalty to Roddenberry's "vision" was legendary; after all, back in 1967 and 1968, fans famously saved the original series from cancellation with "I grok Spock" buttons and assorted Spockamania protests, laying the foundation for the subsequent cultural phenomenon (Whitfield 223). In this context, upon hearing the idea of a sequel series, Leonard Nimoy emotionally wondered, "How can you ever hope to do it without *us*?" (325).

But their resistance, as *Star Trek: The Next Generation* demonstrated, was futile.

While the producers worked over the potential characters and the actors to play them, they had fewer concerns over the actual make up of the 24th century. Roddenberry, armed with full creative control, believed social ills would vanish by the 23rd century, and it seemed intuitive the 24th century projected an even greater masterpiece society. However, the glossy sheen of technowizardry and human harmony belied complex political and social forces constructing the future. Back in the 1960s, even as the original *Starship Enterprise* explored new civilizations, more often than not, the very human (and half-human) crew ended up learning about their own shortcomings and how far humanity had to go. Themes of racism, the World War II/Eugenics War/Cold War parallels, Eden-bound counterculture hippies, and, when they voyaged home in 1986, environmentalism, all found representation in Roddenberry's "*Wagon Train* to the stars" (Whitfield 21). While the Prime Directive applied to developing cultures, including Earth's own history, it was not a "guardian of forever" in terms of protecting the sanctity of the United Federation of Planets. The historical and cultural dynamics of the 20th century clearly shaped the creation of the future.

By the 1980s, then, the development of any *Star Trek* follow-up would surely address the continuation of political and social issues. *Star Trek: The Next Generation*'s 15-year run—comprised of the original 1987–1994 television series and four films from 1994 to 2002—witnessed contemporary concerns only hinted at among Kirk and company. Themes included a government's responsibility to its citizens ("The Hunted"), the rise of terrorism ("Ensign Ro"), the technological revolution ("11001001"; "Q Who"), and the break-up of the nuclear family ("The Bonding"; "Imaginary Friend"). These hot-topic issues at the end of the 20th century influenced the depiction of the Federation flagship, her crew, and her ongoing mission. At the same time, the new show further explored themes prevalent in the original series, such as the marginalization of others ("The Outcast"; "The Drumhead"), eugenics ("The Masterpiece Society"), and the meaning of life and the definition of human rights ("The Measure of a Man"). Captain Picard once characterized 20th century ancestors as hungry, greedy, and infantile in "The Neutral Zone," but he is very much a product of the human condition from ages past. No matter how grim the storyline, though, Roddenberry's optimistic outlook dominated, in which core human values endured and prospered.

Star Trek: The Next Generation's formula resonated with audiences. The series consistently ranked among the top syndicated programs during its original run and finished with an impressive 10.6 Nielsen rating (Nemecek 32; Weinstein H1). The show's success and longevity is a testament to its enduring impact and reflection of American and international popular cultural contexts. However, as a historical document of its time, *Star Trek: The Next Generation* remains underexplored, often overshadowed by the original series, or lumped with its successors: *Deep Space Nine*, *Voyager*, and *Enterprise*.

To mark the 30th anniversary of *Star Trek: The Next Generation*, this volume fills a gap in the literature of popular culture studies. Although several books and documentaries touch upon the series, the majority link *Star Trek: The Next Generation* to the entire *Trek* mythos of Kirk to Kirk—from William Shatner to Chris Pine—while others limit their studies to one theme, such as race (Bernardi; Pounds) or sexual politics (Robin), laws both legal (Chaiers and Chilton) and scientific (Krauss), philosophy (Decker and Eberl), religion (Porter and McLaren), or the franchise's place in television history (Pearson and Davies). This volume is the first book to solely focus on *The Next Generation* as a lens to explore the complexities of 24th century culture, politics, and social mores as reflections of contemporary history.

Several essays examine the foundational structures of the Federation and intergalactic relations in the section Building a Galaxy: Structural Foundations in Interstellar Government. Alex Burston-Chorowicz contextualizes the Federation's foreign policy as a stand-in for international relations at the end of the Cold War. Burston-Chorwicz places Captain Picard at the apex of liberal and progressive ideology and Wilsonian internationalism, especially self-determination and democracy. However, the end of the Cold War also demonstrated the limitations of Federation liberalism as the show explored Starfleet's tumultuous relationship with the Romulans and the Cardassians.

Larry A. Grant also examines foreign policy through the application of the Prime Directive and its "real world" impact. The Federation created the Prime Directive as an information embargo to prevent the corruption of less technologically advanced societies. Grant demonstrates that the Prime Directive's flaws come from a grand strategy that prioritizes state sovereignty, blindness to the underworld and moral failings of Starfleet officers, and a fundamental inability to prevent inevitable information leakage. As an absolutist principle, the Prime Directive fails as an operating system of governance.

Anh T. Tran looks at the Romulan Tal Shiar as a parallel for covert American activities, particularly COINTELPRO, in the latter 20th century. Tran argues *Star Trek: The Next Generation* positions the Romulan Tal Shiar as a secret police in the name of national security. Indeed, the Tal Shiar's reputation even leads Starfleet to violate its own cherished notions of freedom. Tran traces COINTELPRO's legacy into the War on Terror, in which the U.S. government, and secret police forces in general, continue to endanger civil liberties at home.

Mehdi Achouche compares the Borg and the Federation through multiculturalism and colonialism. Achouche argues that the Borg, as the Federation's ultimate nemesis, offers a competing vision of utopia through assimilation and conformity. In contrast, the Federation of the 24th century mirrored contemporary debates about diversity, multiculturalism, the end of the assimilative "melting pot," and the heritage of the civil rights movements.

Justin Ream and Alexander Lee close this section by juxtaposing the Federation against the Other to look inward. Ream and Lee focus on the Federation's technostructure, in which management systems and bureaucracy serve as means of creating order and purpose. This group identity encompasses Starfleet, eliminating ego and maximizing performance, while also creating comparisons with "Other" alien empires as a means of establishing relationships through categorization. At the same time, individuals, such as Wesley Crusher and Q, challenge this form of acculturation.

The next set of essays, Gender and Identity Constructions, examines social dynamics within the Federation, and among the *Enterprise* crew. Simon Ledder, Jens Kolata, and Oonagh Hayes examine biopolitics, pointing out how the series displays a largely positive message about disability by promoting merit-based individualism. This distinction emerges when the *Enterprise* encounters various eugenic/"perfect" societies that regulate aspects of race, gender, and dis/ability contrary to Federation norms. However, the show contains inconsistencies in the Federation's idealized standards, especially the "embedded" gender roles of female nurturers and a hierarchy based on white male privilege.

Olaf Meuther also looks at the intersection between engineered societies and gender roles, with a comparison on the Borg and Lieutenant Commander Data. Meuther argues the Borg and the Federation address the issue of transhumanism, incorporating technology as a means of enhancing human life. The Federation's masculine orientation, with an emphasis on individuality and self-determination, downplay androgyny and femininity, represented by the Borg's matriarchy and collectivist hive mind. Machine life, such as Data, Lal, and Hugh, occupy a middle ground, at times challenging Starfleet's and the Borg's ideologies.

Katharina Thalmann examines the shifts in heroic masculinity and leadership from the 1960s to the 1990s. In comparing Captain Kirk to Picard, Thalmann argues that Picard's physical vulnerability, as demonstrated by his age and baldness, belies his greater mental stamina and prowess. Picard's role as a father figure, rather than a "cowboy," further represents a shift in masculine demeanor, emphasizing stability, continuity, and conservatism. These values reflected a larger contemporary political culture in the post–Cold War years and the television industry.

Bruce E. Drushel looks at homosexuality and deviancy within Starfleet's masculine norms. While the Federation promotes inclusivity in theory, this tolerance is limited to the strict codes of heteronormativity, as displayed in Starfleet's militaristic traditions. Characters outside this paradigm, notably villains such as Kivas Fajo, parody long-established homosexual stereotypes. However, Drushel argues Q's consistent disruptive effects on Starfleet may render Q a queer "hero" of sorts by offering the *Enterprise* crew a side of humanity that challenges their standards of behavior.

Erin C. Callahan provides an overview of the main women characters, Troi, Crusher, and Yar, and points out how the three exemplify the advances of, and backlash against, women in the workforce in the late 1980s and early 1990s. Despite the audience resistance that lead to Troi's sexualization and Yar's death, Callahan argues *The Next Generation* promoted equality in the workplace, allowing women like Crusher to balance professional and personal lives. By contrasting Starfleet with alien cultures, notably the Ferengi, Callahan asserts the series prepared audiences for a woman to assume the captain's chair in *Voyager*.

Joul Smith examines the emergence of mental health in public discourse during the 1980s and 1990s through Counselor Deanna Troi. While many studies of Troi focus on her sexuality, Smith challenges this historiography, arguing Troi was unique in television history; she became a voice for mental health issues at a time when such topics were controversial. Troi provides an emotional and human balance to the overwrought scientific technobabble prevalent in the series, and signifies an American "epic futurism" far more than a gendered sexual trope.

Peter W. Lee offers an alternative reading to feminist gains in *Star Trek: The Next Generation*. Lee contends feminism actually suffered a setback in television in the conservative Reagan era. Using the short-lived character of Tasha Yar as a lens, Lee posits Yar's death reflected the curtailing of strong female characters and silenced concerns about social issues like drug culture and social inequality during the late 1980s.

The final section, Cultural Textures in Twenty-Fourth Century Living, looks at cultural facets of the 24th century. Jared Miracle focuses on martial arts in *Star Trek: The Next Generation*. Although kung fu may seem anachronistic in the phaser/CGI lightshows of the future, Miracle argues martial arts played a key role in the development of masculinity during the 1980s and 1990s. The re-assertion of masculine identity found a home in Klingon/warrior martial arts, empowering men while contributing to a growing subculture with divergent warrior codes.

Tom Zlabinger discusses the importance of music among the *Enterprise* crew. Zlabinger argues music serves two purposes, with "traditional" forms of music extending personality traits. However, music also became a form of cultural exchange and development, as Picard, Data, and Wesley Crusher use music and musical motifs to push the boundaries of their characters' identity construction. Music became an aural component of the *Enterprise*'s mission to explore the frontiers of the crew's creative and personal growths.

Personal growth and exploration are also themes in the show's use of history. Alexander Simmeth points out the series frequently used "good" and "bad" history to impart lessons to the characters and viewers. This type of history often mirrored then-current hot topics in the 20th century, which became a "future past" leading to a bright 24th century. Characters who misuse this narrow appropriation of history, notably Rasmussen from the episode "A Matter of Time" and Reginald Barclay in "Hollow Pursuits," find themselves "corrected" to fit the historiographical narrative of the future.

After *Star Trek: The Next Generation* wrapped in 1994, some critics thought Gene Roddenberry's vision was perhaps *too* perfect, even communistic, with its equality and harmony (Graeber 124; Reeves-Stevens 136). Life aboard the Federation's flagship lacked the grittier edges and personality conflicts that defined other shows, such as *Babylon 5* or *The Next Generation*'s successors: *Deep Space Nine*, *Voyager*, and *Enterprise*. The franchise's attempts to "darken" *The Next Generation*'s tone in the movies, from all-out action in *First Contact* (1996) and *Nemesis* (2002) to government conspiracies in *Insurrection* (1998), met with mixed results among critics and fans. Although the relatively harmonious crew aboard the *Enterprise-D* can be attributed to their captain's capable leadership, we can read the series as the calm eye in a turbulent 24th century. Wherever the *Enterprise* warped to, viewers saw facets of the late 20th century that left culturally encoded marks on this "perfect" utopia.

Space exploration, the omnipotent Q informs Picard in "Q Who," is dangerous. Those who lack courage or cannot tolerate losses might as well stay home and cower in fear. That the stalwart captain instead meets these challenges head on demonstrates the resiliency of Roddenberry's vision of human betterment through exploration. In engaging the historical and cultural legacy of *Star Trek: The Next Generation*, this volume does no less in making it so.

Let's see what's out there.

WORKS CITED

Bernardi, Daniel. Star Trek and *History: Race-Ing Toward a White Future*. Camden: Rutgers University Press, 1998. Print.

"The Bonding." *Star Trek: The Next Generation—The Complete Third Season*. Writ. Ronald D. Moore. Dir. Dennis McCarthy. Paramount Home Video, 2002. DVD.

Chaires, Robert H., and Bradley Chilton. Star Trek *Visions of Law and Justice*. Dallas: University of North Texas Press, 2004. Print.

Decker, Kevin S., and Jason T. Eberl. Star Trek *and Philosophy: The Search for Socrates*. Hoboken, NJ: John Wiley & Sons, 2016. Print.

"The Drumhead." *Star Trek: The Next Generation—The Complete Fourth Season*. Writ. Jeri Taylor. Dir. Jonathan Frakes. Paramount Home Video, 2002. DVD.

"Ensign Ro." *Star Trek: The Next Generation—The Complete Fifth Season*. Writ. Michael Piller. Dir. Les Landau. Paramount Home Video, 2002. DVD.

Graeber, David. *The Utopia of Rules: On Technology, Stupidity, and the Secret Joys of Bureaucracy*. Brooklyn: Melville House, 2015. Print.

"The Hunted." *Star Trek: The Next Generation—The Complete Third Season*. Writ. Tobin Bernheim. Dir. Marvin Rush. Paramount Home Video, 2002. DVD.

"Imaginary Friend." *Star Trek: The Next Generation—The Complete Fifth Season*. Writ. Edithe Swensen and Brannon Braga. Dir. Gabrielle Beaumont. Paramount Home Video, 2002. DVD.

Koenig, Walter. "On Second Thought..." *Star Trek: The Modala Imperative*. New York: DC Comics, 1992. n.p. Print.

Krauss, Lawrence M. *The Physics of* Star Trek. New York: Basic Books, 2007. Print.

"The Masterpiece Society." *Star Trek: The Next Generation—The Complete Fifth Season*. Writ. Adam Belanoff and Michael Piller. Dir. Winrich Kolbe. Paramount Home Video, 2002. DVD.

"The Measure of a Man." *Star Trek: The Next Generation—The Complete Second Season*. Writ. Melinda M. Snodgrass. Dir. Robert Scheerer. Paramount Home Video, 2002. DVD.

Nemecek, Larry. *The* Star Trek: The Next Generation *Companion*. New York: Pocket Books, 1992. Print.

"The Neutral Zone." *Star Trek: The Next Generation—The Complete First Season*. Writ. Maurice Hurley. Dir. James L. Conway. Paramount Home Video, 2002. DVD.

Nimoy, Leonard. *I Am Spock*. New York: Hyperion, 2005. Print.

"11001001." *Star Trek: The Next Generation—The Complete First Season*. Writ. Maurice Hurley and Robert Lewin. Dir. Paul Lynch. Paramount Home Video, 2002. DVD.

"The Outcast." *Star Trek: The Next Generation—The Complete Fifth Season*. Writ. Jeri Taylor. Dir. Robert Scheerer. Paramount Home Video, 2002. DVD.

Pierson, Roberta, and Máire Messenger Davies. Star Trek *and American Television*. Berkeley: University of California Press, 2014. Print.

Porter, Jennifer E., and Darcee K. McLaren. Star Trek *and Sacred Ground: Explorations of* Star Trek*, Religion, and American Culture*. New York: State University of New York Press. 1999. Print.

Pounds, Michael C. *Race in Space: The Representation of Ethnicity in* Star Trek *and* Star Trek: The Next Generation. Lanham, MD: Scarecrow, 1999. Print.

"Q Who." *Star Trek: The Next Generation—The Complete Second Season*. Writ. Maurice Hurley. Dir. Rob Bowman. Paramount Home Video, 2002. DVD.

Reeves-Stevens, Judith, and Garfield Reeves-Stevens. Star Trek: The Next Generation—*The Continuing Mission*. New York: Simon & Shuster, 1996. Print.

Robb, Brian J. Star Trek: *The Essential History of the Classic TV Series and the Movies*. Philadelphia: Running Press, 2012. Print.

Roberts, Robin. *Sexual Generations:* Star Trek: The Next Generation *and Gender*. Urbana: University of Illinois Press, 1994. Print.

Shatner, William, and Chris Kreski. Star Trek: *Movie Memories*. New York: HarperCollins, 1994. Print.

Weinstein, Steve. "Newest 'Star Trek' Zooms at Warp Speed." *Los Angeles Times*, 3 May 1988, H1. Print.

Whitfield, Stephen E. *The Making of* Star Trek. New York: Ballantine Books, 1968. Print.

William Shatner Presents: Chaos on the Bridge. Dir. William Shatner. Vision Films, 2015. Film.

Engage!
Captain Picard, Federationism and U.S. Foreign Policy in the Emerging Post–Cold War World

ALEX BURSTON-CHOROWICZ

From the opening moments of *Star Trek: The Next Generation* (*TNG*) audiences are bedazzled with a continuation of Gene Roddenberry's universe of boundless optimism, adventure, frontier spirit (Pilkington 54–66), and a new captain who embodies this milieu. The new *Enterprise*, a city-like starship (Dyson 90–91), is the embodiment of this universe where technological prowess is underwritten by a distinctive universalism. The first episode, "Encounter at Farpoint," introduces a uniform crew dutifully and collectively working to keep the ship running. Most strikingly, when Captain Jean-Luc Picard enters the bridge, the pivotal locale of all *Star Trek* shows, viewers are casually introduced to Worf, a Klingon. His species was a sworn enemy of the Federation during *The Original Series* but is now an apparently seamless and contributing member of the crew—another nod to this universalism. A few moments later, Q, a being with omnipotent power, appears on board. Q quarrels with Picard over humanity's historical progression, asserting that humanity's legacy as a dangerous, barbaric race precedes them. Consequently, he refuses to let humans continue exploring the galaxy. The captain asserts humanity has come far from its violent heritage through social and political evolution, and says Q should judge humanity as they are now.

Picard's optimistic response characterizes his position as the personified portrait of Federation idealism. His steadfast belief in Federation ideology is a principal theme and highlight of the show. This philosophy is imbued with deeply liberal and progressive values concerning social progress. When Picard's security officers implore him to deal with Q forcibly, he resists, preferring to negotiate with this new life form on rational terms based on mutual understanding. This tension between liberal-universalism and realpolitik is an important aspect of the series. Major interstellar powers in the galaxy, from the Romulans to the Borg, constantly threaten Federation interests and Picard and the *Enterprise* crew always responded by sticking to their cherished ideology.

The Federation and its guiding philosophy reflect American progressive-liberal values. The United Federation of Planets, despite its eradication of market forces, is largely the United States projected into outer space. This relationship was keenly delineated when *Star Trek* first debuted in 1966. Despite his bright view of the future, creator Gene Roddenberry established *Star Trek* as a vehicle of social and political commentary on contemporary matters (Kapell 67). Compared with *The Original Series*, *The Next Generation* (*TNG*) was even more optimistic and utopian in its endeavors (Dyson 91). Nonetheless, its commentary on then-current affairs was an important aspect of the series, especially American foreign policy.

This essay highlights *Star Trek: The Next Generation*'s historical links to American foreign policy through the show's main character, Captain Jean-Luc Picard. Picard's characterization and actions serve to contextualize the show's political commentary and Roddenberry's larger liberal optimism. Placing this political narrative within its historical context is key to understand how the franchise deals with U.S. foreign policy, and *The Next Generation* is no exception. The second part elucidates how *TNG* investigates foreign policy issues within the historical context of the show's run, from 1987 to 1994.

As Q demonstrates in "Encounter at Farpoint," however, the legacy of the Cold War haunts the 24th century. Picard's dealings with the Romulans and Cardassians serve as examples of how political contours during the 1980s and early 1990s impacted the show. Picard and his liberal beliefs were continually tested through these conflicts. Through such contestations, the show explores Roddenberry's take on the legacy of Wilsonian ideals concerning democracy and self-determination. By the 1990s, the show presented the limits of these ideals when dealing with power politics observed from both realpolitik pressures and left-wing critiques in a post–Cold War context.

In 1936, Marxist philosopher Walter Benjamin, in his famous work on art production and reproduction in capitalism, argued:

> Even the most perfect reproduction of a work of art is lacking in one element: its presence in time and space, its unique existence at the place where it happens to be. This unique existence of the work of art determined the history to which it was subject throughout the time of its existence [Benjamin].

The importance of historical context in production and reproduction of art is essential. *Star Trek* was created as a response to a particular historical context. During the 1960s, the Cold War and superpower rivalry served as *Star Trek*'s most stinging and insightful political criticisms offered to its audiences (Gonzalez 29). Contemporary politics, world-affairs, and Gene Roddenberry's progressive criticism shaped these themes throughout the series. In 1987, *The Next Generation* was no different. In a sense, *TNG* was a partial reproduction of *The Original Series*, although Benjamin's insistence on historical context was not lost. *The Next Generation* was a reimagining of its forbearer but, like the original, was self-conscious about its time and place in history. The show is set about eight decades after *The Original Series*, and many large political and technological changes have taken place. It reflects geopolitical transformations from the mid–1960s to the late 80s and early 90s in which old enemies are allies and new technologies offer new avenues for exploration, war, and exploitation. However, Roddenberry and his successors continued to use Starfleet and the Federation as vehicles of criticism and as vision for America's place in the world (Kapell 67–69). The contours of twentieth century global history are the center of *TNG*'s imaginings of humanity's future.

Star Trek *and the American Century*

In February 1941, less than a year before American involvement in World War II, publisher Henry R. Luce coined the term "American Century" in an editorial of *LIFE* magazine. Luce spoke of opportunities the United States had in shaping world politics into something truly internationalist. Luce sensed that the U.S. was in a unique position to remold the world in its own image. Untethered from historical baggage of European politicking and buttressed with a distinct form of entrepreneurial capitalism, America could encourage both democracy and material abundance through free enterprise. He implored the country to create the "first and great American century" (Luce 65). There were undertones of Wilsonian internationalism in his argument, despite Luce's being a Republican and critic of President Franklin Roosevelt.

Luce's aspirations for American power were realized after World War II. Apart from Pearl Harbor, the U.S. was untouched by physical destruction while its economy vastly expanded due to arms production (Herring 596–97). With the devastation of continental Europe and the Soviets dominating Eastern Europe, the world anticipated the U.S.'s enormous Marshall Plan to rebuild Western Europe and promote democracy abroad. Suddenly, the U.S. had unprecedented cultural and political influence (Hook and Spanier 53; Geiger 88).

Most importantly, isolationism, which held significant sway in American politics since 1776 (Hunt 19–45), was laid to rest. The legacy of Pearl Harbor, the U.S.'s prominent influence on the war, and the postwar Marshall Plan made isolationism unfeasible after 1945 (Nordlinger 9–15). Due to its island-hopping campaign against the Japanese, the U.S. had bases throughout the Asia Pacific region, and it also maintained a strong military presence in Western Europe to counter Soviet pressure. Its foreign policy makers, however, faced paradoxical forces. On the one hand, the globe was being divided between the Communist and Western blocs. On the other, the United States pushed to create the United Nations as a means of promoting internationalism and collective security. The world was becoming bipolar, but there also existed a determined effort to establish and empower global institutions to avoid another global conflagration (MacQueen 20–21). The U.S. was finally, and permanently, engaged in world affairs and reveled in its dominant position (Herring 538–39).

By the 1950s, American popular culture gripped much of the world. Television, dishwashers, and other consumer products became hallmarks of post-war domestic and suburban existence made possible by the post-war economic boom (Hobsbawm *Age of Extremes*, 267–70). These products bestowed new cultural weight and significance for American consumer culture worldwide, with television being the most ubiquitous. TV was a new medium, broadcasting American cultural and political values to other parts of the globe. Joseph Nye's theory on soft power—the idea that a country can persuade another to pursue certain actions without coercion through cultural sway—comes to mind. *Star Trek*, with its progressive and critical view of humanity, reflected America's place as a global power. Here, the United States could directly shape world events vis-à-vis the Federation. *Star Trek* and its utopian desires for humanity's future are cultural by-products of the American Century.

When *Star Trek* first aired in 1966, the Cold War was at its height and U.S. involvement in Vietnam was escalating. America's rivalry with the USSR was an ever-present theme in both American politics and culture. *The Original Series* emphasized this conflict with tensions between the Federation and the Klingon Empire (Franklin 173–76). The Klingon Empire was presented as a monolithic totalitarian regime whose expansionism threatened the liberal Federation. Parallels of U.S./Soviet rivalry was shown in plain televisual sight (Sarantakes 78). Episodes such as "Errand of Mercy" and "The Paradise Syndrome" highlight the contradiction between Americans as supporters of self-determination and peace, while engaging in proxy wars overseas. These episodes, with the Klingons as "evil" adversaries, contain moral and political ambiguities echoing the Cuban Missile Crisis and escalation in Vietnam.

In 1991, *Star Trek* resolved the cold war between the Federation and the Klingon Empire, just as the real one ended (Kapell 183). In the final voyage of the original crew, *The Undiscovered Country* (1991; made mid-way into *TNG*) showed the Federation signing a peace treaty with the Klingon Empire. The reform-minded Chancellor Gorkon, named because of its likeness to Soviet General Secretary Mikhail Gorbachev, sued for peace with the Federation in response to a Chernobyl-like environmental disaster threatening his empire (Memory Alpha, Dyson 66). Just as Gorbachev was ousted in a coup in 1991, Gorkon is assassinated by reactionary elements in the Klingon Empire and in Starfleet who hope to continue the conflict. As usual, Kirk and his crew thwart these plans, after overcoming their own prejudices, and the peace treaty is signed. The film deals with complex issues surrounding the cessation of long-term conflict, the emergence of a new historical epoch, and explores the ways people comprehend such tectonic geo-political shifts. It implored contemporary audiences to embrace change and a multi-polar world. The image of the Cold War warrior, the night watchman for freedom and democracy, was now an anachronism and barrier to peace.[1]

The Next Generation's debut in 1987 equally explored dilemmas America faced in the latter twentieth century. The Cold War was ending and the Soviet Union was liberalizing. American power was being challenged, but in different ways than it was previously with Kirk. The U.S. remained the sole superpower, but multi-polar dynamics soon emerged, complicating and contesting U.S. policies and interests. Emerging nationalisms, rising powers, and old conflicts submerged by bipolar politics came back to the fore (Hook and Spanier 172).

This political context impacted the development of *TNG*, especially the Federation's overarching ideology. *Star Trek*'s concept of Starfleet created a hybrid of state-sanctioned exploration with military purposes and hierarchical structures. Starfleet served as Roddenberry's vehicle of conceptualizing and highlighting American power. Despite this military presence, the Federation and Starfleet are duty-bound to espouse liberal and Universalist ideas. It is unmistakably Wilsonian in its outlook and is not so dissimilar to Luce's ambitions. *Star Trek*'s progressive aspiration for American power and influence in the world is shown through this doctrine of "federationism" (Dyson 91). This philosophy is vital in understanding the show's political commentary particularly concerning foreign policy.

Federationism

The Federation is an intergalactic super-state made up of hundreds of worlds. Starfleet is the military, scientific, and exploration branch of the Federation. This is where most of the characters in *Star Trek* are drawn from. Each member-planet has an equal say in the workings of the Federation, sending representatives to the Federation Council. While its inner workings are not highlighted in detail, it acts as a united power held together as a democratic and plural state. There are many humanoids in governmental and bureaucratic positions, although the Federation is arguably skewed towards human and Vulcan representations, both being dominant power blocs.[2] The Federation encourages freedom of expression, individualism, and, through technological innovation, emancipates its citizens from material concerns and desires. In the early episode "The Neutral Zone," Picard fixates on this point, telling three thawed-out, twentieth-century humans that the obsession with material possessions and wealth that drove their lives is irrelevant in the 24th century. Humanity, Picard says, has grown out of such "infancy." The Federation is also "militantly secular" (Barret 61). In "Ensign Ro," Ensign Ro Laren (discussed below) is ordered to remove her traditional Bajoran earring to conform to Starfleet's blunt secularism. There is little mention of religious beliefs on the part of the main characters.[3]

The eradication of market forces, along with the accumulation and production of capital, has led some scholars to view Federationism as a radical socialist imagining. Gonzalez quotes the *Communist Manifesto* as a key document that inspired Federationism. He argues that the abolition of capitalism and the construction of a utopia based on total equality is demonstrative of Marxist inspiration (Gonzalez 32). This is a vulgar reading of Marx and a mistaken view of what Federationism is. Citing the last few paragraphs of the *Communist Manifesto* is hardly a meaningful foray into Marxist canon. The destruction of capitalism through its own contradictions is nowhere to be seen in *Star Trek: The Next Generation*. There is no emphasis on class warfare or violent revolution.[4] Picard and other Starfleet officers deplore the use of violence unless lives are directly threatened. Picard in particular always stresses diplomacy over a show of force. There is little reference to a collectivist ethos in the show apart from the Borg, whose collective consciousness crushes individuality and is an existential threat to the Federation. The entire point of eradicating market forces is justified as a means for individuals to reach their full potential without material incentive. The collective emancipation of the proletariat from the exploitations of capitalism gives way to a larger liberal sanctity of individualism. In *Star Trek*, this is a vital precondition for proper political order, as represented by Starfleet and the many Federation regulations the officers cite. Class warfare and class antagonism, in this framework, is an anathema to such a philosophy.

Instead, capitalism is overcome through technocracy and continual growth and expansion of liberal democracy. Many worlds seek entrance into the Federation as a sign of technological and political advancement. If the *Star Trek* universe is a socialist utopia, it is more akin with technocratic Fabianism—the belief of gradual socialism without revolution—mixed with modern liberalism. Federationism is, at best, liberal or libertarian socialist in outlook. It is utopian, like Oscar Wilde's *Soul of Man under Socialism*, where Wilde contemplated a society based on equality that liberated people from menial work by advanced machines. This allowed for meaningful individualism to be realized. H.G. Wells, in a similar fashion, envisioned state planning aided by sophisticated new technologies to build a society free from capitalism's inequalities (Partington 517–76). Marx rejected such utopian and unscientific socialisms (Hobsbawm *The Age of Capital*, 62, 85, 141). Federationism is, however, deterministic; it sees technological progress as necessary in ending capitalism and its contradictions. Through technological evolution, historical forces that traditionally produce new social, economic, and political realities come to an end. Picard, on a number of occasions, elucidates this. This is an "end of history" thesis (Neuman 45), but it is not Marxist. The scientific element of Marxism, dialectical materialism, is nowhere to be seen. It is a thesis entirely compatible with American politics. It fetishizes individualism and institutions of representative democracy. Consequently, it is able to attract audiences from a number of mainstream political persuasions.

An important aspect of Federationism is the Prime Directive. It stipulates the Federation should not intervene in domestic concerns of other societies, particularly if they are less developed. The Prime Directive is anti-colonial in its outlook, prefacing the importance of political and cultural autonomy (Sarantakes 81; Jameson 265; Whitehall 176).[5] While this essay does not directly deal with these issues, they are nonetheless core aspects of how the Federation conducts its foreign policy. The respect for self-determination is a necessary step towards progressive societal evolution in the *Star Trek* universe. Wilsonian principles and its anti-colonial mentality are again on display here. Captain Picard, the moral and political center of the show, is the prime proponent of Federationism, and serves as a lens to understand how the series deals with politics.

Captain Picard, President Wilson and the Reagan Era

Captain Jean-Luc Picard, commanding officer of the U.S.S. *Enterprise* in *The Next Generation*, is a marked contrast to his predecessor, Captain Kirk.[6] Kirk was a Cold War American hero, libertine, and warrior. Picard cuts a very different, more nuanced figure. His patrician accent, calm demeanor, and intellectual rigor mark him as a proponent of the Federation's liberal attitudes. Before joining Starfleet, Picard seriously considered a career in archaeology. His intellectual rigor makes him out to be a renaissance man. His one archetypal characteristic with the traditional American hero is his willingness to challenge Starfleet if his higher-ups betray the organization's core values. This is first highlighted in the episode "Measure of a Man," where the captain defends Lieutenant-Commander Data's right to be treated as a sentient individual. Members of Starfleet saw the android as property, ordering him to be decommissioned and studied. Picard's rousing final speech, convincing a judge to grant Data the right to choose his own destiny, is the highlight of the episode. Picard asserts that treating Data as property would create a legal precedent that would enslave future androids.[7] By arguing that Data is a sentient being, Picard embraces a radical redefinition of what constitutes an individual and is a typical example of his liberal morals.

Picard's liberalism underscores the many attributes he shares with President Woodrow Wilson, the American president during World War I. Their scholarly passion for history, deeply moralistic outlooks, and desire to project their liberal views are among their defining characteristics. Wilson's "Fourteen Points"—his plan to remodel the world system after the Great War—articulated the sanctity of self-determination, guided and regulated by an international body composed of nation-states. This came to define liberal internationalism (Ambrosius 54–64; Knock 25–52; Layne 54–62). Picard, an ardent supporter of such values, defends them in the show time and time again. When the *Enterprise* responds to various threats and challenges to Federation power, Picard consistently chooses solutions that emphasize individual rights.

Picard's dealings with the Romulan Empire and Cardassian Union exemplify his liberal leaning when implementing Federation foreign policy. At times he comes to log-gerheads with more conservative members of the Federation's security hierarchy. Unlike the Klingon Empire, which, by now had a somewhat stable peace treaty with the Feder-ation, the Romulans and Cardassians were major antagonists in the Alpha quadrant. Klingons were often portrayed as honorable warriors with a complex and well-developed culture, and were admired and respected. Cardassians were depicted as secretive and deceitful, as were Romulans. Klingons who threatened the Federation, like the villainous Duras sisters, did so in collusion with the Romulans. The Cardassians and Romulans, in turn, consistently challenged Federation power. The Federation's tense relationships with the Cardassians and the Romulans allow the creators to create conflict as Picard, captain of Starfleet's flagship, confronts many dilemmas that test his idealism. These plots not only highlight tensions between liberalism and realism, they reflect the rapidly changing world of the late '80s and early '90s.

When *The Next Generation* premiered in 1987, the world was in the midst of rapid change. The Soviet Union was liberalizing and beginning to buckle under pressures unleashed by Gorbachev's *Perestroika* and *Glasnost*. The breakup of Yugoslavia was under-way and became a flashpoint for emerging nationalisms about to engulf the post–Communist sphere. The People's Republic of China was midway through a reform period, introducing market oriented policies ending its autarkic and reclusive conduct; by the mid–1990s it became an emerging and potential super-power (Meisner 514–48). In the Middle East, Palestinian self-determination became a widely accepted notion though it was not yet realized. In South Africa, the release of Nelson Mandela from political prison in 1990 heralded the collapse of Apartheid.

The Republican Party dominated the American presidency throughout most of *TNG*'s run (1987–1994). Hawkish foreign policy rhetoric was the cornerstone of President Ronald Reagan's tenure, and the First Gulf War shaped George Bush, Sr.'s administration. Reagan was a Cold War warrior but his partner in peace, Mikhail Gorbachev, was instru-mental in this new era of détente. The fall of communism and the end of the Cold War were seen as triumphs for liberal internationalism, despite Reagan's skepticism of such institutions.

This period was also a high point for neo-liberalism. Ronald Reagan and British Prime Minister Margaret Thatcher were key world leaders who ushered a renewed empha-sis on free market economics, deregulation, union crackdowns, and shrinking govern-ment services. Neo-liberalism transformed politics on all sides (Hobsbawm *Age of Extremes*, 403–32). In the 1990s, President Bill Clinton's new democrats and British Prime Minister Tony Blair's New Labour confirmed that the mainstream left also embraced this rationale. Most of the former People's Republics became liberal democracies. Their embrace of democratic governance and free market economics strengthened this notion.

The former Communist Bloc's transition to both democracy and capitalism was rocky at best. The new Russian Federation saw depressions set in due to hasty privati-zation. Corruption, which thrived in the Soviet system, was further fueled by the intro-duction of foreign capital and lackluster regulation (Kotkin 125–41). By the end of the show's run in 1994, Russia and the USSR's former republics and satellite states were in the midst of a turbulent decade.

The rise of neoliberalism indicated that the post–World War II's bipolar geopolitical structures were falling away. Thus, *The Next Generation*'s run from 1987 to 1994 marked the end of a major chapter in twentieth century history. Historian Eric Hobsbawm affirms that 1991 marked the historical end of the 20th century. His comments on global change remain poignant: "In short, the century ended in global disorder whose nature was unclear and without an obvious mechanism for either ending it or keeping it under control" (Hobsbawm *Age of Extremes: The Short Twenthieth Century* 562). The end of the Cold War and the Iron Curtain meant that the constant threat of large-scale conflict was no longer on the horizon; in its wake lay a period of uncertainty. America emerged as the sole super power, but this status was tested during its disastrous campaign in Somalia in the early 1990s. America's lack of intervention in Rwanda meant that over a million people lost their lives in genocide and millions more became refugees (Cameron 20–24, 177–78). These two instances demonstrated American limitations despite its mantle as the last super power. This was the global framework of *The Next Generation*.

Unlike its predecessor's geopolitical context, which was dominated by Cold War politics, *The Next Generation*'s milieu was harder to define. *Star Trek* offered its audiences a glimpse into a future where a utopia took shape, loosely infused with values that were now held up as humanity's ideological pinnacle. Francis Fukiyama's thesis that liberal-democracy was the end point of historical evolution comes to mind here, in which contradictions that created new political, social and economic circumstances now ended (Fukuyama xi–xxiii). *The Next Generation* reflected such notions. Nonetheless, prickly issues of power politics, nationalism, dictatorship, and exploitation remained. *TNG* attempted to deal with these issues with Captain Picard serving as the Federationism's voice to explore America's new place in the world, just as he explored the galaxy. The dilemmas Picard faced throughout the show mirrored developments in the post–Cold War period. *Star Trek*, once again, was used as a vehicle for social and political commentary. This time, the world was seemingly more complex and changing, and how the series addressed these issues became the hallmark of *The Next Generation*.

Picard and the Romulans

The original role of the Romulans in *TNG* was to create another Cold War–like scenario in *Star Trek*. When compared to Klingons in *The Original Series*, Romulans are depicted with much more finesse and cunning. In their introductory episode, "The Neutral Zone," they are presented as technologically equal to Starfleet or better: their new warbird dwarfs the *Enterprise*.[8] They are expansionists but realize that outright warfare is costly. Rather, they rely on cloak and dagger tactics to sabotage their enemies. They carried significant diplomatic clout, which consistently tested Picard's status as one of Starfleet's finest diplomats.

The Romulans' internal politics is noteworthy. While few details about the Romulan Star Empire are provided in the series, audiences know the empire is run primarily by the Senate on their home-planet, Romulus. There are elections, but most of its foreign and domestic policies are managed by its military (Manuel 390). When Picard and Data visit Romulus in "Unification," much of their planet is relatively impoverished when compared to its military sophistication. Remus, a sister planet, was conquered by Romulus, and the Remans are used as cannon fodder in wars and slaves in mines. The Tal Shiar is the Empire's intelligence agency, known for its ruthless efficiency.[9] One long-term objective of the Romulan Empire is to break up the Federation-Klingon alliance, thus dividing two of its key rivals.

In "The Neutral Zone," the *Enterprise* responds to reports of missing colonies along the Federation-Romulan neutral zone. The crew realizes the Federation colonies are destroyed, with no trace left of their existence. Security chief Worf and Commander Riker implore Picard to confront the Romulans. When they detect a Romulan ship, Worf and Riker want Picard to attack while the warbird is vulnerable and still under cloak. Picard refuses and his decision is correct when the Romulans contact the *Enterprise* and reveal that their colonies are also missing. They never intended to attack the Federation but, like Starfleet, want to ascertain who attacked their colonies. Both conclude that another force is responsible. Picard's insistence on a diplomatic solution pays off because the Romulans are also seeking a diplomatic solution to this issue. However, at the end of the episode the Romulans announce an end to their period of isolationism and that the Federation take note of their return to galactic politics. This first encounter set the tone for many of Picard's dealing with the Romulans. While he always insists upon diplomatic solutions, such an approach may be problematic in the face of insistent foes intent upon undermining Federation interests. This episode marks the beginning of a renewed Cold War between the Federation and the Romulan Empire.[10]

When the Romulans directly threaten Federation interests, Picard thinks of elaborate ways to stop them without direct confrontation. In the first episode of the fifth season, "Redemption Part 2," Picard sets up a blockade when he realizes the Romulans are supporting an anti–Federation faction in the Klingon Civil War. Through the blockade, Picard exposes the Romulans' involvement. The Romulans retreat upon being detected and the Civil War ends with the pro–Federation faction triumphant. Here, Picard knows his blockade violates the Prime Directive, but nonetheless does so when Federation interests are directly threatened. This example shows Picard's liberalism has limitations. When he detects a greater threat to the Federation, he is willing to forego much of his liberalism in favor of more direct intervention short of actual engagement. In this case, his actions are performed with subtlety since the blockade is not a formal declaration of war. When he does need to intervene, he does so in a way that is not an open confrontation. Even when he acts hawkishly, he demonstrates restraint.

Picard is one to uphold bilateral treaties. In one of the final episodes of the series, "The Pegasus," Picard confronts a senior admiral in Starfleet who violates the Treaty of Algeron with the Romulans, in which the Federation promised not to develop cloaking technology. In this episode, the *Enterprise* is dispatched to retrieve an experimental starship with an illegal cloaking device. When Picard realizes the truth behind the mission, he refuses to cooperate. He even uses the device and de-cloaks in plain sight of a Romulan ship, alerting them to Starfleet's treaty violation. Indeed, Picard performs these actions, directly contravening the orders of his superiors who want to develop the project in secret. Picard is aware that the cloaking device could trigger a wider conflict, but his liberalism shines through as he places the Treaty's stipulations above the Federation's clandestine activities.

The Federation's flagrant violation of such a vital treaty demonstrates that Federation liberalism can be threatened from within. Admiral Pressman, who is in charge of the operation, defends his actions. He claims the treaty holds the Federation back in the Cold War against the Romulans, allowing them to gain the upper hand in the arms race. Pressman has a fair point, since Romulan warbirds dwarf their Starfleet counterparts in both size and technological sophistication. However, Picard sees this argument as barbaric and immoral, asserting that this abandonment of liberal ideals led to a rare case of mutiny among a Starfleet crew when the crew onboard the prototype starship balked against Pressman's orders, leading to its supposed destruction. Riker, who served with Pressman on the prototype starship and who withholds the cloaking secret from Picard until the end, points out that the Federation signed the treaty "in good faith," and that such violations could lead to destructive, open war. Picard's attachment to formal peace treaties is commendable and an example of his commitment to peace and his expectation that Starfleet officers should uphold such treaties. Indeed, the Treaty of Algeron is reminiscent of the various SALT treaties the United States signed with the Soviet Union in the 1970s, and honored by Russia after the Soviet Union dissolved, curbing the likelihood of nuclear war. The episode reminds us that aggressive realpolitik foreign policy is not just conducted by despotic governments. Rather, democracies, too, often justified abandoning their ideals in the name of defending national interests.

The most poignant encounter with the Romulans is the two-part story "Unification." This story guest starred Leonard Nimoy, who plays an older Spock from *The Original Series*. Spock journeys to Romulus to help support the unification movement between the Vulcans and Romulans, since they share the same bloodlines. Romulans, at one stage in their history, broke away from Vulcans. Vulcans, who uphold a bluntly logical and utilitarian philosophy, faced an uprising from those who rejected such values. These dissidents left the planet and formed the Romulan Empire. Spock now comes to give support to a faction that wants to see the reunification of the two societies. He leaves for Romulus without permission from the Federation. Picard is sent to Romulus to look for the missing Spock. The captain lends support to Spock and uncovers a Romulan plot to invade Vulcan. Picard and Spock, of course, spoil this.

The important part is not the Romulan invasion of Vulcan, but the re-unification movement. As Spock points out, unification of the two societies would go a long way in easing tensions between Romulans and the Federation. Picard is neither Romulan nor Vulcan, but he uses his position as an outside player to lend support to Spock's movement. The captain sees a twofold opportunity in supporting a cause that lives up to Federation principles and which also happens to be in their strategic interests. At the end of the double episode, Spock refuses to return to the Federation, wishing to continue his work with the dissidents. Picard allows this, disobeying a direct order. Picard again risks coming to loggerheads with his superiors, regarding Spock's mission as in the interests of Federation principles. The episode first aired in late 1991, only 18 months after the fall of the Berlin Wall and directly references *Star Trek VI*, which showed the end of the Cold War between the Klingons and the Federation. Here, we see a people with a shared history and identity separated by philosophical differences. Picard, sympathetic with this rift, aids liberal reformers amongst his enemy, much like President Reagan's instance on tearing down the Berlin Wall. Once again, *Star Trek* paralleled the end of the Cold War and the triumph of liberal-democracy.

Picard's dealing with the Romulans was *TNG*'s way of reinventing the Cold War at a time when the real-world one was ending. While definitely sympathetic with liberalism, the show offers a more circumspect commentary on power politics. Gonzalez goes as far as to say that the series rejects the role of *The Original Series* in criticizing foreign policy and shifts to a role of support for Reagan's conservative foreign policy (57–75). This is probably an overstatement; self-determination is at the heart of *TNG*'s foreign policy, as is the need for diplomacy and peace, although there is an element of truth in Gonzalez's claim. The key difference is that *TNG* was self-conscious in its effort to demonstrate diplomatic nuances, with Picard being the perfect character for this. Even when there needed to be a more forceful solution to conflict, Picard always opts for either a diplomatic one or a creative military response that does not lead to war. Picard's blockade during the Klingon Civil War fits this pattern. The Romulans serve as the show's great power rival, with all the trappings of another Cold War, but the creators use the Cardassians to more thoroughly explore post–Cold War pressures.

The Cardassians and the Early 1990s

Cardassians were a new enemy *The Next Generation* introduced into *Star Trek* canon. The show uses Cardassians to explore a number of prickly issues U.S. foreign policy faced. The series establishes the Cardassian Union as an empire that just ended a long and brutal conflict with the Federation.[11] A functioning, but fragile, peace between the two powers was established not long before the show's timeline. Although the initial war is never seen in the series, audiences learn that the peace is delicate, as consistent tension from both sides threatens this new relationship. Through these pressures, the show explores nationalism, refugees, and post-colonialism. Picard's Federationism is challenged from both the left and right through his interactions with Cardassians.

The Cardassian Union is a military junta that oversaw a vast empire. Like the Romulans, the Cardassians are roughly equal in strength to the Federation in both territory and technology. In the wake of a crisis that left the home planet poverty-stricken, the military overthrew a civilian government and established a dictatorship. The military turned the economy around through expansion and conquering other civilizations (Manuel 389–90). This was, of course, a reference to the Nazis taking Germany in 1933. Like the Gestapo, the Cardassians have a brutal secret police, the Obsidian Order, although this is not explored until *Deep Space Nine*. Gonzalez argues that the Cardassians represent Latin America, since military coups are a consistent theme in the region's history (Gonzalez 67). While this seems simplistic and vague, the Cardassians' military coup and productive wartime economy offer a ready analogy to real-world historical events.

The Cardassians make for a far more complex adversary than the Romulans. The Cardassians' peace treaty with the Federation involves territorial swaps even though citizens had already colonized those spaces. This relationship is further strained by the fact that the Cardassians oversaw a brutal occupation of the planet Bajor. The Federation was unsure how to handle the Bajoran Occupation since it took place within Cardassian territory and the Federation chose not to get involved. As this narrative develops over the course of the series, it serves as a means to question Picard's and the Federation's policies of non-intervention and liberal internationalism.

In the episode "Ensign Ro," the *Enterprise* responds to an attack on a Federation colony near the Cardassian border. Apparently, a Bajoran terrorist organization carried out the attack to protest Federation inaction vis-à-vis pressuring the Cardassians off their homeworld. Picard and the *Enterprise* investigate a nearby Bajoran refugee camp for information. In doing this, viewers are exposed to a stateless people, hungry and desperate, dwelling and subsisting in poverty for most of their lives—a marked contrast to Federation abundance and utopianism. When the crew makes contact with the terrorists, the audience learns that the Cardassians actually staged the outpost attack and blamed the Bajorans. The Cardassians were waiting for Picard to find the terrorists and then they would step in and violently root them out.

The Cardassian plot is spoiled, but the most important part of the episode concerns the problem of refugees and the complex subject of occupation and terrorism. Picard is sympathetic with the Bajoran terrorists due to their dire situation. Throughout the episode, Picard is constantly questioned by Bajorans, including a new Bajoran crewmember, Ensign Ro Laren (whose surname comes first), about how the Federation's policy of non-intervention was "convenient" (Putman 249–50). The strong-willed and defiant Ensign Ro admits that she, too, lived in such a camp and ran away when she was old enough, joining Starfleet, but her undisciplined behavior led to a court martial. She now has a second chance to make good, but Ro's cavalier attitude towards Starfleet regulations is no doubt shaped by her childhood and the Federation's lackluster efforts in addressing the Bajoran issue.

Picard implores the Bajorans to give up violence and promises that the Federation would pressure the Cardassians to end their occupation through diplomatic channels. Of course, the Bajorans are skeptical and treat him with disdain. After all, it is *they* who need blankets, food, and medical supplies, not more politicking. Most interestingly, the admiral who sent Picard on this mission assigned Ro to quietly make a deal with the Bajorans terrorists, offering them weapons in exchange for targeting Cardassian installations. Ro admits this to Picard, who is outraged that an admiral would flagrantly violate the Prime Directive.[12] In the end, Picard exposes Cardassian involvement in the initial attacks. The issue of terrorism and the future of the Bajorans are left conveniently unanswered—just as the Federation's inaction is never resolved.[13]

Here the show's liberalism is challenged by the emergence of terrorism. Obviously, liberals such as Woodrow Wilson were appalled by the stifling of self-determination, but Wilson sought solace by setting up global institutions like his Fourteen Points' League of Nations to deal with these issues. The establishment of international bodies, however, gives little comfort for starving, desperate, and stateless peoples. The Bajorans offer a left wing critique of such a political philosophy, highlighting the limitations and the elitism that make up liberal morality. Picard and the Federation seem aloof when confronted with such an issue. Institutions like the League of Nations or the United Nations may have grandiose objectives in upholding self-determination and solving refugee crises, but such devotion to institutions has real-world limitations. For example, Palestinian suffering and the Rwandan Genocide were issues the U.N. failed to adequately deal with in the 1990s (Frederking 139–41, 57–58). Likewise, Picard's sympathy with the Bajorans and their freedom fighters is notable, but more noteworthy is his uneasiness with their unlawful violence and that members of Starfleet attempt to arm them. This reflected the uncertainties among the production crew: writers Rick Berman and Michael Piller admitted that the Bajorian issue on *Star Trek* is a reference to a number of stateless people in history, including Jews and Palestinians (Nemecek 247). The episode aired in late 1991, the tail end of the First Intifada and the beginning of the stalled Israeli-Palestinian peace process. Here, we see a thorny post–Cold War issue that continues well into the 21st century. The implication that the United States needed to do more to aid this process is the episode's obvious message.

Postcolonial issues are also part of Federation-Cardassian relations. In order to come to an agreeable border, both cede planets to each other. Planets that are already inhabited need to be evacuated. Some Federation colonists refuse to leave their homes and agree to live under Cardassian rule. In the episode "Journey's End," Picard is tasked with removing a group of Native American colonists from one of these worlds. Picard, deeply uncomfortable with his assignment, must convince the colonists to relocate. Keenly aware of the disturbing historical parallels with colonialism and Native Americans, Picard's liberalism is put to the ultimate test. The Native Americans refuse to leave, citing spiritual connections with their new homeland. Cardassians attack the colonists and Picard is stuck between upholding the treaty while protecting Federation citizens who are, technically, acting illicitly. Eventually, the colonists decide to remain on the planet and relinquish their Federation citizenship. Picard, faced with kowtowing to neo-colonial policy is, despite his best efforts, unable to come to a solution. It is the colonists who decide to surrender their citizenship and remain on their planet. The Federation, with its eye more on the Cardassians, ignores the self-determination of their own citizens who were historically victims of violent imperialism. The audience is left with the issue unresolved and a feeling that tensions could easily be reignited.[14]

Soon after this episode the Cardassians begin quietly supporting militias to attack other former Federation colonists, driving them away from their homes. In response, the more militant and organized settlers form the Maquis to combat this (referencing French resistance during World War II, an appropriate name to combat the Nazi-inspired Cardassians).[15] The Maquis become outlaws of both the Cardassians and Federation. Since Maquis cells are made up of former Federation citizens, including disgruntled Starfleet officers, the Federation is obliged to curb these renegades' activities to maintain cordial relations with the Cardassians. This story is expanded in *Deep Space Nine* and *Voyager*.

In the penultimate episode of the series, "Preemptive Strike," Picard orders Lieutenant Ro to infiltrate the Maquis. Picard, though sympathetic to their cause, is more concerned about upholding the treaty and keeping the peace. Meanwhile, Lieutenant Ro has come a long way from her angry days as an ensign. She was court-martialed for failing to obey Starfleet regulations, but came to accept, even support, its mission and liberal agenda. Picard, having given her a second chance in Starfleet, is a mentor figure to her and this mission is the ultimate test of her newfound loyalty.

Picard, despite his intimate knowledge of Cardassian brutality, realizes that the Maquis' continuing violence would effectively annul the treaty with the Cardassians. Picard goes to great lengths in trying to catch the Maquis and arrest senior cell leaders. To Picard, the Maquis are Federation citizens breaking the law, undermining Federation interests. Ro is sent to gather information on the Maquis and feed information back to Starfleet. She is finally assigned to set up a trap that would deprive the clandestine guerrilla group of both leadership and military hardware. Ro, however, switches sides at the last minute, revealing the trap and betraying Picard and Starfleet. Ro's transformation offers a radical critique of Federation liberalism.

Having experienced Cardassian oppression firsthand, Ro comes to realize that radical and violent actions are the only recourses possible against Cardassian rule. She understands that Federation doctrine is limited and does not have the capacity to halt injustices. Picard, like the Federation, is too committed to institutions and their processes to properly deal with state-sponsored violence the Cardassians are undertaking against Federation citizens. The Maquis, unlike the Federation, is willing to fight for their own rights regardless of how it may play out with higher powers. The Maquis sees violence as a necessity since Federation diplomacy directly led to their predicament and Cardassian violence remains unanswered. The ending shot of this episode, a close-up of Picard's tortured face, suggests more than a personal betrayal. Picard, in a way, acknowledges the Federation's failings in situations like this one inevitably lead to betrayals like Ro's.[16]

While it is difficult to peg the Maquis as either conservative or progressive, they nonetheless represent a post-colonial pressure. Here, two great powers colonize space and then seek to forcibly remove populations to placate each other. The self-determination of whole groups of people is ignored. The overtones with the Israel-Palestine and nationalism in Russian provinces like Chechnya are obvious parallels. In the case of Palestine, a messy withdrawal by the British Empire, coupled with the colonial project of Zionism, meant that the self-determination of Arabs was subjugated (Kimmerling and Migdal 146–66). Chechnya, a republic within the Russian Federation has, since the 1990s, a well-organized succession movement. Russia, since the end of the USSR, waged a number of wars and bloody engagements to quash the rebels (Stone 244–47). Picard, straight-jacketed by liberalism and his petulance for Federation legality, cannot devise a satisfactory answer for this issue other than to nullify the Maquis. The Maquis fall well outside Federation legality, interrupting diplomatic norms and undermining Federation interests. Picard and the Federations thus set out to destroy them. Ro's betrayal and the Maquis' activities make the audience think twice about the noble liberalism Picard and the Federation espouse.

Conclusion

The Cardassians and the Romulans in *The Next Generation* explore tensions between liberalism and realpolik in American foreign policy at the end of the Cold War. More importantly, these antagonists elucidated fissures and tensions in the emerging post–Cold War global order. America's place in this world, though supreme, was nevertheless uncertain. As a result, *TNG*'s political commentary was far more complex than that of Kirk's time, reflecting changes in geo-political dynamics. *The Next Generation* was conscious of its political context and went to great lengths in traversing it. *Star Trek* is undoubtedly one of the most successful sci-fi series, and is so because of its ability to confront its audiences with complex and important questions of history, politics, philosophy and the human condition at large. It is unashamedly American in its identity and its endeavors. Captain Picard's ventures have shown the American experience was never monolithic and *Star Trek: The Next Generation* dived into those cracks and complexities surveying the contradictions in American foreign policy and the country's place in the world in the late 20th century.

ACKNOWLEDGMENT

I would like to thank a few people who were instrumental to me producing this essay. My good friend and colleague, Bronwyn Lowe, alerted me to this project. This would have been impossible without her. I would also like to thank my partner, Karen Freilich, for reading my work; she is always supportive of my endeavors.

NOTES

1. This is alluded to in the *TNG* episode "Unification." Spock, now an ambassador, reminisces to Picard on his experiences with his time with Kirk and how diplomatic niceties and conventions were flouted in what he called "cowboy diplomacy."

2. It is not within the confines of this essay to discuss the power dynamics within the Federation. It is notable that the Federation treats its member states as equals, but the source of power within the Federation

itself is more centralized and opaque. Starfleet headquarters is on Earth, as is the Federation Council and Starfleet Academy. Humans and Vulcans dominate the ranks of Starfleet, including its most senior admirals. There are many non-humanoids in official political positions; however, the main players in the Federation come from Earth and Vulcan.

3. *The Next Generation* is secular in premise, as was *The Original Series*. It was not until *Deep Space Nine* that religion was thoroughly explored. Gene Roddenberry forbade it from being discussed; however, after his death, writers and producers had a much freer hand in tackling the subject.

4. The main inheritors of capitalism in the show, the Ferengi, are portrayed as a greedy race and act as comic foils that seem archaic in the 24th century; they, too, give little attention to class.

5. See Larry A. Grant's essay in this volume.

6. See Katharina Thalmann's essay in this volume.

7. See Olaf Meuther's and Mehdi Achouche's essays in this volume.

8. It is worth noting that the Romulans are not new to the *Star Trek* universe. They featured prominently in *The Original Series*.

9. See Anh T. Tran's essay in this volume.

10. During *The Original Series* there was also a Cold War.

11. The origins of the Cardassian War are not discussed in the show, but given the militaristic nature of the Cardassians, it is certainly implied that they are the ones who started it. In the episode "The Wounded" we learn that Chief O'Brien was involved in this war and was seriously affected by its brutality and civilian deaths.

12. This is no doubt a reference to a similar agreement the CIA made with Palestinian terrorist group Black September in the 1970s.

13. Of course, this is answered in the course of *Deep Space Nine*.

14. See Justin Ream's and Alexander Lee's essay in this volume.

15. The Maquis declare themselves towards the end of the second season of *Deep Space Nine*.

16. In a number of *Deep Space Nine* and *Voyager* episodes, it is made clearer that the Maquis is largely made up of disgruntled Starfleet officers and Bajorans seeking revenge on their Cardassian oppressors.

Works Cited

Ambrosius, Lloyd E. *Wilsonianism: Woodrow Wilson and His Legacy in American Foreign Relations.* Hampshire: Palgrave Macmillan, 2002. Print.

Barret, Michèle. *Star Trek: The Human Frontier.* New York: Routledge, 2001. Print.

Benjamin, Walter. "The Work of Art in the Age of Mechanical Reproduction." 1936. Web. 24 May 2016.

Cameron, Fraser. *US Foriegn Policy After the Cold War: Global Hegemon or Reluctant Sheriff?* New York: Routledge, 2005. Print.

Dyson, Stephen Benedict. *Otherwordly Politics: The International Relations of* Star Trek, Game of Thrones, *and* Battlestar Galactica. Baltimore: Johns Hopkins University Press, 2015. Print.

Franklin, H. Bruce. "Vietnam, *Star Trek*, and the Real Future." Star Trek *and History*. Ed. Nancy Reagin. Hoboken: Wiley, 2013. 87–108. Print.

Frederking, Brian. *The United States and the Secuity Council: Collective Security Since the Cold War.* New York: Routledge, 2007. Print.

Fukuyama, Francis. *The End of History and the Last Man.* New York: Free Press, 1992. Print.

Geiger, Till. "The *Power Game*, Soft Power and the International Historian." *Soft Power and U.S. Foreign Policy: Theoretical, Historical and Contemporary Perspectives.* Eds. Inderjeet Parmar and Michael Cox. New York: Routledge, 2010. 51–82. Print.

Gonzalez, George A. *The Politics of* Star Trek: *Justice, War and the Future.* Hampshire: Palgrave Macmillan, 2015. Print.

Herring, George C. *From Colony to Superpower: U.S. Foreign Relations Since 1776.* Oxford: Oxford University Press, 2008. Print.

Hobsbawm, Eric. *The Age of Capital 1848–1875.* London: Abacus, 1975. Print.

_____. *Age of Extremes: The Short History of the Twentieth Centry 1914–1991.* London: Abacus, 1994. Print.

_____. *Age of Extremes: The Short Twentieth Century, 1914–1991.* London: Clays, 1995. Print.

Hook, Steven W., and John Spanier. *American Foriegn Policy Since World War II.* Thousands Oaks: CQ Press, 2016. Print.

Hunt, Michael H. *Ideology and U.S. Foreign Policy.* London: Yale University Press, 2009. Print.

Jameson, Fredric. *Archaeologies of the Future.* London: Verao, 2005. Print.

Kapell, Matthew Wilhelm. "Speakers for the Dead: *Star Trek*, the Holocaust, and the Representation of Atrocity." Star Trek *as Myth: Essays on Symbol and Archetype at the Final Frontier.* Ed. Matthew Wilhelm Kapell. Jefferson, NC: McFarland, 2010. Print.

Kimmerling, Baruch, and Joel S. Migdal. *The Palestinian People: A History.*: London: Harvard University Press, 2003. Print.

Knock, Thomas J. "Playing for a Hundred Years Hence: Woodrow Wilson's Internationalism and His Would-Be

Heirs." *The Crisis of American Foreign Policy: Wilsonianism in the Twenty-First Century*. Eds. G. John Ikenberry, et al. Princeton: Princeton University Press, 2009. Print.

Kotkin, Stephen. *Armageddon Averted: The Soviet Collapse, 1977–2000*. Oxford: Oxford University Press, 2011. Print.

Layne, Christopher. "The Unbearable Lightness of Soft Power." *Soft Power and U.S. Foreign Policy: Theoretical, Historical and Contemporary Perspectives*. Eds. Inderjeet Parmar and Michael Cox. New York: Routledge, 2010. 51–82. Print.

Luce, Henry R. "The American Century." *Life* 17 Feburary 1941: 61–65. Print.

MacQueen, Norrie. *The United Nations, Peace Operations and the Cold War*. New York: Routledge, 2011. Print.

Manuel, Paul Christopher. "'In Every Revolution, There Is One Man with a Vision': The Governments of the Future in Comparative Perspective." *Political Science Fiction*. Eds. Hassler, Donald M. and Clyde Wilcox. Columbia: University of South Carolina Press, 1997. Print.

Meisner, Maurice. *Mao's China and After: A History of the People's Republic*. New York: Free Press, 1999. Print.

Nemecek, Larry. *The* Star Trek: The Next Generation *Companion*. New York: Pocket, 1997. Print.

Neuman, Iver B. "To know him was to love him. not to know him was to love him from afar": Diplomacy in *Star Trek*." *To Seek Out New World: Science Fiction and World Politics*. Ed. Jutta Weldes. New York: Palgrave, 2003. Print.

Nordlinger, Eric A. *Isolationism Reconfigured: American Foreign Policy for a New Century*. Princeton: Princeton University Press, 1995. Print.

Nye, Joseph S., Jr. *Soft Power: The Means to Success in World Politics*. New York: Public Affairs, 2004. Print.

Partington, John S. "H.G. Wells: A Political Life." *Utopian Studies* 19.3 (2008): 517–76. Print.

Pilkington, Ace G. "Star Trek: American Dream, Myth and Reality." Star Trek *as Myth: Essays on Symbol and Archetype at the Final Frontier*. Ed. Matthew Wilhelm Kapell. Jefferson, NC: McFarland, 2010. Print.

Putman, John. "Terrorizing Space: *Star Trek*, Terrorism, and History." Star Trek *and History*. Ed. Nancy Reagin. Hoboken: Wiley, 2013. 143–57. Print.

Sarantakes, Nicholas Evan. "Cold War Pop Culture and the Image of U.S. Foreign Policy: The Perspective of the Original Star Trek Series." *Journal of Cold War Studies* 7.4 (2005): 74–103. Print.

Stone, David R. *A Military History of Russia: From Ivan the Terrible to the War in Chechnya*. London: Praeger, 2006. Print.

Whitehall, Geoffrey. "The Problem of the 'World and Beyond': Encountering 'the Other' in Science Fiction." *To Seek Out New Worlds: Science Fiction and World Politics*. Ed. Jutta Weldes. New York: Palgrave, 2003. Print.

TV and Film

"Encounter at Farpoint, Part 1." *Star Trek: The Next Generation*. Writ. D.C. Fontana and Gene Roddenberry. Dir. Corey Allen. *Netflix*. Web. 7 Jun. 2016.

"Errand of Mercy." *Star Trek: The Original Series*. Writ. Gene L. Coon. Dir. John Newland. *Netflix*. Web 30 Jun. 2016.

"The Measure of a Man." *Star Trek: The Next Generation*. Writ. Melinda M. Snodgrass. Dir. Robert Scheerer. *Netflix*. Web 3 Jul. 2016.

"The Neutral Zone." *Star Trek: The Next Generation*. Writ. Deborah Mcintyre and Mona Clee. Dir. James L. Conway. *Netflix*. Web. 1 Jul. 2016.

"The Pegasus." *Star Trek: The Next Generation*. Writ. Ronald D. Moore. Dir. LeVar Burton. *Netflix*. Web. 8 Jul. 2016

"Preemptive Strike." *Star Trek: The Next Generation*. Writ. Naren Shankar. Dir. Patrick Stewart. *Netflix*. Web. 9 Jul. 2016

"A Private Little War." *Star Trek: The Original Series*. Wit. Gene Roddenberry and Jud Crucis. Dir. Marc Daniels. *Nextflix*. Web. 4 Jul. 2016.

"Redemption Part 1." *Star Trek: The Next Generation*. Writ. Ronald D. Moore. Dir. Cliff Bole. *Netflix*. Web. 3 Jul. 2016.

"Redemption Part 2." *Star Trek: The Next Generation*. Writ. Ronald D. Moore. Dir. David Carson. *Netflix*. Web. 3 Jul. 2016.

Star Trek VI: The Undiscovered Country. Dir. Nicholas Myer. Paramount 1991, Paramount Home Entertainment, 2009. Blu-Ray.

Star Trek VIII: First Contact. Dir. Jonathan Frakes. Perf. Patrick Stewart, Jonathan Frakes, and Brent Spiner. Paramount, 1996. Paramount Home Video, 2009. Blu-Ray.

"Unification I." *Star Trek: The Next Generation*. Writ. Rick Berman and Michael Piller. Dir. Les Landau. *Netflix*. Web. 6 Jul. 2016.

"Unification II." *Star Trek: The Next Generation*. Writ. Rick Berman and Michael Piller. Dir. Cliff Bole. *Netflix*. Web. 6 Jul. 2016.

"The Wounded." *Star Trek: The Next Generation*. Writ. Stuart Charno, Sara Charno and Cy Chermak. Dir. Chip Chalmers. *Netflix*. 8 Jul. 2016.

An Impossible Standard

*Dangerous Knowledge, Moral Progress
and the Prime Directive*

LARRY A. GRANT

Ignorance is bliss.—Proverb

The Prime Directive exists on two levels. In the series' production world, the Prime Directive was a writers' plot device developed by Gene L. Coon or Theodore Sturgeon and handed down to *The Next Generation* as part of *The Original Series* canon (Adam and Szoka 120n20). Writers used it to motivate characters and complicate their lives by creating tension and forcing action to move the story forward. The Prime Directive was also an expression of the creators' disapproval of American involvement in the war in Vietnam. They viewed the war as an example of the injustice that inevitably follows when powerful nations beset smaller nations, and this belief formed the basis of the Prime Directive. Neither of these aspects of the Prime Directive—plot device or political statement—are the focus of this essay. Instead, the Prime Directive will be examined as a component of "Federation real-world" foreign policy with which Starfleet and its diplomatic personnel must contend as they carried out their duties.[1]

The Prime Directive in the Star Trek Universe

On its face, the Prime Directive, Starfleet's General Order 1, appears to be a rational policy statement. Captain Jean-Luc Picard, with his long experience in Starfleet as a source of authority, provides a basic statement of the policy.[2] History, he says, has repeatedly demonstrated that every time humans interfere with less-developed civilizations—even with the best of intentions—the outcome is "invariably disastrous" ("Symbiosis"). To prevent these inevitable disasters, the Federation has mandated a policy of nonintervention and instituted a strict prohibition on such interactions.[3] The use of history, as suggested by Picard, to "prove" that contacts between asymmetrically developed civilizations lead inevitably to tragic outcomes will play an important part in this examination of the Prime Directive policy and its consequences.

Though the principle of the Prime Directive seems straightforward, closer inspection reveals considerable subjective variation in application of the policy. As the following two examples show, Picard often uses the Prime Directive to achieve a particular outcome that he desires, whether or not his actions accord strictly with the official policy. For instance, strict interpretation of the Prime Directive is the rule when the *Enterprise* rescues the crew of a distressed Ornaran freighter in "Symbiosis," leading Picard to offer the summary of the Prime Directive noted above. Picard discovers that the Ornaran crew is transporting a drug, felicium, because they claim they need it to control a virulent disease on their home world. Alerted by Dr. Crusher, who is unable to isolate an infectious agent for this unusual disease and who concludes from observations of the Ornarans that felicium is a dangerous narcotic, Picard probes further and finds that the Ornarans are the victims of an addiction-extortion scheme by the neighboring Brekkian people. After reason fails to resolve the impasse between the two groups, Picard invokes the Prime Directive and refuses to help to repair the Ornaran ship. Since their addiction has left them incapable of doing the work needed to repair their vessels, the Ornarans will no longer have the means to transport the drug.

Picard reasons that, without their ships, trade will stop, thereby forcing the Ornarans to face their addiction and learn to live without the felicium. However painful and costly that recovery may be for the Ornarans, the Prime Directive permits Picard to avoid complicity in what he judges to be a morally questionable trade. In this case, the desires of both starship commander and Federation policy are served. It is worth noting that, though the principle focus of the episode is the pitiable condition of the Ornarans, the production of felicium is the sole industry of the unsympathetic Brekkian society. The Ornarans, who produce everything they need except felicium, also manufacture all essential goods for the Brekkians, who manufacture nothing for themselves. Arguably, the effect of Picard's action is even more devastating for an entire society where all access to crucial industries is terminated at a stroke. How many members of that society must be held complicit in actions by their leaders, and is their suffering justified? Without ever considering such questions, Picard's decision disrupts two civilizations with likely devastating—perhaps even civilization-ending—consequences for at least one and perhaps both.

Such reinforcing intersections of Picard's personal desires and Federation policy do not always happen, however. While the Ornaran case seems to comport with both the letter and the spirit of the Prime Directive, in effect, Picard employs the Prime Directive as his personal tool to enforce his belief on the Ornarans that their addiction and loss of autonomy are not just incompatible with the higher personal standards that he maintains, but are morally wrong. This interpretation is supported by the episode "Justice" earlier in the season in which *Enterprise* visits the Eden-like planet of the Edo, Rubicun III. Picard instructs an away team to scout the planet's suitability for visits by the *Enterprise*'s crew for rest and recreation. Wesley Crusher joins the team to survey the leisure possibilities for the younger members of the crew. Only after Wesley inadvertently violates a local law does Picard learn that local edicts punish any violation of the law, however minor, with the death penalty. In fact, as Picard will learn, the edicts are literally directions from the Edo god above. Forced to choose between leaving Wesley to his fate and violation of the Prime Directive's non-interference provision, Picard violates Federation policy and Edo law by bringing an Edo representative to his advanced starship. He forces her to confront her god in order to learn what he can of the entity, all the while assuming that the god is nothing more than another technically advanced entity.[4] Then, for some imperceptible reason, the god, perhaps grown bored, acquiesces to Wesley's escape ("Justice").[5]

Picard's violation of the Prime Directive is not simply a refusal to submit to the demands of a weaker culture, knowing they are powerless to object. That alone is sufficient to violate the Prime Directive. However, Picard removes Wesley from the planet knowing that the Edo are the subjects of a powerful entity easily capable of destroying the *Enterprise*. Though he argues with the unresponsive entity that there is no justice if laws are absolute (itself an interesting comment on the Prime Directive), he refuses to surrender Wesley even though he does not know whether or not the god will destroy the *Enterprise*. The entity does not do so, but its reasons are unknown to Picard. Instead, Picard is guided solely by his sense of justice, which supersedes any respect demanded by the Prime Directive for the justice system of indigenous cultures. These two examples, the Edo and the Ornaran episodes, highlight the sort of subjective employment of the Prime Directive encountered repeatedly in the mission records of the voyages of the *Enterprise* and suggest serious defects exist in the policy.

This essay looks for the sources of those defects in the history and character of the Prime Directive to determine if it will produce the desired outcome; i.e., would strict application of the Prime Directive by the Federation and its agents prevent the corruption and destruction of emerging civilizations? "Strict application" includes a ban on exceptions to the policy based on subjective appeals to presumably higher principles. Three aspects of the policy are explored. First, the Prime Directive is examined as another expression of the dynamics and policies that arise to govern relations between civilizations. It is particularly concerned with the question of asymmetrical contact, where the Federation is "superior" to the host planet technologically and socially. Second, the Prime Directive's connection to the data-information-knowledge-wisdom continuum is inspected. The focus of this study is the Federation's ability to exert the desired level of control (i.e., total) over access to all the pathways and stores of information needed to ensure the Prime Directive is effective. Finally, the assumptions that buttress the Prime Directive's threshold standard for contact between civilizations (i.e., the requirement that contact may only follow the attainment of warp drive capability by the emerging civilization) are explored. In this exercise, the definition of the Prime Directive, in the spirit its creators in both the twentieth and 24th centuries envisioned, is defined as a policy prohibiting interference by officials of the Federation in the affairs of developing civilizations to preclude the detrimental effects that "invariably" attend such contact.

Historical Antecedents

Prior to presenting a discussion of the three aspects of the policy, I'll offer the antecedents of the Prime Directive. Little is known of the Federation government, but it is not unreasonable to turn to Earth's history to gain some insight into the Federation Council and its policymaking practices. Aspects of Federation policy can be traced back along the human branch of history that merged with the broader Federation stream after Earth's First Contact with its future Federation partners. Other antecedents could be traced down the histories of other spacefaring civilizations, but these branches are even less well known. It is sufficient for the purposes of this essay to examine the antecedents of the Prime Directive in Earth history, since the continuity of the principles found in human diplomatic policy and practices that appear in the Prime Directive becomes evident. Furthermore, it can be assumed with confidence that, by the 24th century, all of the other members of the Federation have had the opportunity to make their marks on the Prime Directive. If the policy nonetheless maintains considerable similarity with policies from Earth's past, then either the thoughts of Earth's Federation partners are similar to Earth's or Earthly principles won the argument over the issue.[6] Further, it is appropriate to look to history to understand the Prime Directive if for no other reason than that was the source of authority to which Picard appealed to justify it in the first place.

Grand Strategy

Responsibility for the logical development of a policy like the Prime Directive does not rest with Starfleet. While Starfleet ships and officers represent the most familiar face in the Next Generation universe, Starfleet is not the branch of the Federation bureaucracy responsible for the policy. The prerogative for policymaking does not rest with the military or exploring arms of government. The authority to formulate and alter such policies rests with the diplomats and the Federation executives who derive their diplomatic doctrine and policies from the Federation's grand strategy (Rowan 195–196).[7] Grand strategy, as strategist and historian Edward Luttwak defines it, functions at "the level at which knowledge and persuasion, or in modern terms intelligence and diplomacy, interact with military strength to determine outcomes in a world of other states with their own grand strategies" (409). In Earth's Westphalian period, from the mid-seventeenth century to the mid–22nd century, national leaders formulated grand strategy based on state sovereignty to guide their strategic planning and their use of the instruments of national power to achieve long-term national security objectives.

For example, the grand strategy adopted by the United States during the twentieth century comprised five major themes: (1) support the proliferation of democratic governments, (2) preserve a favorable position among the principal powers, (3) create friendly alliances and strengthen their capabilities, (4) intervene to oppose international troublemakers, and (5) defend the homeland (Miller 7–44). Political scientist Peter Feaver adds promotion of economic themes to this list but otherwise is in general agreement (57–70). While the primary emphasis shifted among these national policy themes at various times according to strategic need, together they drove the development and application of subordinate national doctrine statements (e.g., the Truman doctrine). These high-level doctrines, in turn, guided the development of specific diplomatic, military, and economic doctrines and the more tangible strategic, operational, and tactical plans developed at lower levels of government.

These grand themes display an enduring logic, and many fit neatly in revealed Federation practices. From the example above, the general characteristics of a Federation grand strategy might be postulated. The Federation is non-exploitive of the resources of weaker powers. Federation grand strategy is rational and realistic, not driven by greed, malice, jealousy, envy, or similar emotional responses or motivations. Though the specifics of the Federation grand strategy cannot be known with certainty, no long-time observer of the Federation can doubt that it struggles to preserve enlightened democratic government. The Federation and the *Enterprise* have acted on multiple occasions to preserve a favorable position among the principal powers in encounters with Cardassians, Ferengi, Romulans, and various renegades. Diplomats from the Federation routinely travel with Captain Picard, often requiring his personal assistance to create, maintain, and strengthen Federation alliances, as occurred in "Sarek." The *Enterprise* and her crew have intervened repeatedly to oppose galactic troublemakers. Even in their first mission to Farpoint station on Deneb IV, they find that the humanoid Bandi have illegitimately imprisoned an intelligent space-dwelling alien lifeform, and Picard repairs the injustice while also demonstrating to the super-being Q that human civilization is more mature than he suspects ("Encounter at Farpoint"). Finally, defending the homeland is a basic mission undertaken by *Enterprise* even when it might lead to self-destruction, as against the Borg, for example ("The Best of Both Worlds, Parts I and II"). An example can be found in *Star Trek: First Contact* when first officer, Commander William T. Riker, Counselor Deanna Troi, and Chief Engineer Geordi La Forge describe humanity's utopian future to Zefram Cochrane, knowing that the future they have lived is endangered if they fail to convince him to conduct the first warp flight in human history as scheduled. As Troi points out, his launch is necessary to keep the Borg probe from destroying a future where many social ills are eliminated in the fifty years following the flight.

Prime Directive in Human History

Like the enduring themes of grand strategy, the Prime Directive also has many antecedents in Earth's diplomatic history. An early one can be found in the writings of the sixteenth century Dominican priest, Bartolomé de las Casas. In *A Short Account of the Destruction of the Indies*, *In Defense of the Indians*, and other works, de las Casas deplored the harsh treatment of the New World natives by Spanish conquerors. His description of the natives echoes Jean-Jacques Rousseau's noble savage: "These people are the most devoid of rancors, hatreds, or desire for vengeance of any people in the world." He continues, "They are also poor people, for they not only possess little but have no desire to possess worldly goods. For this reason they are not arrogant, embittered, or greedy." Their paradisiacal life did not survive the arrival of the Spaniards, one of whom was Javier Maribona-Picard, a distant ancestor of Jean-Luc Picard ("Journey's End").

> It was upon these gentle lambs … that from the very first day they clapped eyes on them the Spanish fell like ravening wolves upon the fold, or like tigers and savage lions who have not eaten meat for days. The pattern established at the outset has remained unchanged to this day, and the Spaniards still do nothing save tear the natives to shreds, murder them and inflict upon them untold misery, suffering and distress, tormenting, harrying and persecuting them mercilessly [*A Short Account*, 11].

When the Spanish first arrived at Hispaniola, he says, three million people lived on the island. Within a short time only two hundred survived. De las Casas objected strenuously to the physical mistreatment of the natives, but, more crucially, he deplored the damage done to their spiritual beings. Maltreatment, he argued, would alienate them to the point that they would reject the Church's teachings and endanger their eternal salvation.

> Now Christ wanted his gospel to be preached with enticements, Gentleness, and all meekness, and pagans to be led to the truth not by armed forces but by holy examples, Christian conduct, and the word of God, so that no opportunity would be offered for blaspheming the sacred name or hating the true religion because of the conduct of the preachers [De las Casas *In Defense*, 350].

De las Casas' campaign eventually secured a papal encyclical on the enslavement and evangelization of Indians that resonates in the Prime Directive. While he could not prohibit contact between the cultures, the Pope tried to mitigate further harm.

> Desiring to provide ample remedy for these evils, We define and declare by these Our letters ... the said Indians and all other people who may later be discovered by Christians, are by no means to be deprived of their liberty or the possession of their property, even though they be outside the faith of Jesus Christ; and that they may and should, freely and legitimately, enjoy their liberty and the possession of their property; nor should they be in any way enslaved; should the contrary happen, it shall be null and have no effect [Pope Paul III, *Sublimus Dei*].

Unfortunately, this attempt to establish a caring and protective relationship between the cultures had little practical effect.

Indeed, the hope of restraining the historic human desire to meddle in other peoples' affairs and to allow them to live according to their own rules was overwhelmed in the subsequent three or four centuries on Earth by the so-called "civilizing impulse." The civilizing impulse refers to the belief that more enlightened cultures have a missionary responsibility to bring civilization and refinement—suitably defined—to primitive and barbarous cultures everywhere. Widely held in Europe, similar beliefs were also regarded by the Japanese and other aspiring cultures as justification for their expansionist drives (Eskildsen 388). At the same time that they carried out their civilizing mission, these cultural evangelists often managed to earn a tidy profit or secure high position for themselves in the new world or upon their return to the old.

The civilizing impulse faded by the middle of the twentieth century and the whole colonial edifice crumbled as colonies gained independence from their former masters. During this period, as new nations were founded and old nations emerged from the shadows of the Second World War, the reaction against intervention and invasion brought new respect to the concepts of stable borders and inviolable sovereignty. In the wake of World War II, the victorious nations revisited and strengthened state sovereignty in light of the recent aggressions. The victors created a new organization, the United Nations, and included in its Charter a prohibition against unlawful intervention. Article 2(4) confirms the inviolability of state sovereignty, stating, "All Members shall refrain in their international relations from the threat or use of force against the territorial integrity or political independence of any state, or in any other manner inconsistent with the Purposes of the United Nations." The UN International Court amplified this principle, saying that the element of coercion was "the very essence of prohibited intervention," (I.C.J. Reports 108), and Oppenheim's International Law further elaborated that "*Interference pure and simple is not intervention*" (emphasis added)" (Oppenheim 1.1 432).

The human diplomatic principle of unlawful intervention set forth here is much narrower than the Federation standard in that, for the Prime Directive, the question of coercion is irrelevant. *Any* contact with a sovereign civilization posted off-limits by the Prime Directive is forbidden, including contact to prevent or to stop atrocities. While Federation officials argue that this position is necessary for the higher purpose of protecting less-developed civilizations from inevitable disaster, this constitutes a much stronger statement of support for state-planetary-system sovereignty than was the case even in the more primitive times of the twentieth century. At the time of the UN's founding, the concept of inherent individual sovereignty emerged in conflict with state sovereignty, which was forced, at least marginally, to give way to the rights of individual human beings. In the decades following the Holocaust, the belief spread that unlawful violations of human rights—even by state authority—occasionally obliged a response to save the victimized and punish the offender. To that end, some statesmen and theorists began to envision circumstances where a state or group of states could intrude legally into the internal affairs of another state to end human rights violations (Shapiro 29).

Not everyone concurred. Even when carried out only to correct the grimmest subset of circumstances for the best of reasons, humanitarian interventions nonetheless remained controversial, because they were violations of, and threatened to, undermine the entire concept of national sovereignty. That was not a welcome possibility even among the caring nation-states of Earth most likely to practice humanitarian interventions. As professor of international relations Hedley Bull commented in 1984:

> As regards the right of so-called humanitarian intervention… there is no present tendency for states to claim, or for the international community to recognize, any such right. The reluctance evident in the international community even to experiment with the conception of a right of humanitarian intervention reflects not only an unwillingness to jeopardize the rules of sovereignty and noninter-vention by conceding such a right to individual states, but also the lack of any agreed doctrine as to what human rights are [qtd. in Chang 196].

The inability of Earth's international community to reach a consensus to respond to even the clearest instances of genocide (e.g., Rwanda, 1994) offers stark proof that the lack of agreement permitted the destruction of millions of lives. Humans eventually discarded the concept of national sovereignty that enabled such atrocities when Earth achieved a unified planetary government.[8] It is surprising, then, that the Federation's Prime Directive reflects so closely an unenlightened form of sovereignty, bringing all its flaws into galactic diplomatic affairs.[9] The justification for this, of course, is that the underlying Federation prohibition against interference is a necessary condition to ensure the safety of less-developed civilizations. Whatever the justification the practical effect in a contest between respect for sovereignty and prevention of harm to a developing planetary civilization or to its populace, strict compliance with the Prime Directive mandates deference to the principle of sovereignty.

Knowledge Is Dangerous

The Federation's policy of protecting planetary systems from interference and domination by external powers, and from "contaminating" effects generally, has the effect of erecting an information blockade around developing worlds to control the inward flow of information. This embargo is not absolute. As the episode "Who Watches the Watchers" shows, the ban prohibits information flow in one direction—toward the developing system—while allowing limited information to be gathered by covert Federation observers. This is to be expected; some form of intelligence collection on the emerging civilizations' level of technical accomplishment is required by the Federation to judge the proper moment for a policy change. This control mechanism remains in place until the less technologically advanced culture has developed (if it ever does) a warp capability. Until that time, the lesser-developed civilizations remain blessedly uncontaminated by dangerous information.

This characteristic of the Directive turns it into a paternalistic exercise in withholding of knowledge. This impulse also has a long history in human affairs, one even older than the Westphalian nation-state. The concept of forbidden knowledge and the related notion that new knowledge is dangerous is firmly rooted in human culture from the Biblical prohibition against eating the fruit from the tree of knowledge of good and evil onwards. But temptation abounds. In *Star Trek: Insurrection*, the fundamental conflict of the story arises because some members of the Ba'ku civilization were tempted by the off-world bright lights to try to expand their knowledge, leading them to revolt against the stagnant sameness of their society and its life-of-the-mind existence. Their revolt and desire to know the universe were no stronger than Eve's desire to have her eyes opened and to know good and evil. However, the actions of both condemned them to aging and death. Unfortunately for the long term prospects of the isolationist Ba'ku—who seem to offer proof that knowledge is not so dangerous so long as its use is avoided—the attraction of the bright-lights universe endures, as Data's ability to charm their children shows. Like Adam and Eve, the builders of Babel were punished with confusion when they tried to build their tower up to heaven. Prometheus's gift of fire to mankind (a distinctly bipolar bit of knowledge) is another story of the gods' attempting to deny access to knowledge by keeping a powerful tool—fire—out of the hands of mankind and failing. Zeus, fearing that men might challenge the gods, punished Prometheus and created Pandora, who shortly unleashed a torrent of afflictions to keep an incautious humanity in its place.

Even when *knowledge* is acquired, *wisdom* does not always follow. The great superhuman king Gilgamesh was all-knowledgeable, but also an oppressively harsh ruler to his people. Commander Riker also learned this lesson in "Hide and Q." In that episode, Q—playing an acceptable serpent—tempts Riker with the gift of omnipotence. Riker's new power, used at first to achieve what seem to be indisputably good ends—restoring Worf and Wesley to life—soon reveals its dark side. Picard, believing the temptation of such power is too great for any human, challenges Riker not to abuse it. Believing he can control it, Riker agrees but soon regrets his promise after it prevents him from saving the life of a child. Arrogance follows, and after pride comes the fall. Again, the message is that knowledge and the power that comes with it lead to destruction. Ultimately, Riker gives up the power in exchange for wisdom, suggesting that only by gaining *and rejecting* dangerous knowledge can man reach true maturity, a circumstance very like that of the Ba'ku.

The theme in these ancient (and future) stories is neither solely Western nor particularly ancient. The Japanese policy of *sakoku*—national isolation—under the Tokugawa shogunate, and modern Chinese, Cuban, Iranian, North Korean, and other national prohibitions against free access to information reflect a belief that ruin, if only to the reigning political order, inevitably follows exposure to new ideas. The theme features widely in literature. The dangers of curiosity and knowledge seeking often combine with fearful images of rash scientists whose dangerous search for nature's secrets leads to disaster. Mary Shelley's Frankenstein creation, Goethe's Faustian pact, and Huxley's *Brave New World* show the potential dangers, but so do folktales like the Basket Woman story of the Native Americans. This fear has survived into the 24th century. The Prime Directive, an important component of Federation foreign policy, can be interpreted as a 24th century embodiment of the "knowledge is dangerous" theme (Livo xxiv–xxvii.) In the Federation's case, it is Starfleet that occupies the cherubim's guard post to prevent spread of dangerous knowledge, and the "gods" are beings who gain their godlike distinction from the emerging civilizations on the basis of their high technology. As Sir Arthur C. Clarke observed, "Any sufficiently advanced technology is indistinguishable from magic." (Clarke, "Sir Arthur's Quotations") If not quite godlike, the result is much the same.

Moral Advance, Technical Advance

If one species presuming to judge which knowledge to permit another sentient species to access seems condescending, the underlying criterion used to end this paternalistic embargo does not have much empirical evidence to support it. As stated previously, the operative benchmark used by the Federation assumes that technological progress advances alongside moral and ethical progress.[10] Opening access to the emerging civilization once it achieves a particular technical development, warp drive, implies that the related moral and ethical state also has been reached. Earth's philosophers long argued over whether human progress in the sense of steady improvements in human nature—inherent moral and ethical progress—was possible. The late eighteenth century Enlightenment philosopher Georg W.F. Hegel postulated an oscillating dialectical system that delivered a progressively richer synthesis out of the tension that exists between the extremes of thesis and antithesis. Karl Marx also formulated a scientific theory of historical progress, and others have argued similarly that progress is not only possible but certain.[11] Captain Picard offers some anecdotal evidence that humans have made considerable strides in this respect.

While investigating a problem in the Neutral Zone, *Enterprise* rescues three humans from Earth who had been placed in stasis aboard a cryogenic satellite hundreds of years earlier ("The Neutral Zone"). One of them, Ralph Offenhouse, is shocked to learn that he has awakened in 2364. He demands that Picard afford him the means to check on the financial arrangements he made prior to entering stasis. After listening to Offenhouse's demand, Picard tells him that money has become obsolete. Even more startling to Offenhouse than learning that means have been found to replace or eliminate money is Picard's assertion that humankind no longer seeks satisfaction in material possessions. Humanity has, he says, outgrown such infantile materialism. This would be a truly remarkable evolution if one could be assured that it had occurred. The abandonment of lawlessness for willing compliance with mature social and legal norms would make the enforcement of the Prime Directive much easier and perhaps even make the Federation's self-assumed role of arbiter of civilizational development somewhat more acceptable. However, Picard's declaration that human moral progress has reached an advanced stage of ethical maturity is contradicted by considerable evidence. Overwhelming data exist in Federation records that that Humanity 2.0 has not arrived even in the 24th century. If the Federation has made progress, it has been a very uneven achievement.

Hard information about the supposed change in human character is difficult to find, but even a cursory examination of Federation records and of some problems faced by the crew of the *Enterprise* is not reassuring. They show that such criminal activities as smuggling ("Unification, Part I"), genocide and retributory mass murder ("The Survivors"), treason ("Face of the Enemy"), mutiny ("The Pegasus"), and even Picard's own readiness to engage in deadly bar fights ("Tapestry") continue to be problems in Federation space in the 24th century. Though numerous instances can be found of these sorts of activities among average Federation citizens—not all of whom are human—it is telling that some involve individuals at the highest ranks of Starfleet. For example, the *Pegasus* incident in 2358 refers to a mutiny of ship's officers that took place in a Federation starship.

In that instance, the mutiny that erupted against the commanding officer of *Pegasus*, Erik Pressman, was an instance of compounded criminality. Pressman was engaged in secret testing of a cloaking device in violation of the Treaty of Algeron, which had prevented war between the Federation and Romulans for decades. His actions placed his crew in danger, and following a mishap, most of the officers mutinied to prevent the ship's destruction. Will Riker was the only bridge officer who stood by Pressman. Revisiting the *Pegasus* years later, Picard realizes the true and illegal nature of the research, and Admiral Pressman (with others at Starfleet intelligence) is taken into custody. This episode proves that serious crimes and misdemeanors occur at the highest levels of Starfleet, and leaves one wondering how *Pegasus* ever got detailed to carry out the mission in the first place without someone asking a few questions.[12] Are others still in hiding?

Or imagine how the search for profits—material or political or however defined—might undermine the Prime Directive. On Earth in the 21st century, smugglers stole rhinoceros horn in South Africa and shipped it to the Far East, because the horns were more valuable in the Far Eastern market than gold ("Rhino horns"). Similar opportunities would attract adventurers willing to violate the Prime Directive for personal gain. In "Gambit, Part I," Picard himself proves how credible such a scenario is after he discovers that an archaeological site in which he is interested has nearly been destroyed. Picard sets out to find those responsible, leading to his capture by a group of mercenaries. After his capture he takes on the role of a smuggler, Galen, and discovers that the mercenaries are raiding Romulan archaeological sites throughout the sector in search of a specific artifact. The artifact turns out to be an ancient Vulcan device—a psionic resonator—that focuses and amplifies telepathic energy. The weapon is being sought by Vulcan renegades to destroy the Vulcan council. Though the device proves ineffective against peaceful people, the rarity of that condition in the *Star Trek* universe and the obvious danger the device presents to beings with less than perfectly peaceful characters, leads to its destruction. Such activity is unlikely to be limited to artifacts and faux remedies. Drugs—illicit and those with legitimate value—are certain to attract attention. The Ornarans illustrate the illicit attraction, and the Son'a-Federation partnership on display in *Insurrection* provides evidence of the allure that beneficial substances have that can warp reason. The Son'a, developers of the narcotic ketracel-white used to control genetically engineered soldiers, desire the metaphasic particles of the Ba'ku to achieve immortality. The attraction blinds the Federation Council until Picard's revolt highlights the dangers. Who can tell what other possibilities might not arise? Raw medicinal materials scavenged from Earth's jungles and rainforests—often located in poor, less-developed nations unable to protect them—provided components in at least 25 percent of 21st century medicines, and also provided astronomical profits (Tyler 5, 7–8; Gallis 42.) Moreover, as a twentieth century United Nations report noted, "The expanding trade in medicinal plants has serious implications on the survival of several plant species, with many under serious threat to become extinct" (Bodeker, Bhat, Burley, and Vantomme). Illicit drug components, marketable for even greater profits, is also found in the forest, and, as the Ornarans proves, there is a market in Federation space for such compounds.[13]

Clearly some 24th century humanoids—the Ferengi come to mind—are driven by profit, and even a few humans (including Picard's fellow archaeologist/love interest Vash) are susceptible to the thrill-seeking impulses that would be a part of such adventures. If violations of the Prime Directive do occur, what are the consequences if the penalties routinely get waved away, as often seems to be the case? Picard's own behavior on the Edo world is an example of the weak enforcement of the regulations. The consequence of making rules, regulations, and policies whose limits are undermined by ineffective or inept enforcement is to permit and sanction the sort of behavior that undermines all Federation laws, not just the Prime Directive. Even Picard recognizes this. In a slightly incongruous moment in *Insurrection*, when Picard demands that Admiral Dougherty tell him the number of people required before a violation of principle becomes wrong, he is arguing—perhaps not very effectively considering his own personal record—that a democratic society depends on respect for, and compliance with, the laws. This applies to even those in power who believe their violations are in society's best interest. When these things are undermined, crimes may be committed with impunity. If some humans have matured in moral character by the 24th century beyond a need for the prodding of the threat or fact of punishment, not all have. However much progress mankind has made, therefore, empirical evidence shows that "deviant" behavior has not been eliminated from humanity or from the Federation in the 24th century. Even the fact that the Federation maintains extensive machinery for criminal legal proceedings is evidence of this. No truly rational civilization would maintain such a complicated edifice if there was no need. If law breaking—minor and major—continues to hold place in the Federation universe, this is a small thing by comparison to the continued existence of warfare, one of the great evils in human history. Unfortunately, humans continue to fight wars as late as Picard's lifetime ("The Battle") and stand ready to fight others.

Technical Advance

"You can't stop the signal."—Mr. Universe, Serenity (2005)

In view of the foregoing, the Prime Directive appears unlikely to benefit much from the alleged improvements in human character; unfortunately, it might not make much difference to the effectiveness of the Prime Directive in the end if every improvement Picard mentions came to pass. Human agency is less important to the success or failure of the Prime Directive than other factors baked into the structure of the physical universe. This can be illustrated by looking at Starfleet's information handling capabilities.

As humans learned in the nineteenth and twentieth centuries, one consequence of the rise of information technologies is that the cost of information plummets. When something is both cheap and desirable, its reach expands. By the 24th century the improvement in information handling technologies means that Starfleet vessels are equipped with sensors able to scan over lightyears of space and return huge quantities of useable data. As a measure of the amount of information that can be manipulated by the *Enterprise*'s Command, Control, Communications and Intelligence (C3I) systems, La Forge noted that the starship's sensors can search out to ranges of ten light years ("The Wounded"). This amounts to a spherical volume of about 4,200 cubic lightyears. While its resolution is not known, if the long-range sensor sweep is to return useful information at that range, it must be reasonably fine over a significant part of that distance.

When Picard orders a standard sensor sweep, the information acquired is immense. Assuming that the scan is sufficiently sensitive that it can detect the presence of normal interstellar gas in that volume at average densities (about one gas ion per cubic centimeter), a reasonable standard for a vessel concerned with the consequences of traveling at multiples of the speed of light, then the sensor systems—even ignoring dust particles—would have to deal with about 10^{54} gas ions in a volume with a radius of 10 lightyears. In terms of measuring and cataloging whether an ion is or is not present in each cubic centimeter of interstellar space in that volume, the ship must commit about 10^{41} terabytes of memory storage. To 21st century eyes, this is a preposterous number, but even if the *Enterprise*'s sensors are only one millionth that capable, say, by assigning a 0 or 1 to each cubic meter of the scanned space that meets a given threshold, the sensors' memory subsystems still require at that lower level on the order of 10^{35} or so terabytes.[14] Just to examine the stream of data without storing it is not much less daunting considering how fast the process would have to occur.

This is a phenomenal capability, but even more so is the information-handling ability of the ship's transporters. The human body contains about 10^{27} atoms and for the purposes of this discussion roughly 10^{45} bits of information (10^{33} terabyte-sized hard drives).[15] The data transfer rate achieved by the transporter is roughly equal to the amount of data moved divided by the time required to complete the operation, say five seconds of television time. The lower threshold for the data transfer rate for one person in that interval must be about 2×10^{44} bps. Often, however, more than one individual is transported simultaneously in the same amount of time. Obviously, if the transporter moves five red-shirted crewmembers and one Starfleet captain in the same amount of time, the upper limit of the data rate is much higher than the 2×10^{44} bps used to transport a single crewmember.[16] If moving information at that speed and in those amounts is routine, it implies that the process is so inexpensive as to make the question of cost insignificant. The same can be said for the ship's replicators, which also must employ very little energy at very high efficiencies to make Earl Grey (hot) so routine.

The consequences for the Prime Directive should be obvious. With the ability to move information in huge quantities at very low cost commonplace, efforts to contain it will fail. To understand how hard this effort might be, one is only required to imagine the *Star Trek* information equivalent of an ancient USB drive and speculate where that device and its cargo of data might travel in the pocket of a spy or whistleblower. To paraphrase Jeff Goldblum's character, Ian Malcolm, in *Jurassic Park*, information will find a way to escape its confinement no matter how it is guarded. Malcolm would express skepticism in response to any Federation assurance that its information was secure, since the chaos inherent in the universe inevitably intervenes. The smallest changes give rise to great shifts that derail the best-laid plans and policies.[17] Perhaps the Federation that has managed the development of Heisenberg compensators has also eliminated chaos from small portions of the universe, but even that seems doubtful. After all, USS *Enterprise* details crewmembers to its department of quantum mechanics for a reason ("Lessons"). As the Vulcan philosopher T'Plana-Hath notes, chaos underlies Federation civilization (*Star Trek IV: The Voyage Home*).

Some sources of information simply fall outside of the Federation's control. Other life forms might be able to detect Starfleet technology from the nontrivial clues that are likely to be apparent to the gaze of any reasonably alert stargazer. When the Borg tunnel into Earth's past to stop the First Contact by destroying Zefram Cochrane and his ship, the effort to convince Cochrane to continue his work includes showing him the *Enterprise* orbiting overhead through a small telescope (*Star Trek: First Contact*). Earth has had telescopes since Galileo looked at Jupiter's moons in the sixteenth century, and there are other clues considerably more convincing than reflected sunlight that might give away the presence of intelligent life in space.

If accidental exposure proves to be insufficient to alert planet-bound civilizations, any civilization that has progressed to the stargazing stage of development will eventually establish a program designed to seek out extraterrestrial signals. In 1964, while conducting research on satellite transmissions, astronomers Arno Penzias and Robert Wilson discovered an unexpected microwave noise source that turned out to be the signal of the cosmic microwave background radiation associated with the Big Bang (Adams 295). That same year, Gene Roddenberry used Dr. Frank Drake's 1961 equation, which attempted to estimate the number of extraterrestrial civilizations in our galaxy with which humans might be able to communicate, in his successful proposal for the original *Star Trek* series to Desilu Studio executives (Memory Alpha, "Star Trek Is…"). Physicists had speculated for more than sixty years before that time that radio waves might be detected from astronomical sources, and astronomers had observed the sky using radio wavelengths for at least three decades prior to Penzias's and Wilson's discovery. Their work shows how even a very faint signal might surprise an un-alert observer. Such basic technology can also be used in a systematic search for intelligent life. Earth established a program called SETI, the search for extraterrestrial intelligence in 1973 and, in 1977, astronomer Jerry R. Ehman detected the WOW signal, a strong narrowband radio signal that appeared in Sagittarius (Clingbine 209). Speculation about the signal's source has not eliminated the possibility that it was artificial in origin.

Any slightly odd signal in their data will generate significant attention and speculation by astronomers. For instance, an emergency signal from a Federation ship might be high on the list of observable signals. Their character by design must be strong, multispectral, and detectable at great distances. They must also be obviously artificial to stand out against the normal electromagnetic activity of the galaxy. Any signals with these characteristics would immediately attract notice as various episodes show. The *Enterprise* responds to such signals in "Suddenly Human" and in "Power Play." In "A Matter of Honor," Lieutenant Worf provides Riker with a tiny transmitter altered to transmit an omnidirectional emergency signal. Unusual signals attract attention, and many spark immediate speculation that their origin might be the result of intelligent life forms. When astronomers searching for exoplanets noticed something odd in the data from the F-type star (KIC 8462852) in the constellation Cygnus in late 2015, eager speculation began that the regular and significant shifts in luminosity resulted from an alien megastructure like a Dyson sphere circling the star. Later explanations suggested that the dimming was the result of the technological evolution in instruments, but the furor shows how clues about interstellar space—at a distance of almost 1500 light-years!—are observable even to planet-bound civilizations like old Earth at very low levels of technological development (Wright, et.al.). This signal proved to be false, but it is worth noting that the signal was discovered by citizen scientists on Earth, not even professional astronomers, suggesting the vulnerability of such things to detection is high.

How would the radiation from the starships of galactic civilizations compare to these extremely faint signals? This question received some attention from aerospace engineer Robert Zubrin in 1994. He speculated that detection is possible at considerable distances from the observer. Depending on the type of engine used to power a starship and the instruments used by observers, Zubrin suggested that they might be detected at ranges of as little as one lightyear or as much as 300 light-years" (494). Starship signals, deliberate or otherwise, if sufficiently widespread—and Federation records show considerable activity—would be revealed to any civilization approaching 21st century Earth levels of technology that it was not alone in the galaxy. While suggestive, even the level of technology involved in Zubrin's speculation is not needed. In fact it is not even necessary to *watch the sky!*, as the 1951 classic *The Thing from Another World* suggests. Hard evidence of Federation activity might require no more than a shovel and a visit to nineteenth century San Francisco, where a little digging in the final episode of season five revealed the severed head of *the* 24th century android ("Time's Arrow"). There is no better evidence that an advanced civilization's information control systems are flawed than that the head of Starfleet's only android ended up in an ancient cave, waiting for anyone to find. So much for a total embargo on data.[18] Similar examples show up in the previously mentioned accidental exposure depicted in "Who Watches the Watchers" and in deliberate interference for humanitarian reasons in "Homeward." Unlike the criminal possibilities previously mentioned, malice is not required for exposure of information, which is sometimes revealed for the best of reasons.

Finally, all the speculation on whether the Federation could prevent the spread of information and the unaided detection of indications from planetary surfaces simply discounts the possibility that someone is actively searching for Starfleet secrets to bring, Prometheus-like, information to the embargoed planet dwellers. Examples of the existence of a smuggling infrastructure are numerous. For example, in a bar on Qualor II, Riker meets the ex-wife of a smuggler killed by the *Enterprise* while trying to steal deuterium ("Unification II"). In "Chain of Command, Part I" Picard and others arrange to be smuggled to the Cardassian planet, Celtris III, with the assistance of DaiMon Solok. It is possible that a Ferengi would hesitate to smuggle something as profitable as dangerous information, but unlikely. Again, in "Gambit, Part I" Picard and Riker deal with pirates ransacking archaeological sites for a super-weapon—what other possible markets exist for technology? If the Federation has to work this hard to stop fuel and artifact smuggling, and if smugglers will move anything for profit, then the smuggling of valuable information also happens, particularly when even the most closely guarded secrets in history have been susceptible to this vulnerability.

An example of the temptation and the consequences of an information security failure created by agents actively seeking and selling information can be found in the twentieth century Manhattan Project established by the United States in June 1942 to design and build an atomic bomb. The stakes could not have been higher: the triumph of fascism or the triumph of democratic government. Allied scientists won the race against the Nazis, successfully testing their weapon on July 16, 1945. The Manhattan Project was carried out behind multiple overlapping layers of security. Extensive background checks, constant surveillance, layers of security checkpoints, and great diligence were employed to keep the Project a secret, not only from the German enemy, but also from their Soviet ally. Nevertheless, the information restrictions failed. In 1946 the U.S. Army's top-secret counter-intelligence program VENONA revealed that Soviet spies—highly-placed individuals inside the project—had betrayed the Manhattan Project secret, showing that even the most closely guarded secret can be leaked by trusted high-level officials despite the best efforts (Haynes and Klehr 10). The example of Romulan Sub-Commander Selok posing as Vulcan Ambassador T'Pel shows that spying at the highest levels of the United Federation of Planets is also not unknown ("Data's Day").

Notwithstanding the Federation's enormous information infrastructure advantages, its systems inevitably will suffer similar security failings. Even if Federation systems are proportionally more secure than 21st century governments' systems, their improvements will still be asymptotic and not absolute. Sophisticated planetary, state, and capable non-state/planetary-affiliated actors, whose numbers and locations cannot be predicted, will retain the ability to steal, alter, destroy, and misuse sensitive data from both types of systems. Adversaries with varying degrees of sophistication and the intent will intrude, operate, plant collaborators, and withdraw, potentially without leaving any sign of their presence. Actors within known space that will have these capabilities include empires, planetary systems governments, organized crime groups, and others, like the Borg hive mind that surely knows everything that Picard knows, and the god-entity of the Edo that, as Data admits, knows everything he knows. However, the worst examples of this, as with the Manhattan Project, will take place because of the actions of otherwise trusted agents who betray confidences. This was true of the "The Pegasus" incident. The illegal cloaking device testing project aboard USS *Pegasus* was set in motion in violation of the Treaty of Algeron by the very group—members of Starfleet Command—tasked at the highest stratum of the Federation to detect and stop such violations. Instead, the secret Starfleet group covered up the operation for many years ("The Pegasus"). The episode "The Drumhead" also shows that an active fear of spying exists in the Federation and Starfleet bureaucracies. If this fear is rational, it reveals the existence of a threat, though it does not provide details. If it is irrational, it suggests something very unpleasant about the Federation, since a "drumhead court," by its nature, is one that gives little consideration to evidence, legalities, or the protection of defendants' rights.

Justification

The Prime Directive's information embargo seems reasonable and justifiable, particularly in light of Earth's experiences with nuclear proliferation and similar issues. Knowledge is a sharp tool. It can be used to cut, but it can harm the one wielding it if care is not exercised in its use. Refusing to give a sharp tool to a baby is not only a good idea, it is responsible behavior. However, refusing to give the baby a sharp tool until it grows up and invents the tool himself is ridiculous. It is a rejection of the power of reasonable interaction, education, and training; it is an abdication of the duties of a responsible adult. It handicaps the object being "protected" based on the erroneous argument that interaction between those who have attained different levels of development is "invariably" damaging to one party or the other. The successful raising and education of children are only the easiest proof of the opposite case. Mentors are essential in such a relationship to ensure a positive outcome.

Sir Arthur C. Clarke saw technology as containing a self-winnowing mechanism. "As our own species is in the process of proving, one cannot have superior science and inferior morals. The combination is unstable and self-destroying" (The Arthur C. Clarke Foundation). Humanity must get smarter as its technology gets smarter and uncouple its ability to destroy from its will to destroy, or it will end in self-destruction. Civilizational safety, according to Clarke, demands that the two elements evolve hand-in-hand. Unfortunately, like two sine waves slightly out of phase, the curve representing human toolmaking skills—and likely all other intelligent species—has always led the moral and ethical curve. As other parts of the human animal—muscle, bone—attained mature forms long before the human brain, so have human tool-making skills evolved earlier than human moral and ethical skills. The benefits that derive from having a functioning brain must necessarily follow the development of that organ. No doubt engineers will develop, as did Doctor Noonien Soong, all other aspects of a functional humanoid android long before managing to develop a positronic brain for such a system. Despite Isaac Asimov's optimism, the ability of engineers to incorporate the "Three Laws of Robotics" into their creations will almost certainly trail even that development.[19]

The problem with blanket restrictions and ineffective enforcement regimes is that they ignore human motivation, innovation, initiative, and the willingness of individuals to hold and to act on incongruent ideas and beliefs contrary to logic or law or received wisdom. Effective enforcement of such a regime depends on a vigilant Federation overseeing and preventing literally every potential violation when those who might be interested in evading the prohibitions need to succeed only once. Regulations like the Prime Directive overlook the fact that it is impossible to legislate the laws of the physical world when they are found to be inconvenient. There is an apocryphal story from ancient Earth that the Tennessee legislature once tried to enact a law to make the value of pi equal to three (Heinlein 319).[20] Making a policy to prohibit the flow of information in the way envisaged by the Prime Directive is just as ill-advised, since information is a fundamental part of the universe, not amenable in every case to intelligent control.

The conclusion from this evidence is that progress does not end human failings nor can they be legislated away. The answer to the problem the Prime Directive is meant to solve is not negative, requiring more embargoes or censorship or prohibitions on technological advance. That will not work. Instead, positive efforts must be made to phase-shift intelligent beings' moral and ethical development until they come into sync with technological development. For all his lapses related to the Prime Directive, Captain Jean-Luc Picard actually represents the prototype for the best solution to the problems that arise from the shortcomings of the Prime Directive policy. That is, depending on mature, flexible, and intelligent individuals who are empowered to use the skills and instincts they have developed through long experience, like Captain Picard, is more effective than legislation. If non-interventions and prohibitions inevitably fail, the answer is not to double down on ineffective policies but to prepare to prevent the inevitable failures where possible and to mitigate elsewhere. If history, as Picard suggests, "proves" asymmetrical civilizational contact leads to tragedies, it also "proves" that leaders can be found to deal with them.

NOTES

1. In the future (as in the present), Federation foreign policy will almost certainly be guided by a complex combination of state interest, political necessity, and law, both formal and informal. During the early years of the space age, the term "metalaw" was invented by aerospace lawyer, Andrew G. Haley to refer to a system of laws that might one day be applied to all intelligences in the universe. It is possible that the principles of a mature metalaw will become part of Federation policy, but exploring this connection is outside the scope of this essay.

2. See Alex Burston-Chorowicz's essay in this volume.

3. Both non-intervention and non-interference appear in human discussions of international relations, though the term non-intervention is used most often. For a discussion of the Prime Directive, any difference between the two is inconsequential, since all interactions are prohibited. They will, accordingly, be used interchangeably.

4. Troi suggests as much by reminding Picard that the ship's sharing an orbit with god is not a small experience, and Data's report on his mental link with the god-ship confirms this.

5. The episode provides an interesting contrast to military visiting practices from earlier centuries. The arrival of twenty-first century military units in a foreign nation was preceded by a detailed briefings provided by local embassy or liaison personnel with a thorough understanding of local laws and customs. Rules for infractions were often addressed by a formal status of forces agreement (SOFA) before any visiting was allowed to prevent exactly the sort of diplomatic crisis described in this episode from ever arising.

It is unclear why the *Enterprise* crew interacts with the Edo in the first place. The civilization has not developed warp drive capability, nor is there any indication that they have interacted with star-traveling civilizations previously. In particular it seems highly unlikely that previous visitors would have neglected to mention the super-entity that protects the Edo people.

6. The *Star Trek: Enterprise* episode "These are the Voyages..." and *The Next Generation* episode, "Best of Both Worlds, Part I," reinforce the assertion that Earth is central to the Federation. It is the location where the signing of the Charter took place, and it is also the strategic point of attack selected by the Borg in their effort to destroy the Federation.

7. Not a great deal is known about the inner workings of the Federation bureaucracy or how Federation policy is made. Founded in the mid-twenty-second century and headquartered on Earth, the United Federation of Planets is an interstellar federal republic. The one hundred fifty members of the Federation are planetary governments who retain governing authority in their own systems. A president presides over the Federation in conjunction with the Federation Council, which functions as the legislature. A Federation Supreme Court occupies the third branch of government. Unlike other galactic entities extending over many lightyears of space whose members included systems subjugated by force, the members of the Federation joined freely together for common defense and other endeavors like trade, exploration, and scientific research. They acknowledge universal principles of liberty, equality, peaceful cooperation.

Beyond this bare outline of the structure of the United Federation of Planets, many important questions remain unanswered. If each planetary or system government sends delegates to the apparently unicameral legislative body, how many do they send? Is representation based on population or on a one planet-one vote model or on some other model? How is representation in the Federation bureaucracy and the various governing bodies—legislative, executive, and legal—apportioned? Does the Federation's Council decide important legislation as a committee-of-the-whole or in some smaller executive forum similar to the United Nations' Security Council, where some members are afforded more power than others? Is there a veto power and who exercises it? Beyond scientific, exploratory, and defense functions, what other functions does the Federation perform? Answers to these questions are uncertain or, at best, incomplete.

8. A planetary United Earth was formed in the twenty-second century following First Contact with Vulcan in the preceding century.

9. It is clear that the structure of the Federation permits each member state to retain some level of autonomy. How and to what degree members' sovereignty is limited is unclear. If planetary systems give up their right to employ violence against fellow members, the extent to which they can do so within their own planetary or system boundaries is vague. Equally unclear is how and where limits of Federation authority to intrude planet-side end. What seems to be certain, however, is the difficulty of harmonizing a rejection of humanitarian aid and strict planetary-state sovereignty to an advanced rational culture.

10. The link postulated here between the "particular technical development, warp drive" and a "related moral and ethical state" is only implied in the series. At no point—for obvious reasons related to dramatic storytelling—do the actors and writers of TNG stop the action to describe in detail the show's underlying philosophies.

Nevertheless, the notion that human progress is a driving force in the TNG universe can easily be demonstrated by example. The connection is fundamental to the storyline from the very first show, "Encounter at Farpoint." In that episode, Q places Picard (and humanity) on trial specifically to determine whether or not humans should be permitted in space (or even allowed to survive). In particular, Q references humanity's misuse of some technologies, to which Picard responds by claiming that humanity has "outgrown" that primitive brutal past (i.e. the behavior, not the technology), a clear allusion to the progress humanity has achieved subsequently.

The Ornaran episode might be construed as another (negative) example of the Prime Directive's technology-moral development nexus. When Picard refuses to repair the Ornaran ship, he has, in essence, revoked their spacefaring credentials until they can overcome their moral failing (i.e. their addiction to felicium). Other episodes make the same point. "Gambit" links advanced technology to physical destruction for even thinking the wrong ("immoral" or hateful) thoughts, and the Enterprise crew's encounter in "The Arsenal of Freedom" presents the lesson that civilizations that fail to advance both attributes simultaneously end in ruins.

11. Unitarian minister Theodore Parker's collection of sermons from 1853 states: "I do not pretend to understand the moral universe, the arc is a long one.... But from what I see I am sure it bends toward justice." Since its use by Martin Luther King in a slightly modified form, this has become frequent shorthand for the notion that progress is inevitable and universal (Parker 84–85).

12. See Alex Burston-Chorowicz's and Anh T. Tran's essays in this volume.

13. Even games, the modern addiction, are a concern as the *Enterprise* crew learns in "The Game," when they are addicted to a mind-controlling video game Riker brings aboard after taking shore leave on Risa.

14. This is likely a reasonable estimate. In the opening scenes of *First Contact*, the *Enterprise* is assigned to patrol a sector near the Romulan Neutral Zone instead of joining the fight against the Borg. Picard examines the results of a local scan and comments sarcastically on the few particles detected in the otherwise empty space.

15. Various scientists have attempted to estimate the number of atoms and the amount of information in a human being and have not yet arrived at a definitive answer. According to a 2016 revised estimate by Ron Sender et.al. the number of human cells in the 70 kg "reference man" is 3.0×10^{13}. (Ron Sender, Shai Fuchs, Ron Milo. "Revised Estimates for the Number of Human and Bacteria Cells in the Body." PLOS Biology, August 19, 2016. http://dx.doi.org/10.1371/journal.pbio.1002533.) This figure does not include 3.8×10^{13} bacterial cells that also ride along with each human being.

There are 10^{10} protein molecules per cell and many additional lipids, DNA, RNA and other molecules (Gary C. Howard, William E. Brown, Manfred Auer, eds., *Imaging Life: Biological Systems from Atoms to Tissues*. New York: Oxford University Press, 2014, 229). The generally accepted total number of atoms in each cell is on the order of 10^{14} atoms. This does not account for the millions of processes occur continuously within each cell that presumably need to be included in the accounting during transport. A reasonable minimum, then, for the total number of atoms in a reference human is about 10^{27} atoms.

Similar calculations can be performed to determine the amount of information in the human body. Theoretical physicist Sidney Dancoff and Austrian radiologist Henry Quastler made one of the first estimates of the information contained in a human body. Their estimate was 10^{25} bits. This value was not uncontroversial, but taking it as a starting point, and assuming a margin of 10^{20} bits or so in the transporter buffer for safety's sake, generates an information requirement of about 10^{45} bits. (Izrail I. Brekhman. *Man and Biologically Active Substances: The Effect of Drugs, Diet and Pollution on Health*. J.H. Appleby, trans., New York: Pergamon Press, 1980, 13.)

16. This compares rather favorably with the average internet connection in a twenty-first century home.

17. Malcolm was not the first observer to point this out, though he may have been the first to try to offer a theoretical explanation in a major motion picture on the back of an actor's hand. The basic precept occurs in many other contexts. For instance, one of the most famous sayings in military affairs is Helmuth von Moltke's "No operation extends with any certainty beyond the first encounter with the main body of the enemy" (113.6). Likewise, U.S. Marine Corps General James Mattis pointed out, "No war is over until the enemy says it is over. We may think it over, we may declare it over, but, in fact, the enemy gets a vote" (Mattis Q&A). If the enemy represents chaos, the meaning is identical to Malcolm's: certain things are beyond control.

18. It could be worse. Ryan Whitwam, writing at ExtremeTech, points out that some warp drives might wipe out on arrival the civilization they intended to visit. "The instant the Alcubierre drive is disengaged, the space-time gradient that allows it to effectively move faster than light goes away. All the energetic particles trapped during the journey have to go somewhere, and the researchers believe they would be blasted outward in a cone directly in front of the ship. Anyone or anything waiting for you at the other end of your trip would be destroyed" ("The downside of warp drives: Annihilating whole star systems when you arrive" http://www.extremetech.com/extreme/140635-the-downside-of-warp-drives-annihilating-whole-star-systems-when-you-arrive accessed 14 Jun. 2016).

19. The "Three Laws of Robotics" as formulated by science and science fiction author Isaac Asimov are: (1) a robot may not injure a human being or, through inaction, allow a human being to come to harm; (2) a robot must obey orders given it by human beings except where such orders would conflict with the First Law; (3) a robot must protect its own existence as long as such protection does not conflict with the First or Second Law. Asimov credits science fiction writer and editor John Wood Campbell, Jr., with the original formulation in his 1979 autobiograph, *In Memory Yet Green: The Autobiography of Isaac Asimov, 1920–1954* (New York: Doubleday, p. 286).

20. This bit of fiction was included by Robert A. Heinlein in his 1961 science fiction masterpiece, *Stranger in a Strange Land* (New York: Ace Books) and later was duplicated in an April Fool's Day prank in 1998 by Sandia National Laboratories physicist Mark Boslough, but it never appeared on a legislative calendar.

Works Cited

Adams, David John. *An Introduction to Galaxies and Cosmology*. New York: Cambridge University Press, 2003.

Asimov, Isaac. *In Memory Yet Green: The Autobiography of Isaac Asimov, 1920–1954*. New York: Doubleday, 1979. Print.

"The Battle." *Star Trek: The Next Generation*. Writ. Herbert J. Wright and Larry Forrester. Dir. Rob Bowman. *Netflix*. Web. 7 Jun. 2016.

"The Best of Both Worlds, Part I." *Star Trek: The Next Generation*. Writ. Michael Piller. Dir. Cliff Bole. *Netflix*. Web. 7 Jun. 2016.

"The Best of Both Worlds, Part II." *Star Trek: The Next Generation*. Writ. Michael Piller. Dir. Cliff Bole. *Netflix*. Web. 7 Jun. 2016.

Bodeker, et.al., eds. *Medicinal Plants for Forest Conservation and Health Care*. Rome: United Nations Food and Agriculture Organization, 1997. Web.

"Chain of Command, Part I." *Star Trek: The Next Generation*. Writ. Ronald D. Moore and Frank Abatemarco. Dir. Robert Scheerer. *Netflix*. Web. 7 Jun. 2016.

Chang, Chih-Hann. *Ethical Foreign Policy?* Farnham, UK: Ashgate, 2013. Web.

Clarke, Arthur C. "Sir Arthur's Quotations." *The Arthur C. Clarke Foundation* n.d. Web.

Clingbine, Graham. *Release from Stasis: The Future Is Now*. Leicestershire, UK: Troubador Publishing Ltd., 2015.

de las Casas, Bartolomé. *In Defense of the Indians: The Defense of the Most Reverend Lord, Don Fray Bartolomé De Las Casas, of the Order of Preachers, Late Bishop of Chiapa, Against the Persecutors and Slanderers of the New World Discovered Across the Seas*. Trans., ed., Stafford Poole. DeKalb: Northern Illinois University Press, 1974. Print.

_____. *A Short Account of the Destruction of the Indies*, London: Penguin, 1992. Columbia University Libraries Virtual Reading Room, 2002. Web.

Eisner, Bruce. *Ecstasy: The MDMA Story*. Berkeley, CA: Ronin Publishing, 1989, 1994. Print.

"Encounter at Farpoint, Part 1." *Star Trek: The Next Generation*. Writ. D.C. Fontana and Gene Roddenberry. Dir. Corey Allen. *Netflix*. Web. 7 Jun. 2016.

"Encounter at Farpoint, Part 2." *Star Trek: The Next Generation*. Writ. D.C. Fontana and Gene Roddenberry. Dir. Corey Allen. *Netflix*. Web. 7 Jun. 2016.

Eskildsen, Robert. "Of Civilization and Savages: The Mimetic Imperialism of Japan's 1874 Expedition to Taiwan." *American Historical Review*, 107.2 (2002): 388–418. Web.

"Face of the Enemy." *Star Trek: The Next Generation*. Writ. Naren Shankar and René Echevarria. Dir. Gabrielle Beaumont. *Netflix*. Web. 7 Jun. 2016.

Feaver, Peter. "American Grand Strategy at the Crossroads." Eds. Richard Fontaine and Kristin M. Lord. *America's Path: Grand Strategy for the Next Administration*. Washington, D.C.: Center for a New American Security, 2012. Web.

Gallis, Christos, et.al., "Forest Products with Health-Promoting and Medicinal Properties," in Nilsson, Kjell, et.al. eds., *Forests, Trees and Human Health*. New York: Springer, 2011.

"Gambit, Part I." *Star Trek: The Next Generation*. Writ. Naren Shankar and Christopher Hatton. Dir. Peter Lauritson. *Netflix*. Web. 7 Jun. 2016.

Haynes, John Earl and Harvey Klehr. *Venona: Decoding Soviet Espionage in America*. New Haven: Yale University Press, 2000.

Heinlein, Robert A. *Stranger in a Strange Land*. New York: Ace Books, 1961, 2003. Print.

"Hide and Q." *Star Trek: The Next Generation*. Writ. C.J. Holland and Gene Roddenberry. Dir. Cliff Bole. *Netflix*. Web. 7 Jun. 2016.

International Court of Justice (I.C.J.) *Reports*, 1986. Web.

"Journey's End." *Star Trek: The Next Generation*. Writ. Ronald D. Moore. Dir. Corey Allen. *Netflix*. Web. 7 Jun. 2016.

"Justice." *Star Trek: The Next Generation*. Writ. Ralph Willis and Worley Thorne. Dir. James L. Conway. *Netflix*. Web. 7 Jun. 2016.

"Lessons." *Star Trek: The Next Generation*. Writ. Ron Wilkerson and Jean Louise Matthias. Dir. Robert Wiemer. *Netflix*. Web. 7 Jun. 2016.

Luttwak, Edward. *The Grand Strategy of the Byzantine Empire*. Cambridge, MA: Belknap Press, 2009. Print.

Mattis, James. "Gen. James Mattis Q&A." *Defense News*. n.d. smallwarsjournal.com, May 24, 2010.

Miller, Paul D. "Five Pillars of American Grand Strategy." *Survival*, 54.5 (2012): 7–44. Web.

Moltke, Helmuth von, Graf. *Moltke on the Art of War*. Trans., Daniel J. Hughes and Harry Bell. Ed., Daniel J. Hughes. New York: Presidio Press, 1993. Epub file.

"The Neutral Zone." *Star Trek: The Next Generation*. Writ. Maurice Hurley, Deborah McIntyre, and Mona Clee. Dir. James L. Conway. *Netflix*. Web. 7 Jun. 2016.

Norma J. Livo, *Who's Afraid...? Facing Children's Fears with Folktales*. Englewood, CO: Teacher Ideas Press, 1994. Print.

Oppenheim, Lassa, and Robert Yewdall Jennings, Arthur Watts. *Oppenheim's International Law*. 9th ed. Ed. Robert Jennings, Arthur Watts. Vol. I. Oxford: Oxford University Press, 1992, 2008. Web.

Parker, Theodore. "Of Justice and the Conscience." *Ten Sermons of Religion*. Boston: Crosby, Nichols and Company, 1853. Web.

"The Pegasus." *Star Trek: The Next Generation*. Writ. Ronald D. Moore. Dir. LeVar Burton. *Netflix*. Web. 7 Jun. 2016.

Pope Paul III. "Sublimus Dei, May 29, 1537." *Papalencyclicals.Net* n.d. Web. 7 Jun. 2016.

"Rhino Horns Worth $2.75 Million Stolen from Safe in South Africa." *New York Daily News*, 6 Apr. 2013. http://www.nydailynews.com/news/world/rhino-horns-worth-2-75-million-stolen-south-africa-article-1.1309499.

Rowan, Terry. *Adventures in Outer Space Film Guide*. lulu.com, 2016. Web.

Ruditis, Paul, ed. *The Star Trek Book*. London: Dorling Kindersley Publishing, 2016. Web.

"Sarek." *Star Trek: The Next Generation*. Writ. Peter S. Beagle, Marc Cushman and Jake Jacobs. Dir. Les Landau. *Netflix*. Web. 7 Jun. 2016.

Shapiro, Ilya, ed. *Cato Supreme Court Review, 2008–2009*. Washington, D.C.: Center for Constitutional Studies, Cato Institute, 2009. Web.

Star Trek: First Contact. Dir. Jonathan Frakes. Perf. Patrick Stewart, Jonathan Frakes, and Brent Spiner. *Netflix*. 1996. Web.

Star Trek IV: The Voyage Home. Dir. Leonard Nimoy. Perf. William Shatner, Leonard Nimoy, and DeForest Kelley. *Netflix*. 1986. Web.

Star Trek: Insurrection. Dir. Jonathan Frakes. Perf. Patrick Stewart, Jonathan Frakes, and Brent Spiner. *Amazon*. 1998. Web.

"Star Trek Is..." *Memory Alpha* n.d. Web. 8 Aug. 2016.

"The Survivors." *Star Trek: The Next Generation*. Writ. Michael Wagner. Dir. Les Landau. *Netflix*. Web. 7 Jun. 2016.

"Tapestry." *Star Trek: The Next Generation*. Writ. Ronald D. Moore. Dir. Les Landau. *Netflix*. Web. 7 Jun. 2016.

"These Are the Voyages..." *Star Trek: Enterprise*. Writ. Rick Berman and Brannon Braga. Dir. Allan Kroeker. *Netflix*. Web. 7 Jun. 2016.

The Thing from Another World. Dir. Christian Nyby. Perf. Kenneth Tobery, Margaret Sheridan, and James Arness. Warner Home Video, 2005. DVD.

Tyler, Varro E. "Natural Products and Medicine: An Overview," in M.J. Balick, E. Elisabetsky, and S.A. Laird (eds.), *Medicinal Resources of the Tropical Forest—Biodiversity and Its Importance to Human Health*. New York: Columbia University Press, 1996.

"Unification I." *Star Trek: The Next Generation*. Writ. Jeri Taylor, Rick Berman, and Michael Piller. Dir. Les Landau. *Netflix*. Web. 7 Jun. 2016.

"Unification II." *Star Trek: The Next Generation*. Writ. Rick Berman and Michael Piller. Dir. Cliff Bole. *Netflix*. Web. 7 Jun. 2016.

"Who Watches the Watchers." *Star Trek: The Next Generation*. Writ. Richard Manning and Hans Beimler. Dir. Robert Wiemer. *Netflix*. Web. 7 Jun. 2016.

"The Wounded." *Star Trek: The Next Generation*. Writ. Jeri Taylor, Stuart Charno, Sara Charno, and Cy Chermak. Dir. Chip Chalmers. *Netflix*. Web. 7 Jun. 2016.

Wright, Jason T., et.al. "The Search for Extraterrestrial Civilizations with Large Energy Supplies. IV. The Signatures and Information Content of Transiting Megastructures." *The Astrophysical Journal*, 816.1 (2016). Web.

Zubrin, Robert. "Detection of Extraterrestrial Civilizations Via the Spectral Signature of Advanced Interstellar Spacecraft." *Aip Conference Proceedings*, 301, 1407–1413 (1994). Web.

Policing Loyalty
Comparing the Tal Shiar and the FBI's COINTELPRO

Anh T. Tran

Through a combination of administration, brute force, and legitimizing ideologies, states attempt to produce citizens who obediently participate in economic production without demanding systemic change. History's most powerful empires have reinforced such imperatives through secret police forces, the most notorious of which include the Soviet *Cheka*, the East German *Stasi*, and the Japanese *Kempeitai*. These organizations rise to their peaks in times of war, when state leaders—feeling flanked by external foes and homegrown defectors—mobilize civil society and the entirety of the state's domestic infrastructure to support war efforts abroad. The secret police represent an especially aggressive and effective component of this vast warring network.

The subject of this essay is a secret policing program in an unlikely place: The United States, an empire boasting to be one of the world's most consolidated liberal democracies. Beginning in 1956 and continuing through the height of the Cold War years, the Federal Bureau of Investigation (FBI) conducted a top secret COINTELPRO (COunterINTEL-ligence PROgram) to extra-legally surveil, infiltrate, and sabotage dissident political movements throughout the country. "War necessity" gave COINTELPRO a powerful mandate to subvert constitutional and democratic rights at home, ironically in defense of democracy (and capitalism) against the unwelcome popularity of socialist and communist ideas inside and outside the U.S.

The counterrevolutionary role of COINTELPRO during the Cold War was perfectly dramatized in *Star Trek: The Next Generation* by the Tal Shiar, the Romulan Star Empire's premier counterintelligence agency, feared and respected for their no-holds-barred approach to protecting the Empire's national security interests.[1] High on the Tal Shiar's agenda was to co-opt Ambassador Spock's underground reunification movement on Romulus for a far more sinister purpose: to take over Vulcan, a key Federation member (as told in the two-part story, "Unification"). While traversing the final frontier, we could also detect fissures in the liberal-democratic utopianism of the United Federation of Planets as it engaged in some of the same morally questionable practices as the Tal Shiar and the FBI in the name of safeguarding freedom and moral values.

Several points of convergence between the practices of the FBI's COINTELPRO and the Tal Shiar demonstrate how insecure states resist the centrifugal pressures of war through monitoring and enforcing their citizens' allegiances to the existing political order. Both the FBI and Tal Shiar latched onto wartime ideologies regarding peaceful citizen activists as existential threats to the state, rather than as participants in healthy civic life. These ideologies enabled the agencies to pursue their "enemy others" without legal restraint or public oversight. The FBI and Tal Shiar were motivated by deep-seated apprehensions that the brewing counterhegemonic movements within their respective domains would not only undermine the authority and autonomy of the empires they sought to protect, but would fundamentally alter the meaning of American or Romulan identity as well. Allegations that domestic activists had ties to foreign conspirators further magnified perceptions of the risk these activists posed to national security (Finman and MacCaulay 633). The Tal Shiar identified Spock as the outside agitator principally responsible for brainwashing Romulans with his proselytizing on Vulcan-Romulan reunification, while the FBI believed Russian Bolsheviks were aiding the American Left in its purported crusade to overthrow the American government (Sullivan and Brown 149; Senate Select Committee, "Hearings on Intelligence Activities" 377).

Upon developing their ideological frameworks, the Tal Shiar and FBI both relied on conventional counterintelligence strategies to monitor the political affiliations of their respective citizenries and internally disrupt the activities of social movement organizations, to destroy them from the inside out. The two agencies also broke new ground in counterintelligence work by weaponizing ideas and using them to discredit activists in the eyes of the mass publics. To illustrate, this essay examines how National Security Council Report 68—the primary security directive of the Cold War era—established the ideological framework for subsequent COINTELPRO operations against the Communist Party–USA, the Socialist Workers Party, the Black Panther Party, New Left organizations and institutions foundational to American liberal democracy (e.g., democratic elections, rule of law, a free press, and academic freedom). COINTELPRO activities against these targets will be detailed using information from Senate reports, declassified COINTELPRO memos, and secondary sources. Comparisons are drawn to the modus operandi of the Tal Shiar.

"Face of the Enemy"

In the sixth season *TNG* episode entitled "Face of the Enemy," Counselor Troi awakens on a strange vessel to find her appearance had been surgically altered to resemble Romulan physiology, and that she dons the uniform and regalia of a Romulan military officer. Romulan Sub-commander N'Vek enters, informing Troi that she must pose as the deceased Major Rakal of the Tal Shiar and pull rank to forcibly take command of the ship from Captain Toleth. Troi eventually learns that her mission is to smuggle into Federation space a prominent Romulan government official and his aides who had defected to the reunification movement. While this is the first and only time we hear the Tal Shiar name explicitly uttered on *TNG*, there are indications that, since the outbreak of the Klingon civil war two seasons earlier, the Tal Shiar had been lurking behind the scenes, intervening in various political affairs of interest to the Romulan Empire.

In "Face of the Enemy," we discover that the struggle for reunification was one of the most contentious chapters in Tal Shiar history. Loyalists likely perceive this domestic political challenge to be a graver danger than anything emanating from the Romulans' interstellar enemies, because reunification threatened to negate the essence of Romulan identity and the empire built upon that identity (recall that Romulans are distinguished from their Vulcan cousins by the former's violent emotionality, having rejected the Vulcans' turn to logic and pacifism during the Time of Awakening millennia ago). Romulan loyalists must have realized that the greatest empires in history have fallen, not by the hands of outside invaders, but by their own internal contradictions. Nevertheless, it is convenient to blame domestic crises on foreign manipulation. Consequently, the Tal Shiar, under Sela's command, struck the reunification movement with an iron fist to prevent the empire from fragmenting and to prevent Vulcan/Federation meddling in Romulan affairs.

Likewise, the U.S. government's assessment of Soviet material capabilities was inseparable from emotions, identity, and economics. For much of the twentieth century, American leaders dreaded what they understood as the coming of an inexorable tide of communism, threatening to swallow up American identities and traditions rooted in individualism, liberalism, and democratic politics (Tuathail and Agnew 201). Economic elites feared that communism would destabilize the functioning of international capitalism, a system for which the U.S. served as guarantor, and from which it disproportionately benefited (Cox 35). Indeed, President Harry Truman's desire to maintain open markets seemed to initially guide his actions more consistently than any commitment to containment policy (Larson 10, 144). American leaders fed a "missile gap" narrative to the public that exaggerated the scale of the Soviet military threat and depicted the U.S. as a defensive—rather than offensive—war. This was due to uncertainty over the U.S.–Soviet strategic balance and to maintain an economic military hegemony.

While Soviet weapons undoubtedly undercut U.S. military dominance, the Soviet Union lacked a standing army and navy (Cox 26). Even by Western estimates, the Soviet Union possessed only a quarter of American economic power and was on no trajectory toward parity. Therefore, the extreme lengths taken by the U.S. to assist right-wing counterinsurgencies, to stage military coups against left-wing governments, to repress political dissent at home through COINTELPRO and other initiatives, could not be explained by the balance of material power between the two superpowers alone. A more plausible explanation is that American leaders believed the socialist conflagration sparked by the 1917 Russian Revolution would imperil American identities and economic interests, leading them to conclude that national security was also in jeopardy, and to react in ways that aggravated the security threat, in a self-fulfilling process. Likewise, the non-violent, bush-league reunification movement was no match for the Tal Shiar's superior military and intelligence capabilities. Rather, the perceivably powerful threat posed by the movement stemmed from an alluring idea—the idea that the Vulcans and Romulans shared enough in common to peacefully coexist.

A Framework for Counterrevolution

National Security Council Report 68 (NSC 68) formally articulated the principles and strategies of "containment" that many consider the U.S. "master plan" for the Cold War. The State Department engineers of NSC 68 re-imagined warfare as something more than military combat on foreign soil by linking the enemy abroad to the enemy at home (National Security Council 11). In other words, the American socialist, communist, or anti-establishment dissidents embodied Bolshevism's projected dangerously charismatic appeal, no matter if these Americans actually held any ties to international socialist organizations. U.S. Cold War strategists hoped to defeat the menace by "expos[ing] the falsities of Soviet pretensions" and "fostering the seeds of destruction within the Soviet system" (National Security Council 21). This strategy of ideological containment concretized in the forms of covert intelligence and counterinsurgency operations, diplomacy efforts, cultural exchanges, and propaganda projects around the world, complemented by policing political loyalties inside the U.S.

While the Tal Shiar did not have a document comparable to NSC 68, we can infer from its actions that the agency employed a similar strategy of limitless and borderless war. In an effort to precipitate a war between the Klingon Empire and the Federation in "The Mind's Eye," the Tal Shiar brainwashed Lieutenant Commander La Forge into trying to assassinate a Klingon governor. In the two-part episode "Redemption," Sela and her minions once again intervene in external affairs to secure the Romulan national interest, this time aiding the Duras family to illegally seize control of the Klingon High Council, resulting in a civil war. Both the U.S. and the Romulan Empire treated internal and external political developments as two sides of the same coin, which necessitated a war strategy that connected the domestic battleground to the international (or intergalactic) one.

But NSC 68 was more than just a strategy document. It helped shape the historical memory and discourse surrounding the Cold War by framing the U.S.-Soviet conflict in apocalyptic proportions, taking place between absolute binaries of good versus evil, civilization versus barbarity, individualism versus collectivism, and freedom versus slavery. Based on such abstractions, the document drew a most dire conclusion: "The issues that face us are momentous, involving the fulfillment or destruction not only of this Republic but of civilization itself" (National Security Council 4). In the NSC 68 narrative, the American and Soviet systems were primordially antithetical and irreconcilable; thus, total war was inevitable. By accentuating the enormity of the stakes, the framers of NSC 68 could justify sweeping programs like COINTELPRO, which would have been unconscionable in peacetime. Likewise, the Tal Shiar's objectives of eradicating the prospect of reunification and destabilizing Klingon-Federation relations were considered so vital to the survival of the Empire that the agency could supersede norms of Romulan Senate oversight and civil protections for Romulan citizens.

The Practice of Counterrevolution

For the U.S. to protect its ideological, military, and economic interests, American intelligence agencies must be free to intervene wherever socialist and communist ideas courted hearts and minds, even if this meant bringing the Cold War home. But since armed repression of the political opposition is considered unacceptable in advanced democracies—especially for preventive purposes—agents of the state turned to ideological repression instead. The focus on ideological repression did not preclude the state using armed repression in certain desperate historical moments.

The suppression of anti-establishment ideas was by no means unique to the Cold War. During the Philippine-American War of 1899–1902, the U.S. government censored anti-war media and branded critics of the war as "liars and traitors" (Miller 166). Throughout World War I, more than 21,000 people were indicted under the Espionage Act of 1917 and the Sedition Act of 1918 for publicly opposing U.S. involvement in the war (Goldstein 108). During World War II, the U.S. defended dragnet Japanese internment under the rationale that since it was impossible to conclusively differentiate "loyal" Americans from "disloyal" ones, all Japanese people had to be detained (*Korematsu v. U.S.*). Romulan citizens also live inside an intensely guarded and paranoid society that tolerates little internal dissent, detests other species, and is constantly mobilizing for war, all of which are mutually reinforcing conditions.[2]

The U.S. track record of revoking political rights from American citizens for the sake of wartime national security forecasted the shape of things to come under COINTELPRO. With Director J. Edgar Hoover at the helm, the FBI launched COINTELPRO initially to disrupt and eliminate the Communist Party–USA's (CP-USA) "influence over the masses, ability to create controversy leading to confusion and disunity, [and] penetration of specific channels of American life where public opinion is molded" (J. E. Hoover to D. Anderson 7/29/55[3]; Senate Select Committee, "Intelligence Activities" 66). The scope of COINTELPRO expanded palpably over time to target the Socialist Workers Party (SWP), black nationalist organizations, the "New Left," and, to a lesser extent, the American Indian Movement, Puerto Rican *independentistas*, and white supremacist groups.[4] The Tal Shiar's list of nemeses was just as lengthy, and included the reunification movement on Romulus, also included the Dominion Founders, Obsidian Order operatives, the Federation, and the Klingon House of Gowron.[5]

COINTELPRO incorporated the repressivwe and anti-communist infrastructure that first emerged after World War I, consisting of Palmer Raids, the House Un-American Activities Committee, the American Protective League, and the surveillance, denaturalization and deportation of CP-USA and SWP members. Two key pieces of legislation reinforced the imperatives of anti-communist repression and gave it the air of universality, rationality, and beneficence to the public good. First, Truman's 1947 Executive Order 9835 permitted the Justice Department to maintain a list of "subversive organizations" and conduct "loyalty investigations" of federal employees. Second, the Internal Security Act of 1950 and its subsequent iterations forced communist organizations to register with the Attorney General's office, barred its members from citizenship and international travel, strengthened exclusion and deportation laws, authorized the president to detain political dissidents in cases of national emergency, preempted grassroots counterorganizing by making it a felony to picket courthouses, and eventually outlawed the CP-USA entirely.

The warring networks of the Romulan Empire were even more expansive in scope. The Tal Shiar operates an entire fleet of warships, allowing it to conduct unlimited covert operations within and beyond the Empire's borders.[6] The episode "Balance of Terror" in *Star Trek: The Original Series* reveals that a warring network covers the entirety of Romulan society, which is characterized by total militarization and war preparedness. One's military rank determines one's social status. Defending the Empire is a matter of honor and of highest personal priority, even when national defense came at great cost to personal political freedoms and community protections.

The FBI's Counterrevolution Program

COINTELPRO—legitimated but not necessarily legalized by Truman's Executive Order and the Internal Security Act—carried out NSC 68's edict of preventing "internal political and social disunity" with exceptional vigor (National Security Council 61). The program relied on five tactics of psychological terror to achieve its objectives: (1) gathering information on targets through informants, infiltrators, wiretaps, bugs, tails, burglaries, and mail tampering; (2) spreading derogatory information about targets ("gray propaganda") or disseminating controversial and divisive publications made to look like they were produced by the targets ("black propaganda"); (3) using agent provocateurs to stir up controversy, create splinter factions, criticize rival organizations, advocate that their leadership be eliminated, plant information to make targets appear to be FBI informants ("snitch jacketing"), or otherwise incite conflict among members of the same group or between members of different groups; (4) making arrests on false charges, bribing or threatening witnesses, and framing targets for crimes they did not commit; and (5) collaborating in or encouraging the assaults and assassinations of target individuals (Saito 1081–1088).

The FBI directed its activities against the same American institutions that NSC 68 designated as vulnerable to communist influence and most likely to be converted into instruments of communist propagandizing:

> Every institution in our society is an instrument which it is sought to stultify and turn against our purposes. Those that touch most closely our material and moral strength are obviously the prime targets, labor unions, civic enterprises, schools, churches, and all media for influencing opinion. The effort is not so much to make them serve obvious Soviet ends as to prevent them from serving our ends, and thus to make them sources of confusion in our economy, our culture, and our body politic [National Security Council 34].

By policing civil society organizations and institutions, as opposed to investigating or prosecuting actual crime, the FBI snuffed the conventional understandings and functions of law enforcement: "The unexpressed major premise … is that the Bureau has a role in maintaining the existing social order, and that its efforts should be aimed toward combating those who threaten that order" (Senate Select Committee, "Supplementary Detailed Staff Reports" 6–7). Countless pages of COINTELPRO records consisted of verbatim copies of speeches, internal debates, and newspapers from the organizations it investigated (Ryter, "Corrupting American Institutions" 2), a testament to COINTELPRO's fixation on the ideological content that it regarded as dangerous to the political status quo, but which posed zero or minimal physical threat to U.S. national security and American laws.

In pursuit of their targets, COINTELPRO frequently collaborated with private and public entities beyond local law enforcement, such as banks, motor vehicle registrars, the Internal Revenue Service, and the Bureau of Alcohol, Tobacco, Firearms, and Explosives (Ryter, "FBI Lawbreaking and Violence" 2). The Tal Shiar also conspired with their Cardassian counterpart, the Obsidian Order, to attack the Founders' homeworld and assassinate a former Obsidian Order operative ("Improbable Cause"). These practices displayed the broader information-sharing networks and militarized societies within which these agencies worked—war was not bound by rules regarding who can become an ally and who can become an enemy. A closer look at the experiences of groups entangled in COINTELPRO's crosshairs further shows the similarities of methods used by the FBI and Tal Shiar against their political opponents.

The Targets of COINTELPRO

Communist Party–USA (CP-USA)

The first COINTELPRO streamlined previously ad hoc FBI operations against CP-USA. Its tactics against CP-USA ranged from mundane (e.g., banning members from their usual meeting spaces) to mischievously crafty (e.g., inventing a fictional organization called the Committee for Expansion of Socialist Thought in America to attack CP-USA with ideas from the Marxist Right, or snitch-jacketing a leading CP-USA official in New York State, which contributed to disintegrating the entire chapter) (Goldstein 447–448). In another operation dubbed "Hoodwink," the FBI attempted to provoke a mafia hit against key CP-USA leaders by designing leaflets appearing to originate from CP-USA, and which rebuked the labor practices of the American Mafia (F.J. Baumgardner to W.C. Sullivan 10/4/66).

Operation Hoodwink exemplified how the FBI used psychological manipulation to produce violent results without the direct application of violence. Intimidation served a similar function for the Tal Shiar, allowing it to coerce compliance without resorting to blunt physical force, although the Tal Shiar did not shy away from the latter. Returning to "Face of the Enemy," we find Captain Toleth annoyed and frustrated by Major Rakal's/Troi's commandeering of her vessel, but Toleth is unable to defy the Major, lest she meet the same fate as her father (as a child, Toleth witnessed Tal Shiar operatives abduct her father and drag him out of their home at night, and he was never to be seen again). Troi exploits the fearsome reputation of the Tal Shiar to her own advantage, and in so doing, demonstrates the ways in which the existing climate of fear and paranoia established by the Tal Shiar's previous activities enables it to pursue its goals with only the implicit threat of violence. The same can be said for COINTELPRO, whose tactics of psychological warfare proved powerfully effective; in the end, COINTELPRO was partly if not largely responsible for reducing the ranks of CP-USA from 80,000 to 2,800 members, with FBI informants filling approximately one-third of this dwindling remainder (Goldstein 407).

Socialist Workers Party (SWP)

The SWP COINTELPRO, also known as the "SWP Disruption Program," relied extensively on "poison-pen" letters to propagate misinformation severing SWP's relationships with groups like Malcolm X's Organization of Afro-American Unity (SAC–New York to J.E. Hoover 6/15/65) and widening rifts between SWP and New Left organizations (SAC–New York to J.E. Hoover 2/13/70). The FBI even meddled in the electoral process—the cornerstone of democracy and a measure of the U.S.'s moral superiority over the Soviet Union. In 1965, FBI agents masqueraded as "A Concerned Mother" in a public letter designed to red-bait SWP candidates running for the Denver School Board (SAC-Denver to J.E. Hoover 5/1/65). In 1966, the FBI conducted a campaign of libel against New York gubernatorial candidate and SWP member Judy White, swaying the state to revise its election laws to prohibit candidates under 30 years of age, like White, from running for the governorship (SAC–New York to J.E. Hoover 10/24/66).

Over the course of 20 years, the FBI conducted 20,000 days of illegal wiretaps, 12,000 days of bugging, and 208 burglaries against SWP (*SWP v. Attorney General*). Between

1960 and 1966, agents stole and photographed over 8,000 pages of SWP members' personal letters and financial records, adding to the trove of over one million documents ultimately collected on the organization (Jayko 6). At any given point between 1960 and 1976, FBI informants composed two to eleven percent of the total SWP membership. Yet despite its decades-long investigation and infiltration into SWP, the FBI could not unearth any prosecutable evidence (*SWP v. Attorney General*), suggesting that COINTELPRO constituted little more than the machinery for a witch hunt.

The SWP Disruption Campaign closely parallels not a Tal Shiar operation, but, rather, a dark event in the Federation. In "The Drumhead," Admiral Norah Satie boards the *Starship Enterprise* to investigate an explosion in the dilithium chamber hatch. In addition to arresting J'Dan, a visiting Klingon officer who confesses to being a Romulan spy but not causing the explosion, Satie also accuses medical technician Simon Tarses of being J'Dan's co-conspirator. Satie bases this accusation on her Betazoid assistant's intuition that Tarses is hiding something out of fear and guilt. Tarses admits to Captain Picard that he lied on his Starfleet Academy application when he stated that his grandfather was Vulcan rather than Romulan. Even after the explosion is determined to be an accident, Satie continues to publicly interrogate Tarses. To rationalize her actions Satie references an earlier event when a Tal Shair when a Tal Shair spy successfully masqueraded as a respected Vulcan ambassador and escapes with Federation secrets ("Data's Day"). When Picard and Worf voice their objections to the hearing, Satie criticizes Picard for failing to capture the spy and reminds Worf that his own father (allegedly) betrayed his people to the Romulans.

Satie bases her accusations against Tarses and Worf on their guilt by Romulan association (albeit generations removed). Her methods are akin to COINTELPRO's persecution of SWP, not because the organization violated any laws, but because it was associated with socialism. And Satie does not act as a lone ranger; Starfleet Command wholeheartedly approves her methods, just as the witch hunt against SWP represented a continuation, rather than an aberration, in a long history of political policing in the U.S., authorized at the highest levels of power. Tarses' experience, and that of SWP members, attested to a systematic pattern of painting "the enemy" with strokes so broad, anyone could become trapped in it. Satie and COINTELPRO stubbornly persisted even when no incriminating evidence was found, since the goal was not to prosecute criminal activity, but to root out unassimilated identities and suppress unapproved ideas.

Black Panther Party (BPP)

In a top-secret report to President Richard Nixon, FBI Director Hoover declared the BPP to be "the most active and dangerous" of the black nationalist organizations (Hartman 20–21). Consequently, BPP alone was targeted for 233 out of 295 total documented COINTELPRO operations against black nationalist groups (Senate Select Committee, *Supplementary Detailed Staff Reports* 406–407). While other black nationalist organizations engaged in more frequent and extreme acts of violence, BPP posed a unique danger to powerholders because the group coupled black nationalism with socialist internationalism and received widespread support in black communities, especially among youths (Bloom and Martin 212). The foremost priority of the FBI was to discredit BPP's ideology, unsurprisingly at a time when Martin Luther King, Jr., other prominent civil rights leaders, and many rank and file black activists were gravitating toward democratic socialism (Sturm 80–81). For these reasons, COINTELPRO's campaign against the BPP signified not only a reaction to the Civil Rights Movement, but also the trepidation felt by powerholders over the popular reception given to left-wing thought received by marginalized sectors in American society.

The FBI worked with the media to mold public impressions of BPP by describing the party and its supporters as "cold blooded" (O'Reilly 258), "preening ghetto generals" (O'Reilly 297), a "nihilistic terror" (O'Reilly 322), "killers" (O'Reilly 323), "predatory" (Ryter, "Corrupting American Institutions" 3), and a "black army for a white revolution" (Ryter, "Corrupting American Institutions" 3). These labels insinuated that the Panthers were self-serving agents of the Soviet government rather than true social justice warriors, just as the Romulan High Command and the Tal Shiar consider reunification activists to be malcontents duped by Vulcan outside agitators as opposed to devotees of a noble cause.

Another attractive target for COINTELPRO was the BPP's Breakfast for Children Program, which provided free food and alternative schooling to low-income children, and became an important source of the group's popular legitimacy. COINTELPRO operatives circulated rumors that the program's volunteers were infected with venereal disease, and printed coloring books promoting violence against the police, made to appear as if the program had distributed them (Senate Select Committee, *Supplementary Detailed Staff Reports* 210). When the BPP leadership learned of the books' existence, they ordered them destroyed immediately. COINTELPRO operatives nevertheless mailed copies to the corporate donors of the Breakfast for Children Program (e.g., Safeway Stores Inc., Mayfair Markets, and the Jack-in-the-Box Corporation), urging them to withdraw.

Although COINTELPRO specialized in ideological warfare, its operations were calculated to produce violence. For example, the Los Angeles FBI exacerbated animosity between BPP and its rival, the United Slaves, by sending an anonymous letter to United Slaves describing a fictional BPP plot to assassinate the United Slaves leader (SAC–Los Angeles to J.E. Hoover 11/29/68). Undercover agents also circulated crude cartoons between the two groups depicting the lynching of their leaders. In subsequent months, armed skirmishes between United Slaves and BPP left at least four Panthers dead (Freed 65), an outcome apparently intended by the FBI:

> Shootings, beatings, and a high degree of unrest continues to prevail in the ghetto area of southeast San Diego. Although no specific counterintelligence action can be credited with contributing to this over-all situation, it is felt that a substantial amount of the unrest is directly attributable to this program [in reference to the FBI's use of black propaganda cartoons]. In view of the recent killing of SYLVESTER BELL, a new cartoon is being considered in the hopes that it will assist in the continuance of the rift between BPP and US [SAC-San Diego to J.E. Hoover 8/20/69].

We are reminded of the toll the Tal Shiar's divisive methods had on Romulan society. In the "Unification" episodes, Captain Picard and Commander Data disguised themselves as Romulans and follow Ambassador Spock to Romulus as he walks into a trap set up by Romulan Senator Pardek, a popular peace advocate whom Spock had befriended eighty years earlier. On Romulus, Data and Picard discover a pervasive climate of wariness and suspicion among the populace, and even more so among members of the reunification movement, who distrust any new face. As the BPP could attest, it was difficult, if not impossible, to build movements strong enough to effectively challenge central power if one was distracted with infighting and searching for spies in one's midst (although given the proportion of FBI informants and infiltrators within the ranks of the CPA-USA and SWP, perhaps groups under COINTELPRO investigation should have prioritized spy-hunting). Indeed, Hoover's vision for COINTELPRO was to create the sense that "an FBI agent [was] behind every mailbox" (Churchill and Vander Wall, *Agents of Repression* 39–40), as to compel movement activists to self-police and self-censor, thus stunting their forward momentum.

The event epitomizing state terror under COINTELPRO was the December 1969 Chicago police raid of BPP deputy chairman Fred Hampton's apartment, coordinated by COINTELPRO's Special Agent in Charge (SAC) in Chicago (Wolf 12). On the night of the raid, Hampton's bodyguard (who was an undercover FBI agent) drugged Hampton with secobarbital. As Hampton lay unconscious, the police fired hundreds of bullets into the corner where they knew Hampton's bed was located, according to floor plans provided to them earlier by Hampton's bodyguard. Hampton was eventually killed by one bullet in the chest and two in the head at point-blank range. Four days later, COINTELPRO and the Los Angeles police joined forces in another thinly-veiled assassination attempt against BPP leader Geronimo Pratt, in circumstances unnervingly similar to those of Chicago.[7]

A total of 28 Panthers were killed in just two years between 1967 and 1969, many in police raids directed by FBI operatives or in FBI-engineered confrontations with rival organizations (Foner 257–258). Ironically, it is the Panthers who are remembered as violent murderers despite Senate investigations and declassified documents revealing that the FBI had invented the most cringe-worthy stories about the BPP that are still repeated in scholarship and public discourse today. The undetectable manipulations of COINTELPRO liken to those of the Tal Shiar, whom Captain Picard hints at in a conversation with the Duras sisters. As the infighting between the House of Duras and the House of Gowron escalate, Picard warns the Duras sisters that the Tal Shair were master manipulators who could shape actions and attitudes to discredit or disgrace their enemies without anyone suspecting their presence ("Redemption, Part I"). However, Picard's warning is moot; at that point, the captain did not know that the Duras sisters had already formed an alliance with Sela's agents. Even though Starfleet ultimately prevents the Duras sisters from controlling the Klingon High Council, the Tal Shair still brought down the once-powerful House of Duras (thus breaking their alliance) and destabilizing Klingon politics under Gowron, a relatively weak leader who depends on Federation aid to maintain power.

The New Left

By 1968, COINTELPRO's formal "New Left" targets included activists and organizations that promoted revolution in the U.S. or withdrawal from Vietnam (C.D. Brennan to W.C. Sullivan 5/9/68). In practice, the New Left was the FBI's catch-all category for activists, organizations, and community spaces which challenged American values, traditions, and lifestyles (Cunningham 52). The net was cast so wide that it encompassed student clubs, peace organizations, anarchist groups, black protest groups, LGBT groups, environmental organizations, and the fundamental institutions of social life, including "food co-ops, health clinics, child care centers, schools, bookstores, newspapers, community centers, street theaters, rock groups, and communes" (Glick 12). The FBI demarcated its New Left targets based on arbitrary cultural indicators such as embracing a "hippie" lifestyle, reading poetry, or listening to rock-and-roll. The Bureau even considered "the dirty anti-social appearance and behavior of a large number of students, who can be seen to have the fullest beatnik image" as a sign of radicalism at Antioch College in Ohio (Cincinnati office to J.E. Hoover 6/3/68), which the Bureau later used to justify its crackdowns on student organizing at Antioch, despite acknowledging that the students posed no threat to national security (Cunningham 53).

The focus of the New Left–COINTELPRO was Students for a Democratic Society (SDS), in which Hoover was convinced communists were involved in because members of the group "were saying things similar to what is being said in Peking" (Finman and MacCaulay 677). The breadth of COINTELPRO's New Left targets, its actions against Antioch students, and Hoover's statement regarding SDS confirmed that foremost on COINTELPRO's agenda was the policing of identities and loyalties, not the policing of crime. Returning to "The Drumhead," Admiral Satie's unrelenting pursuit of Tarses and her accusations against Worf make sense in light of concerns over what Tarses' and Worf's identities might express about their loyalty to the Federation, as opposed to concerns over any violations of Federation statutes.

Civic Institutions

The anti-communist crusade extended into civic institutions at the heart of American democracy. This essay has already noted how the FBI obstructed free and fair elections in their operations against the SWP. In addition, COINTELPRO operatives flouted due process and the rule of law by paying witnesses to give false testimonies in court and framing individuals for crimes as serious as murder. For example, FBI infiltrator Julius Butler was the only witness to testify against BPP leader Geronimo Pratt for the 1968 robbery that resulted in the murder of a white woman and injuries to her husband (Wolf 55–56). Pratt served 27 years in prison for a crime of which the FBI knew he was innocent, having surveilled him while he was 400 miles away from the scene. A year later, three Panthers were tried for robbery, attempted murder of police officers, and illegal weapons possession, based on the testimony of a police infiltrator who planted the shotgun in the Panthers' car and who drew up the hotel floor plan comprising the only available evidence tying the Panthers to the conspiracy (Goldstein 527). The Bureau linked another BPP leader, Dhoruba Bin Wahad, to the 1971 killings of two NYPD officers, for which the Black Liberation Army had already claimed responsibility (Wolf 61–64). Bin Wahad was wrongfully imprisoned for 20 years before his conviction was overturned.

The press also lost its freedom to maneuver. Most mainstream media outlets enthusiastically repeated baseless rumors about the communist connections or the moral depravity of blacklisted individuals and published the private internal political debates of leftist organizations to further fractionalize them (Bernstein). While the Bureau marshaled the mainstream press as a foot soldier in its anti-communist crusade, it sought to decimate the infrastructure of the underground press. Convinced that alternative newspapers were "a type of filth that could only originate in a depraved mind" (SAC-Newark to J.E. Hoover 5/23/69), the FBI conducted numerous warrantless raids on the offices of alternative media outlets, during which the Bureau confiscated and destroyed printers, typewriters, records, and other materials; threatened the lives of the newspaper workers; and arrested countless on false charges (Leamer 138–141).

Finally, throughout the 1960s, the FBI violated the principles of academic freedom by sabotaging their teaching appointments and public speaking engagements [defaming radical scholars like Morris Starsky, Staughton Lynd, and Angela Davis] (Memo to J.E. Hoover 11/15/68; SAC-Phoenix to J.E. Hoover 10/1/68; Memo to SAC-Charlotte 3/11/65). Sometimes these operations escalated to blood-letting, as when Howard Berry Godfrey— a notorious FBI informant and head of the FBI-funded and anti-communist Secret Army Organization—conducted a drive-by shooting at the home of San Diego State University professor Peter Bohmer, injuring a v*San Diego Street Journal* reporter (Zoccino; Parenti 24). Godfrey's SAC shielded him from prosecution by hiding the gun under his couch while local police investigated the shooting.

TNG gives too little information to adequately assess how the Tal Shiar affects core institutions in Romulan society, but we can turn instead to the Federation, which often uses the same warring tactics as its enemies. The Federation prides itself on the advancement of science and exploration, but these foundational institutions are not spared from corruption in the name of national security. In "The Pegasus," viewers learn that on more than one occasion Starfleet Command endangered the entire crew aboard the *Starship Pegasus* as they tested a secret, experimental cloaking device, in violation of the Algeron Treaty with the Romulan Empire. Even after the experiment killed most of the *Pegasus* crew and fused the starship into an asteroid, Admiral Raner, head of Starfleet Security, sought to revive the experiment on the premise that it is a defensive technology critical to the security of the Federation. Starfleet Security's relentless pursuit of this weapons technology takes the Federation to the precipice of war with the Romulans, from which they only narrowly escaped.[8] This is cause to wonder whether similar excessive courses of action taken by the FBI and other American counterintelligence agencies at home and around the world made Americans more insecure and worsened the security dilemma with the Soviet Union.

The Legacy of COINTELPRO

The FBI successfully disrupted political organizing during critical years of the Cold War thanks to a skillful balancing of covert psychological methods and conventional intelligence gathering. COINTELPRO inflamed paranoia, mistrust, and animosity within leftist circles, crippling their solidarity and organizational power for generations to come. As Noam Chomsky observed in 1975:

> Alone among the parliamentary democracies, the United States has had no mass-based socialist party … no socialist voice in the media, and virtually no departure from centrist ideology within the schools … at least until the pressure from student activism impelled a slight departure from orthodoxy. All this is testimony to the effectiveness of the system of controls that has been in force for many years, the activities of the FBI being only the spearhead for far more extensive, substantial, and effective—if more low-keyed—measures enforced throughout American society [Blackstock 35].

It is just as likely that the Tal Shiar paralyzes or rolls back the momentum for reunification at potential turning points. For instance, Commander Sela conspires with Proconsul Neral and Senator Pardek to lure Spock onto Romulus with the promise of endorsing reunification, and then constructs a hologram of Spock urging Vulcan to receive a "peace envoy" from Romulus containing thousands of troops on a Trojan horse mission to conquer Vulcan ("Reunification"). While new generations of Romulans are increasingly receptive to reunification, the movement still faces an uphill battle against the overwhelmingly powerful machinery of the Romulan state.

After fifteen years of operation, the FBI finally terminated COINTELPRO in 1971. Afterward, as part of a broader investigation into the abuses of U.S. intelligence agencies, the Senate Select Committee to Study Governmental Operations with Respect to Intelligence Activities—better known as the Church Committee—combed over 20,000 pages of COINTELPRO documents and oversaw numerous depositions of COINTELPRO agents. Despite some serious shortcomings in the investigative and accountability process,[9] the committee concluded that COINTELPRO amounted to "a sophisticated vigilante operation" with no legal basis (Senate Select Committee, *Supplementary Detailed Staff Reports* 27). Its tactics may have generated more violence than it intended to prevent, especially through inflaming tensions and rivalries among targeted organizations. The Church Committee deemed COINTELPRO's techniques of arrest-on-suspicion and selective prosecution to be "intolerable in a democratic society even if all the targets had been involved in violent activity" (Senate Select Committee, *Supplementary Detailed Staff Reports* 3). At best, COINTELPRO targets had "no conceivable rational relationship to either national security or violent activity" (Senate Select Committee, *Supplementary Detailed Staff Reports* 7). Despite these searing indictments, only two COINTELPRO operatives were charged with wrongdoing, only to be pardoned by President Ronald Reagan before either had spent a day in prison (Saito 1101).

The Tal Shiar enjoys comparable immunity from prosecution, bound neither to Romulan law nor Romulan Senate oversight. The agency commands the total cooperation and resources of the government and military to carry out its missions. This is why, in the guise of Major Rakal, Counselor Troi only needed to flash her insignia badge to override Captain Toleth's authority, seize the *Warbird Khazara*, and threaten the captain's life if she displays any opposition. The license enjoyed by the Tal Shiar and COINTELPRO sent a message that state agents who violate political rights are guaranteed immunity from prosecution as long as they veil their actions in the language of wartime necessity and patriotism.

Without accountability, intelligence agencies are encouraged to repeat their abuses. Indeed, Cold War–era state violence persisted into the War on Terror, accompanied by the same rhetorical mission to "uphold the values of America, and remember why so many have come here … they [al-Qaeda] hate what we see right here in this chamber—a democratically elected government. Their leaders are self-appointed. They hate our freedoms—our freedom of religion, our freedom of speech, our freedom to vote and assemble and disagree with each other" (Bush, "State of the Union Address"). Yet the U.S. government has transgressed these core principles in its crusade against terrorism just as it did against communism. The War on Terror has featured the policy and surveillance of anti-war protests and urban Muslim-American communities, and the government has failed to protect Muslims who experience religious or racial discrimination and hate crimes. Captain Picard's warning to his crew and superiors during the interrogation of Simon Tarses resonates forcefully here: that the first act of political censorship can easily descend into wholesale political repression, whereby we forget what it is we are purportedly defending in the first place.

Conclusion

Because we watch *TNG* mainly through the eyes of the Federation, it is easy to dismiss the existence of an all-powerful secret police force like the Tal Shiar as an idiosyncrasy of a totalitarian enemy. Yet, in the more foreboding *Deep Space Nine* series, Starfleet unveiled that it has its own intelligence agency, "Section 31," deriving its name from Starfleet Charter's Article 14, Section 31, which permitted security operatives to sidestep normal rules of conduct under the same "war necessity" dogma as COINTELPRO. Glossing over the existence of Section 31, Federation ideologues often spoke of the Federation as being more rational, judicious, and virtuous than their interstellar adversaries. Yet Section 31 usurped the efficacy and ruthlessness of even the Tal Shiar, conducting campaigns of brainwashing, torture, assassinations, chemical warfare, and genocide outside the purview and control of any Starfleet or Federation leadership body. With the Dominion War threatening the Federation's existence, Starfleet sets aside Gene Roddenberry's vision in its struggle for survival—as did the United States.

However, Section 31's existence actually predates the Federation; the *Enterprise* episode "Divergence" reveals that Section 31 began in the 22nd century to protect United Earth from outside threats, likely drawing from the legacy of the Cold War two centuries earlier. The historian John Lewis Gaddis assures Americans that, unlike the countries which embraced Marxist-Leninism during the Cold War, the U.S. avoided an authoritarian turn: "Despite the military-industrial complex, the nation maintained its markets; despite McCarthyism, it sustained and ultimately strengthened civil liberties; despite the excesses of Vietnam and Watergate, the strategy of containment never came close to corrupting fundamental American values ("The Legacy of George Kennan"). Stepping into the era of the War of Terror, President George W. Bush declared that the U.S. was squarely on the side of an incorruptible good: "There can be no neutrality between justice and cruelty, between the innocent and the guilty. We are in a conflict between good and evil. And America will call evil by its name" (Bush, West Point Commencement Address).

The words of these statesmen reverberate with irony when juxtaposed against the U.S. government's chilling record of policing loyalty to the social order and repressing speech, assembly, and due process rights during almost every war the U.S. has fought in since its conception as a nation. American and Federation practices of political and ideological containment have perverted the ideas of "freedom" that it intended to promote by first blurring then eventually demolishing the line between criminal and political policing. Striking the proper balance between national security and protecting the political rights that compose the bedrock of any democratic order will remain a defining policy challenge in the 21st century, as the U.S. faces new security challenges in a globalized world.

NOTES

1. For the Federation's foreign policy concerning the Romulan Empire, see Alex Burston-Chorowicz's essay in this volume.

2. See TNG episodes "Data's Day," "Neutral Zone," and "The Enemy."

3. FBI records on COINTELPRO take the form of memos between Director Hoover and Special Agents in Charge (SACs) of local offices or among COINTELPRO agents. Unless otherwise cited, memos are acquired from the FBI's digital vault of records found at https://vault.fbi.gov/cointel-pro.

4. COINTELPRO investigations into the Ku Klux Klan differed considerably from its approach toward left groups—the FBI took a permissive attitude toward the KKK, even assisting them in planning attacks against civil rights activists (FBI Vault, G.C. Moore to W.C. Sullivan 7/20/70; W.C. Sullivan to A.H. Belmont 8/30/63).

5. For more on Tal Shiar operations against the Founders' homeworld and former Obsidian Order agents, see *Star Trek: Deep Space Nine* episodes "Improbable Cause" and "The Die Is Cast." For the Tal Shiar's intervention in the Klingon Civil War, see TNG episodes "Sins of the Father," "Reunion," and "Redemption:

I & II." For the conflict between the Federation and Romulan Empire, see the Tomed Incident in "The Neutral Zone," "The Pegasus," and "The Defector."

6. See TNG episodes "Yesterday's Enterprise," "Sins of the Father," and "The Mind's Eye."

7. An FBI informant named "Cotton" Smith, chief of Los Angeles BPP security, provided the detailed floor plan that the FBI used to raid the local Black Panthers headquarters where Pratt was housed (Durden-Smith 134–135). The only reason Pratt emerged alive was because he slept on the floor, rather than in his bed, due to an injury he sustained as a veteran fighting in the Vietnam War. The raid was headed by a Panther-focused unit of the LAPD, working with the local COINTELPRO section overseen by the son of the Chicago SAC that planned the raid on Hampton's apartment.

8. See Larry A. Grant's essay in this volume.

9. The Church Committee accounted for a total of 2,679 COINTELPRO operations, including 2,305 warrantless wiretaps, 697 buggings, and 57,846 mail openings, among a deluge of other activities of questionable legality (Senate Select Committee, "Supplementary Detailed Staff Reports" 301, 632 and "Hearings on the FBI" 601). However, these figures are probably dramatically deflated. By itself, the New York office conducted over 1,000 operations in just a three-year span between 1959 and 1963 (Ryter, "Corrupting American Institutions" 2). A former agent revealed in an interview with *Seven Days* that he completed more warrantless searches (or "black bag jobs") than the figure reported for the entire FBI. Another FBI whistleblower confirmed that the numbers were manipulated based on the requirements of the FBI at any given time. It is safe to assume that a countless number of COINTELPRO operations have vanished from history, having been withheld by the Bureau or were never documented in the first place. Further sanitizing the recorded history of COINTELPRO is the fact that the Church Committee often repeated the FBI's statements verbatim and allowed the FBI to abridge its records before turning them over (Church and Vander Wall, *COINTELPRO Papers* xiv). The Committee never completed their investigations before being "temporarily suspended." The investigation still remains suspended, over 40 years later.

Works Cited

"Balance of Terror." *Star Trek: The Original First Series—The Complete First Season*, written by Paul Schneider and Gene Roddenberry, directed by Vincent McEveety, Paramount Pictures, 2004. DVD.

Bernstein, Carl. "The CIA and the Media." *Rolling Stone* 20 Oct. 1977. Web. Accessed 11 Apr. 2017.

Blackstock, Nelson. *COINTELPRO: The FBI'S Secret War on Political Freedom*. New York: Monad Press, 1975. Print.

Bloom, Joshua, and Waldo E. Martin, Jr. *Black Against Empire: The History and Politics of the Black Panther Party*. Berkeley: University of California Press, 2016. Print.

Bush, George W. "Commencement Address at the United States Military Academy in West Point, New York." *The American Presidency Project*. 27 May 2006. Web. Accessed 4 Jan. 2018.

_____. "President Bush Addresses the Nation." *Washington Post* 21 Sept. 2001. Web. Accessed 7 Apr. 2017.

Churchill, Ward, and Jim Vader Wall. *Agents of Repression: The FBI'S Secret Wars Against the Black Panther Party and the American Indian Movement*. Boston: South End Press, 2002. Print.

_____. *The COINTELPRO Papers: Documents from the FBI'S Secret Wars Against Domestic Dissent*. Boston: South End Press, 1990. Print.

Cox, Michael. "From the Truman Doctrine to the Second Superpower Détente: The Rise and Fall of the Cold War." *Journal of Peace Research* 27.1 (1990): 25–41. Print.

Cunningham, David. "State Versus Social Movement: FBI Counterintelligence Against the New Left." *States, Parties, and Social Movements,* Ed. Jack A. Goldstone. Cambridge: Cambridge University Press, 2003. 45–77. Print.

"Data's Day." *Star Trek: The Next Generation—The Complete Fourth Season*, written by Harold Apter and Ronald D. Moore, directed by Robert Wiemer. Paramount Pictures, 2002. DVD.

"Divergence." *Star Trek: Enterprise—The Complete Fourth Season*, written by Judith and Garfield Reeves-Stevens, directed by David Barrett, Paramount Pictures, 2004. DVD.

"The Drumhead." *Star Trek: The Next Generation—The Complete Fourth Season,* written by Jeri Taylor, directed by Jonathan Frakes, Paramount Pictures, 2002. DVD.

Durden-Smith, Jo. *Who Killed George Jackson? Fantasies, Paranoia, and the Revolution*. New York: Alfred A. Knopf, Publishers, 1976. Print.

"Face of the Enemy." *Star Trek: The Next Generation—The Complete Sixth Season,* written by Naren Shankar, directed by Gabrielle Beaumont, Paramount Pictures, 2002. DVD.

Federal Bureau of Investigation. "FBI Records: COINTELPRO." *FBI Vault* 5 Sept. 2016, Web. Accessed 5 Sept. 2016.

Finman, Ted, and Stewart MacCaulay. "Freedom to Dissent: The Vietnam Protests and the Words of Public Officials." *Wisconsin Law Review* (1966): 632–723. Print.

Foner, Philip S., editor. *The Black Panthers Speak*. Philadelphia/New York: J.B. Lippincott Co., 1970. Print.

Freed, Donald. *Agony in New Haven: The Trial of Bobby Seale, Erica Huggins, and the Black Panther Party*. New York: Simon & Schuster Publishers, 1973. Print.

Gaddis, John Lewis. "The Legacy of George Kennan in the Age of Terrorism." *The New Republic* 17 Apr. 2005, Web. Accessed 4 Jan. 2018.

Glick, Brian. *War at Home: Covert Action Against U.S. Activists and What We Can Do About It.* Cambridge, MA: South End Press, 1989. Print.

Goldstein, Robert J. *Political Repression in Modern America from 1870 to 1976.* Champaign: University of Illinois Press, 2001. Print.

Hartman, Andrew. *A War for the Soul of America: A History of Culture Wars.* University of Chicago Press, 2015. Print.

"Improbable Cause," *Star Trek: Deep Space Nine—The Complete Third Season.* Written by René Echevarria, directed by Avery Brooks, Paramount Pictures, 2003. DVD

Internal Security Act. 50 USCA. Sec. 781 et seq. 1950. Print.

Jayko, Margaret. *FBI on Trial: The Victory in the Socialist Workers Party Suit Against Government Spying.* New York: Pathfinder Press, 1988. Print.

Korematsu v. United States. 323 U.S. 214. 1944. *Justia,* n.d., Web. Accessed 22 Apr. 2017.

Kuklick, Bruce. "U.S. Intellectual History." In *American Cold War Strategy: Interpreting NSC 68,* Ed. Ernest R. May. Boston: Bedford Books, 1993. 156–159. Print.

Larson, Deborah Welch. *Origins of Containment: A Psychological Explanation.* Princeton: Princeton University Press, 1989. Print.

Leamer, Laurence. *The Paper Revolutionaries: The Rise of the Underground Press.* New York: Simon & Schuster Publishers, 1970. Print.

Miller, Stuart C. *"Benevolent Assimilation": The American Conquest of the Philippines, 1899–1903.* New Haven: Yale University Press, 1982. Print.

"The Mind's Eye." *Star Trek: The Next Generation—The Complete Fourth Season,* written by Ken Schafer and René Echevarria, directed by David Livingston, Paramount Pictures, 2002. DVD.

National Security Council. "NSC 68: United States Objectives and Programs for National Security." *Truman Library* 5 Sept. 2016. Web.

O'Reilly, Kenneth. *"Racial Matters": The FBI's Secret Files on Black America, 1960–1972.* New York: Free Press, 1989. Print.

Parenti, Michael. *Democracy for the Few.* New York: St. Martin's Press, 1980. Print.

"The Pegasus." *Star Trek: The Next Generation—The Complete Seventh Season,* written by Ronald D. Moore, directed by LeVar Burton, Paramount Pictures, 2002. DVD.

"Redemption, Part I." *Star Trek: The Next Generation—The Complete Fourth Season,* written by Ronald D. Moore, directed by Cliff Bole, Paramount Pictures, 2002. DVD.

Rogin, Michael. *"Ronald Reagan" the Movie: And Other Episodes in Political Demonology.* Berkeley: University of California Press, 1988. Print.

Ryter, Mark. "COINTELPRO: Corrupting American Institutions." *First Principles* 3.9 (1978a): 1–5. Print.

_____. "COINTELPRO: FBI Lawbreaking and Violence." *First Principles* 3.10 (1978b): 1–6. Print.

Saito, Natsu Taylor. "Whose Liberty? Whose Security? The USA PATRIOT Act in the Context of COINTEL-PRO and the Unlawful Repression of Political Dissent." *Oregon Law Review* 81.4 (2002): 1051–1132. Print.

Senate Select Committee to Study Government Operations with Respect to Intelligence Operations. *Foreign and Military Intelligence, Book I,* 94th Congress, S. REP. NO. 94–755. Washington, D.C.: U.S. Government Printing Office, 1976. Print.

_____. *Hearings on Intelligence Activities, Volume 6: The Federal Bureau of Investigation,* 94th Congress, S. REP. NO 66-077. Washington, D.C.: U.S. Government Printing Office, 1975. Print.

_____. *Hearings on the Federal Bureau of Investigation, Volume VI,* 94th Congress. Washington, D.C.: U.S. Government Printing Office, 1975. Print.

_____. *Intelligence Activities and the Rights of Americans, Book II,* 94th Congress, S. REP. NO. 94-755. Washington, D.C.: U.S. Government Printing Office, 1976. Print.

_____. *Supplementary Detailed Staff Reports on Intelligence Activities and the Rights of Americans, Book III,* 94th Congress, S. REP. NO. 94-755. Washington, D.C.: U.S. Government Printing Office, 1976. Print.

Socialist Workers Party v. Attorney General of the United States. 642 F. Supp. 1357 (S.D.N.Y 1986): 1357, 1379–80.

Sturm, Douglas. "Martin Luther King, Jr., as Democratic Socialist." *Journal of Religious Ethics* 18.2 (1990): 79–105. Print.

Sullivan, William C., and Brown, Bill. *The Bureau: My Thirty Years in Hoover's FBI.* New York: W.W. Norton Co., 1975. Print.

Truman, Harry S. "Executive Order 9835." *Harry S. Truman: Library and Museum 21* Mar. 1947. Web. Accessed 4 Jan. 2018.

Tuathail, Gearóid Ó, and Agnew, John. "Geopolitics and Discourse: Practical Geopolitical Reasoning in American Foreign Policy." *Political Geography* 11.2 (1992): 190–204. Print.

"Unification I." *Star Trek: The Next Generation—The Complete Fifth Season,* written by Jeri Taylor, directed by Les Landau, Paramount Pictures, 2002. DVD.

"Unification II." *Star Trek: The Next Generation—The Complete Fifth Season,* written by Michael Piller, directed by Cliff Bole, Paramount Pictures, 2002. DVD.

Wolf, Paul. "COINTELPRO: The Untold American Story." Report presented to UN High Commissioner for Human Rights, Mary Robinson at the World Conference against Racism in Durban, South Africa, 2001. Print.

Zoccino, Nanda. "Ex–FBI Informer Describes Terrorist Role." *Los Angeles Times* 26, January 1976. Print.

"You will be assimilated"
Multicultural Utopianism in the 24th Century

Mehdi Achouche

Despite its narrative focus on the future, science fiction (SF) is often more revealing of its own present, even of that present's contradictions and tensions. As writer and critic Samuel R. Delany argues, "SF is not about the future. SF is in dialogue with the present. It works by setting up a dialogue with the here-and-now, a dialogue as rich and intricate as the writer can make it" (Delany). Science fiction is not so much extrapolation of the future as it is a metaphor for the present, allowing its readers or viewers to gain the necessary distance from their own society and time. This allows its practitioners to reach a better, higher vantage point and see familiar things from an unfamiliar angle, which can be either or both entertaining and enlightening. The genre is most revealing of a given society's values, dreams, and aspirations in its utopian form; one era's definition of the perfect society is rarely the same as another, as progress, the key notion at the heart of the science fiction and utopian genres, is constantly refined and redefined.

That progress may have a lot to do with science and technology, but also often—if not most of all—deals with or reflects contemporary social trends and issues as well. For instance, early 20th century science fiction often imagined the world unified under a single government, typically under the auspices of Great Britain or the United States, or even some "Anglo-Saxon" Empire. The chosen nation would remake the world, and soon the universe itself, in its image—transplanting its own language, institutions and universal values onto other societies in a Social Darwinian process.[1] Societies and races were thought to compete against each other just like animals and species did (evolution being equated to progress), and thus one of them would eventually come out on top and impose its own model. It is precisely this traditional, colonial model that *Star Trek: The Next Generation* (ST: TNG) criticizes through the civilization of the Borg.

The original *Star Trek* (1966–1969) already defied these traditional characteristics of the genre. It no longer imagines an Empire, but a Federation that benignly rules over a multicultural interplanetary territory. Its enemies are, by contrast, warmongering Empires—a word that is systematically associated with wrong purposes in *Star Trek* (Meyer 37)—like the Klingons or the Romulans, who only use violence to integrate new races and planets into their possession and were thus used by the series as a counter-example to the Federation. Similarly, virtually each new weekly civilization the *Enterprise* encounters fails in one way or another when compared to Kirk and his crew, who then needs to show the aliens—and, through them, viewers—what the right values and model are. Kirk often ends the show lauding self-determination, individualism, democracy, tolerance, and other values equated with an ideal American model.[2]

The utopian quality of the 23rd century is first and foremost demonstrated through the multiracial, multicultural composition of the crew. The future is, above all, a question of getting along with each other in spite of racial or cultural differences, a crucial and progressive message in the midst of the civil rights movement. Humanity in the 23rd century finally manages to achieve that progress by uniting around the common goal of space exploration, creating "a utopia where cultural differences are combined productively" to confront common challenges and enemies (Pounds 86). In *Star Trek*'s terms, this philosophy is represented by IDIC (Infinite Diversity in Infinite Combinations), in which differences combine to create meaning and beauty ("Is There in Truth No Beauty").

Yet, as scholars have shown, this multicultural utopia has its limits. The leaders and the main characters of the original show—Kirk, Spock and McCoy—are still white men (even if with pointy ears), while the minority characters are relegated to very peripheral roles and never grow beyond simple one-dimensional characterizations, essentially bringing "background color," or an exotic foreign accent, to the show (Kwan 61). The captain is an American, the ship's designation and name is a reference to the U.S. Navy, while much in the representation of the "United Federation of Planets" is reminiscent of the "United States of America." As Jutta Weldes writes, "despite its appearance of liberal multiculturalism, […] the *Star Trek* universe rests on and serves to naturalize a series of differences that produce a hierarchical ordering of cultures, races, species, and life forms" (qtd. in Meyer 29).

Others do see more progressivism in the franchise, especially in *Star Trek: The Next Generation*, produced twenty years later. The new series is both the product of the original series' legacy and philosophy and the result of its own time's values and debates, yet it still uses the space opera subgenre to dramatize its own vision of race relations in an ideal society. Influenced by increased awareness of minorities and their importance within society, as well as by contemporary debates over the new concept of multiculturalism, the show tries to depict a more genuinely inclusive future by offering more diversity within the crew and by giving its minority characters more narrative weight, while adopting a more thoughtful attitude toward alien cultures, especially in its later seasons. This is why Russell and Wolski correctly observe that "a self-critique and reflection on this colonial mission develops through the seven seasons of ST: TNG" (Russell & Wolski).

Crucially, the series also adopts the same strategy as the original series in its use of an arch-enemy civilization as an inverted mirror image of the crew and the Federation, making it possible for the show to underline in dramatic fashion the qualities and values at the heart of its own updated version of *Star Trek*'s multicultural utopia. The original series did this week after week, while ST: TNG never does so more compellingly than through the Borg, the Federation's new recurring arch-nemesis who explicitly promote their own competing version of progress, utopia and race relations. The Borg also serve to invert the traditional colonial encounter, putting the Federation and the Enterprise in the role of the potential victims of a superior and imperialistic civilization murderously intent on enlightening the galaxy.

Repudiating Assimilation

ST: TNG was produced in an era that experienced significant changes since the original series ended. If the original show was heavily influenced by the civil rights movement and the unrest of its time, with even Martin Luther King, Jr., remarking on the importance of the series (Weitekamp 27), then the sequel was very much influenced by the debates still raging over other races and cultures and their proper places and roles in the United States. Minorities were becoming more visible in American culture, including on television (a presence which the first series pioneered), and in society, such as affirmative action policies. At the same time, a new concept, multiculturalism, was at the heart of contemporary debates. The word, first coined in 1965 and the direct progeny of the civil rights era, conveyed a new social philosophy and ideal, one that was officially adopted as national policy by Canada in the early 1970s (Richter 36).

Rather than promote a singular culture (one language, one religion, etc.) within one country and the need for new immigrants to adapt to and adopt that culture, multiculturalism, in the words of the 1988 Canadian Multiculturalism Act, is based on cultural diversity, with each member of society having a right to "preserve, enhance and share their cultural heritage" (Article 3(1)(a)). In the United States, this soon meant reforming educational curricula to give minorities a more prominent share in, for example, history courses. The assumption was that, in the words of philosopher Charles Taylor in 1992, "a person or group of people can suffer real damage, real distortion, if the people or society around them mirror back to them a confining or demeaning or contemptible picture of themselves" (25). Multiculturalism, in essence, states that Western societies have long ignored minorities living in their midst and should finally acknowledge their presence and contributions, while lauding and protecting their differences from the dominating culture as strengths rather than threats to national unity. It was born out of the Civil Rights Movement of the 1960s, but also out of the contemporary decolonization movement across the world. If, minorities were long victimized by Western powers trying to impose their own supposedly superior culture on others, it was thought, they should now make efforts to accept cultural differences among nations. This included ethnic groups crossing their borders, as large numbers of immigrants were making former colonial powers such as Britain and France, along with the United States, immigrant nations.

This apology of cultural pluralism is often opposed to the more traditional American paradigm of the "melting pot," a belief that peoples from all nations would come to the United States and see their cultural, and even genetic, characteristics melt into a new alloy—a new American, as John Hector De Crèvecoeur famously wrote in 1782: "Here individuals of all nations are melted into a new race of men" (44). This meant the accumulation of peoples into something greater than the sum of their parts—"the fusion of all races, perhaps the coming superman," in the words of the 1908 play, *The Melting Pot,* which made the metaphor popular (Zangwill). A debate soon arose in the United States, but also in Canada and soon in Western Europe, over how to tackle immigration and the minorities living in their midst—by eradicating their cultural differences or by protecting those differences.

In the U.S., the 1980s witnessed the rise of a conservative movement intent on promoting a more traditional vision of America. As the "openly anglo-conformist" (Washburn et al. 75) conservative administrations of Presidents Reagan and Bush tried to limit or even roll back earlier reforms (Hewitt, loc. 61), a chorus of voices rose to condemn multiculturalism and defend the older idea of assimilation. During this time, "a full-scale attack on multiculturalism was mounted," which "particularly focused on educational issues and attempted to link it to other 'politically correct' policies such as affirmative action" (Hewitt, loc. 187). In 1990, historian Arthur Schlesinger warned against the "repudiation of the melting pot," deploring the fact that "the contemporary ideal is not assimilation but ethnicity. [...] We used to say e pluribus unum. Now we glorify pluribus and belittle unum. The melting pot yields to the Tower of Babel" (Schlesinger A14). A 1987 critique of the new "minorities-friendly" academic curricula became a best-seller, while a later book called multiculturalism a "Trojan horse in America"—conveying the idea that foreigners were trying to undermine the country (Schmidt xiii). Meanwhile, the word "multiculturalism" went from no mentions in major newspapers in 1988 to more than 100 items in 1990, more than 600 in 1991 and 1500 in 1994—the period during which ST: TNG gave center stage to the Borg menace (Glazer, *Multiculturalists* 7). Multiculturalism and assimilation were now part of the so-called "culture wars" identified in a 1991 book of the same name: a struggle to define the ideal America of the future—an ideal which ST: TNG depicted each week on television.

The stinging criticism of the melting pot paradigm by the multiculturalists, who felt it meant denying and destroying minorities' identities to impose an oppressive uniformity over all citizens, made the word "assimilation" an increasingly loaded one by the early 1990s. As Nathan Glazer wrote in 1993, "Assimilation is not today a popular term. [...] Indeed, in recent years it has been taken for granted that assimilation, as an expectation of how different ethnic and racial groups would respond to their common presence in one society [...], is to be rejected" (*Assimilation* 123). Yet ST: TNG chose to use it repeatedly during the same period in relation to the Borg (starting with the 1990 double episode "The Best of Both Worlds"). *The Oxford English Dictionary* defines assimilation as "the action of making or becoming like; the state of being like; similarity, resemblance, likeness" (OED Online, 1.a.). Such a nightmare of uniformity and conformity sums up well the nature of the Borg "utopia." In the episodes "The Best of Both Worlds" and "I, Borg," the Borg repeatedly state their intentions to assimilate not just individuals but other "cultures" as well, to eradicate any semblance of racial difference and cultural diversity throughout the galaxy—the caricature of the contemporary debates over cultural diversity within the United States.

If the present situation of the country was the object of controversy between the multiculturalists and the assimilationists, the future of the nation was even more controversial. Again in 1990 (ST: TNG's fourth season had just launched with "The Best of Both Worlds, Part II"), *Time* ran a cover on "America's Changing Colors," announcing that in the near future (the 21st century) whites would no longer be the majority in the country. The lead article, entitled "Beyond the Melting Pot," informs its readers that "history suggests that sustaining a truly multiracial society is difficult, or at least unusual" and tries to identify the risks and opportunities offered by the "browning of America" (Henry 28). For its November 18, 1993, issue, the same magazine's cover featured "Eve," a computer generated image introduced as "The New Face of America" because it was digitally created by mixing several races to come up with a convincing—and harmonious—melting of those races. The subtitle explained "how immigrants are shaping the world's first multicultural society," even though the synthetic face corresponds to the ideal at the heart of the melting pot idea—thus illustrating the confusion that has often characterized the debate over the integration of immigrants and over the definitions of the various concepts behind the words "melting pot" and "multiculturalism" ("Eve"). This confusion reflects the ambiguity at the heart of the Federation and the franchise: promoting diversity, but always under the auspices of thinly veiled American institutions and ideals.

This is the context in which ST: TNG was produced from 1987 to 1994. The show continued to represent the same racial harmony as the original series by featuring diversity on the bridge of the *Enterprise*—even including a Klingon, Worf, among the main cast to denote the progress the Federation made since Kirk's times one century earlier. Throughout ST: TNG and then in *Deep Space Nine*, Worf repeatedly confronts the tensions between his loyalty to the Federation and his attachment to Klingon culture. This allowed *Star Trek* to explore the issue at the heart of multiculturalism—harmony and unity within diversity—even though the Federation and Starfleet are rarely compared unfavorably to any outside model. The captain is now identified with French culture (even though his references—and the show's—are more often to Anglo-American history and culture, with Picard citing Shakespeare, Melville, Admiral Nelson, etc.), while the minorities making up the crew are both more numerous and given more narrative importance. In a demonstration of how important the representation of minorities in the *Star Trek* universe is, the next spin-offs went even further, with *Deep Space Nine* featuring an African American captain and *Voyager* boasting a (white) woman as captain. The franchise thus follows in the footsteps of the original series by illustrating the progress its fantasized humanity had made through the racial and sexual diversity among its crew, depicting within its imagined future and in the production of the franchise itself multicultural progress in action. Its three main African American actors, Michael Dorn, LeVar Burton and Whoopi Goldberg, also frequently mentioned the importance of *Star Trek* as an inspiration for minorities.

Like its predecessor, ST: TNG tries to find various ways to depict an inverted reflection of the Federation and the metonymical *Enterprise* crew, to dramatize by contrasting the qualities and values of Picard and his staff with the antagonists they encountered. This strategy allows the series, like its 1960s precursor, to connote the nature of its futuristic utopia without having to actually show its society in any detail. The Federation thus remains vague enough that it hardly offends anyone, which it inevitably would have if it addressed specific political or social issues of its times. One way ST: TNG found to tackle contemporary society is through an ideal nemesis and "evil twin" of the Federation—the Borg.

Diversity Is Futile

First encountered in the second season episode "Q Who," the Borg is a race composed of enhanced humanoid cyborgs made up of organic and artificial components, and whose brains are constantly connected to other Borg. As Troi remarks in that same episode, the Borg do not have individual minds nor do they have a single leader. They share a collective consciousness, which is underlined by the Borg constantly using the first person pronoun "we." As the crew explores the Borg ship in that episode, it becomes rapidly clear that each Borg individual is only a drone and has no individual existence, as dramatized by the tricorder not picking up any life signs aboard the Borg ship, even though tens of thousands of Borgs are there. As Data explains, the devices do not detect any life readings because when the Borg connect to their alcoves, they become part of a whole and no longer read as separate life forms. The episode "I, Borg" makes clear that the Borg are always connected to the group and their collective consciousness, even when not inserted in their slots, by hearing the million voices of their fellow drones. Picard reminds Dr. Crusher and the audience in that same episode that the crew should think of them as a single collective being. A Borg, he adds, is no more an individual than a single body part.

The Borg thus belong to the traditional science fiction representation of the "hive mind," aliens often paralleled with insects and which do not acknowledge any form of individuality, with Crusher making the connection clear when she uses the word "hive" in "I, Borg." An online encyclopedia of science fiction defines the hive mind theme as "referring to any situation in which minds are linked in such a way that the whole becomes dominant over the parts" (Stableford & Langford). Insectoid civilizations are often used in science fiction (*Starship Troopers*, *Ender's Game*) to create an enemy that denies individuality and difference in favor of a totalitarian, uniform and (literally) inhuman social structure. They also make it possible to play on the idea of evolution, showing how another species follows another evolutionary path toward its own social model and its own version of Progress. The same encyclopedia entry notes "a hive mind is the organizing principle of the community in those insect species of which the basic reproductive unit is the hive, organized around a single fertile female, the queen" (Stableford & Langford). The eighth *Star Trek* film, *First Contact* (1996), introduces the Borg Queen, completing the insect analogy and the characterization of the Borg as an oppressive civilization intent on dehumanizing human beings by transforming them into drones.[3]

Such a civilization is, in the words of Stableford & Langford, the "ultimate totalitarian dystopia," the exact opposite of individualist democracy that the Federation champions. Given the ideological underpinnings of science fiction as a whole, and of *Star Trek* in particular, it is perhaps inevitable that the genre and the franchise repeatedly stages the struggle of democracy, liberty, and individualism against oppression, imperialism, and collectivism among the stars in order to vindicate a certain version of progress and of the ideal society.

The key episodes here are the two-part "The Best of Both Worlds," aired in June and September 1990. As indicated in the (ironic) title, the two civilizations are contrasted in the episode, thanks to Picard, who is assimilated by the Borg, becomes Locutus of Borg, gives the *Enterprise* and viewers an insight into the Borg civilization, and ultimately uses his newly acquired knowledge to defeat them. Whereas their introductory episode stresses how the Borg are only interested in technology, we now learn that they also take control of the bodies and minds of conquered species, adding the sum of their knowledge to theirs and thus growing in the process. The Borg integrates newcomers into their civilization by giving their prey cybernetic appendages and linking their minds to the hive. *First Contact*, the film sequel to this storyline, plays especially well on that theme, depicting the horror of Borg creatures transforming human beings into lifeless, monstrous, zombie-like automatons.

Yet "The Best of Both Worlds" goes beyond the horrific aspect of the vampirization of human beings to include the macroscopic and societal level: how the Borg absorbs whole cultures to benefit theirs. This is what the opening teaser of the episode dramatically expounds, as we witness not just the devastation of a Federation colony, but its disappearance into thin air at the hands of the Borg. As their introductory episode underlines, the Borg are the ultimate user, treating human beings and their cultures, technology, and knowledge as pure raw materials, exploiting them for the benefits they can draw from them and destroying everything and everybody in the process—the ultimate definition of assimilation. Additionally, the collective tells Picard that all cultures will adapt to service theirs, a statement which essentially captures the spirit of colonialism. The Borg are indeed the ultimate colonialist power, in the first and strongest meaning of the term; they colonize other worlds with their own kind and soon replace the original culture with theirs, absorbing it into their collective in the name of progress and perfection. This is what *First Contact* illustrates when the *Enterprise* travels through time to the past to prevent alternate reality where Earth is entirely populated by Borg drones.

The film's story thus allows dramatizes the stark choice which awaits Earth: assimilation by the Borg and thus uniformity and lack of any free will, or diversity and democratic harmony through the Federation—two competing versions of the future and progress, which is what is at stake every time the *Enterprise* encounters the Borg. That narrative echoes the dichotomy in Earth's past: a planet faced with the prospect of debilitating conflict and nuclear annihilation, or collaboration, peace, and prosperity. "The Best of Both Worlds" uses Picard and his Borg persona, Locutus, to dramatize the idea of competing versions of society (good Picard vs. his evil twin), while *First Contact* uses Data and his possible allegiance to the Borg Queen for the same reasons. But these narrative patterns also allow the show to draw the larger parallels between the Federation and the Borg, to show how close, and yet how vastly different, both civilizations and models are.

Through the Looking Glass, Darkly

The Borg collective serves the Federation's evil twin, ST: TNG's own version of the original series' mirror universe, which shows an alternate reality where the main characters belong to a fascist version of the Federation. This time, viewers are given a glimpse of Picard's, Data's and even Earth's totalitarian counterpart.

The Federation is confronted with an enemy that strangely resembles it in its relationship to the ideas of Progress and the "final frontier": going from planet to planet to discover, learn, and integrate new societies into their political system for the betterment of all parties. This analogy is pointed out by Hugh in his discussion with La Forge in "I, Borg," an episode which opens with Picard explaining that the *Enterprise* is on a mission of reconnaissance for possible future "colonization" on desert planets. When La Forge tells Hugh that part of what the Federation does is learn about other species, Hugh answers that the Borg do the same thing—by assimilating them against their will, which is more expedient and efficient. La Forge gets the final word when he stresses the importance of self-determination and embracing differences, proving to viewers the superiority of the Federation's model.

In "Best of Both Worlds," the Borg collective tells Picard how they wish to improve themselves and how, in order to do so, they seek to incorporate humanity's biological and technological properties into theirs. The Borg Queen says the same thing in *First Contact*, explaining how her civilization's objective is the same as the Federation's, namely, evolving increasingly closer toward a state of perfection for the entire hive. She adds that the Borg were like humans at one point, which she derisively calls organically limited and imperfect, but overcame such weakness due to biotechnology and their philosophy of assimilation. By insisting on the theme of evolution, the Borg Queen harkens back to the old Social Darwinian/colonial theme typical of early science fiction, with one superior race or civilization destined to replace all the others. As Data remarks to the Borg Queen, however, her model of progress is not so much evolution as it is conquest—the way for ST: TNG to dramatize the paradoxically old-fashioned approach represented by the Borg, as opposed to the Federation's more modern, enlightened attitude of voluntary inclusiveness and respect of racial and cultural diversity.

Later *Star Trek* spin-offs make the parallels between the Federation and the Borg even clearer, showing how popular and useful the Borg are to help reflect on the Federation and contemporary societal issues. Characters frequently would accuse the Federation of being no different from the Borg, thus allowing the franchise to further its apology of the Federation. In *Deep Space Nine*, one character accuses the Federation of being even worse than the Borg because they, too, assimilate people but only much more pervasively and hypocritically, while another critic in *Voyager* points out how the Federation could be itself guilty of assimilation and "colonization" (qtd. in Russell and Wolski). That both characters expressing this criticism belong to the Maquis, a dissident organization which feels the Federation betrayed its own ideals by compromising with the Cardassian Empire, first introduced in ST: TNG, show how the latter series are willing to create mirror organizations to test core Federation ideals.[4]

The proximity between the Federation and the Borg is again underlined when, in "Best of Both Worlds," Picard becomes the Borg's spokesperson, Locutus. The figurehead of the Federation and captain of the Starfleet's flagship turns into a spokesman of forced assimilation, while Riker and the *Enterprise* must battle one of their own who knows them better than they know themselves. Locutus soon confronts the *Enterprise*, telling the crew that they will shortly be assimilated and that the Borg's only intention is to raise quality of life—that is, to impose progress. Observing the diversity aboard the ship, including Worf, he again promises to erase all forms of diversity in preparation for what he calls "the New Order." His focus on Worf is particularly telling, since Worf is the most obvious example of integration aboard the *Enterprise*. As the sole Klingon in Starfleet, Worf balances his commitments to Starfleet and his Klingon heritage. Earlier episodes, such as "Heart of Glory," demonstrate how Worf often feels like an outsider among the crew, but he remains dedicated to his position and responsibilities. When Locutus faces Worf and promises him assimilation as a kind of elevation from a single-minded warrior race, ST: TNG contrasts two models for integrating "minorities." Worf fiercely rejects the "melting pot" model, asserting the Klingon Empire will never accept the Borg.

It is revealing that Picard, often connoted to a European heritage, is the character who is assimilated by the Borg and then threatens the Federation with assimilation, while the consistently white-faced Borg are repeatedly seen discussing the merits of assimilation with minority characters: La Forge and Guinan in "I, Borg," or the dark-skinned Worf (who is played by an African American actor) in "The Best of Both Worlds." Guinan explains to the Borg named Hugh that her people resisted when the Borg came to assimilate them, which cost them dearly as they abandoned their home world and scattered throughout the galaxy, finding refuge in the diverse Federation, which points to a parallel with the history of African Americans.

In this parallel with colonialism, Locutus caricaturizes the Federation's and Picard's own designs, a "harsh parody of white assimilationist and colonialist practices" (Wilcox

79). He is Picard's darker side the way the Borg are the Federation's negative double. By seemingly turning the tables and putting the *Enterprise* and the Federation in the position of being assimilated by a superior culture (because the Borg have superior technology and consider themselves to be superior), and by having Picard himself state these intentions, the episode thus holds a mirror to the *Enterprise* and to viewers. They refer back to the old colonialist ideology, including a reliance on technological superiority.

Like colonial empires of old, the Borg rely on their technological prowess to both justify and facilitate their propagation. The Borg are, in fact, the caricatures of scientific hubris, where scientists—famously Victor Frankenstein onwards—believe so much in scientific progress that they literally lose their humanity by merging life with technology. The collective only equates progress with science and technology, offering a satire of hyper-rationality, as their cubic spaceship dramatizes. The original series, through Spock, and ST: TNG through Data, show (often in a humorous ways) the risk of science and reason leading to inhuman hyper-rationality, especially how Spock and Data learn to respect and admire human beings and understand that cold logic cannot address everything. The Borg, on the other hand, have not learned this lesson, and thus again illustrate what the Federation has managed not to become. The discussions between the Borg Queen and Data in *First Contact* serve to underline the contrast, with Data, the android that aims to be human, showing how the Federation has a wiser relationship to technology. Apparently very close from one another, Data and the Borg are in fact at opposite ends of the spectrum: technology is the means for the Borg to eradicate their biological differences in order to become interchangeable, while for the Federation it remains subservient to humanist values of knowledge, self-development and diversity.

By having the Locutus inform Worf in "Best of Both Worlds" that they only wish to raise quality of life for all species, the episode satirizes the traditional trope of the imperialist civilization that strives at all costs to export its supposedly universalist and enlightened values to other societies, even if that means using force and coercion to achieve that objective. The Federation/America is better, implies Picard in his answer to the hive mind, because it is based on freedom, self-determination, and diversity. Individuals belonging to other cultures join the United Federation of Planets and serve Starfleet of their own free will because they are truly convinced of the greatness of its social and philosophical model. Furthermore, they know they do not have to abandon any of their cultural or personal characteristics in order to do so. The Federation, like the *Enterprise*, manages to find an ideal equilibrium between "pluribus" and "unum," an ideal balance between (cultural, individual) diversity and unity, a compromise which lies at the heart of its utopian model and which only the Borg can dramatize to full effect.[5] This also implicitly answers the criticism mentioned earlier of the limitations of the *Star Trek* utopian model, by showing how the Federation respects and treasures cultural differences everywhere. This is also the way ST: TNG reconciles aversion toward imperialism, colonization, and uniformity with the dream of an ever-expanding, ever-improving political body that peacefully and harmoniously brings all races and cultures.

The ideal society can only be reached, in the view of both the Federation and the Borg, when all societies have reached a harmonious relationship with one another. Yet, for the Borg, it is only when the galaxy is like the nightmarish alternate reality Earth glimpsed in *First Contact*—with all difference eradicated—that conflict is extinguished and harmony reached. This alternate reality Earth is a window into what society might have looked like had colonialism run its course, while the double episode "Descent" shows how easy it is for the Borg, once their own harmony is disrupted and they prove incapable of dealing with individuality, to fall under the sway of a fascistic leader. That this leader is none other than Lore, Data's evil twin brother, reinforces the parallels between the Borg and the *Enterprise*, especially when Data himself crosses over to join Lore—just as he would join the Borg Queen in *First Contact*.

Given how deep and far the parallels between the assimilationist Borg, colonialism and the melting pot paradigm go, it is not surprising how often viewers draw out ST: TNG's metaphors of assimilation and multiculturalism. They frequently make the show's parallels explicit after ST: TNG's original run, repeatedly using the Borg as a tool in debates over multiculturalism.

Popular Re-appropriation

Creators of popular culture have not failed to see ST: TNG's use of assimilation as a commentary on contemporary times. Political activists and critics have appropriated the Borg as a rhetorical tool to further those discussions. Feminist scholar Diana Relke, for instance, quotes a women's washroom graffiti that appeared in 2003, in the run up to the 2003 Iraq War:

> You will be assimilated. We will add your political and military distinctiveness to our own. Your armies will adapt to service US. NATO is irrelevant. The UN is irrelevant. Anti-war protest is irrelevant. Hell, even Saddam's compliance is irrelevant! Resistance is futile. Have a nice day. George W. Borg [Relke 3].

Similarly a 2008 blog entry shows a smiling George W. Bush wearing the typical Borg laser headgear, reminding viewers of Picard/Locutus and drawing another parallel between the Bush administration's invasion of Iraq (and its attempt to export democracy there) and the Borg (Reed). Many online debates on assimilation and multiculturalism similarly mention the Borg, often sarcastically, such as in the following question: "Which integration model do you prefer, the Melting Pot, the Salad Bowl, Lunchables, or the Borg?" (Ludgate). Likewise, when debate.org organized a debate asking, "Is multiculturalism a better social model than assimilation?," the Borg soon appeared in the discussion. First-generation immigrants or their descendant bloggers also use the Borg when reflecting upon their experiences integrating U.S. culture. In 2012, one blogger reflected "on assimilation & family" and described himself, wistfully, as an "American Borg" (Steele). Earlier, immediately in the wake of the 9/11 attacks (November 2001), another blogger used the same phrase, "American Borg," to denounce the singling out of Muslim immigrants on the grounds that they had supposedly failed to assimilate to U.S. society (Fleishmann). A 2015 entry on the popular social network LinkedIn, addressing the same issues and examples of racism in Europe, where similar debates over assimilation and multiculturalism are raging, again uses an image of the Borg to illustrate the "sinister connotations" the word "assimilation" has for many people nowadays (Hope).

Authors, including the essayist Thomas M. Sipos, addressing the issue and defending the melting pot paradigm, even mention the Borg in discussion—even if it is not clear if they have actually seen any Borg episode. This shows how "pervasive" the Borg have become in popular culture and how easily they are associated to the assimilation vs. multiculturalism debate, including outside of the United States (Sipos). Whereas *Star Trek* can sometimes be perceived, especially abroad, as a vehicle for a typically American worldview, the Borg collective does not present the same ambivalence because their campaign against cultural diversity easily resonates throughout the world. In drawing an imperialist caricature of the Federation, *Star Trek* allows many viewers to find an outlet for widely shared anxieties over the extinction of cultural diversity and the imposition of one predominant model.

Other viewers, finally, even receive their first education in multiculturalism through ST: TNG. Another blogger in 2016 shared her thoughts on assimilation by recounting the experience of her six-year-old-self watching ST: TNG and being scared by the Borg and their assimilationist policies: "To six-year-old me, that was *terrifying*. To 31-year-old me, it is *still* terrifying, but for different reasons." She continues:

> The first time I heard someone tell me that immigrants should learn English because otherwise they're not *assimilating*, I physically recoiled. Because, when I was little, the word "assimilate" was a bad thing. That association has stuck with me since I was six, and I hope beyond hope that it will continue until I'm dying [Tasha].

She concludes: "I will not become the Borg. Gene Roddenberry made me terrified of them at six years old, and I think he did so for a good reason, because he knew the melting pot analogy was bullshit. I will not become them, and I will not allow those around me to become them" (Tasha). Given the number of likes and shares this entry garnered (1,151 to date), her sentiment about the Borg and assimilation seem to have been widely shared.

Many other examples can be mentioned, but all point to the same re-appropriation of the Borg by popular culture to address the issue of multiculturalism. The questioning of the melting pot and assimilationist paradigms grew in the 1970s and really came of age at the time ST: TNG was originally broadcast, but the issue has never left the public arena and has in fact, if nothing else, grown and become more pressing with time. The 2016 presidential election has itself given the issue much prominence, especially as some members of the Republican Party were keen to defend the old assimilationist model. In 2015, Republican candidate Bobby Jindal, himself the son of immigrants, repeatedly addressed the issue, declaring, "Immigration without assimilation is not immigration; it's invasion," thus repudiating multiculturalism and calling for a return to the melting pot (McHugh). Critics were quick to denounce and mock those comments by reiterating the now-familiar Borg civilization, with one Twitter user facetiously asking: "So Bobby Jindal is Borg?" (Mackey).

Conclusion

The use of the word "assimilation" has become political in itself. Since the late 1980s, assimilation served as a useful, if caricatured, signifier of one large set of ideas, a euphemism to connote one specific ideology and to polarize the debate over immigration and integration into two clear-cut camps. That ideology might be multiculturalism, mixing all races and cultures into one harmonious whole, or an imperative for newly arrived immigrants to conform to pre-existing norms rather than the possibility of changing them. ST: TNG is sometimes criticized as being too conservative in its vision of a multiracial, multicultural utopia, and "advanc[ing] the neoconservative project that was the zeitgeist of the 1980s" (Bernardi 117). Yet the series demonstrates how the Borg are often equated with an even greater conservative ideal, especially given how the Borg analogy resonate among fans and the public alike. It is more useful to see ST: TNG as offering a middle ground between models of integration which may not be antithetical after all; adaptation might be necessary, but does not necessarily entail the total disappearance of any and every cultural and individual specificities and differences. The real utopia conveyed by ST: TNG is the way individuals and societies reach a good compromise, even though we do not know, we cannot know, the specifics of the achievement. In spite of clear limitations, then, ST: TNG uses the large legacy of space opera and *Star Trek* to weigh in on a societal issue which is both topical and timeless to science fiction, utopia, and the United States.

NOTES

1. On the creation of "perfect" societies, see Simon Ledder, Jens Kolata, and Oonagh Hayes' essay in this volume.

2. See Katharina Thalmann's essay in this volume.

3. See Olaf Meuther's essay in this volume.

4. On the Federation's "frontierism" and foreign policy, see Alex Burtsyn-Chorowicz's essay in this volume.

5. On the technocratic make-up of the Federation, see Justin Ream and Alexander Lee's essay in this volume.

WORKS CITED

Episodes

"The Best of Both Worlds Part 1." *Star Trek: The Next Generation—The Complete Third Season.* Writ. Michael Piller. Dir. Cliff Bole. Paramount Home Video, 2002, DVD.

"The Best of Both Worlds Part 2." *Star Trek: The Next Generation—The Complete Fourth Season.* Writ. Michael Piller. Dir. Cliff Bole. Paramount Home Video, 2002, DVD.

"Descent Part 1." *Star Trek: The Next Generation—The Complete Sixth Season.* Writ. Ronald D. Moore. Dir. Alexander Singer. Paramount Home Video, 2002. DVD.

"Descent Part 2." *Star Trek: The Next Generation—The Complete Seventh Season.* Writ. René Echevarria. Dir. Alexander Singer. Paramount Home Video, 2002. DVD.

"Heart of Glory." *Star Trek: The Next Generation—The Complete First Season.* Writ. Maurice Hurley. Dir. Rob Bowman. Paramount Home Video, 2002. DVD.

"I Borg." *Star Trek: The Next Generation—The Complete Fifth Season.* Writ. René Echevarria. Dir. Robert Lederman. Paramount Home Video, 2002. DVD.

Star Trek: First Contact. Dir. Jonathan Frakes. Perf. Patrick Stewart, Jonathan Frakes, and Brent Spiner. Paramount Home Video, 1998. DVD.

"Q Who." *Star Trek: The Next Generation—The Complete Second Season.* Writ. Maurice Hurley. Dir. Rob Bowman. Paramount Home Video, 2002. DVD.

Books and Articles

Abott, Carl. *Frontiers Past and Future: Science Fiction and the American West.* Lawrence: University Press of Kansas, 2006. Print.

"Assimilation, N." *OED Online.* Oxford University Press, September 2016. Web. 11 October 2016.

Bernardi, Daniel Leonard. Star Trek *and History: Race-Ing Toward a White Future.* New Brunswick, NJ: Rutgers University Press, 1998. Print.

Bernstein, Richard. "The Arts Catch Up with a Society in Disarray." *The New York Times,* 2 September 1990. Print.

Bloom, Allan. *The Closing of the American Mind.* New York: Simon & Schuster, 1987. Print.

Booker, M. Keith. "The Politics of *Star Trek.*" *The Essential Science Fiction Television Reader.* Ed. J.P. Telotte. Lexington: University Press of Kentucky, 2008. 195–208. Print.

Canadian Multiculturalism Act, R.S.C., c. 24 (4th Supp.), 1985, assented to 21 July 1988. Web.

Chametzky, Jules. "Beyond Melting Pots, Cultural Pluralism, Ethnicity—Or, Deja Vu All Over Again." *Melus* 16:4 (1989): 3–17. Print.

Clute, John. David Langford, Peter Nicholls and Graham Sleight (eds.). "Hive Minds." *The Encyclopedia of Science Fiction,* 2 Oct. 2015. Web. 4 May 2016.

Crèvecoeur, J. Hector St. John De. *Letters from an American Farmer*. Ed. Susan Manning. Oxford: Oxford University Press, 1997. Print.

David, Peter. *Star Trek: The Next Generation Giant 2: Vendetta*. London: Titan Books, 1991.

Delany, Samuel R. "On Triton and Other Matters: An Interview with Samuel R. Delany." *Science Fiction Studies*, 52, Volume 17, Part 3, November 1990. Web. April 1 2017.

"Eve." *Time*, 18 Nov. 1993, cover.

Fleishmann, Glenn. "American Borg." *Glog*. 2 Nov. 2001. Web. 19 June 2016.

Ghorra-Gobin, Cynthia. "Du Melting Pot au multiculturalisme: L'impératif d'une communication intégrant le spatial," *Quaderni* 22 (1994): 157–165. Print.

Glazer, Nathan. "Is Assimilation Dead?" *The Annals of the American Academy of Political and Social Science* 530 (1993): 122–136. Print.

_____. *We Are All Multiculturalists Now*. Cambridge: Harvard University Press, 1997. Print.

Gross Edward, and Mark A. Altman Mark. *Captains' Logs: The Unauthorized Complete Trek Voyages*. Boston: Little, Brown and Company, 1995. Print.

Henry, William A. "Beyond the Melting Pot." *Time*, 9 April 1990: 28–31. Print.

Hewitt, Roger. *White Backlash and the Politics of Multiculturalism*. Cambridge: Cambridge University Press, 2005. Kindle.

Hope, Tracy. "What Does Cultural Integration Look Like to You?" *LindekIn*, 25 Nov. 2015. Web. 28 June 2016.

Hunter, James Davison. *Culture Wars: The Struggle to Define America*. New York: Basic Books, 1991. Print.

Huntington, Samuel. *The Clash of Civilizations and the Remaking of World Order*. New York: Simon & Schuster, 2011 [1996]. Kindle.

Kanzler, Katja. *Infinite Diversity in Infinite Combinations: The Multicultural Evolution of Star Trek*. Heidelberg: Universitatsverlag Winter, 2004. Print.

Kwan, Allen. "Seeking New Civilizations: Race Normativity in the *Star Trek* Franchise." *Bulletin of Science, Technology & Society* 27.1 (2007): 59–70. Print.

Lacorne, Denis. *La Crise de l'identité américaine. Du Melting-pot au multiculturalisme*. Paris: Fayard, 1997. Print.

Langer, Jessica. *Postcolonialism and Science Fiction*. New York: Palgrave Macmillan, 2011. Print.

Ludgate, April. "Question #86728." *The 100 Hour Board*. Brigham Young University, 21 May 2016. Web. June 24 2016.

Mackey, Rich (richmackey). "So Bobby Jindal Is Borg? 'We must insist on assimilation—immigration without assimilation is invasion,' Jindal Said." 6 Aug. 2015, 5:12 p.m. Tweet.

McHugh, Katie. "Bobby Jindal: 'Immigration without assimilation is an invasion,'" *Breitbart*, 4 Nov. 2015. Web. 2 June 2016.

McKitterick, Chris. "Resistance Is Futile: How Gene Roddenberry Made Me Recoil at Racism—Yeah, Basically Wtf?" *The Stars My Destination*. Tumblr, 13 January 2016. Web. 18 June 2016.

Meyer, Uwe. *We Only Want to Be Your Partners*: Star Trek: Enterprise—*Politisch-Ideologische Dimensionen Einer Fernsehrie Zwischen Kaltem Krieg Und War on Terror*. Frankfurt: Peter Lang Gmbh, 2008. Print.

Mogen, David. *Wilderness Visions. The Western Theme in Science Fiction Literature*. 2nd ed. Rockville, MD: Borgo Press, 2008. Print.

"The New Face of America," *Time*, November 18, 1993. Print.

Pounds, Michael C. *Race in Space: The Representation of Ethnicity in* Star Trek *and* Star Trek: The Next Generation. Lanham, MD: Scarecrow, 1999. Print.

Reed. "Treknobabble #43: We Come in Peace; Unfortunately, You Will Be Assimilated." *Film Junk*, 4 December 2008. Web. June 18, 2016.

Relke, Diana M.A. *Drones, Clones and Alpha Babes: Retrofitting* Star Trek's *Humanism, Post-9/11*. Calgary: University of Calgary Press, 2006. Print.

Richter, Miriam Verena. *Creating the National Mosaic: Multiculturalism in Canadian Children's Literature from 1950 to 1994*. New York, Rodopi, 2011. Print.

Rieder, John. *Colonialism and the Emergence of Science Fiction*. Middletown, CT: Wesleyan University Press, 2008. Print.

Russell Lynette, and Nathan Wolski. "Beyond the Final Frontier: Star Trek, the Borg and the Post-Colonial." *Intensities: The Journal of Cult Media* 1 (2001): n. pag. Web. 15 May 2016.

Said, Edward. *Orientalism*. London: Penguin Books, 2003. Print.

Schlesinger, Arthur A. "When Ethnic Studies Are Un-American." *Wall Street Journal* 23 April 1990: A14. Print.

Schmidt, Alvin J. *The Menace of Multiculturalism: Trojan Horse in America*. Westport, CT: Praeger, 1997. Print.

Sipos, Thomas M. "The True Melting Pot. A Nation of Assimilated Immigrants." *Salvo Magazine* 2016, Web. June 3, 2016.

Stableford Brian, Langford David. "Hive Minds." *The Encyclopedia of Science Fiction*, October 2, 2015. Web. April 2, 2017.

Steele, Benjamin David. "American Borg; on Assimilation & Family." *Marmalade*. Wordpress, 17 May 2012. Web. June 23, 2016.

Tasha. "Resistance Is Futile: How Gene Roddenberry Made Me Recoil at Racism." *Yeah, Basically Wtf?* January 4, 2016. Web. April 1, 2017.

Taylor, Charles. "The Politics of Recognition." *Multiculturalism.* Ed. A. Gutmann. Princeton: Princeton University Press, 1994. 25–74. Kindle.

Trombold John. "The Uneven Development of Multiculturalism." *Profession, Modern Language Association* (1999): 236–247. Print.

Turner, Frederick Jackson. *The Frontier in American History.* 1953. New York: Dover Publications, 1996. Print.

Washburn, David E., et al. *Multicultural Education in the United States.* Philadelphia: Inquiry International, 1996. Print.

Weitekamp, Margaret. "More Than Just 'Uhura': Understanding *Star Trek*'s Lt. Uhura, Civil Rights, and Space History." *Star Trek and History.* Ed. Nancy Reagin, Hoboken, NJ: Wiley, 2013. 22–38. Print.

Wilcox, Rhonda. "Miscegenation in Star Trek: The Next Generation." *Enterprise Zones: Critical Positions on Star Trek.* Eds. T. Harrison, S. Projansky, K. Ono and E.R. Helford. New York: Westview Press, 1996. 69–94. Print.

Zangwill, Israel. *The Melting Pot.* New York: The American Jewish Book Company, 1921. Project Gutenberg. Web. 4 March 2016.

Material Agency
The Limits of Technostructure in the 24th Century

JUSTIN REAM *and* ALEXANDER LEE

Star Trek: First Contact marked the 30th anniversary of *Star Trek* with what is arguably the best of the *Star Trek: The Next Generation* films. What made *First Contact* so compelling is the scope of what is at stake. This movie is really about humanity's struggle concerning the kind of relationship it will have with the "Other," in this case, literal aliens represented by the Borg and the Vulcans. Although *First Contact* has a split plot structure (Worf, Data, Crusher, and Picard struggle with the Borg on the *Enterprise* while the away team attempts to guarantee the historic (re)enactment of Zefram Cochrane's initial encounter with the Vulcans), both stories center around this crucial turning point in human history. As emphasized over and over, the event of first contact with the Vulcans awaken humanity as a single rational, self-governed and self-aware whole. *First Contact* not only defined humanity's outlook in Zefram Cochrane's future (as Starfleet and the Federation), it also provides the template for how humans interact with other species, as well as how humans expect other species should naturally grow. First contact becomes the definitive basis for the Prime Directive, the governing basis when Starfleet encounters the Other: "To boldly go where no man has gone before."

To understand *First Contact*/first contact better, we can turn to the German philosopher Georg Wilhelm Friedrich Hegel. Starfleet's policy of first contact is related to what Hegel calls "Spirit." Hegel describes the true Spirit as

> *for itself* in that it preserves itself in reflection in individuals, and it is *implicitly* Spirit, or substance in that it preserves them within itself. As *actual substance*, it is a nation as *actual consciousness*, it is the citizens of that nation. This consciousness has its essence in simple Spirit, and the certainty of itself in the *actuality* of this Spirit, in the nation as a whole; it has its truth, therefore, not in something that is not actual, but in a Spirit that exists and prevails [*The Phenomenology of Spirit* 267].

As a philosopher of the state, Hegel defines the reification of Spirit as a concrete substance. Material provides the basis for conscious self-awareness, which manifests through the Spirit. Spirit is materially expressed ideology that provides a baseline for subjects to calibrate their subjectivity. Conversely, subjectivity within Spirit requires the freedom of self-determination. With this freedom, subjectivity becomes self-aware. In this way, Spirit is essential to self-determination because Spirit is a shared metric for selves to reify in selfhood. In the context of the film, First Contact is only possible through the Vulcans, since self-awareness is not present in the Borg. Within the Borg hive mind, Borg have a collective awareness, but not freedom or selfhood.[1] The freedom of a clear awareness of self is only possible with an encounter with the Other. This encounter of the Other is the ethical metaphysical basis that defines Starfleet.

This metaphysical concept is expressed in the Prime Directive, General Order 1, from which all other directives derive.[2] After first contact, humans devised legislation eventually forming the larger bureaucracy of Starfleet. The Prime Directive limits Federation agency by guaranteeing non-interference for any pre-warp species. The essence of the Prime Directive allows species to achieve the same ideological realizations humans did: to develop their own awareness and selfhood without "contamination." Materially, this is expressed as the formation of fledging bureaucracies. It's no accident that "official" initial encounter with "junior" species is also called first contact. Essentially, first contact is the defining event for the Federation because from it, the totality of human endeavor becomes subsumed under a technostructure, one that is equal parts Spirit, material agency (technology), hierarchy, and bureaucracy.

Cowboys, Klingons and the New Technocractic Order

As evidenced by *First Contact*, much of *Star Trek* is about an idealized future for humanity. David Alexander notes Roddenberry believed that "much of the value of the *Star Trek* property and its mass audience reputation comes out of the fact that it has been kept scrupulously clear of religion and political theory" (567). *Star Trek* was meant to be a materialist utopia "without conflict" as the final progression of twentieth century Earth's material economy. According to this narrative, pure technology eliminates the need for humans to fight among themselves, which leads to material abundance for all. Yet, without ideological content, or even capitalism, what is left for humans to organize around? How humans organize is the main difference between *Star Trek: The Original Series* (*ST*) and its sequel, *Star Trek: The Next Generation* (*TNG*).

Without overt ideological content (as viewed from the 20th century), *ST*'s organization presents a hierarchy that appears to be equal parts military and bureaucracy. Roddenberry, however, insisted "*Star Trek* was *never* a military show" (Alexander 543, original italics). This gets to the heart of *Star Trek*. *ST* presents a utopia of bureaucracy. David Graeber writes:

> Consider *Star Trek*, that quintessence of American mythology. Is not the Federation of Planets—with its high-minded idealism, strict military discipline, and apparent lack of both class differences and any real evidence of multiparty democracy—really just an American vision of a kinder, gentler Soviet Union, and above all, one that actually "worked"? [124].

This working entails a human organization in which there is clearly defined procedures to do anything. These procedures are decided beforehand and the crew merely implements these set procedures. In *ST*, "political problems are always addressed solely through administrative means" (Graeber 125). As a result, *TNG* does not show the political process since that process is already defined by bureaucracy.

Although most of us would consider bureaucracy as merely administrative busywork, John Kenneth Galbraith notes there is no aspect of contemporary life that is untouched by bureaucracy. Military, corporations, universities, government and other institutions form a continuous bureaucratic structure Galbraith calls a technostructure, which he defines as the core group of decision makers in any organization. In a corporation, this group includes the chairman, board members, and those with "specialized knowledge, talent, or expertise" to aid in the decision-making process (693). All others, especially workers, are relegated to carrying out these decisions in a mechanical manner.

> [Technostructure] is a collective and imperfectly defined entity; in the large corporation it embraces chairman, president, those vice presidents with important staff or departmental responsibility, occupants of other major staff positions [all the way to] the outer perimeter [of] white- and blue-collar workers whose function is to conform more or less mechanically to instruction or routine. It embraces all who bring specialized knowledge, talent or experience to group decision-making. This [totality], not the narrow management group, is the guiding intelligence—the brain—of the enterprise [Galbraith 693].

When Galbraith introduced the concept of technostructure (and its administrative leadership, the technocrat) in the 1960s, he was describing the ways the Soviet Union and the United States approached the global capitalist market. Both superpowers used a technostructure to distribute and manage material wealth.

Galbraith put forth the concept of the technocratic state in the 1960s, which coincided with the rise of modern corporations. This model removed the owner/entrepreneur as an individual from the actual enterprise (693). This downplaying of individualism countered the legacy of the "cowboy" myth that symbolized the American character in previous decades. Galbraith explains that throughout American history the public identified business leaders as those who were "entrepreneurs"—men who controlled the capital, organized and ran production, and had the capacity to innovate. After World War II, the United States came of age, redefining its national identity, notably through the proliferation of cowboy dramas. Although the Wild West genre was not new, it took on new importance through "superwestern" movies "to cover up incompetence and justify imperialism" (Gilman n.p.). The rise of the technostructure coincides with the extension of World War II planning as the military industrial complex. Galbraith explains that the rise of the technostructure presented the next step in the organization of production, shifting from the entrepreneur to the latter 20th century emphasis on bureaucracy.

Gene Roddenberry adapted this transition into his conception of *Star Trek*. Roddenberry removed capitalism and material, leaving only the technostructure in place through the organizational structure onboard the *Enterprise*. In the *Star Trek* universe, technostructure is the key organizational modality as a means of rational planning without ideological content, which leads to a maximization of will, a minimization of ego, and pure material utopia. Only when *TNG* was introduced in the 1980s was the technostructure expressed in its entirety. This transition from cowboy to technocrat, from ST to *TNG*, is often characterized by various contemporary debates about who is the better captain: James Kirk or Jean-Luc Picard. This debate centers on the effectiveness of two kinds of leadership, Kirk's intuition and guts or Picard's calm rational calculations. Unlike Picard, Kirk is often away from the technostructure of Starfleet as he explores the wild reaches of deep space, whereas Picard is often in contact with admirals who dictate their bureaucratic decisions for Picard to execute. While both captains operate within the technostructure, Kirk has more autonomy, having more in common with the Wild West loners practicing what Spock later characterized as "cowboy diplomacy" ("Unification II").[3]

Thus, *TNG* differs from *ST* in that *TNG*'s technostructure is all encompassing. In *ST*, the crew goes into deep space, leaving their families behind; family life is separate from the adventures of the *Enterprise*. In *TNG*, families travel aboard the ship, because, by the 24th century, technostructure *is* human culture.[4] Furthermore, in *TNG* there is a procedure for everything. The bridge crew continually presents their findings to the captain, even in the midst of red alert crises. Picard then synthesizes a decision to enact a material change, to direct action for the crew to execute. Although Kirk conducts officer meetings, the episodes' climaxes usually involve a different means of conflict resolution. Kirk's fist fights and wrestling matches almost always resolve the issues whereas Picard's meetings often present resolutions requiring technological, procedural executions. The resolution of conflict in *TNG* is less about physical face-offs with antagonists inasmuch as it is about the correctness of committee-based decision making followed by perfect execution by the crew. Correct bureaucratic procedure of the crew's part is the key to solving problems in *TNG* as much as the crew's submission to the hierarchy.

For example, in the episode "Where Silence Has Lease," the *Enterprise* is trapped by a mysterious alien called Naglium who threatens to kill up to half the crew as part of an experiment about death. Rather than submit his crew (and their families) to the control of an alien agency, Picard sets the ship to auto-destruct. This gamble ultimately pays off when Naglium releases the *Enterprise*. However, one of the key moments occurs when Troi and Data personally urge Picard to abort the autodestruct and submit to Naglium's will. Picard recognizes "Troi" and "Data" are actually facsimiles created by Naglium. The captain realizes this deception when they attempt to circumvent the chain of command through personal desire. While Naglium appears to have tipped his hand too far, his ruse actually serves his purpose. He explains to Picard that he released the ship because the *Enterprise*'s autodestruct was not necessary since he learned everything he wanted to know. Naglium learns that how humans face death is how they face life: through the hierarchical and bureaucratic confines of technostructure.

Bureaucratic Realism

Obviously, technostructure, by its very name, includes technology, so this begs the question: why are bureaucracies important? Ideally, bureaucracies are supposed to streamline a process by removing human subjectivity, thereby making it colorblind, consistent, and impersonal. The generic roles within bureaucracy are meant to eliminate excess ego so that people "can do their duty," that is, to maximize performance as directed by the hierarchical structure. For example, early in *TNG*, Worf, repeatedly states what constitutes a dignified way for a Klingon warrior to die. But towards the end of the series, Worf begins to curb his pride as a warrior when he starts to consider the needs of others to the point where he even accepts his son's desires to step outside the Klingon tradition. Worf's own romance with Troi—a "non-warrior" whose primary duty is catering to the crew's emotional well being—highlights how far Worf is integrated in the Federation technostructure.

Non-Federation hierarchies, however, do not have an ego check. Riker's participation in an officer-exchange program onboard a Klingon ship in "A Matter of Honor" shows that Klingons integrate pride with physical combat in order to maintain the hierarchy, even when their ship is threatened. The Cardassian hierarchy appears much like Starfleet's hierarchy except without the ego check; in *Deep Space Nine*, Gul Dukat thinks the Bajorans should have worshipped him because he allowed them to have minimal cultural preservation during their occupation. His excessive ego leads him to literally become a false prophet at the end of the series. From Starfleet's (and the audience's) perspective, these excessive behaviors of "Others" exemplify the need to remove ego to maximize the hierarchy's operations.[5]

When Starfleet's excessive ego does occur, the process has an ethical justification of the Other to check it. In "Drumhead," Picard proves to be the master of Starfleet ethics when he goes against Starfleet hierarchy. Rear Admiral Norah Satie attempts to crucify a young ensign who tries to hide his stigmatized Romulan blood (blood of the Other) to satiate her own desire for her father's validation. To check her ego, Picard breaks rank and opposes her. When he is put on trial, he presents her father's own words, warning that denying one person freedom becomes an attack on all. Admiral Satie's excessive reaction in the courtroom highlights her underlying bias, that she is driven by personal validation rather than preservation of the hierarchy. In the final scene, Worf, a semi-outcast himself, learns about the difference between ferreting excess ego and correct hierarchy calibration. Worf expresses remorse that he believed and helped Satie's witch-hunt. Picard explains that villains with stereotyped behavior, are easy to identify. Others who disguise themselves through good words and actions, however, are much harder to recognize.[6] Picard asserts Admiral Satie and her ilk are always present, waiting for public insecurity to give them an opportunity. Starfleet must be vigilant against those who would undermine its hierarchy. With this moral lesson, we get a sense of the fragility of the Federation's bureaucracy. Time and again, problems within Starfleet result from excessive ego, requiring that officers and subordinates check each other's actions appropriately. In another episode, "The Wounded," Miles O'Brien confronts his former captain, Benjamin Maxwell, about Maxwell's one-man war against the Cardassians. Maxwell, who lost his family during a previous Federation-Cardassian war, denies any suggestion of PTSD or vendetta. He asserts the Cardassians are preparing for another war. Although Picard eventually realizes that Maxwell is correct, Maxwell still faces a court-martial for refusing to work within the bureaucratic hierarchy of Starfleet.

The hierarchy is integral to the series because it provides direction for the technostructure to be implemented. Recall Hegel's conception that Spirit is both ideological and "real." A Starfleet officer understands her place in the world reflexively, by realizing her place within Starfleet's/the Federation's hierarchical bureaucracy, and her relationship to others in the same system. Philosopher Slavoj Žižek neatly explains this relationship, stating that "the frame itself is always also a part of the enframed content" (469). Literally, by joining Starfleet and meeting other aliens (both in and outside Starfleet), can one find oneself. For the *Enterprise* crew and the audience, this contact defines the boundaries for how Starfleet works, what the show considers the "norm," and how these standards relate back to the characters. Indeed, in "Disaster," a wounded Picard establishes order among three panicking children by "promoting" them to Starfleet ranks. Once the children are "absorbed" into the hierarchy, Picard is able to deal with them as officers. In turn, the children behave as such, controlling their emotions and following his orders. At the end of the episode, he rewards them by granting their initial wish to tour the off-limits part of the ship. Thus, hierarchy does more than incorporate the children; the hierarchical frame allows Picard to acknowledge the children as subjects and "officers"—the eldest child, whom Picard made his "Number One," even responds when the captain tells Riker to take charge of the bridge. With the children integrated into Starfleet's subjectivity, Picard is willing to forgo bureaucratic prohibitions that he initially applied to them.

This self-relating position is another kind of agency, one "hidden" in the hierarchy, and one which Picard warns Worf to be "vigilant" about because hierarchical relationships are subject to corruption, despite their supposed bureaucratic rigidity. While we may conceive of hierarchy as a series of bureaucratic positions pre-defined by law, theoretical physicist Karen Barad defines agency as more than the ability to do something. She raises the concept of agency to a level of performance as realism.[7] Agential realism is crucial to understanding that the bureaucratic hierarchy is a constantly constructed edifice, enacted at every level of interaction simultaneously. This enactment is why Admiral Satie is able to subvert the values of Starfleet hierarchy by utilizing Starfleet. As agency relationships are negotiated between parties in the system, Barad's key insight is that "reality" is a produced phenomenon, performed but not necessarily mandated: "specific material practices, that is, specific dynamic material configurings of the world, *causally* produce specific material phenomena, as part of the ongoing differential performance of the world" (331). Thus, "phenomena," be it individuals and/or Starfleet, are actually a series of specific, interacting performances.

Recall the episode "Second Chances," where Riker encounters his double from a transporter mishap. The main confrontation occurs when Lieutenant Riker "goes above" Commander Riker to make mission recommendations to Captain Picard. When Picard agrees with Lieutenant Riker's recommendations despite Commander Riker's objections, the first officer has to make the chain of command clear to stop his junior version's subversion of the hierarchy. Commander Riker tells his Lieutenant self that he is not disciplining Lt. Riker simply because the captain overruled him. As "Number One," Riker respects the chain of command, but he demands his lower-ranking self to do the same. The first officer ends by stating those who cannot follow this edict have no place in his away team, i.e., the system. Only after a subterranean bridge collapses and their lives are threatened is peace established between the two Rikers as each acknowledges the other's uniqueness and value. Commander Riker and Lieutenant Riker must be separated in the hierarchy in order to reconcile outside the hierarchy.[8] We see this in a literal way as Commander Riker submits to his captain and demands submission from his lower-ranking self through the same mechanism. When the officers re-affirm the hierarchy, they acknowledge a shared self-reflexive "Spirit." That enables them to relate to each other and operate in their defined roles. Barad concurs:

> The agential realist account does not position human concepts, human knowledge or laboratory contrivances as foundational elements [...]. On the contrary [...], agential realism calls on the theory to account for the intra-active emergence of "humans" as a specifically differentiated phenomena, that is, as specific configurations of the differential becoming of the world, among other physical systems. ["H]umans" themselves emerge through specific intra-actions [352].

Thus, each of the different organizations, be it Romulan, Cardassian, Klingon, or Starfleet, all have different ways of co-existing in the galaxy. In "A Matter of Honor," Riker's successful integration in a Klingon starship requires that he interacts with the Klingons kind in kind, such as eating their food and beating up his superior officer. This calibration of *kind in kind* acts as an ego check in Starfleet, but exacerbates ego as integral to the Klingon hierarchy. As demonstrated throughout the series, whenever someone cites Starfleet regulations—or, as Riker realizes when he serves as an exchange officer in "A Matter of Honor"—the system only works when people behave in a manner that reifies it and perpetuates it. Žižek offers a physical analogy:

> Take the case of using a stick to find one's way around a dark room: we can treat the stick as a measuring apparatus; as a prolongation of our hand, as a tool enabling us to "measure" (recognize) the contours of the room; or complementarily, if we already know the contours of the room very well, we can treat the stick itself as the object to be measured (when it touches a wall which we know to be a certain distance from where we stand, we can determine the length of the stick [933].

What we cannot do is directly measure the apparatus of measurement itself, because that requires a new object of measurement to determine new agential relations. Whatever we pick as our "base" metric is only understood as such in relation to other kinds of the same kind. We need hardness to measure hard things. We need lengthy things to measure length. Starfleet officers need other officers in order to know who they are. Humans fit together by "being human" as Klingons fit together by being "Klingon." It is this relation of *kind in kind* that determines our concepts and calibrates agential interactions. In this manner, each species' bureaucratic hierarchy is a performance its members enact in a kind of Spiritual topography, but not some kind of foundational ontological (immutable) substance, as though being Klingon or being human were pre-defined (after all, anyone can be a Borg, or, as Worf shows, even Klingons can join Starfleet). In sum, the hierarchical bureaucratic realism as expressed materially in starships, rankings, starbases, and colonies *is* the technostructure. What makes this technostructure uniquely human is the manner of its reification in Spirit. Starfleet/Federation not only actualizes its subjects within its hierarchy, but also seeks (through fledging bureaucracies and first contact with junior species) to reify the Other as well.

Deviations in Alien Technocratic Form

The Federation is not the only political body that undergoes a technocratic makeover from *ST* to *TNG*. As Starfleet became more technostructural in operation, its antagonists did as well. In *The Original Series*, Klingons are the main foes with Kirk, often competing with the *Enterprise* crew in a contest of will. As Kirk's cowboy diplomacy is left behind in *TNG*, contention between Klingons and Starfleet are no longer the major area of conflict. Throughout *TNG*, different species/empires are introduced in an attempt to expand the area of conflict. As the area of contention progresses from Kirk's individualism to increasing technocracy, the show's conflict develops along a line of group identity between alien species.

Each of the Federation's competitors highlights a different aspect of human identity, contrasting the Federation's lack of a single dominating human trait. The one-dimensional aliens (i.e., "greedy" Ferengi, "fascist" Romulans) thus present conflicting forms between governmental technostructures. The alien technostructures in *TNG* can be broken into two groups: technostructures "castrated" by the material abundance of the Federation and technostructures in conflict with the Federation.

"Castrated" technostructures cannot disrupt the Federation's technostructure. For instance, the first antagonists introduced in *TNG* are the Ferengi. The Ferengi's main characteristic of greed, however, is unable to disrupt the human organizational scheme because the rejection of capitalism within the Federation's technostructure leaves no room for Ferengi-induced corruption. As Galbraith points out, the technostructure created in the postwar years was used to manage capitalism and its disruptive influences. The series thus eventually dismisses the Ferengi as unworthy of being a true antagonist to Starfleet and the Ferengi are relegated to comic foils.

While the Ferengi are "demoted" outright, the original antagonists from ST, the Klingons and Romulans, are also "castrated" through various forms of assimilation in *TNG*. Interestingly, throughout the series' run, both of these aliens become incorporated. Concerning the Klingons, Worf represents the possibility of Klingon integration into the Federation. Worf's primary relation to other Klingons seems to consist largely of their urging him to circumvent Starfleet hierarchy to help the Empire. By rebuking this circumvention, Worf proves he can be in the Starfleet hierarchy while being far more "Klingon" than other Klingons.[9] Worf fits the structure of the modern self, by reserving his Klingon essence as a private matter while fulfilling his public Starfleet duty. This allows him to accept his family's discommendation when other Klingons would not, thus preserving the Klingon Empire. This splitting of self into public and private is a mark of bureaucracy, allowing Worf (and his son Alexander) to show that Klingons can live with humans on human terms while still maintaining their Klingon heritage. The show contrasts the success of Worf's incorporation into the Federation with that of the Romulans.

In *ST*, the Romulans consist largely of unincorporable Vulcans. In *TNG*, Romulans are a competing organization to the Federation. The introduction of Tasha Yar's daughter, Sela, as the spokesperson for the Romulans mark their same-but-different status as another technostructure equal in strength to Starfleet's. Some essential quality of Tasha Yar is compatible with the Romulan hierarchy, such as her fierceness. Yet as *TNG* progresses, the Romulans become more interested in incorporating their Vulcan cousins to achieve an internal completeness of Spirit rather than expanding outwards in direct military competition with humans (as the Cardassians do with the occupation of Bajor).[10] The split between the Vulcans and the Romulans becomes a major plot point in the series between the Federation and the Romulans. This split between Vulcans and Romulans can be understood as a failure of the Romulan side of the Vulcans to have a first contact–like event. In a sense, the Romulan "First Contact," that is, the defining moment of the Romans, is the split between Romans and Vulcans. In "Unification," Spock, as a Vulcan and as ambassador for the Federation, spreads the study of non-aggressive Vulcan ways within Romulus, subverting the Romulan hierarchy's ethnic justification for the Romulan technostructure. We assume that once Romulans adopt the neutrality of Vulcans they, too, would see no problem with joining the Federation. Thus, the Romulans are too weak to be a true antagonist to humanity because they are internally fractured.

The two conflicting technostructures that are not compatible with Starfleet, the Borg and the Cardassians, function as critiques of the Federation. Each species highlights a different area of human identity as a limit to human conduct. As each new species challenges humans, that challenge presents an opportunity for humans to change their modes of engagement to match this external Other. We can boldly go where no man has gone before, but what then? Do we change who we are in response to our encounters?

The first true critique of the Federation technostructure comes from the Borg. In "Q Who," Q offers to join the crew of the *Enterprise* but is rejected by Picard. The episode frames the Borg conflict by introducing an enthusiastic new ensign, Sonya Gomez, assigned to the *Enterprise* straight from the Academy. In her initial excitement, she spills hot chocolate on Picard, whose impersonal response as the technocrat of the *Enterprise* disturbs her; she thinks she already botched her new position. Later, when the death of several crewmembers distracts Gomez from her duties, her commanding officer, Geordi La Forge, tells her to focus on her work; the green ensign must align herself to the hierarchy to perform well; to give in to mourning and human sentiment disrupts the bureaucracy. In the same episode, Picard also acts in the interest of the technostructure when he rebuffs Q's offer to assist the *Enterprise* in their mission of exploring the unknown. The captain intuitively understands that Q, with his excessive powers, would likely disrupt the hierarchy of the ship.[11] Perhaps not ironically, in response, Q introduces the Borg, who, as an absurd expression of technostructure, is unrecognizable to humans as even being alive (the Borg do not initially register as life forms to their sensors).

This same-but-alien quality of the Borg is subtly emphasized again with in "Best of Both Worlds Parts" when Picard, who thus far is presented as the perfect technocrat, is assimilated by the collective. As captain of the Federation's flagship, Picard's role in the Starfleet hierarchy is to represent the "voice" for Starfleet, internally to his crew and externally as a Federation's diplomat. Picard's often crucial monologues show his mastery of ethical expression, as he normalizes existing relations internally and externally. The Borg, who are presented as interested in technology (and not in other life forms) eventually come to value Picard's expert agency in modifying human-other relations when they kidnap him and turn the captain into a spokesperson to facilitate the assimilation of humans. Without his humanity, Picard becomes another Borg, repeating Borg values, rather than the human ones. Locutus of Borg parodies Picard's consistent ethical expression for what makes humanity worthwhile by only repeating why Borgs are superior. Despite the seemingly resolution to the Borg storyline when their impersonal expression give way to individuality in "Descent," the Borg are the first full critique of 24th century technostructure.

Ironically, the Borg's absurd repetition of "resistance is futile" parodies the Federation's own organization's mission. To enjoy the material abundance guaranteed by the Federation's trade and technological superiority, aliens must submit to Federation standards of ethics and social organization. While the Borg do not respect the individual agencies of Others as Starfleet tries to, the Borg transform Others by assimilating their differences into a technostructure, mirroring Worf's and Data's acculturation into Starfleet. In this sense, the Borg are colonists; the collective is a self-reflection of Starfleet as a pure technostructural society that has no other identity than the singular mission of material incorporation.[12] Thus, humanity's rejection of the Borg reifies the acceptance of the Other. Recalling *First Contact*, acceptance of the Vulcan's rational neutrality of greeting Others with wishes for long life and prosperity foreshadows Starfleet's eventual formation of the Prime Directive. The *Enterprise*'s revisiting this crucial moment when humanity makes its official initial encounter with the Other is fitting—the crew's witnessing First Contact assures them they not only saved the future from the Borg, but confirms the ideology and reality of Starfleet.

The Cardassian critique of the Federation's technostructure is a response to Roddenberry's statement that *Star Trek* is not a military show. Here, the Federation must cope with an explicit military regime. The Cardassians are first introduced as the oppressors of the Bajorans. As the Bajorans are a deeply spiritual and artistic people, the Cardassians are shown as a threat due to their excess militarism—a kind of anti–Bajorans. Unlike the Romulans, who become muddled in an internal struggle to dominate and resist the Vulcans, the Cardassians are more interested in external domination, establishing colonies for their people, and extending their technostructure.

The Cardassians explain their philosophy in "Chain of Command Part 2." Here, a high-ranking officer, Gul Madred, shows his tortured captive, Picard, his love for his child. Madred tells his daughter that humans are not the same as Cardassians; they are not people. Picard questions the wisdom of Madred's allowing his daughter to see the devaluation of life, telling him that a desensitized child can grow up devaluing anyone, including her own parents. Madred responds by saying that the military solved all their material problems, such as starvation; hence, an enhanced military means better lives for Cardassians. When Picard points out that excessive military leads to spiritual poverty, perhaps indirectly referencing the Bajorans, Madred has no response except to begin torturing Picard again. It's significant that this torture isn't about military information. Madred's torture of Picard refers back to Orwell's *1984* as a sign of the oppressive technostructure (Lapidos). He tortures Picard simply because doing so is a crucial part of a military regime, an aspect of daily life the Cardassian officer openly displays before his child. The excessive militarization of Cardassian Union is its unifying Spirit, giving all Cardassians a singular vision of who they are.

While Romulans and Cardassians appear to have a fairly similar military technostructure, the contrast between these groups and the Federation is characterized by how shared space between political bodies is described. The Romulans and the Federation have a "neutral zone," a "no man's land" buffering their boundaries, which either side cannot enter. Contrast the neutral zone with the Cardassian-Federation demilitarized zone. With the Romulans, neutrality means no incursion. With the Cardassians, neutrality means no military aggression; both sides are allowed to establish colonies in the demilitarized zone, which leads to problems later on when the Federation's colonies go up against a military regime bent on expansion. The difference in how each buffer zone is characterized highlights how Spirit of each alien is characterized. This characterization later becomes the area of contention for the latter seasons of *TNG* and its spin off series, *Star Trek: Deep Space Nine* (DS9).

To Boldly Know...

While Starfleet hierarchy is presented as superior and the ideal for humanity's future, its hierarchical arrangements are necessarily limited by its own immanent limits. Starfleet's limits are best explored through the indoctrination of Wesley Crusher. Introduced as a "boy genius," Wesley's precocious abilities are eventually acknowledged by even the stoic Picard, who candidly admits he is uncomfortable around kids. Wesley's constant dabbling in technology shows his super science capabilities are wildly extensive, often both threatening and saving the *Enterprise*. As early as the sixth episode, "Where No One Has Gone Before," Picard promotes Wesley to the rank of acting ensign due to his outstanding performance. In this episode, a mysterious being called the Traveler tells Picard to encourage Wesley's pursuits so that the boy can realize his gifts for energy, time, and propulsion. Picard eventually becomes a surrogate father for Wesley (Picard was originally a friend of Wesley's father and a romantic rival for his mother's affections) so that the captain's acknowledgment of Wesley indirectly parallels a father's nurturing his son. As Wesley works within the constraints of the ship's/Starfleet's hierarchy, he begins to achieve impressive results, which leads to Picard promoting Wesley to the rank of full ensign in the episode "Ménage à Troi." In this episode, Wesley misses an opportunity to enroll in Starfleet Academy to help save the day. In return, Picard makes up for Wesley's loss by showing young Crusher does not need the Academy; in a sense, he is already indoctrinated in the hierarchy. By giving Ensign Crusher a standard uniform, Picard rewards Crusher through the established bureaucratic channels for services rendered. This culminates when Wesley saves his father figure's life in "Final Mission." In this way, Wesley and Starfleet have a reciprocal relationship through the technostructure as he matures into full adulthood.

Although hierarchy works to normalize its members for specific tasks, it requires the matching of "kind in kind" of agential relations between its participants. Wesley's excessive potential renders him superior to Starfleet's bureaucracy and eventually leads him to reject the hierarchy. In "Journey's End," Wesley encounters the Traveler again, this time after being led to a vision quest in which he sees his dad releasing him from the bounds of Starfleet; the elder Crusher states that Starfleet is not for his son. Wesley's inner struggle with Starfleet is matched by Picard's own conflict when, against his better judgment, he attempts to follow direct orders from Starfleet Command to relocate colonists off a planet. A Starfleet-Cardassian treaty gave the colonists' planet to the Cardassians, but the colonists refuse to leave. Picard resolves the situation with the colonists by allowing Federation citizens to leave the hierarchy. Picard tells the colonists that, while they are free to leave, the severance will be complete; they will have no Federation protection should the Cardassians persecute them. In essence, the colonists have no real recourse to resist the Federation's hierarchy except to leave it. Here, the catchphrase "resistance is futile" applies to Federation citizens. Those who try to resist, either ideologically or physically, ultimately leave the hierarchy.

While Picard preserves the technostructure by releasing people who do not care for it, Wesley takes the Traveler's advice to embark on his "final journey." This "final journey" is from Starfleet's perspective, as Wesley's agency exceeds that of the hierarchy's ability to contain him.[13] He realizes this when a firefight breaks out between the Cardassians, the colonists, and Starfleet, leading Wesley to freeze time. When Wesley asks the Traveler how this happened and if the Traveler did this, the Traveler tells Wesley he did not; rather, Wesley did it on his own by stepping out of the confines of "reality" in the limiting terms of time, space, and energy.

At this point, Wesley's Spirit is no longer with that of Starfleet's. How Wesley's agential interactions in the future work and what that would bring him, is unknown and perhaps limitless. Wesley's ability to stop time shows that his abilities are far beyond Picard's experience—and may even approach Q's level of power. Just as Q has no place in Starfleet, neither does Wesley. Wesley's super-agency will lead him to identify differently among others, even his former associates. With this new way of existing in mind, the Traveler tells Wesley that neither can interfere with the episode's plotline and that Wesley should trust Picard/Starfleet to solve their problems by themselves. The Traveler's statement signifies that different beings have different investments. Where Wesley's agency leads him, at least in *TNG*, is beyond the technostructure. Fittingly, Wesley and the Traveler walk off screen, we imagine, to a higher plane, letting the firefight continue. It becomes Picard's sole responsibility to work with the Cardassians to order a cease fire and implement the treaty.

Having seen the end of Wesley's Starfleet-story-arc, the series concludes with Q and

Picard in "All Good Things…" Wesley exceeds Starfleet's technostructure, and in a way, Q attempts to discover this hidden potential in Picard. Throughout the series, Q focuses on showing Picard the limits of hierarchy, at first by mocking human endeavors, and then later by forcing new information onto Picard. Up until the last seasons, Picard, being the technocrat extraordinaire, is still extremely effective in justifying human organization, even when confronted with an all-powerful being like Q. Picard's ability to stand up to Q shows the power of Starfleet's ethical conviction as the captain not only grounds his crew as the embodiment of Starfleet ethics, but also as the immovable block to Q's unlimited force.

Q frames *TNG* by appearing in both the first and last episodes. In the first episode "Encounter at Farpoint," Q judges humanity by focusing on the human ego, urging that Picard take excessive action as a response to facing the unknown.[14] In "Hide and Q," Q returns to try to dissolve Riker's commitment to the hierarchy by bestowing upon him Q-like powers.[15] Picard, however, rightly appraises Riker's character and the character of his crew. Picard authorizes and supports Riker to exercise his powers, thereby presenting a veneer of legitimacy from a hierarchical authority. When Riker realizes that he cannot satiate his ego by bribing his crewmates, Picard welcomes him back to the crew. Having failed to stoke the human ego because of Picard's mastery of ethics, Q then focuses his attention by offering his services as a guide; in "Q Who," Q dons a captain's uniform and wants to be incorporated into Starfleet as a member of the crew. Picard rejects Q's offer, claiming the existing hierarchical structure has no place for someone, a mischievous life form that continually does not respect Starfleet rules and discipline. By rejecting Q, Picard maintains the status quo. After Q introduces the crew to the Borg to demonstrate that Picard's ethics has limited applicability when facing the unknown,[16] Picard admits he is wrong about not needing Q's help. Although this admission resolves the episode, Picard's response to the Borg's introduction shows that he misunderstands Q's lesson. Instead of adjusting Starfleet's hierarchy and being more open to the unknown, Picard states that the presence of the Borg requires an intensification of material agency. He sees Q's actions as a warning of what is out there and he turns defensive to protect the Starfleet hierarchy already in place. Of course, Picard proves to be ineffectual against the Borg's collectivism. Only Riker, who is more flexible, is able to resist assimilation.

In "Tapestry," Q shows Picard how merely following hierarchical bounds would lead him to a dreary and dull life. Picard learns that even willful ego has a place to counterbalance hierarchy, gaining a renewed sense of connection between the man he is and the man he might have become if he always played it safe. Nonetheless, while Q allows Picard to sidestep hierarchy in a personal way, in "Tapestry," Picard's actions only affects himself and doesn't apply the lesson elsewhere. In "All Good Things…" Picard comes to realize the lesson Q presented during the "trial" in the first episode, "Encounter at Farpoint." In "All Good Things…" Picard is thrown relentlessly across time and space, he briefly sees the limitless possibilities of exploration as a concept. Only after Picard sees three views of hierarchy simultaneously—his past, present, and future—does he realize the material agency necessary to counteract the anomaly threatening to destroy humanity. Picard has to simultaneously (in narrative time) use technocratic agency (in the present), hierarchy (in the past) along with a short monologue of ethical justification to his new and suspicious crew, and his own ego-enforced will to sidestep hierarchy (in the future, when everyone thinks he is suffering from dementia). In the future, an aged Picard has to surpass Admiral Riker's entrenched position as a leader in Starfleet. Despite this accomplishment, Picard sticks to his small mindedness, nearly missing the lesson. Q sums it up best, telling Picard that, even after saving humanity from a crisis the captain started, the initial trial continues because the Q Continuum sees the potential in humanity. That minuscule moment when the captain opens his mind to new concepts represents the ultimate form of exploration. Rather than the routine business of mapping stars, Picard should broaden his horizons to consider the unknown, and infinite, possibilities of individual (and hierarchical) existence, just as Q did in the past two television hours as he threw the captain across various alternate timelines. Losing hierarchy isn't the answer, but neither is maintaining its endless stasis.

Where Wesley exceeded bureaucratic hierarchy through increased material agency, Q shows Picard, an ordinary human, that truly exploring what is "out there" requires, given agential realism as a performance, an exploration in here. The best way to learn the unknown is to be flexible enough to really interact with it, rather than retreating to the confines of a familiar hierarchical bureaucracy. While Q doesn't suggest an arrangement that will benefit humankind's future, he does to point to the problem, which, like the time anomaly, is self-causing: humanity's reliance on its "solution" post–First Contact has a shelf-life. The last episode of *TNG* begs the question: are we ready for the next unknown?

Technocrats: The Next Generation

An over-determined bureaucracy like Starfleet charts the unknown by making it in kind to what it knows, namely, a repetition of itself. Such a calibration of like-with-like leads humans to consistently miss the unknown, because the "star trekkers" seek patterns of familiarity and do not consider what they may not yet recognize. This exposure to the unknown is, of course, exactly what Galbraith means when he states that "the enemy of the market is not ideology but the engineer" (657). In a historical, post–World War II context, the Western dominance of major corporations ensure market stability since "[p]roduction is not in response to market demand but given by the overall plan" (657). In this context, bureaucracy works best to maintain the structure of large corporations internally while keeping markets stable externally. While market domination makes sense in terms of capitalism, what could possibly be the need for keeping stasis in the 24th century? Certainly deep space exploration requires that a massive number of humans cooperate for extended periods of time. Bureaucracy and hierarchy keeps individuals focused on probing the limitless expanse of the final frontier. But if the exploration of the unknown is the goal, do we not sometimes need to vary our standards and approaches to gain new perspectives?

We cannot avoid the obvious conclusion that *Star Trek*, while about the 23rd and 24th centuries, relates to the 20th century in its methods of human organization and cognizance. So far, 20th and 21st century acceptance of the Other leads us to multicultural situations wherein Others are boxed according to their unique lifestyle. By categorizing Others according to consumer demand, we analogize all colors as merely shades of the same cardboard cutout. Shows like *The Mighty Morphin' Power Rangers* or *Captain Planet and the Planeteers* present ethnicities as an idyllic unity, whose spectral difference is merely a variant of some deeper type.[17] Can we reduce the *Star Trek* to a kind of enclosure where each hierarchy is only some exaggerated aspect of the same humanoid in a harmless bout of misunderstanding and easy community resolution?

This is the problem with the ending of *TNG*: it is too final, with a message that the *Enterprise* carries on as before. Q's interest in Picard is, as Data put it, like a pet ("All Good Things…"). In a way, Picard is a wise sage of technocracy, at the height of its limit. With Q showing an old Picard new tricks, it becomes unclear what happens to the technostructure when it is too stagnant. Two easy choices appear, to increase or decrease Starfleet's technostructure by throwing it into new environments. Is this not the split between *Deep Space Nine* and *Voyager*? *DS9* presents an overbearing bureaucracy. The space station is literally stuck between Starfleet's ideological technostructure, the Bajoran bureaucratic government, and the Cardassian military regime. To find balance, Commander Benjamin Sisko eventually retreats into mysticism to deal with competing bureaucracies. In *Voyager*, the premise of a ship lost in the Delta Quadrant leads Captain Janeway to enforce the bureaucratic impetus even more so, this time, with a group of renegades who initially reject the Federation in the aftermath of "Final Journey." After all, there is no Starfleet without hierarchy. Yet, there is a third option open to *Voyager*, one that was rejected from *First Contact*, where the crew becomes nothing more than mindless drones of a technostructure run amok. Starfleet resists the Borg and their frightening critique of (im)personalism by sublimating their fears into a personality: the Borg Queen. With the establishment of a queen, Starfleet can now negotiate (and manipulate) the collective. Janeway is able to continually elude the Borg, even recovering a piece of humanity the Borg assimilated, Seven of Nine. In this sense, Q's critique of Starfleet's technostructure is lost, since the Borg becomes just as another enemy for Starfleet to thwart, enabling the Federation to emerge triumphant and unchallenged.

In a strange way, due to its isolation, *Voyager* gives audiences the reality TV aspect at its fullest as the *Star Trek* universe is reduced to minimal surface differences.[18] Analogously, *Voyager* serves as an enclosed house for Alpha Quadrant types. Here, Ronnie Romulan, Kenny Klingon, Bobby Bajoran, Clarissa Cardassian, and Vicky Vulcan all cohabitate with main leads Henry Human and Hollie Human, sometimes visited by Benny Borg and Freddie Ferengi. The sitcom format is apt here, as their repetitious conflict through their bureaucratic procedures go nowhere with nothing ever truly at stake. At the same time, the co-habitants all operate under "house" rules, that of Starfleet regulations. Ironically, even lost in the Delta Quadrant, the crew is at home with familiar tropes of operation. Without the interjection of a great "unknown," eventually all of these "types" will have their own story arc, but the characters are defined by a celebration of their superficial differences, challenged only by a mindless sameness that ranks characters according to some Intergalactic rating for endless syndication. The television industry, like bureaucracy, keeps things well-oiled, but after material abundance is secured, should we not seek more than a repetition of the same clichés? With bureaucracy, going where no man has gone before transforms into a matter of going where man has gone yet again, and again, and again.

NOTES

1. See "I, Borg" when a Borg is recovered by the *Enterprise* crew and only achieves self-awareness through interactions with the crew. The Borg may be aware of self-awareness but they do not value it, or allow it the self determining agency in order for it to be fully reified.

2. See Larry A. Grant's essay in this volume.

3. See Katharina Thalmann's essay in this volume

4. Galbraith notes that with the post-industrial society, families become units of consumption, as the technostructure manages lifestyle choices to families as a way of guaranteeing profit. Although the bridge crew generally lacks families (with the exception of the Crushers and later, Worf with his son), the inclusion

of families on the *Enterprise* in *TNG* signifies the lack of limits, just as the technostructure today manages all aspects of human culture.

5. There is a limit to how hierarchy functions. In "Allegiance," Picard is replaced by an imposter. When the imposter orders the *Enterprise* too close to a dangerous pulsar, the crew mutinies. Meanwhile the actual Picard unites with other kidnapped prisoners in a makeshift hierarchy and they effectively challenge his captors. By the end of the episode, when Picard reunites with his crew, he covertly directs the hierarchy and captures his former captors, much to their dismay. Even without his crew, Picard is an effective hierarchical director.

6. See Anh T. Tran's essay in this volume.

7. Barad writes that "*agency is a matter of intra-acting; it is an enactment, not something that someone or something has*" (178, original italics).

8. In this way, bureaucracy is a way of policing oneself in public and private spaces to fit in society, as seen with Wolf's splitting his public Starfleet duties and private Klingon traditions. Public separation is needed to create the opportunity for private reconciliation. This echoes Michel Foucault's and Judith Butler's works on subjectivity.

9. Likewise, in "A Matter of Honor," Riker transfers as an exchange officer onto a Klingon ship. He also proves to be just as "Klingon" as his hosts. Riker eats what appears to be living worms, "gagh," in order to fit into the Klingon structure, makes jokes with other Klingons about women, and otherwise bonds with them. By the end of the episode, however, Riker demonstrates that the Starfleet orientation on material is superior to the Klingon orientation on pride. Riker not only succeeds in "defeating" the *Enterprise*, thus allowing the *Enterprise* to save the Klingon ship, but also saves face for his Klingon captain by taking a punch to the face. As a Starfleet officer, Riker calibrates his actions on the need to preserve material agency (seen here as the elimination of some space bugs eating the Klingon ship), placing that above his own ego. Contrast this material attention with the Klingons' immediate response that the presence of this bug justifies attacking the *Enterprise*. By fulfilling the needs of the Klingon hierarchy and saving both ships, Riker proves that Starfleet's calibration to material is superior to the Klingon's, whose limitation is their excessive tie to ego validation. In essence, the Klingon technostructure is no threat to Riker, who saves everyone, fulfills his Starfleet duties, and exceed the social needs of the Klingon technostructure by leaving it intact.

10. See Alex Burston-Chorowicz's essay in this volume.

11. In "Déjà Q," Q bitterly remarks that he is just as capable as any other human on Picard's ship and Data explains that Picard is simply concerned with Q's ability to successfully interact with others. Q responds that he is not interested in forming human relationships. Data replies that to work onboard a Starfleet vessel, or, any human activity, the outsider must form such relationships. The most important part is one's ability to function within a group setting. Q's struggle with working with humans when he has lost his powers justifies why Picard rejected Q's suggestion that he join his crew in "Q Who." Increased personal agency has no place within the hierarchy because it imbalances the bureaucratic system. The border between self (ego) and other is as essential to the calibration of hierarchy just as hierarchy is important to calibrate agency, which is why the technostructure of Starfleet is also a method to regulate social behavior for individual officers/citizens and within the larger Federation.

12. See Mehdi Achouche's essay in this volume.

13. It's important to note that while hierarchy is meant to curb ego, Wesley's leaving Starfleet suggests that hierarchy contains minimal ego. Without the reflexive coherency of seeing oneself in hierarchy, hierarchy becomes meaningless and groundless. Only after Wesley releases his ego (which also severs his tie to Starfleet hierarchy) is he ready to begin finding himself again as he leaves the viewers' plane of existence.

14. It's interesting to note Picard does not revoke Farpoint's application to the Federation. Instead, he resolves the situation by telling its applicants to rebuild Farpoint Station per his/Starfleet's instructions. One imagines this means Picard left a bureaucratic structure with administrators behind.

15. On Q, see Bruce E. Drushel's essay in this volume.

16. Ironically the Borg's methodology as pure "users of technology" mirrors the Federation's incorporation of hierarchy without the ethical limits. The *Enterprise* is not only ineffective at reaching an understanding with the Borg, but the Borg's material agency also exceeds the current ability of Starfleet to resist assimilation.

17. "The Chase" reveals that all the humanoid species throughout the galaxy originated from ancient humanoids. These ancient humanoids seeded various planets, leading to the evolution of the familiar humanoids in *Star Trek*.

18. Interestingly, Alexander notes that, when developing *TNG*, Roddenberry, along with being concerned about excessive militarism, wanted to avoid *TNG* becoming like "Animal House in outer space" (544).

Works Cited

Alexander, David. *Star Trek Creator: The Authorized Biography of Gene Roddenberry*. New York: Penguin Books, 1995. Print.

Barad, Karen. *Meeting the Universal Halfway: Quantum Physics and the Entanglement of Matter and Meaning.* Durham: Duke University Press, 2007. Print.

Berardinelli, James. "Star Trek: First Contact | Reelviews Movie Reviews." *Reelviews,* http://www.reelviews.net/reelviews/star-trek-first-contact. Accessed 25 August 2016.

Ebert, Roger. "Star Trek: First Contact Movie Review (1996) | Roger Ebert." Rogerebertwww, http://www.rogerebert.com/reviews/star-trek-first-contact-1996. Accessed 25 August 2016.

Galbraith, John Kenneth. *Galbraith: The Affluent Society & Other Writings, 1952–1967: American Capitalism/ The Great Crash, 1929/The Affluent Society/The New Industrial State,* 1st Edition. New York: Library of America, 2010. Print.

Gilman, Sean. "A Short History of the Western Genre, and Why the Wild Bunch Was Ahead of Its Time." *Metro Classics.* 7 Sept., 2009, Web. 30 May, 2016. http://metroclassics.blogspot.com/2009/09/short-history-of-western-genre-and-why.html.

Graeber, David. *The Utopia of Rules: On Technology, Stupidity, and the Secret Joys of Bureaucracy.* New York: First Melville House, 2015. Print.

Hegel, G.W.F. *Phenomenology of Spirit.* Trans. A.V. Miller. New York: Oxford University Press, 1977. Print.

_____. *The Philosophy of History.* Trans. J. Sibree. New York: Prometheus Books, 1991. Print.

Lapidos, Juliet. "There Are Four Lights!: Revisiting *Star Trek: The Next Generation*'s Eerily Prescient Torture Episode." *Slate.* May, 2009, Web. 5, June, 2016. <http://www.slate.com/articles/arts/culturebox/2009/05/there_are_four_lights.html>

Žižek, Slavoj. *Less Than Nothing.* New York: Verso 2012. Print.

TV and Film

"All Good Things..." *Star Trek: The Next Generation.* Writ. Brannon Braga and Ronald D. Moore. Dir. Winrich Kolbe. *Netflix.* Web. 4 Jun. 2016.

"Allegiance." *Star Trek: The Next Generation.* Writ. Richard Manning and Hans Beimer. Dir. Winrich Kolbe. *Netflix.* 4 Jun. 2016.

"Best of Both Worlds, Part 1." *Star Trek: The Next Generation.* Writ. Michael Piller. Dir. Cliff Bole. *Netflix.* Web. 4 Jun. 2016.

"Best of Both Worlds, Part 2." *Star Trek: The Next Generation.* Writ. Michael Piller. Dir. Cliff Bole. *Netflix.* Web. 4 Jun. 2016.

"Chain of Command, Part 2." *Star Trek: The Next Generation.* Writ. Michael Piller. Dir. Cliff Bole. *Netflix.* Web. 4 Jun. 2016.

"The Chase." *Star Trek: The Next Generation.* Writ. Joe Menosky. Dir. Jonathan Frakes. *Netflix.* Web. 4 Jun. 2016.

"Déjà Q." *Star Trek: The Next Generation.* Writ. Ricard Danus. Dir. Les Landau. *Netflix.* Web. 4 Jun. 2016.

"Disaster." *Star Trek: The Next Generation.* Writ. Ronald D. Moore. Dir. Gabrielle Beaumont. *Netflix.* Web. 4 Jun. 2016.

"Drumhead." *Star Trek: The Next Generation.* Writ. Jeri Taylor. Dir. Jonathan Frakes. *Netflix.* Web. 4 Jun. 2016.

"Encounter at Farpoint, Part 1." *Star Trek: The Next Generation.* Writ. D.C. Fontana and Gene Roddenberry. Dir. Corey Allen. *Netflix.* Web. 4 Jun. 2016.

"Encounter at Farpoint, Part 2." *Star Trek: The Next Generation.* Writ. D.C. Fontana and Gene Roddenberry. Dir. Corey Allen. *Netflix.* Web. 4 Jun. 2016.

"Final Mission." *Star Trek: The Next Generation.* Writ. Ronald D. Dir. Corey Allen. *Netflix.* Web. 4 Jun. 2016.

"Hide and Q." *Star Trek: The Next Generation.* Writ. Maurice Hurley. Dir. Cliff Bole. *Netflix.* Web. 4 Jun. 2016.

"I, Borg." *Star Trek: The Next Generation.* Writ. René Echevarria. Dir. Robert Lederman. *Netflix.* Web. 4 Jun. 2016.

"Journey's End." *Star Trek: The Next Generation.* Writ. Ronald D. Moore. Dir. Corey Allen. *Netflix.* Web. 4 Jun. 2016.

"A Matter of Honor." *Star Trek: The Next Generation.* Writ. Burton Armus. Dir. Rob Bowman. *Netflix.* Web. 4 Jun. 2016.

"Ménage À Troi" *Star Trek: The Next Generation,* Writ. Fred Bronson and Susan Sackett. Dir. Robert Legato. *Nexflix.* Web. 4 Jun. 2016.

"Q Who." *Star Trek: The Next Generation.* Writ. Maurice Hurley. Dir. Rob Bowman. *Netflix.* Web. 4 Jun. 2016.

"Second Chances." *Star Trek: The Next Generation.* Writ. Rene Echevarria. Dir. LeVar Burton. *Netflix.* Web. 4 Jun. 2016.

Star Trek: First Contact. Dir. Jonathan Frakes. Perf. Patrick Stewart, Jonathan Frakes, and Brent Spiner. Paramount, 1996. *Netflix.* Web. 4 Jun. 2016.

"Tapestry." *Star Trek: The Next Generation.* Writ. Ronald D. Moore. Dir. Les Landau. *Netflix.* Web. 4 Jun. 2016.

"Unification, Part 1." *Star Trek: The Next Generation.* Writ. Jeri Taylor. Dir. Les Landau. *Netflix.* Web. 4 Jun. 2016.

"Unification, Part 2." *Star Trek: The Next Generation*. Writ. Michael Piller. Dir. Cliff Bole. *Netflix*. Web. 4 Jun. 2016.

"Where Silence Has Lease." *Star Trek: The Next Generation*. Writ. Jack B. Sowards. Dir. Winrich Kolbe. *Netflix*. Web. 4 Jun. 2016.

"The Wounded." *Star Trek: The Next Generation*. Writ. Jeri Taylor. Dir. Chip Chalmers. *Netflix*. Web. 4 Jun. 2016.

Perfect Society and Flawless Human Beings

The Biopolitics of Genetic Enhancement, Cloning and Disability in the 24th Century

SIMON LEDDER, JENS KOLATA *and* OONAGH HAYES

According to *Star Trek: The Next Generation (TNG)*, the contemporary issue of biopolitics continues into the 24th century. When Captain Jean-Luc Picard confronts his villainous clone Shinzon in *Star Trek: Nemesis*, he asks himself the old question regarding "nature versus nurture" to reason whether, if under other conditions, he would have developed in the same way Shinzon had. Thirteen years earlier, the *Enterprise* faced another issue of biopolitics when they encountered the genetically engineered children of the Darwin Genetic Research Station in "Unnatural Selection." In another episode, "The Enemy," when chief engineer Geordi La Forge realizes that his VISOR is not working due to the radiation on the planet Galorndon Core, he says he is blind. Three examples, three different phenomena, and yet they all fall under the rubric of biopolitics.

Biopolitics refers to a framework that regulates diverse aspects of gender, race, class and dis/ability, not the least through certain technological means. Such categories, especially genetics, reproductive medicine, and disability, are recurring topics in *TNG* (Jenkins and Jenkins 105–124, Andreadis 191–216, Lehman, Kerry 699–714). Although *Star Trek* is known to have a very active fan community with their own participatory culture (Jenkins), we focus on the field of the "canon" representations. *TNG* reproduces, but also produces, a certain view, specifically, the connection between society and medicine. This is not surprising, given that this relationship was an essential part of biopolitics in the late 20th century. To point out the ways biopolitics works on different levels in *TNG*, we start with an analysis of social dimensions, which includes the entanglement of gender, sexual orientation, class, race, and species. By using the theories of Michel Foucault and other theorists, this paper analyzes the biopolitical use of reproductive technologies, sexuality, concepts of family, birth control, abortion, and eugenics in the series and movies. Two reproductive technologies in particular—genetic enhancement and cloning—are predominantly represented in four *TNG* episodes: "Unnatural Selection," "The Masterpiece Society," "Rightful Heir," and "Up the Long Ladder." According to our analysis, *TNG* often represents biopolitical practices of other societies as negative, while the biopolitical means of the Federation are shown as natural and positive.

Biopolitics

The theoretical basis for this essay is the concept of biopolitics, as established by Michel Foucault and further developed by Jürgen Link, David Mitchell, and Sharon L. Snyder. According to Foucault, in the early modern period, Western societies developed practices to discipline human bodies in certain institutions, such as schools, hospitals, barracks, or prisons. This form of social disciplining of individuals was also the basis for a governmental perspective on the population as a whole, constructed through statistics on factors such as birthrate, mortality and migration.

Biopolitics attempts to optimize these processes through means of regulation, such as decreasing mortality rates by introducing sanitation or regulating the birthrate by changing the legal age of marriage. Biopolitics—like the concept of power in general in Foucault's works—is not centered in powerful institutions of the state. Instead, he interprets power as a fluid network that connects all members of a society like relays. Thus, there are many different agents that have an impact on biopolitics, including scientists, associations, physicians, and employers (Foucault 1998, 133–160; Foucault 2003, 239–264; Foucault 1977).

One example is the heterogeneous network of political parties, scientific organizations, public health officers, and pro-eugenic associations that argued for the introduction of eugenic measures like sterilization and genetic counseling in the first half of the 20th century in practically all Western nations (Bashfort and Levine). All these are, according to Jürgen Link, processes of normalization. In different discourses, a field of "normalcy" is established, which relies on comparisons of different phenomena via statistical means and drawing boundaries between "normal" and "abnormal." This field serves as an orientation for the individual; to become a member of the society, one has to "self-normalize" (Link 2004a, 14–32).

According to Foucault, within biopolitics, various forms of positive and negative discrimination are legitimated by resorting to socially-determined categories based on biological factors. For instance, people with certain disabilities or nationalities are discriminated because they are depicted as threats to the supposed "purity" of a given population. This discrimination, in turn, reinforces a biological hierarchy and the social status quo (Foucault 1977, Esposito 2008).

While Foucault's early works on biopolitics concentrate on the role of various institutions, his later publications focus on concepts of subjectivity. Not only are the actions of individuals regulated by numerous institutions and agents, the subjectification process itself is inseparably intertwined with processes of power (Foucault 1982, 208–226). For example, some employers offer their employees the possibility of social freezing (i.e., the freezing of human egg cells for later conceptions) to allow these individuals to prioritize their professional careers before having children. That an employee has this option available supposedly speaks to her self-determined order of priorities. Nevertheless, such decisions are made within a network of power and interests, in this case, the employer's (Cattapan et al. 2014). *TNG*'s use of biopolitics explores the dynamics between societal regulation of individual life processes in a population—especially concerning the reproductive culture—through various organizations, agents, and modes of subjectification.

Interdependent Categories of Social Inequality: Class, Race, Species and Gender in TNG

Categories of social inequality, such as class, race, species, and gender are heavily represented in *Star Trek: The Next Generation*. While there are many studies about the representation of race and gender in *Star Trek* in general, and in *TNG* in particular (Pounds; Bernardi; Kerry), the aspect of social inequality through class is largely under-explored (Barrett and Barrett 70f). The Federation claims to have abolished poverty. It seems the Federation provides its citizens with all basic needs. Since technological progress facilitates all necessities, and the accumulation of wealth is relegated as obsolete, this system is represented as a functional one ("The Neutral Zone"; "Time's Arrow, part Two"; *Star Trek: First Contact*).

Does this absence of poverty mean that, within the Federation, social inequality is extinct, too? This leads to the question of whether there are different classes concerning economic and social status as represented in the series. Social hierarchy onboard the *Enterprise* is coined in military terms: Beside the bartenders of Ten Forward and family members of Starfleet personnel, nearly everybody on the ship—scientists, technical and security staff alike—appears to be a member of Starfleet, thus within the hierarchy of military ranks. Within this hierarchy a social upward mobility is possible. A Starfleet career is built upon accomplishments in the line of duty, and not on social lineage. Still, the series does not describe whether different economic, social, and cultural sorts of capital (Bourdieu) are equally distributed within the population. In addition, forms of social privileges still appear. Ensigns on the *Enterprise*, for instance, have to share quarters ("Lower Decks"), while the senior staff have individual flats with multiple rooms. After all, ordinary crewmen are hardly ever utilized within the series to any extent. When the plot is about hierarchy within the crew, it focuses on ensigns and cadets, thus, officers-to-be ("Lower Decks"). Because of this, it is not surprising that Mark Twain, a visitor from the 19th century, at first assumes the ship is reserved for upper-class citizens ("Time's Arrow, Part Two").

Similarly, classical lower- or working-class characters rarely appear. A few times, mining and construction workers are onboard or are featured in dreams. Most of these workers are represented as male, aggressive, and some are sexually threatening, therefore actualizing stereotypes ("The Perfect Mate"; "Phantasms"). Captain Dirgo, one such visitor to the *Enterprise*, is the only character in the series who is a member of the working-class and who has a large role in one episode ("Final Mission"). But even Dirgo, who has responsibilities as a shuttle captain, cannot cope with adversity, and reveals himself as narrow-minded by refusing to understand the consequences of his decisions. By emphasizing force and refusing to listen to reason, he repeatedly puts Picard's and Wesley Crusher's lives in danger, while actually getting himself killed. In contrast, Starfleet appears in a positive light, as indicated by its discipline, respect, and openness to initiative, whereas the working-class symbolizes the classical other.

In the 24th century, the working-class appears as outdated as the traditional image of the working-class seemed in the neoliberal 1980s and 1990s, when the economic shift from the industrial sector to services left many traditional factory workers unemployed (Kollmeyer and Pichler). While those workers confronted increasing hardship, on television, these obstacles were shown as the results of self-made faults. Raine describes three sitcoms from the Reagan era—*Silver Spoons*, *Who's the Boss?* and *Diff'rent Strokes*—

and concludes: "As presented in these popular sitcoms, the minimization of working class jobs contributed to the ideological erasure of the working class by devaluing the labor they perform and their subsequently related struggles. In these shows, working class jobs are portrayed as expendable" (67). In *TNG*, the devaluation of the working class is combined with the devaluation of the rural community, as seen with the Bringloidi in the episode "Up the Long Ladder." They are displayed as an underprivileged group, as poor and backward farmers, with the males as drunkards. With this reproduction of stereotypes of Irish Catholics, the discipline of Starfleet is highlighted even more. They refer to the image of the Irish Catholics as a white underprivileged group within U.S.-American society.

In contrast to Mark Twain's assumption of Starfleet ("Time's Arrow, Part Two"), the Federation claims to not privilege any race or species among its members. All of them supposedly share equal social and political rights. However, certain political entities outside the Federation, like the Son'a (*Star Trek: Insurrection*), do not follow such egalitarian values and assign enslaved species to socially undesirable and demeaning roles. Similarly, the Romulans force the Remans to work in mining facilities, in the armaments industry, and serve as cannon fodder in their army (*Star Trek: Nemesis*). Here, the interdependence of race and class is obvious in the way that members of certain species are privileged in their professions and living conditions, while others are underprivileged because of their species.

The Federation, consisting of numerous different species, is represented as remarkably heterogeneous. The populations of most non–Federation humanoid species are represented as more phenotypically homogeneous. In most cases they are played by white actors, whose whiteness, as Katja Kanzler describes it, "supposedly provides the required *tabula rasa* on which to project the ethno-racial codes of specific difference" (120). Only the Ligonians ("Code of Honor") are displayed as all-black and only a few species show differences in skin color, like the Boraalans and the El-Aurians ("Homeward"; *Star Trek: Generations*). But overall, the view of the series concerning non-humans is from a white perspective.

Although many different species are part of its plot, *TNG* deals much less with ethnicity and racism as a topic compared to *The Original Series*. As Michael C. Pounds points out, the percentage of episodes dealing with ethnicity in *TNG* is nearly half of the share of its 1960s predecessor (83). In contrast to the claim of equality of all species and races, a dominance of white male officers is represented in *TNG*, too. Although the bridge officers comprise more Terran minority characters and non–Terrans than *The Original Series*, the two commanding officers are both male white humans and the ethnic others are displayed "repeatedly involved in a narrow range of activities," like communication, psychology, technical services, and security, which offer fewer chances for gaining command (Pounds 81, 141). Most species in the Federation are represented as having two, and only two, genders.[1] Only a few species are androgynous, like the Bynars, the J'naii and—in their first contact—the Borg ("11001001"; "The Outcast"; "Q Who"). The J'naii, an androgynous species in "The Outcast," are all played by female actors. Out of curiosity, one of the J'naii, Soren, asks members of the *Enterprise* crew about supposed differences of gender in the human society. First officer Will Riker explains that he doubts the traditional concepts of gender roles; however, he also supposes the existence of certain differences, of which he proposes physical and reproductional differences as examples. Hence, the series reproduces the sex-gender-concept, prominent in the 1980s and 1990s in gender studies, which differentiates between a socially constructed gender role and a supposed biological one, and thus essentially binary physical sex.[2] The J'Naii authorities, in contrast, refuse binary gender identities, pathologize it, and administer therapy to people who consider themselves as male or female ("The Outcast"). By criticizing the intolerant measures of the androgynous J'naii towards individuals who feel male or female (Kerry 704–706, Gregory 187–188), the episode indirectly advocates for the rights of sexual minorities like trans- and intersexual persons.[3]

The early encounters of the *Enterprise*-D especially showcase matriarchal societies like those on Angel I and Betazed, and patriarchal ones, like the Ligonians and the Ferengi ("Code of Honor"; "Haven"; "Angel One"; "The Last Outpost"). The matriarchal societies are represented by white human-alike women, while the Ligonians and the Ferengi are represented by black human-like beings or non–Terran others. Matriarchy and patriarchy, thus, are both displayed as traits of societies in which non-whites or non-males assert hegemonic power and are "othered" because they do not succumb to a norm in which masculinity and whiteness are understood as something not being gendered or racialized.

Most Federation species refuse the domination of one gender and claim to offer similar chances to all genders, for instance, in the working sphere. Compared to *The Original Series* crew there are more women in professional positions on the *Enterprise*-D; however, the three highest-ranking officers are male[4] while the three female senior officers, Troi, Crusher, and Pulaski, work in female-associated fields of caring and nurturing (Kanzler 167f). The female characters Tasha Yar and Ro Laren, who work in the more male-associated areas of security and helm, are featured in only a few episodes.[5] There are many background crewmembers in engineering and on the bridge who have red and gold uniforms, suggesting they are engineers, security officers, or in technical or command track positions. Nevertheless, this diversity of working areas is not represented with senior staff. This unwittingly echoes the "glass ceiling," the phenomenon in which women are not promoted to leadership positions, despite their qualifications (Cotter et al.). On the *Enterprise*, the glass ceiling can be broken through in nurturing professions.

The unequal distribution of care-work within families, another important field of the social construction of gender (West and Zimmerman), seems to have shifted. Full-time family care-work appears to have widely decreased in the depicted future, since the term "homemaker" is not common in the 24th century ("The Neutral Zone"). This probably resulted from the increasing availability of technology for social duties like care, education, etc. Nevertheless, replicating food for the family is still seen as a female domain, as shown by Keiko O'Brien ("The Wounded"), which is only vanishing due to the rise of single-parenthood of men, including Riker's father and Worf ("Time Squared").

Another aspect of social inequality via gender, sexual violence, is represented in TNG in form of a telepathic rape of Deanna Troi by Shinzon in "Star Trek: Nemesis." Tasha Yar mentions male rape gangs, when she describes her home world ("The Naked Now"; "Legacy" 4-06).

The Federation—in contrast to the monolithic Klingon or the Romulan empires—appears to be diverse in its peoples and cultures. Although the Federation claims to have abolished different forms of social inequality within its citizenship, the highest-ranking officers aboard the *Enterprise* are predominantly human, male, heterosexual, white, and middle or upper class.

Disability in the Flexible Normalism of the 24th Century

We will now incorporate perspectives from Critical Disability Studies. This approach does not take the difference between "disabled" and "non-disabled" as a transhistorical, biological given, but asks how these practices and discourses are constructed. The premise is that, although the diversity of body types and mentalities are equally valuable, societies label some forms as "disabled" (Garland-Thompson; Mitchell and Snyder; Shildrick). "Disability" in its modern sense, is an umbrella term for many somatic and psychic variations that are deemed deviant, and is connected to the emergence of capitalist relations in the 18th century (Stiker; Davis). As discussed earlier, "normality" became an important concept with the emergence of biopolitics. With the industrialization of society, new bodily norms were established, which excluded some people from the then-new fields of employment. Segregation and institutionalization were the consequences for many people whose bodies or minds were not adaptable to the new work relations (Oliver and Barnes). This was accompanied by facets in popular culture that shaped the public view on "disability," like living a pitiful, impoverished life and being a burden to others—concepts that were and are criticized harshly by the disability movement (Ledder and Münte). Contemporary society naturalizes this historicity of normality; the "compulsory able-bodiedness" (McRuer), which is deeply intertwined with the "compulsory heterosexuality" (Rich), conceals the dynamic factors that produce categories like "disability" and "homosexuality" in the first place. Instead of realizing "normality" and "abnormality" as construction within different discourses and practices, they appear to be self-evident descriptions.

When *TNG* was first aired, the disability movement had already influenced popular culture and attenuated the negative images of disability. Nonetheless, the term "disability" was—and still is—a signaling for something "other." In this perspective, *TNG*'s representations of disabilities are shown in a casual way. In the whole series, the word "disability" is used only three times (Lehmann 225). However, Geordi La Forge, the ship's blind helmsman and later chief engineer, is a major character who quickly moves through the ranks from Lieutenant junior grade to Lieutenant commander, a testament to his qualifications as an officer, with his blindness turned into an attribute amongst others.

Indeed, La Forge's blindness is integral to his identity and he states he has never been embarrassed about it. But his identity comes with a twist: the audience only gets to know La Forge after he learned to live with his VISOR, which he first received as a child.[6] This piece of technology acts as his eyes; it is a silver curved device worn like a pair of glasses that transmits visual input to La Forge's brain via his optic nerves. It enables him to actually see more than the average human, and is quite helpful to analyze people's heart rates, radiation, and other emissions.[7] Living with a VISOR is a learning process to perceive visual information in general, thus normalizing La Forge's, and the audience's, engagement with it.

The Next Generation, representing the Federation as a liberal and diverse society thus establishing a process where somatic variety is successfully integrated into the community with therapeutic or technological means. This is still a medical model of "disability": "Disability" is seen as a characteristic an individual possesses and not related to social and cultural norms. A large part of the disability movement questions this medical model and focuses on the environmental factors that "disable" an individual in the first place (Goodley). In *TNG*, however, the environment is not changed; rather, the individual is.

Yet, this representation of "normality" is strongly dependent on performance. La Forge himself does not contextualize his disability within the Federation's diversity of life, but frames his disability through his achievements. He criticizes the biopolitically engineered colony in "The Masterpiece Society," which would have terminated an embryo with his supposed dispositions. He bluntly excoriates the "perfect" society, questioning its right to determine whether someone should live or die, or whether a "disabled" person can contribute to society.

The VISOR is often the centerpiece in La Forge-centered episodes. His eyepiece is instrumental in saving the day in "The Masterpiece Society," "Starship Mine," and "The Enemy." At the same time, the silver-coated VISOR is not all gold: In three instances during the 178 episode run and four films, the device is manipulated for foes to gain entry to the ship or attack the *Enterprise* and its crew.[8] In general, then, the Chief Engineer is an exceptional officer who just happens to be blind.

While La Forge's bodily variation is an ongoing, but rarely relevant, element in the show, "disability" is discussed more clearly in other episodes. When Troi loses her telepathic abilities in "The Loss," this is represented as a "disability." Troi claims she is not herself anymore and insults Crusher for not "curing" her fast enough, while the rest of the crew encourages Troi to accept her new state. Picard even tells inspiring tales of how "disabled" people can enhance their performances through the other senses, but Troi dismisses these stories as hearsay told by non-disabled—she uses the term "normal"— people without any scientific basis. Nevertheless, although her empathy is reduced, forcing her to rely on psychological skills alone, Troi still saves the *Enterprise* while simultaneously dealing with an unknown species. The message is clear: Even in a "disabled" state, she still contributes to the needs of the ship. But *TNG* does not go as far as to depict Troi living in this new state as a happy ending, so her telepathic senses are restored by the episode's end.[9]

Disability also affects the cultures of non–Federation worlds. On two occasions, the theme of disability is used to illustrate facets of Klingon society. In "Night Terrors," ongoing hallucinations prompt Worf to try to commit suicide. He does not feel he is a warrior anymore because he has become afraid of an unknown enemy. "Ethics," an episode where Worf breaks his back, confirms that adult Klingons are expected to commit suicide when they can no longer fight. Worf, paralyzed, asks Riker to assist him with this ritual, a request which Riker refuses, based on the Federation's supposedly universalistic ethics.[10] Picard accepts Worf's decision, referring to particularistic ethics, but offers a third choice from Crusher. She wants to implant some technical devices that would allow Worf to acquire sixty percent back of his mobility. This is not enough for him; the Klingon says he will not be caught lurching about the ship's corridors like a half-Klingon machine, subject to ridicule and disgust. Nobody offers him a wheelchair—and Worf, who adheres to the ableism of his heritage, would have refused one. Wheelchairs are not common in the 24th century and are probably regarded as a symbol of suffering by the writers, not as a symbol of freedom, as many wheelchair users perceive them nowadays.[11]

Worf, regarding himself as good as dead, is willing to let a visiting scientist, Dr. Russell, make experimental, possibly lethal, tests, including therapeutic cloning. The experiment goes wrong and kills Worf at first, until his special Klingon anatomy kicks in and resuscitates him. Lehmann puts this into perspective: "Historically, the paternalistic attitude of physicians towards people with disabilities, as exemplified by Russell's belief that Worf has nothing to lose, has demonstrated the low value of life assigned to this group of people. [...] For over a century mental patients, prisoners, and those with *diminished capacity* were routinely used as a source of research subjects" (Lehmann 71f). As with Troi's loss, the writers refused to consider Worf's back injury or rehabilitation permanent. He is fully mobile in the following episode, and his injury is never mentioned again.

In another episode, "Loud as a Whisper," another character marked as "disabled," the deaf ambassador Riva, has a prominent role, although he differs from other representations.[12] Riva must mediate peace between two hostile factions. He has a chorus of three interpreters who vocalize his thoughts and to whom he is telepathically connected.[13] In this episode, *TNG* shifts from the medical to a more social model of disability. As long as everybody talks to Riva or uses sign language, nobody becomes "disabled." This even becomes a peace-bringing feature: After his chorus dies, he makes the two factions learn the sign language he uses. These enemies will learn to communicate with him and thus communicate with one another after years of war. Riva's "disability" is represented as giving an unforeseen advantage.

While disability is the object of therapy and supporting technologies in the Federation, killing disabled or aged persons is a tradition in other cultures. In addition to the aforementioned Klingon customs, the Romulans kill disabled children, because they are seen as burdens and as threats of degeneration of the population ("The Enemy"). On Kaelon II, everybody is expected to commit a ritual suicide, known as the "Resolution," on their 60th birthday, to avoid becoming burdens to their families because of care work ("Half a Life"). In the case of an aged valued Kaelon scientist, Dr. Timicin, Picard accepts the ritual, even though such a rigid form of biopolitics is contrary to Federation values. He sees it as a Prime Directive issue, based on particularistic ethics. Lwaxana Troi takes the opposite view, employing a universalistic ethics argument against the tradition (Gregory 192). At the end, however, she accepts the ritual and accompanies Timicin to his death.

Together with La Forge's critique of the eugenic logic in "The Masterpiece Society," all these different representations of disability are discursive elements in the historical context of a "new" debate about euthanasia and assisted suicide in the Western world, initiated by the Australian philosopher Peter Singer in 1979. Singer proposed to kill certain people he did not recognize as persons, for example, those who are in persistent vegetative states and newborns diagnosed with certain disabilities. In contrast to Singer's attitude, the Federation is presented as one that welcomes people, no matter what shape they are in. In the words of Jürgen Link, this could be called "flexible normalism," broadening the realm of "normality" to individuals such as a blind engineer, so they do not have to be considered as "the other." The boundaries between normality and abnormality are not so rigid anymore. While the Klingons, the Romulans and Benbeck from the colony on Moab IV (see below) uphold strict norms on who is worthy to live, the Federation, and those like-minded, postulate a more humane, inclusive narrative.

Yet, as Link and Waldschmidt emphasize, this does not mean that there are no realms of abnormality. People can still be regarded as outside the zone of normality. In the case of the Federation, inclusion works only when linked to successful performance. La Forge and Riva save the day *because* of their "disabilities," while Troi is valuable *despite* her "disability." With Mitchell and Snyder, we interpret such representations as instances of "ablenationalism": Disabled persons are part of society, as long as they behave according to the competitive rules. While the field of those who are accepted as "normal" expands, boundaries are still set, namely with an emphasis on individual achievement. It is hard to perceive the treatment of disabilities in *TNG* as something other than a neoliberal approach: if one works hard enough, one can be "normal" as well. This is a very typical approach when presenting characters marked as "disabled": Here they serve as inspirational tales for the non-disabled (Kamit).

Regulating Population: Family Structures and Sexuality

According to Foucault, sexuality is the most important field of biopolitics because it is crucial for disciplining the individual bodies as well as regulating the population (Foucault 1977). In *TNG*, sexual relationships are mostly shown as temporary affairs. It seems that the main characters cannot be tied to partners to keep numerous plot developments open. The most displayed sexual relationships occur with characters who appear once or twice, usually from outside Starfleet. Promiscuous sexual behavior aboard is pathologized within the series, such as the result of a ship-wide intoxication in "The Naked Now," or a kind of telepathic merging between Deanna Troi with Alkar in "Man of the People." It comes as no surprise that the only exception to this is a male officer, William Riker, whose extensive flirting—even with subordinate female Starfleet personnel—is accepted as normal behavior. No female main character is displayed as being similarly sexually active and accepted. When Deanna Troi displays a sexual casual behavior without being in an emotional relationship, she is represented as displaying an externally generated pathology that requires her death in order to rehabilitate her ("Man of the People"). In contrast to the sexual morals aboard, promiscuous and hedonistic behaviors are characteristics reserved for the Federation's popular recreational planet, Risa. The sexual services of the Risians, mostly females, are displayed as cultural customs, however, without showing their attitude and actions as forms of sex work ("Captain's Holiday").[14] The series switches between these extremes of promiscuity and the loneliness of main characters ("Booby Trap"; "Attached").

All sexual encounters are represented as heterosexual ones. Several other aspects of sexuality and family life are missing in the series, like bi- and homosexuality.[15] Although the episode "The Outcast" is often interpreted as referring to homophobia (Roberts 117–123), homosexuality is neither mentioned nor displayed. The plot of an androgynous species persecuting heterosexuals, thus the supposed attempt to depict homophobia, is so subtle and un-queer, it ultimately reproduced heteronormative positions (Kanzler 212f). Another episode that implicitly addresses homosexuality is "The Host," in which the Trill are introduced. Beverly Crusher has a romantic relationship to the male Trill Odan, and realizes after the man's death that Odan is a worm-like symbiont. When Odan is temporarily transplanted into Riker, Crusher hesitantly continues the sexual relationship, but she finally discontinues it when the symbiont is transplanted into a female host. She tells Odan she is not ready for such kinds of changes, but it remains unclear whether she refers to inter-host changes or to gender-crossing host-changes (Kanzler 210f), which could be interpreted as a form of transgender identity.[16]

The structure of families and the distribution of care work for children are central aspects of social reproduction. In the 24th century human families are still formed by marriages, like the O'Briens' nuptials in "Data's Day." Marriages are not necessary anymore for financial reasons since poverty is abolished in the Federation ("The Neutral Zone"). Marriage for political reasons is rejected within the Federation and among the *Enterprise* crew ("The Perfect Mate"). Arranged marriages appear to Captain Picard as obsolete, too, even though he accepts the Betazoid tradition ("Haven"). All the human and most non-human families are shown as monogamous. In the episode "When the Bough Breaks," the Aldeans appear to have another form of social reproduction. Their "units" are not structured by biological relationships like families, but by shared cultural interests. But families are still composed of heterosexual couples with children, or possibly by a single mother, which reproduces a conventional, human pattern.

Partnerships and sexual relationships within Starfleet face multiple problems and are thus avoided by the main characters despite the idealization of the family unit ("Haven"; "Lessons"). It is not surprising that Picard and James T. Kirk share these ideals; when they are in the Nexus—an extra-dimensional field where one's wishes become reality—in *Star Trek Generations*, each creates a family life they abstained from because of their careers. Starfleet seems to privilege marriages above other forms of partnership by giving the possibility to live together within the organization; hence, spouses have the option to serve together if they wish to preserve the integrity of the family ("Second Chances").[17]

One significant difference to *The Original Series* is that *TNG* features families and children on board the *Enterprise* ("Encounter at Farpoint, Part I"; "Yesterday's Enterprise"; "Imaginary Friend"). This detail coincides with the significant increase of female crewmembers aboard in *TNG*. This phenomenon matches the rising number of women in professional jobs since the 1960s; however, it associates the increased number of women with the increased number of children aboard. This concept—a woman being the "natural" nurturer for a child—is only featured in the background of the series; within the featured crewmembers, the *Enterprise* promotes a more diverse approach, including father figures.

The classical "nuclear family," consisting of both biological parents and their children, is only one of many family structures in *TNG* and is not the most common. Concerning the main characters, many grew up with a single parent (Riker, Wesley Crusher, Troi, and Alexander Rozhenko), with one or two grandparents (Beverly Crusher and Alexander Rozhenko), or with foster parents (Worf), a role which Starfleet itself served for Data and Yar, and the bridge crew for Wesley Crusher when his mother departed during the second season. Only in the case of Geordi La Forge are both biological parents shown in the series ("Interface").[18] Besides the O'Briens, the represented families on the *Enterprise* mostly consist of single parents and children, like Beverly and Wesley Crusher, Worf and Alexander Rozhenko, and Marla and Jeremy Aster ("Encounter at Farpoint, Part I"; "New Ground"; "The Bonding").

The single-parent households contrast with the concept of the "nuclear family" of the Reagan and Bush Sr. presidential administrations. These administrations' policies notwithstanding, a new father role emerged in the 1980s, notably through divorce. The topic of divorce is avoided in *TNG* as if it is morally condemnable; of the protagonists, only Dr. Pulaski is a divorcee, and she insists she is on good terms with all three of her ex-husbands ("The Icarus Factor"). Since the backstories of *TNG*'s characters derive from the death of one or both parents (often in the line of duty, notably Jack Crusher), and not divorce, the show's single-parent families are compatible with conservative family values; these families are not perfect, but they are not morally reprehensible. In addition, the series makes up for the lack of parents by using the three male highest-ranking officers as temporary father figures: Picard for Jason Vigo and Jono ("Bloodlines"; "Suddenly Human"), Riker for Barash ("Future Imperfect"), and Data for Timothy and Lal ("Hero Worship"; "The Offspring"). These roles last only for the duration of single episodes, but assure the prevalence of a pseudo nuclear family for those shattered by death and, for audiences, divorce. *TNG* thus addresses a 20th century crisis by offering a dramatic explanation to legitimatize single parenthood in the 24th century.

Sexuality and reproduction are not only discussed regarding partnerships, but also in connection with medical practices. The issue of childbirth and reproductive medicine is addressed repeatedly. Compared with the frequent attempts of governments to control biological development in *TNG*, it is astonishing that child conception and concrete means of reproductive medicine are rarely shown.[19] Although sexuality is a topic in several episodes and movies, contraception is never mentioned, not even by a doctor, which suggests that the screenwriters did not wish to openly fall out with contemporary sex morals.

This may also be the reason why another topic of reproductive medicine is all but missing in *TNG*: abortion. It is mentioned in only one episode ("The Child"). When Deanna Troi is impregnated by an alien life form, Worf suggests the termination of the pregnancy to guarantee the security of crew and ship. Troi's pregnancy is not voluntary and can be interpreted as a form of surrogate motherhood.[20] Nevertheless, Worf's suggestion objectifies Troi's body by his addressing all senior officers, all of whom are male except for Troi and the ship's doctor, and without addressing the mother directly. Troi refuses this option and decides to have the child.

The screenwriters of *TNG* avoided abortion, which is remarkable given that one of the most common means of eugenic biopolitics in present-day Western societies—and was widespread during the production of *TNG*—is the abortion of embryos that genetic counseling constructed as having a risk of being disabled (Asch and Wasserman; Caeton). Furthermore, while *TNG* solves everyday problems like transportation and nutrition by technological means, this does not apply to sexuality and reproduction. Reproductive technologies are avoided or represented negatively. This leads to the conclusion that *TNG*, out of consideration for conservative sex morals, shows certain kinds of sexuality and reproduction as natural processes.

So far we have pointed out the family structures and sexualities represented in *TNG*. These follow a specific biopolitical logic that idealizes patriarchal family values. In contrast to the dominant contemporary discourse, these biopolitics incorporate the possibility of a single parent—albeit under devastating premises for the people involved.

Genetics and Eugenics

Within the series, genetics-based technologies are used for reproductive medicine in addition to other medical and non-medical goals. For example, for therapeutic reasons, Federation physicians use nanites—tiny robots—to repair the DNA in a cell core ("Evolution"). Synthetical T-cells are used to build immunity to diseases ("Genesis"). Genetics is used for testing biological kinships ("Bloodlines"; *Star Trek: Nemesis*), as it is in the real world since the late 20th century. The revelation of an ancient primordial species, which seeded humanoid life on several planets, including Earth, is also based on DNA scans ("The Chase"). The knowledge of genetics and its manipulation also allows for cloning and genetic enhancement.

Eugenics is one of the most discussed aspects of biopolitics. The term "eugenics," often synonymously called "qualitative population politics," describes attempts to increase the reproduction of desirable groups of a population and to reduce the reproduction of undesirable groups. The basis for this is a biologistic perspective on population and the biologization of social problems. According to eugenicists, bearers of assumed, unsound genes should not procreate while bearers of healthy genes should have more children. The means to enforce the first, like sterilizations, are called negative eugenics, while the means to increase the number of births of assumed wellborn children is called positive eugenics (Bashfort and Levine).

In *TNG*, the biopolitical means of the Federation are set in contrast to biopolitics of other species. By representing the encountered attitudes and technologies as negative, the values and technologies of the Federation emerge as good and natural, or at least as a neutral reference. But what seems "neutral" might not be neutral. This is especially true when dealing with eugenics. Positive eugenics is partly represented in two episodes in the form of genetic enhancement ("Unnatural Selection"; "The Masterpiece Society"), as shown below. In *TNG*, technological means are used much more to increase and enhance the desirable offspring than to avoid undesirable progeny. Negative eugenics, in contrast, is virtually missing in *TNG* and concepts of degeneration or genetic diseases are hardly mentioned. Exceptions are "The Masterpiece Society," in which negative eugenics are discussed, and the episode "Up the Long Ladder," in which a too-small gene pool leads to degeneration, as discussed below.

TNG's focus on aspects of positive eugenics is based on its teleological and biopolitically optimistic concept of evolution. Evolution in *TNG* is considered a process of progression—biological, technological, social and cultural—without discussing central concepts of Darwinist thought like variation and selection. The concepts of variation and selection do not induce a "progress towards a better future," which would be teleological, but simply describe undirected mechanisms of gradual changes from generation to generation, which subsequently prove advantageous or disadvantageous for survival and reproduction.

The Prime Directive embodies a similar linear view on the development of different humanoid species ("First Contact"). In some episodes, biological evolution is represented as an unavoidable biological step to a higher level ("Transfigurations"). This concept of evolution encompasses the evolution of artificial life forms, including nanites and exocomps ("Evolution"; "The Quality of Life"). The selective aspects of evolutionary theory, including the popular concept of the "survival of the fittest," have hardly any relevance in the portrayal of evolution in *TNG*. Hence, evolution without variation and selection is displayed as an unavoidable linear process.

Genetic Engineering

During the production of the series, the idea of genetically engineered humans was already discussed within academic circles (Glover; Anderson). Nowadays, the term "genetic enhancement" is used to promote such an idea. While still far from immediate application, the idea of genetic enhancement is an important biopolitical tool; as a vision, it has attracted research funds (Ferrari et al.). Back in *The Original Series*, genetic engineering was an important topic. According to *The Original Series* some people with selectively bred, genetically engineered, "superior" abilities, strove for the domination of Earth in the 1990s, leading to the devastating "Eugenic Wars."[21] However, surprisingly, unlike in other *Star Trek* series, the Eugenic Wars are not mentioned in *TNG*, even in episodes in which genetic engineering is a main topic, as in "Unnatural Selection" and "The Masterpiece Society."[22]

In "Unnatural Selection" the *Enterprise* investigates an aging disease that killed the crew of another starship. The crew encounters the research project of the Darwin Genetic Research Station: genetically enhanced children.[23] The children are presented as white teenagers and correspond to the 1980s beauty standard, although they are supposedly much younger. Beyond their increased physical and cognitive abilities, they are also telepaths. Soon it becomes clear that the genetic structure of the enhanced children is responsible for the rapid aging and death of anyone who comes into contact with them. Their aggressive immune system alters the genetic patterns of any pathogen around them, leading to the accelerated aging among "non-enhanced" humans. For this reason, the *Enterprise* crew decides that these children cannot live with other humans and should be kept under quarantine. The Darwin Genetic Research team, headed by Dr. Kingsley, accompanies them, hoping to find a way to make living together possible.

Kingsley, a physician and expert on genetic research, wanted to create perfect and "enhanced" humans, including a stronger immune system. The children would learn and grow faster, becoming "superhumans." While her motives are never made explicit, she does not seem intent on creating a species that will dominate the universe, but rather to accelerate the process of evolution of the human species. Kingsley has a lot of sympathy for the children she doomed to live in isolation. The quest for "perfection," which Kingsley explicitly articulates, has led to a lethal condition for all those who are "imperfect."[24]

The family structure within the Darwin Station differs from the aforementioned variants: Kingsley refers to the experimental children as "our children." Although they are artificially created for genetic research, Kingsley considers them as her family. The researchers, especially Kingsley, claim that the children are innocent and cannot be responsible for the rapid aging. She and Dr. Pulaski both press for a responsible treatment of the lethal children. Picard very reluctantly allows Pulaski to beam one child aboard, under thorough anti-contamination conditions. Pulaski's disregard for her own safety and breaking the quarantine can be interpreted as the representation of an overwhelming "female" solicitude for children. Kingsley's and Pulaski's commitment is closer to female-connoted caring than to the distanced objectivity associated with science which they otherwise exhibit.

While Kingsley is aggrieved about the lethal consequences of her research, most of the *Enterprise* crew, especially Picard, rejects the project's intent as such. Picard counters Pulaski's claim that they are witnessing the future of the human race with a clarification that this "future" is one envisioned by Kingsley alone. In addition, the captain despises genetic engineering in general. While Pulaski is shown as the emotionally misled figure, reflecting a typical feminine stereotype, Picard is the calm, moral instance, devoid of such imbalance, thereby stereotyping masculinity.[25] When Pulaski's empathy for the children leads to her rapid aging and near death, Picard is proven right, and Pulaski's position is therefore invalidated. Under his leadership, the crew works to save her.

Picard's disapproval of genetic engineering is made even more explicit in "The Masterpiece Society." Here, the *Enterprise* discovers a human society on the planet Moab IV that is deliberately designed, including selective breeding and genetic engineering for the eight generation-old colony. The reproductive technologies are never shown, but this technology defines this so-called stable order. The people are born with pre-programmed specific functions. The colony's leader, Conor, a white male, and his second-in-command, Benbeck, a black male, claim that everyone in the colony has freedom, but they all choose to fulfill their societal roles because they were designed to act this way.[26] For instance, Conor is born to be the leader just as Benbeck is born to interpret the founder's word. Conor is characterized as reasonable and diplomatic, admitting his society has its shortcomings, but agrees with its overall purpose. In other societies, he states, people often work in jobs they do not like, which is not the case for Moab IV. Benbeck, on the other hand, is aggressive and emphasizes the necessity of their rigid norms to keep their society "superior" to the rest of human societies.

The premise for such an engineered—one could argue "cybernetic"[27]—society is a closed system. The colony, situated on the distant planet Moab IV, has refused any communication with outsiders since its creation, affirming its founders' desires for isolation. The *Enterprise* crew therefore is only reluctantly accepted, and this is solely because of the imminent danger from a stellar core fragment that threatens to destroy the biosphere shield that physically and symbolically protects the colony from the harsh outside galaxy.

Yet, even within this enclosed system, not every individual performs as "designed." This is shown with Bates, a white female, who is a theoretical physicist and clearly subordinate to Conor and Benbeck. Yet, at the end of the episode she firmly criticizes the colony's structure. She realizes that her society, with its isolation, cannot progress at the same level as the Federation because of its desire to maintain the status quo. She explicitly argues the need to interact with outsiders to get new ideas, because her own society, which she once thought perfect, did not achieve Starfleet's technological progress. In fact, working with La Forge and seeing how a blind man can outperform her "perfection" leads her to see the limits of Moab IV's technological and societal development. Once again, La Forge's disability serves as a useful resource by showing how the Federation's inclusivity of people with disabilities trumps negative eugenics. In the end, she leads 23 other disgruntled colonists who want to leave the planet when the *Enterprise* breaks orbit. Conor is alarmed because this will disrupt the equilibrium of the society, but he lets them go.

This episode shows ambivalence towards genetic engineering. The arguments are different from the dominating discussions in American society, which rely more on the possible economic inequalities or the religious-based concerns about the integrity of Creation. Benbeck is presented as an unsympathetic traditionalist: his norms are inflexible and his dogmatic view of the greater good obstructs humane decisions. Conor upholds the idea of the greater good as well, until the very last sequences, but is overburdened by his own desires for personal freedom. Shown as the "good" leader, he respects the wishes of his people and lets them leave the colony. Bates embodies the individualistic longing to not be constrained by traditional rules. Her openness to change, in contrast to Conor and Benbeck, seems to result from her professional scientific perspective.[28]

The *Enterprise* crew, ever self-reflective, is ambivalent. Picard gives a two minute philosophical monologue to Troi, praising human uncertainty and the chance of self-discovery. Although the Prime Directive dictates he is not allowed to interfere with other planets' development, Picard grants asylum all the same. Yet, the captain ponders if the *Enterprise*'s presence will lead to the colony's destruction, perhaps doing more damage than the core fragment. La Forge, however, articulates a larger point. Voicing the main concerns of the disability movement against prenatal diagnostics and the rise of new negative eugenics (Hubbard 1986; Saxon 1998), La Forge explicitly highlights the irony that the technology that saves the colony, his VISOR, was invented to assist blind people—people who would never have been allowed to live on Moab IV in the first place.[29] This is a very compelling argument for a diverse society. Troi, concerned with the well-being of everyone, points out the value of having a well-functioning society and that giving up the uncertainty of an unwritten future might be better for everyone in the long run.[30]

Cloning in TNG *as a Reproductive Technology*

Cloning is an ordinary and widespread reproduction method for many plants and microscopic organisms. However, cloning mammals and humans became a more controversial topic at the end of the 20th century when the sheep Dolly, the first viable mammal cloned from differentiated cells, was born in 1996. Dolly was not only a milestone in science, the sheep became the symbol of cloning (Jenkins and Jenkins 122ff). Dolly's birth occurred two years after the end of *TNG*'s series, but science fiction latched on to cloning as a hot plot device. In 2002, for instance, *Star Wars: Episode II—Attack of the Clones* and its television spin-off, *Star Wars: The Clone Wars*, heavily uses clones as plot points. In the same year, *Star Trek: Nemesis* featured a clone villain, as did *Star Trek: Deep Space Nine*'s clone army, the Jem'Hadar, first introduced in 1994.

In *TNG*, we find a predecessor to those narratives. Cloning appears several times in *TNG*. For all intents and purposes, these episodes feature the same theme; as Pulaski states in "Up the Long Ladder," cloning is "not the answer." In all instances, a clone is considered a copy and devalues the original. This is even postulated within the fictional "medical babble," such as "replicative fading" from "Up the Long Ladder,"[31] which leads to nonviable clones, and "genetic drift" in "Second Chances,"[32] which, paradoxically, makes a clone detectable by its DNA sequence.

The episode "Rightful Heir" gives a lengthy definition of cloning and what it represents when a mythological Klingon hero, Kahless, "returns" from the dead to take command of the Klingon Empire.[33] Worf learns that this Kahless is a clone created by high priests in a monastery. He asserts that a clone is second rate compared to the original, repeatedly referring to the mythical hero as the "real Kahless," even though, paradoxically, the clone has identical DNA with the original. In this episode, the cloned Kahless not only has the DNA, but also has the memories and experiences of the original mythical figure, thereby not only housing the Klingon hero's nature, but also that of his nurture. The only difference between the mythical figure and the clone is that the new Kahless has not actually lived what he remembers, and his inability to conjure up details thoroughly upsets him and makes him wonder about his own identity. Through a conversation with Data, Worf realizes that the clone, despite its origin, can still become more than just a lab experiment through the faith of Klingon believers. In the end of that episode, the

Klingons come to a consensus, stating that Kahless will fulfill a leading role as a spiritual and political unifier, regardless of his origins in a laboratory. Thus, the Klingons "bend" the legend to fit this new Kahless, even suggesting that the method of Kahless' return is not stipulated in the original legend and that cloning technology might well serve as the modern means of mythical reincarnation. This explanation, which the high priest endorses, serves to justify cloning and is as near an acceptance of cloning as *TNG* gets. Worf overturns this argument but recognizes this Kahless as the rightful heir because Kahless will heal a spiritual gulf in the Klingon Empire. In the end, they decide to make public the background of Kahless' reappearance, yet define his identity by what he represents, rather than how he was created.

Worf's initial devaluation of the cloned Kahless reflects the general disapproval regarding cloning. Worf initially insults Kahless, telling him he was developed in a test tube and compares him to a fungus. This degradation references the circumstances of the clone's origin, which adds to the questions of identity and authenticity of clones. Using such derogatory terms for creating a life in laboratory in a science-fiction series is somewhat astounding: the first test-tube baby, Louise Brown, born in 1978, and others after her, are surely part of the Western collective memory, even if they are not linked to cloning, but to another reproduction technique, in-vitro fertilization (IVF). Worf's casual insult, then, hints at *TNG*'s vision of reproduction as an allegedly natural process only, which leaves an open door for technophobic representations of "unnatural" processes of reproduction.[34]

As in "Rightful Heir," cloning is used for a political intrigue in *Star Trek: Nemesis*, where the Romulans create a clone of Picard to replace him. Their shared DNA is demonstrated by a joint genetic disorder but, moreover, Picard's clone, Shinzon, displays striking personality similarities, which go beyond mere genetics. Like Picard, he reveals outstanding leadership qualities. Here again, in the meritocratic *Star Trek* universe, acquired characteristics are pointed out, even if—or especially when—dealing with a field like genetics, often mostly considered as deterministic. Shinzon's DNA turns out to be flawed and his survival depends on Picard's genetic material. This again underlines the postulated primacy of the original over the "copy."

In "Up the Long Ladder," reproductive cloning plays an essential role in the plot. The *Enterprise* receives an antiquated distress signal that eventually leads to two marooned colonies from the 22nd century. Both have evolved very differently and the story line leads up to the colonies' unification to survive. The members of the first colony, the Bringloidi, are defined by Data as Neo-Transcendentalists, who cling to a simple, agricultural way of life. They are friendly, jovial, curious, but have no modern technology. Their gender roles are conspicuous. The Bringloidi adhere to a traditional patriarchal structure, but the men are sympathetic drunkards, so the practical leader is Brenna Odell, the daughter of their nominal leader. She is in charge of domestic tasks such as food and shelter, and is responsible for the young and elderly. The Bringloidi are portrayed as Irish stereotypes, including large families with many children.

The second colony, Mariposa, is based on reproductive cloning due to an initial accident that left only five survivors. Three males and two females did not suffice for a large enough gene pool to establish a colony, so, being scientists, they embraced cloning as a replacement for sexual reproduction. However, this has created problems three centuries later. Their Prime Minister, Granger, immediately asks the *Enterprise* to assist fighting "replicative fading." Pulaski defines this term as a developmental defect that magnifies through each generation, like a copy of a copy.[35] Pulaski articulates a eugenic fear of a genetic degeneration, which would lead the entire society to soon die out. This inherent characteristic of fictional cloning leads to a plot development: the Mariposans ask Picard's crew to contribute their DNA to help revitalize their gene pool.

Picard, Riker, and Pulaski declare that the crew of the *Enterprise* would unanimously refuse to donate DNA. They cite their uniqueness as the primary reason. Yet, the Mariposans subject Riker and Pulaski unwittingly to cell samplings and steal their DNA. When they learn what happened, Riker shoots his clone with his phaser and then Pulaski's, with her consent. This condemns Mariposa to replicative fading in the short term, but the *Enterprise* crew works out a socially and genetically viable solution to merge both colonies, in which monogamous marriage will be forbidden for several generations; Pulaski explains that every woman in both groups should have at least three children by three different men.[36] Addressing the Mariposan reluctance to merge with the Bringloidi, Picard states that strong resources are found in diversity in general. Praising diversity is very much in accordance with Federation principles. The conclusion of the episode explicitly reinforces the notions of sexual reproduction as natural and implicitly as good and functional. An affirmation of this is the prolonged portrayal of Prime Minister Granger's fascination when he sees a pregnant young woman.

Interestingly, sexuality and reproduction are equated in this episode: cloning seemingly goes together with suppression of the sexual drive. As if reproduction were the only reason for sex, Pulaski asks Prime Minister Granger how they refrained from having sexual intercourse, whether by drugs or punitive laws. He specifies that, in the beginning both played a part, but that after three hundred years, the idea of sexual reproduction itself is deemed disgusting. The concept of contraception is never mentioned; from the Mariposan perspective, cloning negates the purpose of sexuality.

Nevertheless, sensuality, sexuality, and promiscuity all play parts in this episode. From the moment they meet, Riker and Brenna Odell flirt and eventually get involved in a casual relationship. At the end of the episode, after learning about the polygamous deal, Odell quickly turns her attention towards Granger. These elements and the terms to unite both colonies reveal a certain sexual liberality. The equation of sexuality and reproduction in this episode might seem surprising: while contraception is never mentioned in the *TNG* universe, birth control is tacitly implied—Riker's and Odell's relationship certainly does not lead to an offspring. Yet the absence of contraception in the series is remarkable, considering that this separation between sexuality and reproduction is one of the most important elements of contemporary Western biopolitics, due to the gradual accessibility of contraception and abortion during the 20th century. Not only does sexual intercourse not necessarily lead to pregnancy, but, since the birth of the first IVF child in 1978, coitus is not even a necessary condition for procreation.

Holding onto one's uniqueness and how cloning infringes on the value of the originals, are the main motives against cloning in "Up the Long Ladder." Uniqueness motivates Riker to destroy "his" and "Pulaski's" clones. The episode justifies his killing these clones as a case of self-preservation and self-protection.[37] According to this rationale, the existence of clones endangers an individual's identity, of which uniqueness is a crucial component. The right to kill suggests a fundamental (and unalienable) characteristic of a person in the *TNG* universe. The clones' threat to Riker and Pulaski is explained by Riker's arguments about uniqueness and is shown through the process of retrieving cells for the cloning. In this process, several elements violate Federation ethics and principles:

not only does it occur against their will and while they are unconscious, but the needle used for extraction is large and driven slowly and purposefully into their abdomen, which make the process appear particularly invasive and sadistic. This aggression is framed in terms of physical violation, close to rape. Theft is also mentioned to support the claim of the "originals," i.e., the theft of the physical property of sampled cells, on top of the identity infringed upon by the existence of clones. Granger replies that no harm is done to the original, but his argument seems too weak to justify the Mariposans' action. Incidentally, even though La Forge is sent on the same away team, his DNA is not collected. La Forge's omission is not discussed, as if, like in "The Masterpiece Society," his blindness is a self-explanatory reason for not harvesting his DNA.[38]

TNG deals with cloning as an inferior form of reproduction. In "Rightful Heir" cloning is accepted for the lack of an alternative and the absence of the original. But in "Up the Long Ladder," the default position is to reject cloning and to kill the (not fully mature and still unconscious) clones. Sexual reproduction is considered ideal and represented as natural. Just as cloning and (non-reproductive) sexuality, different modes of reproduction are represented as mutually exclusive. Those who would constitute a combination (i.e., the Mariposan women after the merging between the two colonies), are completely absent from the screen. In *TNG*, the primacy of sexual reproduction is unequivocal.

Conclusion

In terms of race and gender, *TNG* has a more diverse crew aboard the *Enterprise* than *The Original Series*. The principles of a meritocratic system are developed further and displayed repeatedly. Ranking and promotion of Starfleet personnel depend on individual achievement more than on social heritage. No one is barred from attaining an officer's position or duties due to disabilities, as shown in La Forge, Riva, and Troi. The liberal society the Federation represents is reinforced by contrasting it with societies like the Klingons and the Romulans, who are depicted as culturally homogeneous. Compared to the approaches of the J'naii, the Moab IV colonists, the Bringloidi, or the Mariposans towards gender, sexuality, or dis/ability, the Federation is presented as an egalitarian society.

Nevertheless, while granting everyone the same rights, only white male humans are on top of the ship's hierarchy. This is a subtle representation of neoliberal society, which is deeply intertwined with sexism and racism (Pounds). But this should not be understood as *TNG*'s stance on contemporary society: there is not a single display of structural discrimination within Starfleet or the Federation. *Star Trek*'s writers likely took non-disabled white males as a seemingly neutral projection space, in which dis/ability, gender, and race only emerge as relevant if a character is not non-disabled, male, or white. Therefore, representing non-disabled white male humans as the ship's two commanding officers probably seemed unproblematic, although critics argued that this latently reproduces ableist, sexist, and racist assumptions.

Regarding biopolitics, *TNG* represents some shifts in the societal discourse towards flexible normalism. While the topic of divorce is avoided, the single parent seems common in the 24th century. Concerning sexual freedom, the show supports different positions. Neither contraception nor abortion—with one exception—are topics in *TNG*. In addition, when *TNG* tries to criticize homophobia in "The Outcast," it simply falls into a heteronormative representation.

TNG also deals with topics of human genetic enhancement and human cloning. Those concepts were science fiction while *TNG* first aired, and still largely are science fiction in 2018. *TNG* deals inventively with these topics, which are not necessarily represented according to their contemporary majority views; for instance, *TNG* presents evolutionary theory optimistically as a law of progress. Instead of taking into account the mechanisms of variation and selection, *TNG* postulates a teleological concept of evolution, which supposes that evolution will give rise to "superior" beings. This is connected to the concept of eugenics, although *TNG* articulates different positions. Regarding *TNG*'s fictional perspective on the process of cloning, a fear against some "defects," based on a limited gene pool, is mentioned. But this does not lead to negative eugenics, which is rarely discussed in the series. Positive eugenics, however, is represented as a potential option and, simultaneously, a threat to human individualism, diversity, and paradoxically, to survival. The uniqueness of the individuals is of such high value that even the killing of a clone is legitimized. At the same time, reproductive technologies are used only in concordance with suppressing sexuality. There is no explicit differentiation between sexuality and reproduction in the 24th century. However, birth control implicitly seems to be common practice. This implicitness is obviously due to cultural tensions in the nonfictional frame about these subjects at the time of creation of the series.

In *TNG* the "Other" is used to point out the positive aspects of the Federation's values. This is clearly displayed when dealing with reproductive medicine. Certain biotechnological means are criticized harshly, while contraception and abortion are not discussed. *TNG* thus presents certain forms of sexual reproduction as natural. This departs from the show's general stance regarding technology as means of social progress. Only in regard to biopolitics is technology represented as negative or not discussed. This dystopian view of biotechnologies has no counterpart in the Federation utopia. As a result, *TNG* falls behind the sexual moral of the 1970s and the reproductive technology of the 1980s.

Taking Foucault's theory of biopolitics into account, *TNG* produces an ambivalent position towards the recognized population. While sexual reproduction is only valid when devoid of technological support, in general, a diverse population is welcome—as long as they behave according to the meritocratic system. We can assert that *TNG* already is part of flexible-normalistic discourses. "Normality" is not restricted to a set group of humans, but includes a variety of people who inherit very different aspects that had been deemed "abnormal" in earlier discourses, especially regarding gender, race and dis/ability. This expanding of the boundary that sets apart "normality" from "abnormality" allows a diverse group of people to become officers aboard the *Enterprise*-D and *Enterprise*-E. Yet, the boundary still exists. In *TNG*, being included is linked to individual achievement; one's performance is the criterion on which one's "normality" is validated. The crew consistently works against the threat of being denormalized; only by sustaining their level of performance are they kept in the realm of "normality." This is typical of biopolitics in the 20th century: The individual is not just subject to processes of normalization, but has to adjust to the given standards that are set within different discourses.

NOTES

1. *Star Trek: Nemesis* is the first and only time that transgender species are mentioned in *TNG*.
2. This approach was dominant in Gender Studies until in the late 1980s/early 1990s, when the alleged

biological category "sex" was criticized by social constructivists and deconstructionists alike (West and Zimmerman; Butler).

3. See Bruce E. Drushel's essay in this volume.

4. The highest ranking officers are Picard, Riker and Data. While the first two are non-disabled white males, Data is an android and the beige-based make-up, mixed with pale gold and bright gold powder (Westmore et al.), made him appear quite artificial. We discuss him here as male, because his figure appears as male, his pure rationality, devoid of any emotions, embodies the enlightenment concept of masculinity, technology in general is coded as male, and the *Enterprise* crew addresses Data as male. But we want to note that Data is othered as well and not simply embodies hegemonic masculinity (Relke; Rashkin).

5. The authors are aware that the presence of Yar and Ro in *TNG* is limited because of production issues with the actors. Nevertheless, the producers, writers, and directors did not seem willing to introduce other regular female characters in male-associated fields. See Alex Burston-Chorocwicz's, Erin C. Callahan's and Peter W. Lee's essays in this volume.

6. Although never mentioned in the series, VISOR stands for "Visual Instrument and Sensory Organ Replacement" (Okuda and Okuda 546).

7. In some episodes, the series displays to the audience what La Forge perceives: a lot of colors that are hard to connect as actual forms. In "Heart of Glory," the VISOR is connected to the main viewer, prompting Picard to ask how La Forge is able to make anything out of this huge amount of input. La Forge points out that he has learned to select the necessary information just as Picard has learned to differentiate between sounds in a noisy environment. La Forge's VISOR is presented as a very "normal" way of learning to perceive the world.

8. In "The Mind's Eye," the Romulans kidnap La Forge and use his neuronal implants to program him. They command La Forge to kill a Klingon governor. La Forge follows these orders and only Data's ability to recognize and interfere with the Romulans' transmissions saves the governor. Here, a very typical motif of human-machine interaction is presented: turning the human into a machine without any free will (Dinello 180–222). For a discussion of the Romulans, see Anh T. Tran's essay in this volume. In "Interface," La Forge is equipped to control a special drone to help to analyze the circumstances that wrecked another spaceship. While La Forge steers this drone via his VISOR, he is tricked by some subspace organism only he can see into risking his life. While this form of manipulation is like a case of classical deception, it only works because of La Forge's human-machine interface. Finally, in *Star Trek Generations*, the evil Duras sisters place a surveillance device inside the VISOR. This allows them to find out the shield frequency of the *Enterprise*, which they then use to execute a devastating attack, resulting in the ship's destruction.

9. See Joul Smith's essay in this volume.

10. As a second step, the Federation's universalism regarding the value of life is trumped by other principles. Loyalty and friendship compel Riker to accept a particularistic point of view and to agree to assist Worf in the Klingon suicide ritual, although Riker rejects it as such. For this reason, Riker tries to wiggle out of it by pointing out that Alexander, Worf's son, is actually the correct person to perform the assisted suicide. Worf is thus eventually pressured into changing his mind, presumably to spare his son, who is still a child. Also, being partly human and because of his upbringing, Alexander adheres to Federation (universalistic) values, for example of self-determination over constraints of tradition, and is not necessarily willing to be fully exposed to the hardest (Federation antagonistic) aspects of Klingon culture.

11. Only once is a wheelchair depicted in *TNG*. In "Too Short a Season," Admiral Jameson passes through a reverse aging process. At the beginning of the episode he is a man of about eighty years of age and his wife pushes him in his wheelchair. After the use of a drug-like substance, he grows younger and younger, firstly symbolized by him getting up from his wheelchair. This representation reproduces the ableist signification of the wheelchair as a symbol for suffering (Papadimitriou 2008). Starfleet's disregard for wheelchairs is stated explicitly in *Deep Space Nine*'s episode "Melora." In contrast to *TNG* with its individualistic notion of disability, in this episode, the environment is what "disables" the individual. While the overall episode is still troubling—the character labeled "disabled" is shown as willing to give up her identity, and "disability" is equaled with suffering—the focus on environmental aspects is a shift from the "medical-individualistic" to the "social" model of disability.

12. We argue that Riva is represented as a person with disability, because this is the hegemonic point of view towards deaf persons and those hard of hearing. Yet, many people who identify themselves as Deaf do not consider themselves "disabled," but part of a linguistic minority. Writing "Deaf" with a capital D refers to those who consider themselves to be part of this cultural group. It is unclear how much of this differentiation takes place in this episode.

13. Still, any communication with Riva should be directed towards him. This mode of interaction is considered decent when using a sign interpreter. This whole episode is much more acquainted with the social model of disability as it shows the importance of other people's behavior in "disabling" someone.

14. Only one other species, the Edo, is represented similarly sexually active ("Justice").

15. Kerry, however, argues that representation and non-representation are not central and that the focus should be put on the gender-queerness of characters (700–703).

16. Representations of lesbian and gay sexual relationships concerning *TNG* can only be found in off-

canon products, like the novels *The Best and the Brightest* (Wright) and *Rogue* (Martin and Mangels). Obviously the producers and screenwriters—like most of their colleagues in the 1980s and 1990s—did not dare to broach these issues openly in the series and the movies, due to anticipated public homo- and transphobia.

17. This does not appear to be always the case. For example, Geordi La Forge's parents are often working on different starships ("Imaginary Friend"; "Interface").

18. Picard's parents are shown in episodes, but they appear as hallucinations ("Where No One Has Gone Before"; "Tapestry").

19. Three births given by crew members are mentioned, two of them shown (Deanna Troi ["The Child"], Keiko O'Brien ["Disaster"], Francisca Juarez ["Data's Day"]). In later seasons, Nurse Alyssa Ogawa becomes pregnant, but does not give birth on screen. In "Up the Long Ladder," several Bringloidi women are expected to give birth while on the *Enterprise*. The unwanted infertility of the Aldeans, a result of UV-radiation on their planet, could be healed if the UV-radiation is stopped, according to Dr. Crusher ("When the Bough Breaks").

20. About surrogate motherhood see Cooper and Waldby.

21. According to the *Star Trek: Enterprise* episode "The Augments" and *Star Trek: Deep Space Nine* episode "Doctor Bashir, I presume," genetic enhancement is banned on Earth and later in the Federation. These series have been produced after "Unnatural Selection," so maybe this guideline was not yet established for the script writers.

22. Genetic manipulation is also a technology the Son'a use to try to delay aging in *Star Trek: Insurrection*. Genetic engineering for purposes other than reproduction or therapeutics also appears in "Bloodlines." Here, a Ferengi Daimon, whose son was killed in a battle against the *USS Stargazer* under the command of Picard, plans revenge by passing off a young man as Picard's unknown son, with plans to kill him soon after. The stratagem is based on the fact that the alleged son's DNA is re-sequenced so that he would be identified as Picard's son. Crusher discovers the ploy because the DNA re-sequencing induces a genetic disease neither alleged parents present, thereby identifying a fundamental contradiction in the young man's initial identification. This plot, characterized by a fascination for the decrypting of genetics, certainly stands in the wake of the human genome project (Jenkins and Jenkins 108ff) started in 1990. One other main element in the general discourse about cloning is the usage of therapeutic cloning. Therapeutic cloning is used in the *TNG* episode "Ethics," in which Worf's spinal cord is grown and replaced, thereby "normalizing" him. In the series *Star Trek: Enterprise* episode "Similitude," a living and feeling clone is created as an organ donor for its "original." Here the moral stance has shifted from the right of the "originals" over the lives of their clones, as in "Up the Long Ladder," to creating clones for their organs, which is presented as murder.

23. Only the neglect of the Eugenic Wars in *TNG* makes something like this research project within the Federation possible in the first place.

24. This is visualized by the representation of those aging rapidly. The supposedly 35-year old doctor is played by actress Patricia Smith who was 50 years of age at the time. This age and the ongoing progress of aging are highlighted by a lot of make-up; the same holds true for the other station's scientists and the infected Dr. Pulaski.

25. The duality shown between Picard and Pulaski can also be read along other lines. As a captain, Picard has the safety of his crew in mind, whereas Pulaski is willing to take risks and put her own life on the line for the sake of scientific research. In this, she is selfless and devoted, in a heroic audacious way, displaying male attributes, rather than displaying stereotypical mother characteristics. Such combined registers provide Pulaski's character with a certain degree of sophistication.

26. It is unclear how far the society is designed concerning the dimensions of gender. The physicist Bates is depicted as a very intelligent woman; her dealings with technology diverge from female stereotypes. But while we have a somewhat more diverse leadership regarding race, femaleness seems to be a disqualifying trait. Not only are Conor and Benbeck in charge of the colony as leaders, but they also are entrusted with all sorts of decision-making. For instance, La Forge and Bates find a solution to alter the core fragment's way, but it requires both of them working on the *Enterprise*. Bates would be the first person ever to leave the planet. The three men, La Forge, Benbeck and Conor, discuss and decide her ability to leave the planet. Later, Bates argues against Conor and Benbeck, stating that everyone has the right to leave the colony. Troi and Picard enter this scene, and Troi takes Bates away, saying they should allow the—male—leaders to discuss this, thereby affirming the male dominance. This happens without gender-roles being a topic of the episode at all. As a matter of fact, it stays implicit and supposedly self-evident, thus it is not used as a valorization of the Federation but rather inadvertently lets patriarchal dynamics of the 20th century slip into the 24th.

27. To be precise, Moab IV sounds like a first-order cybernetics approach, which adheres to the early theorists (Wiener, von Foerster). Later theorists like Bateson, Mead and the older von Foerster argued within a constructivist epistemology that the observer in any cybernetic analysis is a participant observer that also applies feedback-information to the observed system. Hence the need for a "second-order cybernetics" (von Foerster 289). It is unclear how much of this reflexivity seems to be implied in the representation of the "masterpiece society."

28. Bates criticizes the colony's leader's stance on maintaining the status quo because this holds the society back, at least concerning technological possibilities. While this critique is addressed as a matter of

conflicting ideas, one could also argue that the dimension of gender is relevant. The subordinate female colonist fights against the patriarchal norms of her society, which allows her to become a physicist, but not to live up to her full potential.

29. In one scene, this critique is very central. His VISOR initiates a discussion with Bates, prompting her to look at it. La Forge willingly hands it over. The camera captures the VISOR in Bates's hands, with La Forge in the background. Although the discussion is about the VISOR, it is not the focus, either cinematically or topically. Instead, La Forge is in focus, his face and completely white eyes are in sharp detail, while the VISOR, in the foreground, is blurred. They discuss La Forge's life, and Bates admits a blind person would have been terminated in the embryo stage. This is a rare moment that negative eugenics is discussed within *TNG*. Another occurs in "The Enemy," with a similar indication about the Romulan Empire.

30. At the same time, this seems to stem from Troi's feelings for Conor whom she admires. She even falls in love with him, reducing her professional distance. As Picard points out, this is very human—we all make mistakes.

31. "Replicative fading" comes from a reiterative cloning process in which the result is an increasing vulnerability to genetic defects, thereby limiting the clones' lifespan or viability altogether.

32. Crusher's statements about "genetic drift" are vague as to the exact meaning of the term, but it hints at a kind of genetically detectable (and paradoxical) characteristic of cloning.

33. "Second Chances," which is not about cloning, but follows "Rightful Heir" in airdate order, raises the question of a person's uniqueness. Here, Riker discovers and rescues his double, later taking Riker's middle name "Thomas," who was created by a transporter accident. When genetic identicalness is established, Crusher rules out cloning because she finds neurological evidence for identical childhood experiences. Here, as in other occurrences, both nature and nurture are considered when fictional characters discuss cloning in *TNG*, not just the genetic aspects. This is consistent with the values of the Federation as a meritocratic system in which individuals exercise free will. The latent message in this episode is that Thomas Riker's decision to continue a Starfleet career is intrinsically connected to his identity—whether one links the identity to genetics or not stays open to interpretation and is not dwelt upon in this episode. The latent rivalry between the two Rikers lies in their respective claim to being the original Riker—a claim that cannot be settled as with cloning, since they both are originals with divergent life stories. Towards the end of the episode, Data remarks on the value humans place in their uniqueness and how this is endangered in the presence of a double, without mentioning cloning explicitly. But uniqueness is also a main argument in the discourse about cloning, as seen in "Up the Long Ladder" below.

34. There are similarities in the crew's reactions when Troi is impregnated by a non-corporeal life-form ("The Child," see above). This is considered "unnatural" as well. Yet, the process of childbirth is presented in a much more favorable way, without any pain for Troi. After all, the mythology of the Immaculate Conception is evoked at this point. Here we are not confronted with technophobia as in "Rightful Heir," but the *Enterprise* crew expresses some form of xenophobia—this type of reproduction is considered invalid because it deviates from the human methods.

35. Having said this, one could speculate that a technologically-advanced society like Mariposa could preserve the original DNA and use that "unflawed" DNA for reproduction, thus negating the problem. Ignoring this solution serves to underline a fundamental fictional problem with cloning.

36. In the final negotiations, the Bringloidi and the Mariposans only send representatives who are male. They decide the number of children and of sexual partners. Assuming that the female are the ones who will give birth, the actual child-bearers are excluded from these decisions. In this scene, patriarchal norms, in exercising the control about women's lives and bodies, are unquestioned and reproduced.

37. Incidentally, this contradicts the later *Star Trek: Deep Space Nine* episode "A Man Alone," where at the very end, Odo states that killing a clone, even your own, is murder. In "Up the Long Ladder," however, the clones are not yet alive: they are shown in the incubators as unconscious, and their missing hair hints at an unfinished maturation. Under the aspect of representing genders, we may note that Pulaski doesn't shoot her own clone but that it is done for her. She also shudders and painfully looks away, showing empathy for her counterpart, thus introducing ambivalence in the assessment of the decision to kill the clones.

38. Another aspect is the representation of the clones. They are all fully grown and identical in age and in general appearance, which symbolizes identicalness as a fundamental characteristic of clones: neither children nor elderly are shown on Mariposa. Even if sexuality is taboo, one could imagine education and parenting being a societal issue. Of course, cloning, even using cells from adults, would result in embryos. Instead, in "Up the Long Ladder" adults are grown in incubators and questions about cognitive maturing are not raised. The question of the age of clones is recurrent: Shinzon is younger than Picard (earlier out of the incubator) and in "Rightful Heir" accelerated growth is mentioned, thereby going into scientifically plausible details of the cloning process resulting in an adult person. But this episode was created four years after "Up the Long Ladder."

WORKS CITED

Movies and Series Cited

"The Augments." *Star Trek—Enterprise/Season 1–4*. Writ. Michael Sussman. Dir. LeVar Burton. Paramount (Universal Pictures), 2015, Blu-ray.

"Doctor Bashir, I Presume." *Star Trek: Deep Space Nine—The Full Journey*. Writ. Jimmy Diggs. Dir. David Livingston. Paramount (Universal Pictures), 2012, Blu-ray.

"A Man Alone." *Star Trek: Deep Space Nine—The Full Journey*. Writ. Gerald Sanford and Micheal Piller. Dir. Paul Lynch. Paramount (Universal Pictures), 2012, Blu-ray.

"Melora." *Star Trek: Deep Space Nine—The Full Journey*. Writ. Evan Carlos Somers. Dir. Winrich Kolbe. Paramount (Universal Pictures), 2012, Blu-ray.

"The Passenger." *Star Trek: Deep Space Nine—The Full Journey*. Writ. Morgan Gendel. Dir. Paul Lynch. Paramount (Universal Pictures), 2012, Blu-ray.

Star Trek: Enterprise: "Similitude." *Star Trek—Enterprise/Season 1–4*. Writ. Manny Coto. Dir. LeVar Burton. Paramount (Universal Pictures), 2015, Blu-ray.

Literature

Anderson, W.F. "Human Gene Therapy: Why Draw a Line?" *The Journal of Medicine and Philosophy*, vol. 14, no. 6, 1989, pp. 681–93. Print.

Andreadis, Athena. *To Seek Out New Life: The Biology of* Star Trek. New York: Three Rivers Press, 1998. Print.

Asch, Adrienne, and David Wasserman. "Where Is the Sin in Synecdoche?" *Quality of Life and Human Difference: Genetic Testing, Health Care, and Disability*. Eds. David T Wasserman, Robert Samuel Wachbroit, and Jerome Edmund Bickenbach. Cambridge/ New York: Cambridge University Press, 2005, pp. 172–216. Print.

Barnes, Colin. *Disabling Imagery and the Media: An Exploration of the Principles for Media Representations of Disabled People*. Krumlin: Ryburn Publishing, 1992. Print.

Barrett, Michéle, and Duncan Barrett. Star Trek: *The Human Frontier*. Cambridge/Oxford: Polity Press/Blackwell Publishers, 2001. Print.

Bashfort, Alison, and Philippa Levine, eds. *The Oxford Handbook of the History of Eugenics*. New York: Oxford University Press, 2010. Print.

Bernardi, Daniel L. Star Trek *and History: Race-Ing Toward a White Future*. New Brunswick, NJ: Rutgers University Press, 1998. Print.

Bourdieu, Pierre. "The Forms of Capital." *Handbook of Theory and Research for the Sociology of Education*. Ed. John Richardson. New York: Greenwood, 1998, pp. 241–58. Print.

Butler, Judith. *Gender Trouble*. London/New York: Routledge, 1990. Print.

Caeton, D.A. "Choice of a Lifetime: Disability, Feminism, and Reproductive Rights" *Disability Studies Quarterly*, vol. 31, no. 1, 2011, http://dsq-sds.org/article/view/1369/1501. Accessed 01 June 2016.

Cattapan, Alana, Kathleen Hammond, Jennie Haw, and Lesley A. Tarasoff. "Breaking the Ice: Young Feminist Scholars of Reproductive Politics Reflect on Egg Freezing" *International Journal of Feminist Approaches to Bioethics* vol. 7, no. 2, 2014, pp. 236–247. Print.

Cotter, David A., Joan M. Hermsen, Seth Ovadia, and Reeve Vanneman. "The Glass Ceiling Effect" *Social Forces* vol. 80, no. 2, 2011, pp. 655–682. Print.

Davis, Lennard J. *Enforcing Normalcy: Disability, Deafness, and the Body*. New York: Verso, 2006. Print.

Dinello, Daniel. *Technophobia! Science Fiction Visions of Posthuman Technology*. Austin: University of Texas Press, 2005. Print.

Esposito, Robert. *Bíos. Biopolitics and Philosophy*. Minneapolis, MN/London: University of Minnesota Press, 2008. Print.

Ferrari, Arianna, Christopher Coenen, and Armin Grunwald. "Visions and Ethics in Current Discourse on Human Enhancement." *NanoEthics*, vol. 6, no. 3, 2012, pp. 215–29. Print.

Foucault, Michel. *Discipline and Punish. The Birth of the Prison*. New York: Pantheon Books, 1977. Print.

_____. *History of Sexuality Vol. 1: The Will to Knowledge*. London: Penguin Books, 1998. Print.

_____. "Society Must Be Defended." *Lectures at the Collège De France, 1975/76*. New York: Picador, 2003. Print.

_____. "The Subject and Power." *Michel Foucault. Beyond Structuralism and Hermeneutics*. Eds. Hubert L. Dreyfus and Paul Rabinow. Chicago: University of Chicago Press, 1982, pp. 208–26. Print.

Garland Thomson, Rosemarie. *Extraordinary Bodies: Figuring Physical Disability in American Culture and Literature*. New York: Columbia University Press, 1997. Print.

Glover, John. *What Sort of People Should There Be?: Genetic Engineering, Brain Control and Their Impact on Our Future World*. Middlesex: Penguin Books, 1984. Print.

Goodley, Dan. *Disability Studies: An Interdisciplinary Introduction*. London a.o.: SAGE, 2011. Print.

Gregory, Chris. Star Trek: *Parallel Narratives*. Basingstoke/London: Macmillan Press, 2000. Print.

Hubbard, Ruth. "Eugenics and Prenatal Testing." *International Journal of Health Services*, vol. 16, no. 2, 1986, pp. 227–242. Print.

Jenkins, Henry. *Textual Poachers: Television Fans & Participatory Culture*. New York: Routledge, 1992. Print.

Jenkins, Robert, and Susan Jenkins. *The Biology of* Star Trek. New York: Harper Perennial Books, 1998. Print.

Kamit, Ama. "Supercrips Versus the Pitiful Handicapped: Reception of Disabling Images by Disabled Audience Members" *Communications*, vol. 29, no, 4, 2004, pp. 447–66. Print.

Kanzler, Katja: *"Infinite Diversity in Infinite Combinations." The Multicultural Evolution of Star Trek*. Heidelberg: Universitätsverlag Winter, 2004. Print.

Kerry, Stephen: "'There's Genderqueers on the Starboard Bow': The Pregnant Male in *Star Trek*" *Journal of Popular Culture*, vol. 42, no. 4, 2009, pp. 699–714. Print.

Kollmeyer, Christopher, and Florian Pichler. "Is Deindustrialization Causing High Unemployment in Affluent Countries? Evidence from 16 Oecd Countries, 1970–2003" *Social Forces*, vol. 16, no. 3, 2013, pp. 785–812. Print.

Krauss, Lawrence M. *The Physics of* Star Trek. 2nd ed. New York: HarperCollins, 2007. Print.

Ledder, Simon, and Jann C. Münte. "Dis/Ability—On the Construction of Norms and Normality in Popular Culture." *Popular Culture and Biomedicine: Knowledge in the Life Sciences as Cultural Artifacts*. Eds. German Alfonso Nunez Cabal, Arno Görgen and Heiner Fangerau. Stuttgart: Steiner Verlag, 2016 (in preparation). Print.

Lehmann, Ilana S. *All You Need to Know About Disability Is on* Star Trek. Vancouver: Mind Meld Media, 2014. Print.

Link, Jürgen. "From the 'Power of the Norm' to 'Flexible Normalism': Considerations After Foucault" *Cultural Critique* vol. 57, 2004a, pp. 14–32. Print.

_____. "On the Contribution of Normalism to Modernity and Postmodernity" *Cultural Critique* vol. 57, 2004b, pp. 33–46. Print.

Martin, Michael A., and Andy Mangels. *Section 31: Rogue* (Star Trek The Next Generation), New York: Pocket Books, 2001. Print.

McRuer, Robert. "Compulsory Able-Bodiedness and Queer/Disabled Existence." *Disability Studies. Enabling the Humanities*. Eds. Sharon L. Snyder, Brenda J. Brueggemann, and Rosemarie Garland-Thomson. New York: The Modern Language Association, 2002, pp. 88–99. Print.

Mitchell, David, and Sharon L. Snyder. *The Biopolitics of Disability. Neoliberalism, Ablenationalism and Peripheral Embodiment*. Ann Arbor: University of Michigan Press, 2015. Print.

_____. *Narrative Prosthesis: Disability and the Dependencies of Discourse*. Ann Arbor: University of Michigan Press, 2000. Print.

Okuda, Mike, and Denise Okuda. *The Star Trek Encyclopedia: A Reference Guide to the Future*. 3rd Ed. New York Et Al.: Pocket Books, 1999. Print.

Oliver, Michael, and Colin Barnes. *The New Politics of Disablement*. Hampshire/New York: Palgrave Macmillan, 2012. Print.

Papadimitriou, Christina. "Becoming En-Wheeled: The Situated Accomplishment of Re-Embodiment as a Wheelchair User After Spinal Cord Injury" *Disability & Society*, vol. 23, no. 7, 2008, pp. 691–704. Print.

Pounds, Michael C. *Race in Space: The Representation of Ethnicity in* Star Trek *and* Star Trek: The Next Generation. Lanham, MD: Scarecrow, 1999. Print.

Raine, April Janise. "Lifestyles of the Not So Rich and Famous: Ideological Shifts in Popular Culture, Reagan-Era Sitcoms and Portrayals of the Working Class" *McNair Scholars Research Journal* vol. 7, no. 1, pp. 63–78, http://scholarworks.boisestate.edu/cgi/viewcontent.cgi?article=1095&context=mcnair_journal. Accessed 01 June 2016.

Rashkin, Esther. "Data Learns to Dance. Star Trek and the Quest to Be Human" *American Imago* vol. 68, no. 2, 2011, pp. 321–346. Print.

Relke, Diana. *Drones, Clones, and Alpha Babes. Retrofitting* Star Trek's *Humanism, Post-9/11*. Calgary: University of Calgary Press. Print.

Rich, Adrienne. "Compulsory Heterosexuality and Lesbian Existence" *Signs* vol. 5, no. 4, 1980, pp. 631–660. Print.

Roberts, Robin. *Sexual Generations:* Star Trek: The Next Generation *and Gender*. Urbana: University of Illinois Press, 1999. Print.

Saxton, Marsha: "Disability Rights and Selective Abortion." *Abortion Wars, a Half Century of Struggle: 1950 to 2000*, Ed. Rickie Solinger. Berkeley: University of California Press, 1998, pp. 374–393. Print.

Shildrick, Margrit. *Dangerous Discourses of Disability, Subjectivity and Sexuality*. Hampshire/New York: Palgrave Macmillan, 2009. Print.

Singer, Peter. *Practical Ethics*. Cambridge: Cambridge University Press, 1979. Print.

Stiker, Henri-Jacques. *A History of Disability*. Michigan: University of Michigan Press, 1999. Print.

Von Foerster, Heinz. *Understanding Understanding: Essays on Cybernetics and Cognition*. New York: Springer, 2003. Print.

Waldschmidt, Anne. "Normalcy, Bio-Politics and Disability: Some Remarks on the German Disability Discourse" *Disability Studies Quarterly*, vol. 26, no. 2, 2006, http://dsq-sds.org/article/view/694/871. Accessed 01 June 2016.

West, Candace, and Don H. Zimmerman, "Doing Gender" *Gender and Society Vol. 1, No. 2,* 1987, pp. 125–151. Print.

Westmore, Michael, Alan Sims, Bradely M. Look, and William J. Birnes. Star Trek: *Aliens & Artifacts.* New York: Pocket Books, 2000. Print.

Wiener, Norbert. *Cybernetics: Or Control and Communication in the Animal and the Machine.* Cambridge, MA: MIT Press, 1948. Print.

Wright, Susan. *The Best and the Brightest* (Star Trek Next Generation*).* New York: Pocket Books, 1998. Print.

Non–Star Trek *Movies and Series*

Diff'rent Strokes. Cr. Jeff Harris and Bernie Kukoff. Perf. Gary Coleman, Todd Bridges, and Conrad Bain. NBC (1978–1985) and ABC (1985–1986).

Silver Spoons. Cr. Martin Cohan, Howard Leeds, and Ben Starr. Perf. Ricky Schroder, Erin Gray, and Joel Higgins. NBC (1982–1986) and Syndication (1986–1987).

Star Wars: Episode II—Attack of the Clones. Dir. George Lucas. Perf. Hayden Christensen, Natalie Portman, and Ewan McGregor. Lucasfilm, 2002. 20th Century Fox Home Entertainment, 2002, DVD.

Star Wars: The Clone Wars. Cr. George Lucas and Dave Filoni. Perf. Tom Kane, Dee Bradley Baker, and Matt Lanter. Cartoon Network (2008–2013) and Netflix (2014).

Who's the Boss? Cr. Martin Cohan and Blake Hunter. Perf. Tony Danza, Judith Light, and Alyssa Milano. ABC (1984–1992).

Star Trek: The Next Generation *Movies*

Star Trek: First Contact. Dir. Jonathan Frakes. Perf. Patrick Stewart, Jonathan Frakes, and Brent Spiner. Paramount Pictures, 1996. *Star Trek—The Next Generation Movie Collection.* Paramount Home Entertainment 2009, DVD.

Star Trek Generations. Dir. David Carson. Perf. Patrick Stewart, Jonathan Frakes, and Brent Spiner. Paramount Pictures, 1994. *Star Trek—The Next Generation Movie Collection.* Paramount Home Entertainment 2009, DVD.

Star Trek: Insurrection. Dir. Jonathan Frakes. Perf. Patrick Stewart, Jonathan Frakes, and Brent Spiner. Paramount Pictures, 1998. *Star Trek—The Next Generation Movie Collection.* Paramount Home Entertainment 2009, DVD.

Star Trek: Nemesis. Dir. Stuart Baird. Perf. Patrick Stewart, Jonathan Frakes, and Brent Spiner. Paramount Pictures, 2002. *Star Trek—The Next Generation Movie Collection.* Paramount Home Entertainment 2009, DVD.

Star Trek: The Next Generation *Series*

"All Good Things…." *Star Trek: The Next Generation—The Full Journey.* Writ. Ronald D. Moore and Brannon Braga. Dir. Winrich Kolbe. Paramount (Universal Pictures), 2015, Blu-ray.

"Angel One." *Star Trek: The Next Generation—The Full Journey.* Writ. Patrick Barry. Dir. Michael Rhodes. Paramount (Universal Pictures), 2015, Blu-ray.

"Attached." *Star Trek: The Next Generation—The Full Journey.* Writ. Nicholas Sagan. Dir. Jonathan Frakes. Paramount (Universal Pictures), 2015, Blu-ray.

"Bloodlines." *Star Trek: The Next Generation—The Full Journey.* Writ. Nicholas Sagan. Dir. Les Landau. Paramount (Universal Pictures), 2015, Blu-ray.

"The Bonding." *Star Trek: The Next Generation—The Full Journey.* Writ. Ronald D Moore. Dir. Winrich Kolbe. Paramount (Universal Pictures), 2015, Blu-ray.

"Booby Trap." *Star Trek: The Next Generation—The Full Journey.* Writ. Ron Roman, Michael Piller, and Richard Danus. Dir. Michael Wagner and Ron Roman. Paramount (Universal Pictures), 2015, Blu-ray.

"Captain's Holiday." *Star Trek: The Next Generation—The Full Journey.* Writ. Ira Steven Behr. Dir. Chip Chalmers. Paramount (Universal Pictures), 2015, Blu-ray.

"The Chase." *Star Trek: The Next Generation—The Full Journey.* Writ. Ronald D. Moore and Joe Menosky. Dir. Jonathan Frakes. Paramount (Universal Pictures), 2015, Blu-ray.

"The Child." *Star Trek: The Next Generation—The Full Journey.* Writ. Jaron Summers, Jon Povill, and Maurice Hurley. Dir. Rob Bowman. Paramount (Universal Pictures), 2015, Blu-ray.

"Code of Honor." *Star Trek: The Next Generation—The Full Journey.* Writ. Kathary Powers and Michael Baron. Dir. Russ Mayberry and Les Landau. Paramount (Universal Pictures), 2015, Blu-ray.

"Data's Day." *Star Trek: The Next Generation—The Full Journey.* Writ. Harold Apter. Dir. Robert Wiemer. Paramount (Universal Pictures), 2015, Blu-ray.

"Disaster." *Star Trek: The Next Generation—The Full Journey.* Writ. Ron Jarvis and Philip A. Scorza. Dir. Gabrielle Beaumont. Paramount (Universal Pictures), 2015, Blu-ray.

"Encounter at Farpoint, Part I." *Star Trek: The Next Generation—The Full Journey.* Writ. D.C. Fontana and Gene Roddenberry. Dir. Corey Allen. Paramount (Universal Pictures), 2015, Blu-ray.

"The Enemy." *Star Trek: The Next Generation—The Full Journey*. Writ. David Kemper and Michael Piller. Dir. David Carson. Paramount (Universal Pictures), 2015, Blu-ray.

"Ethics." *Star Trek: The Next Generation—The Full Journey*. Writ. Sara Charno and Stuart Charno. Dir. Chip Chalmers. Paramount (Universal Pictures), 2015, Blu-ray.

"Evolution." *Star Trek: The Next Generation—The Full Journey*. Writ. Michael Piller and Michael Wagner. Dir. Winrich Kolbe. Paramount (Universal Pictures), 2015, Blu-ray.

"Final Mission." *Star Trek: The Next Generation—The Full Journey*. Writ. Kacey Arnold-Ince. Dir. Corey Allen. Paramount (Universal Pictures), 2015, Blu-ray.

"First Contact." *Star Trek: The Next Generation—The Full Journey*. Writ. Marc Scott Zicree. Dir. Cliff Bole. Paramount (Universal Pictures), 2015, Blu-ray.

"Future Imperfect." *Star Trek: The Next Generation—The Full Journey*. Writ. J. Larry Carroll and David Bennett Carren. Dir. Les Landau. Paramount (Universal Pictures), 2015, Blu-ray.

"Genesis." *Star Trek: The Next Generation—The Full Journey*. Writ. Brannon Braga. Dir. Gates McFadden. Paramount (Universal Pictures), 2015, Blu-ray.

"Half a Life." *Star Trek: The Next Generation—The Full Journey*. Writ. Ted Roberts Peter Allan Fields. Dir. Les Landau. Paramount (Universal Pictures), 2015, Blu-ray.

"Haven." *Star Trek: The Next Generation—The Full Journey*. Writ. Tracy Tormé and Lan O'Kun. Dir. Richard Compton. Paramount (Universal Pictures), 2015, Blu-ray.

"Heart of Glory." *Star Trek: The Next Generation—The Full Journey*. Writ. Rob Bowman. Dir. Paramount (Universal Pictures), 2015, Blu-ray.

"Hero Worship." *Star Trek: The Next Generation—The Full Journey*. Writ. Hilary J. Bader. Dir. Patrick Stewart. Paramount (Universal Pictures), 2015, Blu-ray.

"Homeward." *Star Trek: The Next Generation—The Full Journey*. Writ. Spike Steingasser. Dir. Alexander Singer. Paramount (Universal Pictures), 2015, Blu-ray.

"The Host." *Star Trek: The Next Generation—The Full Journey*. Writ. Michel Horvat. Dir. Marvin V. Rush. Paramount (Universal Pictures), 2015, Blu-ray.

"The Icarus Factor." *Star Trek: The Next Generation—The Full Journey*. Writ. Davis Assael. Dir. Robert Iscove. Paramount (Universal Pictures), 2015, Blu-ray.

"Imaginary Friend." *Star Trek: The Next Generation—The Full Journey*. Writ. Jean Louise Matthias, Robert Wilkerson, and Richard Fliegel. Dir. Gabrielle Beaumont. Paramount (Universal Pictures), 2015, Blu-ray.

"Interface." *Star Trek: The Next Generation—The Full Journey*. Writ. Joe Menosky. Dir. Robert Wiemer. Paramount (Universal Pictures), 2015, Blu-ray.

"Justice." *Star Trek: The Next Generation—The Full Journey*. Writ. Ralph Willis and Worley Thorne. Dir. James L. Conway. Paramount (Universal Pictures), 2015, Blu-ray.

"The Last Outpost." *Star Trek: The Next Generation—The Full Journey*. Writ. Richard Krzemien. Dir. Richard Colla. Paramount (Universal Pictures), 2015, Blu-ray.

"Legacy." *Star Trek: The Next Generation—The Full Journey*. Writ. Joe Menosky. Dir. Robert Scheer. Paramount (Universal Pictures), 2015, Blu-ray.

"Lessons." *Star Trek: The Next Generation—The Full Journey*. Writ. Ron Wilkerson and Jean Louise Matthias. Dir. Robert Wiemer. Paramount (Universal Pictures), 2015, Blu-ray.

"The Loss." *Star Trek: The Next Generation—The Full Journey*. Writ. Hilary J. Bader. Dir. Chip Chalmers. Paramount (Universal Pictures), 2015, Blu-ray.

"Loud as a Whisper." *Star Trek: The Next Generation—The Full Journey*. Writ. Jacqueline Zambrano. Dir. Larry Shaw. Paramount (Universal Pictures), 2015, Blu-ray.

"Lower Decks." *Star Trek: The Next Generation—The Full Journey*. Writ. Ron Wilkerson and Jean Louise Matthias. Dir. Gabrielle Beaumont. Paramount (Universal Pictures), 2015, Blu-ray.

"Man of the People." *Star Trek: The Next Generation—The Full Journey*. Writ. Frank Abatemarco. Dir. Winrich Kolbe. Paramount (Universal Pictures), 2015, Blu-ray.

"Masterpiece Society." *Star Trek: The Next Generation—The Full Journey*. Writ. James Kahn and Adam Belanoff. Dir. Winrich Kolbe. Paramount (Universal Pictures), 2015, Blu-ray.

"The Mind's Eye." *Star Trek: The Next Generation—The Full Journey*. Writ. Ken Schafer and René Echevaria. Dir. David Livingston. Paramount (Universal Pictures), 2015, Blu-ray.

"The Naked Now." *Star Trek: The Next Generation—The Full Journey*. Writ. John D.F. Black and J. Michael Bingham. Dir. Paul Lynch. Paramount (Universal Pictures), 2015, Blu-ray.

"The Neutral Zone." *Star Trek: The Next Generation—The Full Journey*. Writ. Deborah McIntyre and Mona Clee. Dir. James L. Conway. Paramount (Universal Pictures), 2015, Blu-ray.

"New Ground." *Star Trek: The Next Generation—The Full Journey*. Writ. Sara Charno and Stuart Charno. Dir. Robert Scheerer. Paramount (Universal Pictures), 2015, Blu-ray.

"Night Terrors." *Star Trek: The Next Generation—The Full Journey*. Writ. Shari Goodhartz. Dir. Les Landau. Paramount (Universal Pictures), 2015, Blu-ray.

"The Offspring." *Star Trek: The Next Generation—The Full Journey*. Writ. René Echevarria. Dir. Jonathan Frakes. Paramount (Universal Pictures), 2015, Blu-ray.

"11001001." *Star Trek: The Next Generation—The Full Journey*. Writ. Maurice Hurley and Robert Lewin. Dir. Paul Lynch. Paramount (Universal Pictures), 2015, Blu-ray.

"The Outcast." *Star Trek: The Next Generation—The Full Journey*. Writ. Jery Taylor. Dir. Robert Scheerer. Paramount (Universal Pictures), 2015, Blu-ray.

"The Perfect Mate." *Star Trek: The Next Generation—The Full Journey*. Writ. René Echevarria and Gary Perconte. Dir. Cliff Bole. Paramount (Universal Pictures), 2015, Blu-ray.

"Phantasms." *Star Trek: The Next Generation—The Full Journey*. Writ. Brannon Braga. Dir. Patrick Stewart. Paramount (Universal Pictures), 2015, Blu-ray.

"Q Who?" *Star Trek: The Next Generation—The Full Journey*. Writ. Maurice Hurley. Dir. Rob Bowman. Paramount (Universal Pictures), 2015, Blu-ray.

"The Quality of Life." *Star Trek: The Next Generation—The Full Journey*. Writ. Naren Shankar. Dir. Jonathan Frakes. Paramount (Universal Pictures), 2015, Blu-ray.

"Rightful Heir." *Star Trek: The Next Generation—The Full Journey*. Writ. James E. Brooks. Dir. Winrich Kolbe. Paramount (Universal Pictures), 2015, Blu-ray.

"Second Chances." *Star Trek: The Next Generation—The Full Journey*. Writ. Michael Medlock. Dir. LeVar Burton. Paramount (Universal Pictures), 2015, Blu-ray.

"Starship Mine." *Star Trek: The Next Generation—The Full Journey*. Writ. Morgan Gendel. Dir. Cliff Bole. Paramount (Universal Pictures), 2015, Blu-ray.

"Suddenly Human." *Star Trek: The Next Generation—The Full Journey*. Writ. Ralph Philips. Dir. Gabrielle Beaumont. Paramount (Universal Pictures), 2015, Blu-ray.

"Tapestry." *Star Trek: The Next Generation—The Full Journey*. Writ. Ronald D. Moore. Dir. Les Landau. Paramount (Universal Pictures), 2015, Blu-ray.

"Time Squared." *Star Trek: The Next Generation—The Full Journey*. Writ. Kurt Michael Bensmiller. Dir. Joseph L. Scanlan. Paramount (Universal Pictures), 2015, Blu-ray.

"Time's Arrow, Part Two." *Star Trek: The Next Generation—The Full Journey*. Writ. Joe Menosky. Dir. Les Landau. Paramount (Universal Pictures), 2015, Blu-ray.

"Too Short a Season." *Star Trek: The Next Generation—The Full Journey*. Writ. Michael Michaelian. Dir. Rob Bowman. Paramount (Universal Pictures), 2015, Blu-ray.

"Transfigurations." *Star Trek: The Next Generation—The Full Journey*. Writ. René Echevarria. Dir. Tom Benko. Paramount (Universal Pictures), 2015, Blu-ray.

"Unnatural Selection." *Star Trek: The Next Generation—The Full Journey*. Writ. John Mason and Mike Gray. Dir. Paul Lynch. Paramount (Universal Pictures), 2015, Blu-ray.

"Up the Long Ladder." *Star Trek: The Next Generation—The Full Journey*. Writ. Melinda M. Snodgrass. Dir. Winrich Kolbe. Paramount (Universal Pictures), 2015, Blu-ray.

"When the Bough Breaks." *Star Trek: The Next Generation—The Full Journey*. Writ. Hannah Louise Shearer. Dir. Kim Manners. Paramount (Universal Pictures), 2015, Blu-ray.

"Where No One Has Gone Before." *Star Trek: The Next Generation—The Full Journey*. Writ. Diane Duane and Michael Reaves. Dir. Rob Bowman. Paramount (Universal Pictures), 2015, Blu-ray.

"The Wounded." *Star Trek: The Next Generation—The Full Journey*. Writ. Stuart Charno, Sara Charn, and Cy Chermak. Dir. Chip Chalmers. Paramount (Universal Pictures), 2015, Blu-ray.

"Yesterday's Enterprise." *Star Trek: The Next Generation—The Full Journey*. Writ. Trent Christopher Ganino and Eric A. Stillwell. Dir. David Carson. Paramount (Universal Pictures), 2015, Blu-ray.

The Borg

The Antithesis of Lieutenant Commander Data

OLAF MEUTHER

An antithesis is the exact opposite of a thesis. To characterize and describe the Borg as the antithesis of the Federation, and Lieutenant Command Data in particular, suggests dualities concerning cybernetics that cannot coexist at the same time, in the same body, and at the same place without threatening both the Borg and Starfleet. According to Katarina Boyd, the Borg and the Federation "embody a postmodern version of radical difference" (95). The conflict is complicated by the fact that the show presents cyborgs and androids on both sides. For instance, having injured his heart during a fight with a vicious Nausicaan, Captain Jean-Luc Picard has a mechanical heart, Lieutenant Commander Geordi La Forge can see only by using a VISOR, and Lieutenant Worf's backbone is reconstructed after an accident ("Tapestry"; "Ethics"). Lieutenant Commander Data himself is an android who was found during a Starfleet mission, was socialized at its Academy, and now serves as the second officer on board the Federation's flagship. In contrast, the Borg consists of cyborgs formed by microscopic, invasive "nano probes" reconstructing the bodies of assimilated beings, solely for the purpose of mechanically optimizing the Borg collective. Their use of assimilation destroys other cultures, which is the show's equivalent to the genocide of other species.

The Borg appear in only six episodes of *Star Trek: The Next Generation*, but they left a lasting impression on the *Enterprise* crew and the audience because they are an overwhelming enemy that seemingly cannot coexist with others. This is made clear in their pilot episode, when the mischievous Q demonstrates to Picard that Starfleet is not nearly as prepared to face the unknown as the captain claims. The episode tantalizes the audience with little background information about the Borg; Q introduces them as an asexual species only interested in new technology, Counselor Deanna Troi senses that the Borg have a collective mind, and Guinan points out that their roots go back thousands of years because their use of assimilation allows them to store foreign knowledge built up over time. Despite Picard's initial attempts at peaceful communication, the Borg invade the ship and carve out a section of the ship, incorporating Starfleet technology and killing several members of the crew. At the last second, Picard asks Q for help to save the ship and the crew ("Q Who").

The next season, Starfleet and the Borg meet near the devastated colony New Providence. During the fight, Captain Picard is kidnapped and assimilated as Locutus of Borg.

This name does not correspond to any regular Borg identification, but is indicative of his extraordinary position in the collective as a spokesman until they assimilate all human beings. The crew manages to free the captain, and to restore his former appearance ("The Best of Both Worlds Part 1"; "The Best of Both Worlds Part 2").

The next several encounters revolve around Borg individuality and identity. In "I, Borg," the *Enterprise* finds a single shipwrecked Borg. Geordi LaForge helps salvage his individuality and give him a name, Hugh. Captain Picard initially plans to use the drone to plant a virus into the collective, but decides that Hugh's individuality entitles him to respect as a person. Hugh prefers to remain with the crew, but, knowing the Borg will return for him, decides to return to the collective rather than risk his friends ("I, Borg"). However, his individuality became a form of virus anyway; in the next season, the crew encounters a special "branch" of the collective infected by the virus of individualism Hugh introduced. Disorganized, they become followers of Lore, Data's "evil" brother. The destruction of the collective by using the idea of individuality did not lead the drones to freedom, but to chaos without the structure of the collective to give them purpose. For a short time, Lore exploits this vacancy for his own purposes by offering them stability and guidance ("Descent Part 1"; "Descent Part 2"). The issue of individuality versus the hive mind becomes the focus of *Star Trek: First Contact*, in which Data's loyalty is tested, and Picard squares off against the Borg Queen and the legacy of his own time within the collective.

Technological progress determined the course of modern history and is certainly a driving force today. Technology is also the center of controversy between Starfleet and the Borg, as people question the extent that technology influences the meaning of life. Where and what are its limits? How far might people go in incorporating robotics without becoming inhuman? Another question is whether or not, and under what conditions, do cyborgs—or androids like Data—challenge the concept of humanity. How do these answers relate to individuality, as represented by the Federation and Data's ultimate goal, with the Borg, who seek to absorb the Federation into themselves?

These questions lead to the answer that Data is the antithesis of the Borg in spite of all the similarities between them. The differences are crucial to understanding *Star Trek: The Next Generation*'s philosophy regarding the development of transhumanism and artificial intelligence. This distinction can be observed between the depiction of two seemingly identical brothers—mechanical in construction, but who "matured" differently. The relationship between Lore and Data becomes a case study of the Federation's acculturation.

To answer these questions we look at the five pillars of Federation philosophy and compare them with the Borg's basic characteristics. The components of Federation life—as presented on the *Enterprise* and through their own actions and words—represent a masculine environment based on humanistic ideals in freedom, individualism, and self-determination. In contrast, the Borg, as represented by the Queen, challenges these ideals through femininity and matriarchy as an alternative form of leadership.

The Federation and Data

The Federation itself represents a form of social progression. However, its view of modern life centers on the masculine-oriented Starfleet, which refutes matriarchy's contribution to the social order (Boyd 102f). The distinction between patriarchy and matri-archy coincides in the perceived differences concerning feminine and masculine gender roles. Mary Philips identifies "two different ways of leadership" based on the two different sexes' physicality (156). Julia Kristeva points out "the female sexual body is the unspoken other of leadership" (Philips 157). The characteristics of this "otherizing" process define the ways Starfleet operates, and also defines its relationship to the Borg.

In *Sexual Generations: Star Trek: The Next Generation and Gender*, Robin Roberts analyzes the relationship between femininity and masculinity within the context of encounters between the Federation and outside aliens. In her view, femininity is one of the frontiers the *Enterprise* confronts regularly. She observes that the *Enterprise* is espe-cially threatened if their adversaries question Starfleet's and Federation's patriarchy, the first pillar of its philosophy (Roberts 2–3). Indeed, on board the *Enterprise*, the differences between male and female are subsumed by their military ranks and a corresponding dress code. The exceptions are two women: Beverly Crusher, the Chief Medical Officer; and Deanna Troi, the ship's counselor. They occupy positions in which empathy, a fem-inine and maternal quality, plays an important role.[1] Viewers see them wearing typical clothes emphasizing their gender. In the first episodes, Troi is often asked to analyze and comment on situations using her Betazoid empathy, which reflect both her duties and her femininity. During the series' run, however, she becomes more assertive. Under orders, she changes her feminine leotard for a standard uniform and this opens the gate for her to seek a promotion and command the ship ("Chain of Command Part 1"; "Chain of Command Part 2"). As in the case of the androgynous[2] security chief, the downplaying of Troi-styled femininity provides Tasha Yar with an opportunity to take over a tradi-tionally masculine-dominated position onboard the *Enterprise*.[3]

The second pillar of Federation ideals is the ability to lead one's own life. Relating back to the principles of freedom, a Federation citizen can decide for him- or herself how to live and prosper, as long as he or she does not interfere in the lifestyles of others. In its most extreme form, individual self-determination even contradicts the "goodness" of the Federation. In "The Enemy," Worf refuses to donate his blood to save a Romulan's life. The Klingon is aware that a Starfleet officer has an obligation to preserve life, but he cannot be persuaded to act accordingly because of his personal hatred for the Romulans and the thought of becoming a symbolic blood brother. Picard could have ordered Worf to donate blood, but the captain respects his decision. The tension between self-determination and ethical necessity was a tricky balance, and Picard upholds his junior officer's identity and beliefs more than his obligation as a Starfleet captain.

A very important part of the concept of individual self-determination is the right to control one's own body. In "The Child," Troi has a baby and the initial conception, in which she is unknowingly impregnated, violates her right of self-determination. In these episodes, an entity invades another person against their will (Roberts 168–170). The rea-sons are many, ranging from scientific curiosity and egotism in "The Schizoid Man," to forms of "memory rape" in "Violations," to the infiltration of Federation brass by space cockroaches, as in "Conspiracy." The series clearly presents the sanctity of physical and psychological identities.

Within this context, Data appears as a blank slate. Importantly, he is not initially a product of Starfleet. He was constructed and built by Noonian Soong, an independent cyberneticist who gave the machine his own appearance and code of ethics. As a result, Data resembles a sentient adult male. However, he has the curiosity of a child; when

Soong first activated his android, Data did not see the need to wear clothes because he realized his mechanical body could not be damaged by the environment and thus saw no purpose for protective clothing. Despite his child-like innocence, however, he is clearly superior to his creator. His photographic memory; powerful positronic brain, which allows him to perform 60 trillion arithmetic operations per second; and his physical powers exceed that of any normal human. The colonists of Omicron Theta feared Data because of his superiority, as well as the memory of his brother, Lore, who ultimately delivered the inhabitants to the malevolent Crystalline Entity ("Datalore"). As a result, Data is aware that people feel uncomfortable in his presence and that they do not know how to respond or react properly to him.

Until his deactivation and deconstruction, Data lived on Omicron Theta. After the Crystalline Entity struck, he was found and re-activated by the crew of the USS *Tripoli*. He attended the Starfleet Academy between 2341 and 2345 and abides by Starfleet rules and customs. After serving on the USS *Trieste* he joined the crew of the *Enterprise* in 2363 ("Data"). The following year, the issue of his self-determination occurred as Starfleet wanted to examine Data's physiognomy and build new androids for their own purposes ("The Measure of a Man"). For the first time, the show asks if Data was a life form or the property of Starfleet.

The issue of Data's rights centers on the third pillar of the Federation, which is the idea of equality. The question arises as to whether or not the android is a life form and therefore equal before the law to other sentient Federation members. Significantly, the idea of gender equality is never brought up. Starfleet is based on the supremacy of masculinity and Data's body is shaped like a man's. Indeed, as discussed below, in the following season, when Data creates an offspring that takes on the appearance and mannerisms of a female, the issue of sentience returns.

If liberty and equality are set in contrast to each other, it is noticeable that the *principle* of equality remains a hallmark in Starfleet's philosophy. In theory, all people are equal when it comes to access to needed resources and information or to equality before the law. If equality is not deemed as important as freedom, then equality—in this case, gender equality—does not truly exist. In Starfleet, women attain true equality only when she "defies" femininity, like the androgynous Yar, or when Troi wears a standard uniform. The notion of women as the "weaker sex" is reinforced even through variations of the "mind meld," one of the most intimate contacts when two minds become one. Regarding women, this mental intimacy occurs as forms of sexual violence, such as Troi's ordeal in "Violations" or "Man of the People." This depiction of merging minds contrasts sharply with the familiar Vulcan mind meld, which debuted in the original *Star Trek* series. Spock uses the mind meld with females, but only for "good" causes, such as communicating with the Horta in "The Devil in the Dark," the whales in *Star Trek IV: The Voyage Home*, and invading Valeris's mind to save a peace conference in *Star Trek VI: The Undiscovered Country*. In contrast, mental connections from those outside Starfleet, as in the case of "Violations" or "Man of the People," lead to mental illness or death. However, between men, mind melds are shown as a form of intellectual bonding between esteemed figures, or a service to help someone to fulfill his duty, such as Picard's mind melds with Sarek and Spock ("Sarek"; "Unification II").

The series establishes Data as equal to that of his biological crewmates, but the android regards himself as inferior to humans because of his lack of emotions. In "Brothers," he is summoned by Noonian Soong shortly before the scientist's death to install an emotional chip. When Data arrives, Soong speaks about his expectations for him, telling him he thought his son would become a scientist in his father's image. He is disappointed that Data joined Starfleet. However, the call does not only reach Data, but his reactivated brother, Lore, too. Although Noonian Soong explains that the brothers are equal, Data doubts these statements. The puzzlement on his face suggests that he cannot reconcile how Lore's amorality causes him to act like a completely different person. This idea of equality confuses Data because, as an android, the conflict between identical mechanical construction and different personalities/lifestyles negates Soong's definition of equality. The inconsistency is never fully resolved, even with Lore's death. Their relationships to others and their completely different socializations seem marked since their birth, with Lore immediately assuming a superior attitude towards biological beings. In contrast, Data's initial nudity suggests a lack of emotions and symbolizes his vulnerability as a blank slate ("Inheritance"). However, even when he accepts Starfleet as a career, he does not fully obey its directives. In his resistance, Data demonstrates the potential for human individuality.

Data and the Limits of Starfleet Philosophy

Individuality is the fourth pillar on which Starfleet's philosophy is based. Its purpose is the development of selfhood, an individual's place in society, and the collective growth of society enhances each participant in return. While the promotion of individual behavior is at the forefront, it has a reciprocal relationship with the welfare of larger whole. This is embodied in Data's musical pursuits as a violinist.[4] After one concert, Captain Picard lauds his interpretation of a classical piece. In his response, Data explains that he used two different interpretations to play the part. He does not apparently realize he had made an individual choice in regards to playing that piece of music ("The Ensigns of Command"). By making such a choice, however, he participates in the evolution of musicology as a whole, as recognized by Captain Picard. In other instances, Data uses individual actions for the greater good, even if his decisions challenge his duties and violate the Prime Directive. He is able to use individual behavior to promote human goals beyond a blind obedience to rules and commands (*Insurrection*; "Pen Pals").

How free is Data? His status as an individual is often questioned. In the episode "The Measure of a Man," he is placed on trial to determine his sentience. If he is not sentient, then Data belongs to Starfleet as property and Starfleet can do what it likes with him. The episode asks viewers to determine whether Data is a commodity or a person. If he lacks freedom, then he must submit to Starfleet's dissecting him in order to duplicate Soong's designs. They know that the work of a genius like Noonian Soong cannot be reconstructed from scratch and believe the scientist is killed by the Crystalline Entity. However, a mass production of mechanical men means a devaluation of the original, its individuality, and its freedom. Data will be reduced to a single role as a replicable instrument to be used in life-threatening situations in which Starfleet does not want to expose (human) beings. The court selects Riker to act on Starfleet's behalf and he does a commendable job. The first officer is also an ironic choice; in "Up the Long Ladder," he strongly protests when the Mariposans steal his DNA to create new viable clones because they are not able to re-produce themselves naturally. An outraged Riker uncovers this plot and kills his and the doctor's clones to preserve their identities.[5]

At the end of the trial, the court supports Data's status as a human person, even though Riker demonstrates that the android can be deactivated and reactivated simply by flipping a switch.[6] Although the episode establishes that Data has freedom as an individual, his rights remain inconsistent. Later episodes of *The Next Generation* suggest machine exploitation is the norm for the Federation, even when the machines may be alive. In "Evolution" and "The Meaning of Life," Data points out that artificial life has individuality and must be respected. By pointing out these flaws, he shows the Federation can change and grow to accept new forms of life. But the definition of life remains anchored to the plot line, as these ethical dilemmas often center on the *Enterprise* and its crew in life-threatening situations. When it comes to beings like Moriarty (Sherlock Holmes' arch-nemesis who becomes sentient on the holodeck), who twice threatens the ship, his iconic role as a literary "villain" allows Picard to deny him individuality and rights. This contrasts with "Evolution," when the crew awards the rights of sentience to microscopic robots, the nanites, which show all signs of a life form, are able to communicate, and feel compassion for other creatures.

However, this situation is always a murky one. Data has rights, but those rights do not extend to his child, Lal. In "The Offspring," Data creates an asexual android, with no identifiers as male or female. In contrast to his own design, he offers it the possibility to define its own sex and appearance. This choice occurs before socialization; in other words, the offspring chooses a sex before it really knows what it means to be a woman or a man. Picard initially reacts with suspicion, firstly because the offspring is reminiscent with the Borg's robotic appearance and, secondly, because by choosing a female appearance, she signalizes a gendered threat for the Federation. Indeed, Picard expresses irritation, stating Data should have consulted him before undergoing this "project" and Picard does not want Lal considered a child on par with biological life. Picard's actions underscore Starfleet's position. Indeed, unlike the female Judge Advocate General in "The Measure of a Man" who rules that Data has sentience after learning he had sexual relations with a woman; and Counselor Troi, who supports Data's decision to procreate; the admiral in "The Offspring" is an older male who regards Lal strictly as a military tool.

Given the masculine dominance and the lack of gender-free entities in Starfleet, it seems that the Federation marginalizes gender-neutral beings.[7] When Lal chooses to become a woman, Starfleet is troubled. Data acquired sentience in "Measure of a Man," but Starfleet's patriarchy does not extend such freedoms to his daughter. Like Seven of Nine's experience on *Voyager*, Starfleet regards Lal with mistrust and more as a machine that can be turned on or off. Her status as a machine is heightened by her earlier appearance as a gender-free robot. Even though she ultimately looks more human than her father in terms of skin tones, Lal's ability to choose (and perhaps re-choose) her sex and appearance is a powerful new concept in the show because it allows the third option of preserving neutrality. Indeed, Lal decides early in the episode to accept a particular sex, even before understanding what it meant to be a human woman, as evidenced by Data explaining courtship rituals and teaching her how to blink. Thus, her appearance reads more like happenstance than a mature decision, which reflects Picard's and the admiralty's discomfort with accepting her as a person. She fulfills the expectations of the patriarchal crew by acting as a biological female, but this is not enough. The breakdown of her positronic brain at the end of the episode reflects this inner struggle over her innate and societal programming.

Lal presents a unique take on gender norms and sexuality in *Star Trek*. There are previous female robots/androids in the franchise, dating back to *The Original Series* in the episodes "I, Mudd," "What Are Little Girls Made Of?," and "Requiem for Methuselah." However, an android created as a female and one who chooses to become female are different topics. In "Inheritance," for instance, Data learns Soong rebuilt his wife, Juliana Tainer, with her engrams reflecting those of a woman. The android Tainer assumes she is the biological original, thus negating her need for socialization. She does not have to face the decision to become a female or a male, and the crew agrees to keep her identity a secret. By this point, however, Lal is a distant memory and Data sees no need to bring up his offspring. At this point, the decision to choose, which Lal opens, has closed, as did the larger question of gender-neutral beings. In choosing to be a woman, Lal made the "wrong" choice, which leads to her destruction.

As Lal and other living machines show, the Federation never resolves the issue of individuality and sentience. Even when Starfleet gives Data the right of sentience, they have limits restricting the individual within a hierarchical order. Throughout the series, Data comes up with unusual solutions to machine life, often serving as an advocate. At times, those solutions challenge Federation regulations. He does this for the greater good, which the Borg collective mind cannot imitate. But even when Starfleet recognizes Data, Hugh, or others as individuals, the Federation does not necessarily treat them as equals. As an android and as a woman, Lal is twice damned for defying Federation norms.

Defining the Borg

The series uses femininity and masculinity in two different ways: to identify gender and to describe in an abstract manner the power-based relationship between two social groups. If the philosophy of these groups reflects diametrically different ideas, the clash between femininity and masculinity take on the characteristics of good and evil. Since Starfleet is patriarchal in its outlook (the men do not wear dresses and, in addition to their femininity, the women must adhere to masculine characteristics when other officers address them as "sir" or "mister"[8]), the Borg represents the opposite of Starfleet. As a species, its philosophy and politics are based on matriarchy. The Borg Queen literally embodies this hierarchy, offering order and security because of her ubiquity. In her introduction in *First Contact*, she characterizes herself as the origin point for the Borg, in addition to the end point where everything would find its completion and perfection. Throughout this process, she "mothers" the hive mind, linking all the drones to her will. She identifies herself as the essence of the Borg using the words found in the Revelation of John (Rev. 12, 13). She refers to a messianic promise of salvation that frees each individual from the dependence on everyday concerns. Thus, her position is like that of a bee queen. The Borg reinforces this matriarchy through their assimilation process. They inject nano probes in a manner reminiscent of insects laying their eggs under the skin of other insects and animals to ensure the larvae have enough nutriment to eat after hatching. Hence, the Borg's reproductive manners echo an insect mother's habit. By doing so, the drones bring their assimilated "children" up under a collective hive united by the Borg Queen's singular consciousness. Without her, no drone can survive on its own because she offers them direction and order in exchange for their subordination under her will. No other species in the Star Trek universe do this.

The series originally introduced the Borg drones as asexual beings due to their implants that castrated both sexes, depriving them of sexual organs ("Q Who"). The removal of sexuality allows the two sexes to become equals of sorts: the former female is not defined by her body and the male is denied of his manhood and the symbolic phallic power. All power becomes centralized in the Borg Queen; her relationship to the drones is a maternal one which, on the surface, contradicts the supposed equality between men and women. The excising of a Borg drone from its collective relegates it into the old male-dominated power structures, and drones such as Hugh initially experience loneliness and confusion after living in "perfect" equality. The Borg's matriarchy not only violates Starfleet social norms, they also conflict with the audiences' acceptance of patriarchy. When a Borg leaves the collective to rejoin humanity, males, such as Hugh or the all-male drones under Lore in "Descent," have a much easier time to reassert their individualities.[9]

The structure of the Borg cube reinforces the collective's security under a queen. Each drone is equal to the others within the entire collective. Only a numeric identification tag distinguishes them, and even this is more of a serial number than an individual name. The identifier is created during the assimilation process, as are their specific tasks. By performing a specific task repeatedly, each drone contributes to the greater working of a vessel with no opportunities for promotion, career changes, reassignments, or other means to enhance their lives. The drones' equality means that, like a part in a machine, they can be easily replaced should a drone fail or is destroyed; indeed, drones disintegrate "dead" Borg simply by removing a few crucial components, leaving no sign of its existence. The one exception is Locutus, who has a name to represent his function as a "spokesman." During his assimilation process, Picard recognizes the erasure of his individuality and his manhood. A tear trickles down his cheeks as Picard's male characteristics and sexuality are erased. The Borg remove all sense of patriarchy, preventing his Starfleet training and his sense of individuality as a Starfleet officer from rising above that of the collective. As an equal, Picard is treated the same as all the others drones.

Compared with the Federation's respect for self-determination, members of the collective focuses their attention on a higher goal manifested in a shared group identity. The development of a single person must reflect the entire community and its needs. As a result, there are immediate penalties for misbehavior. The Borg Queen is the incarnation of this concept. Like a bee queen, she holds together the mass of drones and punishes them for deviancy. But unlike a bee queen, the Borg Queen lacks the ability to reproduce a new colony and a new queen. Her origin reflects the needs of the hive mind. Although canon sources never fully explain her background, there are several possible explanations. First, one drone might develop into the Borg Queen when the need arises. In the *Voyager* episode "Unimatrix Zero," she explains that she was a young drone who grew to become the leader of the Borg. Another possibility is that there are many clones of the Borg Queen. If one queen is destroyed, another clone replaces her seamlessly. Third, there might be a female species that is somewhat separate from the collective and are predetermined as leaders of the Borg. At this point, all of these possibilities are open to conjecture. Nevertheless, for the collective itself, the franchise makes it clear that the Borg drones enjoy a level of equality denied to gendered norms in the Federation.

Resisting the Collective: Hugh and Lore

The concept of a Borg Queen and a beehive mind undermines Starfleet's ideas of individuality. As an individual, Data can disobey orders because he recognizes morality and the greater good. However, not carrying out commands in a collective is an immediate threat against its welfare and requires immediate reprisals if order is to be maintained. The delinquent must be corrected or eliminated to maintain the cohesive whole.

In the episode "I, Borg," the crew finds a stranded Borg drone who initially identifies himself as "Third of Five." Crusher insists on bringing the drone aboard the *Enterprise*, despite Picard's protests. Picard, recalling his painful experiences as Locutus of Borg, prefers that the away team to destroy the drone immediately. However, La Forge and Crusher find a way to remove the Borg implants and they slowly re-build his individuality. La Forge succeeds, telling the Borg in a long conversation why humans do not want to be assimilated. A milestone of the conversation is the Borg's adaption of a specific name, Hugh.[10] For a male Borg, it is possible to accept individuality as better than a collective mind. Having been separated from the collective, he re-learns what individuality is and ends up championing these values. While aboard the *Enterprise*, he opposes Picard/Locutus's command to be re-assimilated and to help Locutus do the same to the ship and his friend, La Forge. By testing Hugh's reactions during this mock interrogation, Captain Picard recognizes the former drone's individuality, especially Hugh's using "I" instead of "we" when he refuses to assimilate Geordi, with whom he is on a first name basis. However, Hugh knows that the Borg will try to find their lost drone and that it is dangerous for the crew to help him resist. He decides that he must return to the collective. He chooses to sacrifice himself, which he views as a necessary evil, but he later changes his mind in the seventh season. In Hugh's last appearance, "Descent, Part II," he tells Captain Picard that the liberated Borg cannot return in the hive. But he conjectures they will find a way to live as individuals and work together as a society.[11] Picard, seeing the Borg "evolve" into a state closer to that of the Federation, wishes them luck.

Hugh, as the representative of a new individualized Borg, is the Borg's last appearance on *The Next Generation*, and viewers might assume they are no longer a threat. Indeed, that the crew of the *Enterprise* endorses them and—after removing Lore's corrupting influence—leaves them be, suggests that the Borg now fall under the Prime Directive, the Federation's non-interference regulation, ensuring and promoting the freedom and individual development of foreign civilizations.[12] Supposedly, the Federation considers the Prime Directive its primary guiding principle, even if it conflicts with the interests of the Federation on several occasions. However, up to this point, the Federation never applied the Prime Directive to the Borg because they had no intention of letting the collective develop "naturally." Instead, the Federation, acting in the name of self-preservation, only sees them as a threat. During their first encounter in "Q Who," Picard immediately judges the Borg as a source of danger, mostly due to Guinan's insight. After their narrow escape from the Borg, Picard and the Federation quickly reject all means of communication or peace. Starfleet eliminates all other options because the "collective" is not compatible with the Federation's value of individualism.

Instead, Starfleet recognizes that individuality is a weapon to destroy the Borg collective. Starfleet actually has a history of using machines to fight wars. In *The Original Series* episode "The Ultimate Computer," a super-computer arguably gains sentience and battles its human creators—but Kirk pulls the plug before the issue comes up. In *Star*

Trek: The Motion Picture, the *Enterprise* encounters a machine-world, *V'ger*. However, it turns out its central computer is an ancient human probe sent to collect knowledge. It was damaged on its journey, repaired by an alien species, and re-interpreted its instructions to return to its origin to fulfill it task. The transformation of *Enterprise* crewmember Ilia into a machine to serve as a liaison between *V'ger* and its human creators not only gives the machine a type of human individuality (alongside a mate), it serves as an early precedent for Starfleet's encountering the Borg. In Ilia's case, she, and her human lover choose to become "one" with *V'ger*.

When re-assimilated by the Borg, individuality itself is not sufficient to thwart the collective's invasive reprogramming. Rather, it requires a combination of the other pillars, such as freedom and self-determination. In the case of Hugh, his final individuality coalesces from the freedoms given to him by La Forge, affirmed by Picard, and took place in an environment conducive to the exploration of self-determination, preconditions which do not exist aboard a Borg cube. The two incompatible ideas of automated guidance and individuality cannot be reconciled ("I, Borg"). Indeed, Picard even says the *Enterprise* would fight to the death to protect Hugh if he wants asylum. In light of the Federation's and Borg's gender norms, a return to matriarchy under the Borg Queen would lead to "Hugh's" death and the return of Third of Five.

Thus, the Federation's individuality becomes a conduit for the Borg to escape their matriarchy. Hugh quickly gives up his collective obedience, by taking up a friendship with La Forge and not wanting him to be assimilated. He adopts his new name quickly, as do other male Borg when Lore takes them over in "Descent." Lore re-establishes a new order by re-uniting the infected drones under a redefined the role of leadership, under the guise of individuality. He is not a king/Borg Queen, but the "primus inter pares," in that, as a machine, he is more advanced than any other drone. Lore's self-hailed leadership becomes the ultimate goal for the drones to reach by competition and the assimilation of worthy races—of which he excludes humans in his drive to destroy the Federation. For Lore's Borg, perfection is achieved not only by assimilation, but by conditioning the physical body, in which weaker species are eliminated. Thus, Lore defines individuality as the contribution a single drone can make to the community, but one strictly under his vision of exclusion. This consists of using Borg individuality for experiments, and setbacks and malfunctions are excised from the community. "Sacrifice," a word that the original hive mind does not comprehend, becomes Lore's noble term to provide for the benefit of all. This initiation into individuality even elicits sympathy from the viewer; when the camera shows the "failed" Borg experiments, twitching in pain and helplessness, Riker looks horrified. Lore's fratricide of his followers illustrates the extent he goes to create and secure a community, but one modeled on his twisted behavior. It is clearly shown that Data, too, realizes Lore's brand of individuality is too dangerous, even for the vulnerable Borg, and deactivates his brother.

Transhumanism: A Bridge Between Borg and Humanity?

The fifth pillar of Starfleet's philosophy is humanism. The Borg are clearly *Star Trek*'s greatest challenge to humanism, with their artificial components and lack of individual selfhood. But how does humanism change when faced with technology that can "enhance" people beyond simple biology? Initial responses might argue that the Borg reflect transhumanism or post-humanism. But it is not clear-cut whether the Borg are transhuman or post-human and this dialog plays into the show's human adventure.

Transhumanism assumes that a higher and better quality of life is created by augmenting the human body with artificial parts. In this regard, transhuman life forms are found among the Borg and Starfleet because of the use of synthetically-produced organs, such as Picard's heart and La Forge's VISOR.[13] The artificial parts raise the question about how a society must accommodate those who cannot are wary of technological enhancements, up to the point of rejecting technology completely. For the most part, the series ignores the potential tension between individualism and self-determination versus the presumed benefits of a technology-driven lifestyle. The most prominent example of this conflict, *Star Trek: Insurrection*, features a race called the Ba'ku, who reject technology and Picard sides with them to resist their forced relocation when the Federation learns their planet possessed the secret to eternal youth. However, the film does not resolve the issue, but leaves it in the hands of the Federation Council and, as of this writing, the fate of the Ba'ku remains unknown. On the whole, however, because of the Prime Directive, Starfleet and the Federation accept those who refuse technology, even though Starfleet clearly believes in technological progress. In "Ethics," for instance, Crusher and a guest-star, Dr. Russell, discuss how far a doctor should go to treat Lieutenant Worf after he broke his back in an accident. Crusher ultimately allows Russell to proceed with a dangerous procedure that kills Worf, and it is only because of the Klingon's natural body reserves that bring him back to life. For Crusher, the happy ending does not justify risking an otherwise healthy patient who could live a full life. However, Russell remains vindicated and Worf is fully mobile by the next episode. In contrast, the Borg do not have this dilemma because of their compulsory assimilation and bodily transformation. They can technically live forever, whereas death remains a part of life for the organic-based members of the Federation.

In posthumanism, humans no longer need to advance physically and naturally because they consider themselves fully developed biological beings. Instead, they turn to artificial intelligence as the next stage to transfer the spirit of man into an artificial intelligence and become immortal. Data and Lore are post-human machines. Lore has the memories of the colonists where he was "born," and he also has the possibility to create a new purpose and mindset for the individualized, aimless, and conflicted Borg. Lore ultimately rejects both societies, which leads to his dismantlement in the former and death in the latter.

Data also has the potential to be the next step for human consciousness. He retains the life experiences of Soong's fellow colonists, has the memories of his daughter Lal, and, at one point, is commandeered by the aging, dying scientist Ira Graves, who tries to live forever by forcibly transferring his spirit (and enormous ego) into Data's mechanical body. Graves's violent takeover of the android's body points to a second form of posthumanism, the dominance of one species by acquiring another, artificial body, even against the other's will ("The Schizoid Man"). Data might retain some of Graves's memories when the takeover ends, but it is never referenced again. Even when Data dies in *Nemesis*, his consciousness arguably lives on in another Soong prototype, B-4. Despite all this potential for immortality, however, Data still idealizes humanity, and even mortality, as preferable to his android state.

Star Trek: The Next Generation thus raises the possibility of post-human immortality, although the series never develops this premise. Theorist Rosi Braidotti argues in favor of a post-human society which individuals, their community, and their species develop a new definition of self and, on that basis, create a new set of ethics. Following Katherine Hayles's critical remarks about the scientific papers on post-humanism, Braidotti creates a counter-proposal to the binary between the Borg and the Federation (45–47). Neither posthumanism nor transhumanism are incompatible with humanism. While posthumanism overcomes the sense of human supremacy in and about their environment, transhumanism merges nature and technology. By choosing one of these positions, society reconciles the divide between machine and man by creating new ethical guidelines. According to Briadotti, in a post-human society, the term *humanism* itself is no longer adequate because it is associated with obsolete, and no longer relevant, thoughts and ideas. Therefore, she introduces the term *zoe*. Zoeism is the counterpart of humanism in a post-human world that overcomes the supremacy of humans (Braidotti 103). The Federation in *TNG* reflects these values. Soong's androids, Data and Lore, are a middle-ground approach because they do not lose their status as androids, but blend facets of humanism into their construct. They reference a post-human society in which their innate mechanical superiority is incomplete without human elements. Data sees himself as inferior to humans while Lore cannot exist without his very human traits. Together, their characterizations reflect the Federation's universal ethics based on axiomatic, anchored ethical principles and disciplinary actions for violating those principles. In the end, Data executes Lore.

The Borg are also post–human beings, but not in the sense Briadotti advocates. The assimilation process requires the abandonment of the self and the idea of individual species, the surmounting of death, and the abolition of sciences—all of which are subsumed in the Borg collective under the Queen. However, the Borg completely abandon humanism and, through their assimilation process, force other species to accept posthumanism against their will. Under these circumstances, the collective insists it wishes to promote "perfection" for all, but this uncompromising dominance renders their ethical and moral foundation moot. Rather than seek to co-exist, the Borg attempt to lead everyone to accept their ideals of perfection predominated by the idea of the supremacy of a "collective" species—themselves—above all the others.

In *ST: TNG*, the Prime Directive is not only important for defining the relationships between Starfleet and foreign powers, it guarantees the uninfluenced development of undeveloped species inside the Federation and its territories. This policy, General Order 1, condemns the predominance of one species over any other species on ethical grounds. However, the Federation has trouble applying the Prime Directive toward their own mechanical creations. Looking at androids or holograms in the series, it seems the Federation "protects" living technology as long as it operates within the given parameters— mostly as tools, like the exocomps. Lore is initially dissembled after he operated independently from social norms, ignoring and despising his fellow colonists, and then executed in "Descent, Part 2" when he directly attacks the Federation. His death is significant, because it is a form of capital punishment. That his own brother carries out the death sentence shows that, even though Data and Lore constitute a new species of artificial life, recognized as sentient and having full legal rights, Data's affiliation with the Federation takes priority over all else. Lore's final words are a claim that he loves his brother, but, without emotions, the stoic Data cannot respond in the same way and simply bids him good-bye.

Conclusion: "The Measure of a Man"?

The Borg collective serves as an antithesis to Commander Lieutenant Data and the Federation. They share a common base. Both of them have transhuman and post-human members who use technology for improving their quality of life. While the Borg supplement their organic bodies with nanotechnology so they can survive and to carry out their duties in deadly environments, including outer space without hazard suits, members of the Federation maintain their largely fragile, biological forms of existence by developing and deploying life-prolonging medical technology. At the same time, organic beings include the concept of death as part of life. For the Borg, death is irrelevant because one drone can easily replace a dead Borg's vacant position to fulfill the same tasks without any noticeable change.

As an antithesis of Starfleet's patriarchal system, matriarchy arose as the most important criterion for the Borg. The dualism between matriarchy and patriarchy bleeds into other characteristics, such as Starfleet's patriarchal structure championing freedom, individuality, self-determination, and humanity. In comparison, the Borg hive operates under a queen who oversees a collective based on equality, heteronomy and anonymity. This juxtaposition characterizes the tensions between the two groups in the Star Trek franchise. The transition from the matriarchy into the patriarchy receives special attention because it highlights the limits of Starfleet's ideology of self-determination, individualism, and equality, especially when it came to gender. When a Borg left the collective, such as Third of Five, he not only gains one pillar—such as freedom—he acquires the entire patriarchal order. Hugh's initial freedom does not allow him to sever his connection to the collective. Only after Hugh adopts the responsibilities of Starfleet's ideals of individuality and self-determination (as a new Borg leader) under the *Enterprise* crew's approval, does he become his own man. In addition, the position of women in Starfleet vessels must be taken into account, because they, too, subscribe to this patriarchal system. The re-conversion of female drones into human women, such as *Voyager's* Seven of Nine, included assimilation into Starfleet's gender hierarchy; Seven immediately embraces Starfleet's regulation for skin-tight outfits. Ultimately, Starfleet's patriarchy and the Borg's matriarchy take on the characteristics of a struggle between good and evil, with Starfleet suffering enormous losses in various altercations, but defeating the Borg each time.

Freedom, individuality, and self-determination are closely linked and limited only by the liberty of the others. These liberties are irrelevant for the Borg inasmuch as the hive subjugates everything in its path.[14] However, the android in Starfleet, Data, finds his niche to develop his freedom, individuality and self-determination. But this depends on others granting him this space. After his trial in "The Measure of a Man," he becomes legally "approved" to develop his identity, albeit in Starfleet's terms. Nevertheless, this applicability proves limited when the crew encounters other forms of machine life and conflicts arose in accordance to Prime Directive. From Data's daughter to the exocomps, to Professor Moriarty, and then the *Enterprise* itself in "Emergence," the series consistently addresses the definition of rights, and even of life, in a post-human society as technology continued to advance. As the series struggles to re-define life and rights, this process appears to be an everlasting task. Data's exceptional case over whether or not an android would or should have the same rights like any other organic beings continues in *Voyager* through the struggle of the holographic Doctor. Re-defining these rights means Starfleet has to re-evaluate how they equate matriarchy with the Borg; this gender role play is backward for the Federation, and makes this utopia seem archaic rather than futuristic. The marginalization of women and facets of femininity, in particular, makes the Federation unattractive to 21st century sensibilities.

Looking back at our set of questions, we find that technology is only one set of tools and methods for mastering life and its circumstances. However, the relationships between people are more important than any piece of technology, as the *Enterprise* crew proves time and again when their humanity triumphs over the cold behavior of the Borg. This is seen in "Q Who," when Picard mourns the loss of life from the *Enterprise*'s first encounter with the Borg. Q chastises Picard, perceiving the captain's humanism as a sign of weakness. But Q misunderstands that Picard's sense of exploration is part of a human drive to seek out the unknown, not conquer it. For Starfleet, this drive is part of its mission of self-betterment and a reflection of universal human values. For the Borg, efficiency and immortality require them to surrender all else; the sense of self gives way to the perpetuation of the status quo. To set other priorities, as Hugh did, means to lose sight of the general objective and to betray the other drones. As Hugh's, Lore's, and Data's journeys show, post-human and technology-based lifestyles end up reflecting or challenging human values in accordance with individual personal choices.

In the course of *Star Trek: The Next Generation*, the Borg and the Federation clash in the Alpha Quadrant, but never neither side achieves final victory in any decisive battle.[15] The end of the Borg, fittingly, occurs at the border between their home turf and the Federation's. In the finale of *Star Trek: Voyager*, Captain Janeway's crew and a Starfleet armada finally end the Borg threat when the gathered forces of the Federation destroy the Borg Queen for good. Appropriately, by leaving the Delta Quadrant to return to the Federation, Janeway ends her autonomy in favor of rejoining the male dominated status quo. Just as Picard and Starfleet battle the Borg matriarchy throughout the series, it is apt that *Star Trek*'s much-heralded first female lead, Kathryn Janeway, saves the Federation from the only matriarchy in the franchise.[16] In the end, the "good" order is restored.

Notes

1. On women as nurturers, see Simon Ledder's, Jens Kolata's, and Oonagh Hayes' essay in this volume.
2. Androgyny is not limited to a particular sexual orientation. Rather, a person shows both male and female characteristics. Tasha Yar has a more masculine hairstyle, short cut hair. She wears the same uniform as her male colleagues. At the same time, however, she shows her full femininity in "The Naked Now."
3. On Troi and Yar, see Erin C. Callahan's, Joul Smith's, and Peter W. Lee's essays in this volume.
4. See Tom Zlabinger's essay in this volume.
5. See Simon Ledder's, Jens Kolata's and Oonagh Hayes' essay in this volume.
6. Data's ruling apparently has limits. The holographic Doctor in *Voyager* is also subjected to a trial to judge his sentience.
7. On gender and sexual "others," see Bruce E. Drushel's essay in this volume.
8. In the first episode of *Star Trek: Voyager*, Kathryn Janeway rebels against this tradition, stating she does not like the title "sir" and prefers the neutral term "captain" rather than "ma'am" ("Caretaker").
9. *Voyager*'s Seven of Nine has a very complicated reintegration with humanity and the crew. She is transformed directly in a Barbie doll, dressed in tight clothes to underscore her sexualized body. Her implants are removed to accentuate her curves, except for some ornamental ones (Zur Nieden 113f). According to the series, Seven was assimilated at the age of six without full cultural socialization. She did not known what individuality was because she only changed her childhood need for parental guidance into a maternal dependency on the Borg Queen without the natural emancipation from the family to live independently. Both relationships do not stand on a sexual basis. The absence of masculinity and a male-dominated structure in her youth does not enable her to respond and act adequately in the male-dominated Starfleet. Analyzing her situation after her emancipation, Seven wonders whether or not her position in the Borg collective would differ from that on *Voyager* ("The Gift"). Seven changes into a new dependency: her freedom, independency, and individuality are limited by the bylaws of masculinity. The Borg Queen sums it up when she says Seven

underwent an operation, received new clothes, and was stylized into a human female ("Dark Frontier, Part 2"). She asks whether or not Seven was simply re-assimilated by Starfleet.

10. At, first, the German word "du," meaning "you," was used as Hugh's name. Hugh was originally supposed to say, "We are you," which tantalizingly hints at the Borg's origins.

11. In *Voyager*, the Borg has some semblance of individuality by tapping into "Unimatrix Zero." When the Borg Queen realizes the existence of Unimatrix Zero, she cracks down on the collective, correctly recognizing that it threatens the collective because it is a haven for Borg to enter a private zone of individualism. Furthermore, the Borg Queen cannot communicate with the drones, hear their thoughts, or control them when they are there ("Unimatrix Zero Part 1"; "Unimatrix Zero Part 2").

12. On the Prime Directive, see Larry A. Grant's essay in this volume.

13. On La Forge's VISOR and the concept of disability and biopolitics, see Simon Ledder's, Jens Kolata's and Oonagh Hayes' essay in this volume

14. Fittingly, in *Voyager*, the Borg met their match with Species 8472, a biological "collective" intent on destroying inferior life forms, including the Borg and Kathryn Janeway's ship.

15. See Justin Ream's and Alexander Lee's essay in this volume.

16. In "All Good Things…," audiences actually see a female captain played by a regular in Captain Beverly Picard. However, she loses her ship aiding her ex-husband. Even worse, she willingly sacrifices her ship even though she initially thinks Picard was on a delusional quest to save the universe.

Works Cited

"All Good Things… Part 1." *Star Trek: The Next Generation—The Complete Seventh Season*. Writ. Ronald D. Moore and Brannon Barga, Dir. Winrich Kolbe, Paramount Home Video, 2002, DVD.

"All Good Things… Part 2." *Star Trek: The Next Generation—The Complete Seventh Season*. Writ. Ronald D. Moore and Brannon Barga, Dir. Winrich Kolbe, Paramount Home Video, 2002, DVD.

"The Best of Both Worlds Part 1." *Star Trek: The Next Generation—The Complete Third Season*. Writ. Michael Piller, Dir. Cliff Bole, Paramount Home Video, 2002, DVD.

"The Best of Both Worlds Part 2." *Star Trek: The Next Generation—The Complete Fourth Season*. Writ. Ronald D. Moore, Dir. Les Landau, Paramount Home Video, 2002, DVD.

Boyd, Katarina G. "Cyborgs in Utopia: The Problem of Radical Difference in *Star Trek: The Next Generation*." *Enterprise Zones: Critical Position on* Star Trek. Ed. Harrison, Taylor, Projansky, Sarah, Otto, Kent A., Helford, Elyse Rae, Oslo: Westview, 1996, S. 95–113. Print.

Braidotti, Rosi. *The Posthuman*. Cambridge, Malden, MA: Policy, 2013.Print.

"Brothers." *Star Trek: The Next Generation—The Complete Fourth Season*. Writ. Rick Berman, Dir. Rob Bowman, Paramount Home Video, 2002, DVD.

"Caretaker." *Star Trek: Voyager—The Complete First Season*. Writ. Michael Piller and Jeri Taylor. Dir. Winrich Kolbe, Paramount Home Video, 2004, DVD.

"Chain of Command Part 1." *Star Trek: The Next Generation—The Complete Sixth Season*. Writ. Ronald D. Moore, Frank Abatemarco, Dir. Robert Scheerer, Paramount Home Video, 2002, DVD.

"Chain of Command Part 2." *Star Trek: The Next Generation—The Complete Sixth Season*. Writ. Frank Abatemarco, Dir. Les Landau, Paramount Home Video, 2002, DVD.

"Dark Frontier Part 2." *Star Trek: Voyager—The Complete Fifth Season*. Writ. Brannon Braga, and Joe Menosky, Dir. Terry Windell, Paramount Home Video, 2004, DVD.

"Data." *Memory Alpha*, 2017, Web. 21 Apr. 2017. <http://memory-alpha.wikia.com/wiki/Data>

"Descent Part 1." *Star Trek: The Next Generation—The Complete Sixth Season*. Writ. Ronald D. Moore, Jeri Taylor, Dir. Alexander Singer, Paramount Home Video, 2002, DVD.

"Descent Part 2." *Star Trek: The Next Generation—The Complete Seventh Season*. Writ. René Echevarria, Dir. Alexander Singer, Paramount Home Video, 2002, DVD.

"Emergence." *Star Trek: The Next Generation—The Complete Seventh Season*. Writ. Brannon Braga, Dir. Cliff Bole, Paramount Home Video, 2002, DVD.

"The Enemy." *Star Trek: The Next Generation—The Complete Third Season*. Writ. David Kemper and Michael Piller, Dir. David Carson, Paramount Home Video, 2002, DVD.

"The Ensigns of Command." *Star Trek: The Next Generation—The Complete Third Season*. Writ. Melinda M. Snodgrass, Dir. Cliff Bole, Paramount Home Video, 2002, DVD.

"Ethics." *Star Trek: The Next Generation—The Complete Fifth Season*. Writ. Ronald D. Moore, Sara Charno and Stuart Charno, Dir. Chip Chalmers, Paramount Home Video, 2002, DVD.

"The Gift." *Star Trek: Voyager—The Complete Second Season*. Writ. Joe Menosky, Dir. Anson Williams, Paramount Home Video, 2004, DVD.

"I, Borg." *Star Trek: The Next Generation—The Complete Fifth Season*. Writ. René Echevarria, Dir. Robert Lederman, Paramount Home Video, 2002, DVD.

"I, Mudd." *Star Trek*. Writ. Stephen Kandel and David Gerrold. Dir. Marc Daniels. *Netflix*. Web. 8 Sept. 2016.

"Inheritance." *Star Trek: The Next Generation—The Complete Seventh Season*. Writ. Dan Koeppel, René Echevarria, Dir. Robert Scheerer, Paramount Home Video, 2002, DVD.

"The Measure of a Man." *Star Trek: The Next Generation—The Complete Second Season*. Writ. Melinda M. Snodgrass, Dir. Robert Scheerer, Paramount Home Video, 2002, DVD.

"The Offspring" *Star Trek: The Next Generation—The Complete Third Season*. Writ. René Echevarria, Dir. Jonathan Frakes, Paramount Home Video, 2002, DVD.

"Pen Pals." *Star Trek: The Next Generation—The Complete Second Season*. Writ. Melinda M. Snodgrass and Hanna Louise Shearer, Dir. Winrich Kolbe, Paramount Home Video, 2002, DVD.

Philips, Mary. "Leadership, Eroticism and Abjection: *Star Trek and the* Borg Queen." *The Physicality of Leadership: Gesture, Entanglement, Taboom Possibilities*. Ed. Donna Ladkin and Steven S. Taylor. Bingley: Howard House, 2014. 155–75. Print.

"Q Who." *Star Trek: The Next Generation—The Complete Second Season*. Writ. Maurice Hurley, Dir. Rob Bowman, Paramount Home Video, 2002, DVD.

Roberts, Robin. *Sexual Generations:* Star Trek: The Next Generation *and Gender*. Champaign: University of Illinois Press, 1999. Print.

"The Schizoid Man." *Star Trek: The Next Generation—The Complete Second Season*. Writ. Tracy Torné, Richard Manning and Hans Beimler, Dir. Les Landau, Paramount Home Video, 2002, DVD.

Star Trek: First Contact. Dir. Jonathan Frakes. Perf. Patrick Stewart, Jonathan Frakes, and Brent Spiner. Paramount Home Video, 1998. DVD.

Star Trek: Insurrection. Dir. Jonathan Frakes. Perf. Patrick Stewart, Jonathan Frakes, and Brent Spiner. Paramount Home Video, 1998. DVD.

Star Trek: Nemesis. Dir. Stuart Baird. Perf. Patrick Stewart, Jonathan Frakes, and Brent Spiner. Paramount Home Video, 2002. DVD.

"Tapestry." *Star Trek: The Next Generation—The Complete Sixth Season*. Writ. Ronald D. Moore, Dir. Les Landau, Paramount Home Video, 2002, DVD.

"Unimatrix Zero Part 1." *Star Trek: Voyager—The Complete Sixth Season*. Writ. Brannon Braga, Joe Menosky and Mike Sussmann, Dir. Allan Kroeker, Paramount Home Video, 2004, DVD.

"Unimatrix Zero Part 2." *Star Trek: Voyager—The Complete Seventh Season*. Writ. Brannon Braga, Joe Menosky and Mike Sussmann, Dir. Mike Vejar, Paramount Home Video, 2004, DVD.

Zur Nieden, Andrea. "Schönheit ist Irrelevant? Die Sexualisierung von Cyborgs in *Star Trek*" *Data, Body, Sex Machine: Technoscience and Science Fiction aus feministischer Sicht*. Ed. Karin Giselbrecht and Michaela Hafner. Vienna: Tunia-Kant, 2001. Print.

"It's Kirk vs. Picard!"

Changing Notions of Heroism
from the 1960s to the 1990s

Katharina Thalmann

In 1991, *TV Guide*'s August 31 issue pitted captains James T. Kirk and Jean-Luc Picard against each other to celebrate *Star Trek*'s 25th anniversary. "It's Kirk vs. Picard!," the magazine declared on the front cover, which also featured an image of the two captains in their signature poses: Picard looking intently ahead, Kirk with arms crossed and sporting a barely perceptible smile. Prominent commentators, including science-fiction writer Isaac Asimov and astronaut Buzz Aldrin, weighed in on who was "best." Although they offered different perspectives on the two captains, the jurors did not determine a winner, and instead agreed that each captain was a hero of his time. As Mary Henderson, curator at the Air and Space Museum in Washington, described it: "Kirk is a man of the '60s. Picard is a man of the '90s" (qtd. in Marin 5).

In this essay, I do not intend to debate which of the two *Enterprise* captains is "best." Instead, I compare and contrast the representations of Kirk in *The Original Series* (*TOS*) and Picard in *The Next Generation* (*TNG*) to trace changing notions and articulations of heroism between the 1960s and 1990s. In line with Henderson's quote above, the two are fictional representations of larger cultural and political developments and products of conventions in the television industry. While Kirk is seen as a classic Western hero and a representative of the heroic ideals associated with the Kennedy presidency and its mythical narratives about the New Frontier, Picard has a different function in *TNG*. He is constructed as a skilled diplomat who has to secure the Federation and maintain its survival and as a paternal authority figure. Like George Washington, who was heroized as *pater patriae* in the Early Republic, Picard is heroized as *pater navis*, as the metaphorical father of his ship and crew, with the *Enterprise* quite literally representing the nation, the "Ship of State."

Picard is also emblematic of a new notion of heroism that emerged in television productions of the 1990s. On the one hand, he is a much more multi-dimensional character than Kirk, which has to do with changes in the television industry that moved from the classic network into the multi-channel era. Television shows began to place a heightened emphasis on complexity, visual effects, and seriality; while *TOS* can be conceptualized as a TV series, with the plotlines resolved by the end of each episode, *TNG* increasingly featured elements of the TV serial (cf. Allrath, Gymnich, and Surkamp 5–6).

On the other hand, Picard is also a much more vulnerable and flawed hero. As his body is increasingly subjected to physical tests, torture, and transmutations, undergoing pain and suffering, Picard does not simply assert his physical strength in phaser fights or hand-to-hand combat, as was the case in *TOS*. Rather, he is exceptional because of or despite his vulnerability, due to his mental strength, his tolerance for pain, his endurance and perseverance. In this context, Picard can be read as a post–Cold War and post–Reagan hero who stands in contrast to the overly masculine, tough action heroes prevalent during the 1980s and who prefigures the complex, flawed television (anti-)heroes of the 1990s to 2000s.

Heroism in TOS: *Space Cowboy on the Frontier*

When *Star Trek* debuted on American television in 1966, the pilot episode "Where No Man Has Gone Before" differed significantly from the original pilot "The Cage," written by Gene Roddenberry and produced by Desilu Studios. "The Cage" featured an enigmatic but sensitive captain called Christopher Pike, a female first officer, and, in a minor role, a pointy-eared but not yet unemotional Vulcan by the name of Spock.[1] It was ultimately rejected by NBC executives because they feared it might be too "cerebral" and the role of a rational, cold female officer too unconventional for viewers in the 1960s (Gregory 26; Pearson and Davies 25). While elements of "The Cage" were recycled in the first-season two-parter "The Menagerie," the later pilot starred a very different cast and followed a different plotline. The character Spock now had a much more prominent role, the actress who played the first officer was relegated to play a nurse, the captain went by the name of James Kirk, and overall the episode relied more heavily on the action-adventure genre.

A product of the interplay (and power plays) between network executives, producers, writers, and consumers, *TOS* illustrates the workings of television productions in general. As Christopher Anderson writes, in popular culture, "Meaning develops according to a delicate operation of similarity and difference. In this process a single story gains significance both through its identification with stories that preceded it and through its disruption of those stories" (qtd. in Gregory 17). In the classic network era of the 1960s, the delicate maneuvering between the familiar and the unfamiliar, the known and the unknown, was particularly important since the three major networks aimed to attract a very broad viewership.[2] As a television show about life in space, *the* genuine unknown at the time, *TOS* was already based on a very different premise than most television productions in the 1960s. Consequently, it is not surprising that the *TOS* producers rejected some of the unconventional elements and characters of "The Cage" or Roddenberry's early plans for the series. It is also not surprising that it mixed tropes recurrent in the genres of science-fiction, the Western, and melodrama to present a narrative about a heteronormative male, white hero who was not too different from the (pop) cultural and political icons of the time: the presidential hero John F. Kennedy and the classical Western hero.

As an allegory of the Cold War conflict of the 1960s, *Star Trek* has, as Rick Worland convincingly argues, "carried the mythos of the New Frontier to the final frontier" (20). John F. Kennedy's campaign slogan of a "New Frontier," calling on Americans in the 1960s to face "the uncharted areas of science and space, unsolved problems of peace and war, unconquered pockets of ignorance and prejudice, unanswered questions of poverty and surplus" ("Address"), was already echoed by the *Enterprise*'s mission statement "to boldly go" and explore the final frontier of space. The *Enterprise*'s weekly intergalactic and utopian explorations, while ostensibly serving to discover and map the unknown, in fact, mostly revolved around similar challenges to those that Kennedy identified: unsolved problems of war with the belligerent Klingons and Romulans, assisting aliens and human(oid)s in need, and overcoming prejudices, racism, and sexism—above all its own. Each episode served as a foray into the frontier of the future and another allegorical foray into the New Frontier of the 1960s. Because of the conventions of television in the 1960s and the show's classical dramatic structure, of course, the problems that the *Enterprise* crew faced were usually resolved by the end of each 45-minute episode and the crew continued on its journey, continuing to extend the New Frontier.

As several scholars point out, structurally, these episodic journeys of the *Enterprise* bear many similarities to the heroic journeys of classic Greek mythology and the hero's journey that Joseph Campbell describes in *The Hero with a Thousand Faces* (cf. 224–25; Bernardi 91). For these scholars, the mythical hero in *TOS* is not just the captain of the *Enterprise*, but the entire crew. According to John Shelton Lawrence and Robert Jewett, the crew performs "the role of cosmic sheriff, problem-solver, and plenipotentiary" (229). In the same vein, Donald Palumbo argues, with regard to the early *Star Trek* films, the protagonist is actually an "ensemble hero," defined as "a collective hero combining attributes and experiences of several [characters]" (144).

Although it is true that much of the plot and moral discussions in *TOS* are driven by, and much of the humor derives from, the dynamics between Kirk, the overly logical Spock, and the overly humanist McCoy, Kirk is nevertheless the sole hero protagonist of the show. I agree with Stephen McVeigh that "Spock and McCoy [a]re presented as different elements of Kirk's psyche" (202) and often serve to emphasize Kirk's exceptionalism. In many episodes, while McCoy and Spock bicker about the limits of rationality, Kirk has already moved on, formed his opinion, and issued commands that propel the plot. The symbolism of the captain's chair also stresses his exceptionalism and individualism (cf. Johnstone 59). While the bridge contains seats and stations for several other leading officers, the captain's chair is clearly at the center of the bridge and there is a spatial distance between Kirk and all other characters. In similar fashion, while many episodes place Kirk in risky situations on board the *Enterprise* or on planetary missions, he is always reinstated in both his seat and command by the end of the episode. In "The Enemy Within," for instance, Kirk is split into two selves, the good and the evil sides of his character, by a defective transporter beam. After the two selves are merged to form a whole captain, the conclusion of the episode features an overhead shot of Kirk at the center of the bridge, sitting in his chair, and reinstated as the leader of the *Enterprise*.

The "hero-tales" (Slotkin 3) of *TOS* revolve around and hinge on the heroism of the *Enterprise*'s captain, just as Kennedy figured as a heroic leader in his narrative about the New Frontier. Quite literally, Kirk thus functions as a fictional representation of and successor to Kennedy. As Henry Jenkins writes, "James T. Kirk, the youngest captain in Star Fleet [sic] history, was the fictional embodiment of the heroic myths surrounding John F. Kennedy, PT boat captain, the youngest president in American history" (151). Kirk adheres to the heroic virtues and habitus fashioned by representations of Kennedy in the mythology of the New Frontier or his Camelot presidency: he is equally versed in literature and military strategy, highly versatile and intelligent, uninhibitedly optimistic about the future but unrelenting in the face of the enemy (Worland 24–25). Furthermore, Kirk also inhabits a highly heteronormative and virulent male role, leading one critic to call Kirk "the James Bond of interstellar travel" (Cranny-Francis 274). In the television series, Kirk's masculinity is both emphasized in his (numerous) relationships with female characters (cf. Helford 11–12), but also through "the gaze" of the camera that often lingers on Kirk's upper naked body (e.g., in "Charlie X," when he teaches a young man self-defense) or shows his virile body in full shots during action sequences ("Where No Man Has Gone Before"; "Court Martial").

Kirk's intellectualism is seldom made explicit by showing his face buried in (electronic) books, but signature close-ups of his face that appear in almost every episode clearly establish him as an intellectual, reflective leader in the Kennedy tradition. Close-ups show him looking intently ahead with a brooding expression and his head tilted slightly to the side; the shots that follow almost always show him giving commands. Furthermore, altero-characterization helps to portray Kirk as an intellectual, for instance, when a former fellow student from Starfleet Academy refers to him as a walking stack of academic books ("Where No Man Has Gone Before"). Other characters also underline Kirk's exceptionalism as a leader. In "Charlie X" McCoy informs a young man who witnesses Kirk in command for the first time that the *Enterprise* captain is an exceptional leader and, in "Balance of Terror," even the hostile Romulan leader grudgingly admits that Kirk is a cunning commander and savvy military strategist.

Kirk combines the heroic attributes embodied by Kennedy with those of the classical Western hero (cf. Worland 20). Tellingly, Gene Roddenberry had pitched the first pilot for the series as "'Wagon Train' to the Stars" (Whitfield and Roddenberry 21). In the series, the red-colored surfaces, papier-mâché rocks, and backdrops of great vistas that often serve as environments for away teams provide the symbolic landscape for Kirk's frontier heroism. Similarly, the *Enterprise*'s view-screen offers a view of the final frontier that is evocative of 19th-century landscape paintings of the American West. As Jan Johnson-Smith points out, the screen "fram[es] the stars outside and creat[es] the kind of artificial composite vista [Albert] Bierstadt and [Frederic Edwin] Church created in their depictions of the western frontier" (107). In return, the screen also casts the *Enterprise* crew and their captain as daring frontiersmen (and women) looking out at uncharted territory.

Kirk thus represents the cinematic cowboy hero who rides into a troubled town and saves its population and the damsel-in-distress, only to disappear into the sunset again—because of *TOS*'s episodic structure, of course, he repeats this on a weekly basis. Consequently, as in the classic Western, many of the episodes feature climactic fights between Kirk and human or alien villains. "Where No Man Has Gone Before" culminates with a fight between Kirk and his former close friend, Commander Gary Mitchell, who has turned into an absolutist godlike figure. Set against a dark-bluish sky and a rugged landscape with sandstone buttes, Kirk kills Mitchell after a prolonged fight scene that involves phaser rifles, fists, and several rocks; it leaves the Western hero with a torn shirt,[3] but also clearly vindicated. In another nod to 1960s geo-politics, Kirk's virulent and almost ruthless individual heroism in this episode prevents Mitchell from spearheading an absolutist regime of supreme beings.

The third-season episode "Spectre of the Gun" literally places Kirk and some of his crewmembers in the mythical West when they are forced to reenact the 1881 gunfight at the OK Corral in Tombstone, Arizona.[4] Again, the episode ends with a climactic fight in which Kirk demonstrates both his physical and moral superiority, but the episode also borrows from Western cinematography. The barren landscape, complete with the occasional tumbleweed, refers to the mythical old West, while only the red sky reveals that this frontier town is located in space. Full shots show Kirk and his crew preparing for the fight with the Earps, their holstered guns clearly visible, and close-ups show them looking at their enemy in combat. In these shots, the composition always places Kirk at the center of the group. In one full shot, for instance, he is standing slightly in the foreground, his upper body turned to the camera, while the other characters are all turned to the side or standing slightly behind the captain.

"Spectre of the Gun" establishes Kirk as a successor to the pioneers of the mythical West—at one point, he even mentions that his ancestors were pioneers themselves. But while the action scenes serve to underline Kirk's bodily supremacy, they also show a difference to the heroes of the Old West; he overcomes the urge to use violence as he refrains from killing his opponent in the end. Both Kirk and the nation as a whole, the episode suggests, have evolved from the problematic conjectures and violent character of Western expansion, despite, or due to, their retaining their innate heroic and virtuous quality.[5] The episode thus underlines both Kirk's and the nation's exceptionalism.

Through *TOS*'s nods to Kennedy's promise of the New Frontier and the mythology of the old frontier, Kirk serves as the individualistic Western hero and exceptional leader who is able to defeat the show's many villains, especially the thinly-veiled allegorical representations of the totalitarian communists, the Romulans and the Klingons, and who is able to assert himself in the wilderness of space. In the following, I offer a close reading of another allegorical episode, in which Kirk is worshipped by the indigenous inhabitants of a distant planet, in order to further illustrate how the show constructs Kirk's heroic habitus. The episode also helps to point out similarities and differences between Kirk and Picard as there is a *TNG* episode in which Picard goes through a similar experience.

The Hero's (Double) Audience: Kirok vs. the Picard

In the third-season episode "The Paradise Syndrome" Kirk loses his memory and is left stranded on the planet Amerind, home to descendants of Native American tribes, while the rest of the *Enterprise* crew deal with an asteroid threatening to annihilate the native population (and Kirk). Framed by natural sunlight, Kirk quite literally appears as a *deus ex machina* in front of two female natives who believe him to be their planet's legendary savior. When he performs the "miracle" of reviving a child through CPR—a technique that he miraculously remembers—the tribe's elders quickly decide to make "Kirok" their new medicine man, much to the chagrin of the previous one and much to the delight of the tribe's priestess, Miramanee. As tradition has it, Kirok marries her, and soon they live a rather picturesque life on Amerind, until the looming arrival of the asteroid makes the tribe realize that Kirok is not a god and they attempt to stone him and his wife. Only when Spock and McCoy save both Amerind and their captain-in-distress does Kirk regain his memory, assisted by Spock performing a Vulcan mind-meld. Together, they stop the asteroid and restore the planet's asteroid-deflection system, but Kirk's pregnant wife dies in the arms of the *Enterprise*'s captain without ever learning his true, very human, identity.

The episode's ending and the overall representation of the natives as a slightly backwards, simplistic, and superstitious people not only illustrate some of *TOS*'s problematic racist underpinnings, but, once again, emphasize Kirk's standing as the heteronormative hero and protagonist of the show. As Daniel Bernadi argues, "The Paradise Syndrome" is a classic narrative about white and Indian miscegenation in which the "native girl dies so that Kirk, the white male hero, isn't shown unheroically and immorally leaving her and their unborn baby behind" (qtd. in Johnston-Smith 85). In other words, while the noble savage dies at the end, the colonizer returns to his ship and continues on his heroic journeys through space, completely uninhibited by the events on Amerind. Through the mind-meld, Kirk immediately remembers who he is; there is not a shadow of doubt about his identity as Captain James T. Kirk and not even his marriage to Miramanee or his brief stint as medicine man has changed this. In the following episodes, no reference is made to Miramanee or her people (mostly due to the episodic nature of the series). Finally, although one of the final shots in "The Paradise Syndrome" shows a grieving and conflicted Kirk holding the dying Miramanee, the closing shot shows the *Enterprise* flying into space right before the end credits' uplifting music begins.

Kirk's heroism is further underlined by having the audience within the diegetic world of the episode, that is, the Native American tribe, heroize and worship "Kirok." To be constructed as heroic, heroes need an audience to witness their deeds and adventures (Asch and Butter 11), but in this episode the hero has a "double audience": first, the cinematic strategies and plotline of the episode already construct Kirk as a hero for the television audience; second, the audience within the fictional world also constructs Kirk as a hero by worshipping him as "Kirok." The episode thus creates discrepant awareness between, on the one hand, television viewers who are very much aware of Kirk's human nature and, on the other one, members of the native population who are convinced that Kirk is a god—and even Kirk himself. He not only welcomes the hero worship but also eventually becomes convinced of his god-like status when he tries to stop the asteroid by yelling that he is Kirok and menacingly throwing his arms into the air. While the scene serves as a source of humor and irony, the episode leaves no doubt that Kirk, although he might not be a god, is still a heroic character.

The *TNG* episode "Who Watches the Watchers" also works with this double audience and draws attention to the differences between *Enterprise* captains Kirk and Jean-Luc Picard. In this episode, the crew of the *Enterprise* rushes to assist a group of Federation researchers on Mintaka III who are studying the planet's inhabitants from a holographic observation outpost. The Mintakans bear a striking resemblance to the Vulcans, but they are also portrayed in a similar way to the natives of "The Paradise Syndrome" as they are not very technologically advanced and quick to fall back on long-lost beliefs in the supernatural. When an injured Mintakan is beamed onboard the *Enterprise* by Dr. Crusher to save his life, he believes that Picard has supernatural powers and has brought him back to life. "The Picard," as the Mintakans call the captain of the *Enterprise*, spends most of the episode trying to convince the Mintakans that he is anything but a god—at first, from orbit, as he sends Troi and Riker to persuade the natives that the vision of "The Picard" was only a dream and, later, by himself, as he beams down to talk to the Mintakans. In the end, he willingly lets one of the Mintakans shoot him with an arrow in order to show that he bleeds and suffers like a mortal.

On the one hand, both "The Paradise Syndrome" and "Who Watches the Watchers" serve to heroize the respective captains of the *Enterprise*. Even though neither Picard nor Kirk are gods, they are nevertheless heroes who are easily recognized as such. For the natives in "The Paradise Syndrome" one look, or "heroizing gaze," suffices to recognize Kirk as a god-like figure and heroic leader and, in "Who Watches the Watchers," the injured Mintakan immediately recognizes Picard as the leader of the *Enterprise* although, technically, Crusher and her team save his life. On the other hand, the episodes also highlight the differences between the two captains and thereby also changing notions of heroism between the 1960s and 1990s. While Picard angrily refuses to be worshipped as "The Picard," Kirk, as a true frontiersman, embraces and even exploits his status as god-like medicine man—in a way, this marks Picard as even more heroic than Kirk. While Picard spends much time and many resources to persuade the Mintakans that he is not a god and on educating them that superstitious beliefs in the supernatural are wrong, Kirk never challenges the natives' belief system and instead confidently assumes his place therein. While Picard scolds Crusher and others for violating the Prime Directive and "contaminating" the Mintakan culture, Kirk does not hesitate to interfere or procreate with the native culture. Some of these differences can be traced back to Kirk's loss of memory in the episode, but nevertheless Kirk never questions his role as the tribe's god-like medicine man or actively tries to recollect his memory. Therefore, as I show in the following, the different reactions are also emblematic of the two characters in general.

Heroism in TNG: *Space Diplomat in a Brave, Familiar World*

TNG reflects an entirely different cultural and political landscape in the U.S. than the Kennedy-Johnson era that served as the historical backdrop to *TOS*. The "alpha quadrant" of *TNG* is largely mapped and the frontier motif that was so prevalent in *TOS* has almost completely disappeared. For the new *Enterprise* crew, as Jan Johnson-Smith puts it, "there is little left to explore. Far from going boldly 'where no one has gone before,' under Jean-Luc Picard the *Enterprise* mostly potters around a secure little galaxy delivering medical supplies, dropping off passengers and supplying Q with frivolity and amusement" (107). Only the metaphorical frontier between wilderness and civilization, between good and evil, still exists in the Federation's wars and quarrels with a set of new opponents, such as the Ferengi or the Cardassians, but only to a degree. Now, there is even peace with the Klingons and a Klingon works on the bridge of the *Enterprise* (Worland 31). By and large, the *Enterprise*'s task in this brave, not-so-new world consists of maintaining the status quo and guaranteeing the survival of the bureaucratic United Federation of Planets (Pounds 83).[6] The captain's voice-overs at the beginning of each episode accordingly also emphasize continuity: while the signature text of *TOS* is mostly retained, it is only modified slightly to make it gender-neutral ("Where no one has gone before…") and to point out that the *Enterprise* is no longer on a limited, five-year mission, but on a continuous voyage through space (83).

Some scholars read *TNG*'s emphasis on continuity and stability as reflective of the neo-conservative tendencies of the Reagan-Bush era during which the series aired. Daniel Bernardi argues that, although the spinoff appears to present an even more diverse and multicultural cast, it "capitulates to a utopian future where 'race' is determined by biology, miscegenation is still a taboo, and difference is either whitewashed or exaggerated and punished" (117). With regards to gender, Jan Johnson-Smith points out that women in *TNG* still mostly perform roles and jobs that are traditionally connoted as feminine, such as caregivers and emotional experts, while there are still very few female captains (81).[7] The hairstyles of the female cast members also support this reading of *TNG*. In *TOS*, Janice Rand's hairstyle was consciously designed as "futuristic" to signify to the audience that she was a woman from a different century and utopian world (Vettel-Becker 153). By contrast, with the exception of Tasha Yar, many women in *TNG* sport rather conservative, feminine hairstyles very much in fashion during the late 1980s to early 1990s.

Of course, *TNG* often remains ambivalent and vague in its representation and articulation of race, gender, and sexuality, offering enough narrative "blank spaces" that can be interpreted differently. As Henry Jenkins concludes about *Star Trek* in general, *TNG* "is neither consistently progressive nor consistently reactionary, neither operates fully within a utopian tradition […] nor remains fully complicit with American […] politics" (149). Nevertheless, the emphasis on continuity, stability, and conservatism in *TNG* also influences the construction of the hero in the series. As in *TOS*, the hero in *TNG* is again the captain of the *Enterprise* rather than an "ensemble hero."[8] But Picard performs two roles that stand in contrast to Kirk's interventionist politics and impulsive leadership in *TOS*: first, as a sort of space diplomat Picard is tasked with protecting and securing the Federation; and second, he has to protect his ship that is now also home to the crew's families and, thereby, to future generations of Federation citizens.

Once again, the command chair in *TNG* already symbolizes the changing style in leadership between Kirk and Picard. In the *Enterprise-D*, the captain's seat is still at the center of the bridge, but First Officer William Riker and Counselor Deanna Troi are seated almost democratically next to Picard, accompanied by two smaller chairs (cf. Johnstone 61). They are often visible in shots that frame the commanding center of the *Enterprise*, whereas in *TOS*, the camera often features close-ups or medium shots of Kirk in his command chair. More than Kirk, Picard actually listens to and actively seeks the advice offered by his staff; he delegates tasks rather than doing everything himself, and only seldom goes on "away missions." In *TNG*, "the hero is no longer characterized by a willingness to risk personal safety, the ship, and crew […] to make contact with 'new life, new civilizations'" (Pounds 83). Instead, the focus lies on Picard's abilities as a skillful diplomat, negotiator, and rhetorician. The episode "Chain of Command," for instance, introduces a character foil to underline Picard's exceptionalism as a diplomat: while Picard is on an undercover mission, a substitute captain takes over the *Enterprise* and endangers negotiations with the Cardassians through his reckless tactics, impolite and aggressive behavior, and dismissal of Troi's and Riker's advice.

In *TOS*, Kirk is never reluctant to engage with other civilizations or interfere in other planets' affairs. His interventionist politics becomes manifest in the episode "Errand of Mercy" when he offers the seemingly backward Organians military assistance in the fight against the Klingons, in addition to monetary, educational, and technological assistance—only to discover later on that the Organians are much more advanced than humans. Through cross-cutting, the episode reveals parallels between Kirk and his Klingon counterpart, as both are equally indignant about the Organians' self-sufficiency and independence, and thereby also caricatures Kirk's interventionism to some degree. Picard, by contrast, sometimes violates the Prime Directive, for instance in "Justice" when he intervenes to save Wesley Crusher's life, but he repeatedly stresses its importance in front of his crew and tries to uphold it at all costs. For Picard, noninterference and noninterventionism are not just "a set of rules" but a "philosophy" ("Symbiosis").[9] Whenever one of his crewmembers breaks the Prime Directive, he reacts furiously, as he does in "Who

Watches the Watchers" when reprimanding Crusher for allowing one of the Mintakans on board the *Enterprise*. In the two-part "Unification," in which Picard argues with guest-star Ambassador Spock about the future of the Romulans, he explicitly voices his criticism of *TOS*'s interventionism as he calls Spock out on his "cowboy diplomacy." As Timothy Sandefur argues, "Where Kirk pursues justice, Picard avoids conflict": he is "commit[ted] to non-commitment" (10)—and, above all, to securing the survival of his crew and the Federation.

Parallel to his function as the defender of the Prime Directive and protector of the Federation as a whole, Picard is also portrayed as the paternal leader and protector of his ship and crew. In *TNG*'s pilot episode "Encounter at Farpoint," his explicit self-characterization as someone who neither likes nor feels comfortable with children stands in contrast to the episode's cinematography that establishes him as the "father" of the *Enterprise*. There are three different scenes in which point-of-view shots show the new ship, the *Enterprise-D*, from the perspective of one of the characters: in the beginning, Picard is shown as a silhouette only and then slowly walks toward the camera, almost looking at the audience, before the camera presents (parts of) the ship through his eyes; later on, the camera follows Riker and teenager Wesley Crusher as they explore the ship and the bridge, respectively. Thereby, Picard is not just directly established as hero-protagonist, but also as a paternal figure who leads, takes care of, and educates future generations of Starfleet commanders and captains in the form of Riker and Wesley.

Much like George Washington's legacy as *pater patriae* of the United States (Butter 36–37), Picard functions as *pater navis*, as father of the ship. Like Washington, he has no (biological) children of his own; rather, his task solely consists of taking care of the metaphorical children placed under his command and of protecting the freedom and unity of the nation as a whole—the "ship of state" that is the Federation. Like Washington, and also to some degree like Kirk, his heroic habitus derives from his military leadership and experience, moral integrity, and intelligence. There is also, as with Washington, a certain elusiveness to his character. He is often shown standing in his quarters or in his ready room by himself and looking out at space, but the full-body shots do not allow for a closer look at his face ("Sarek"; "The Best of Both Worlds I & II"; "Darmok"). In similar fashion, the episode "Darmok" features images of Picard wandering lonely through an idyllic pasture shortly before he is made, quite literally, a mythical hero in the folktales of the Tamarians. More than Kirk in *TOS*, Picard functions as the solitary moral and heroic hub of *TNG*; the other characters do not represent different elements of his psyche, but underline his superiority.

Picard's age and baldness also establishes him as a paternal authority figure. In addition, these characteristics indicate he is a much more gender-neutral character than Kirk and does not perform an overly masculine role. As Brian Ott and Eric Aoki argue, while Kirk "embodies traditional tough, rugged space-cowboy clichés, Picard emerges as sensitive, refined. His favorite activities include listening to classical music, reading Shakespeare, and sipping Earl Grey tea in his quarters, which are not stereotypically masculine" (58).[10] Although Picard is characterized as a womanizer in the flashback episode "Tapestry," he only fosters a handful of relationships over the course of *TNG* and often ends them because of his sense of duty to his crew and ship ("Lessons"). In the time-bending episode "The Inner Light," he is married and has children; yet, this episode also foregrounds the generational theme and Picard's function as a father figure who helps to preserve the cultural memory of an extinct population and, therefore, metaphorically speaking, their survival in the future.

As an older, paternal leader and diplomat, Picard can be read as a fictional representation of the Reagan presidency much in the same way that Kirk is a fictional successor to Kennedy. On the contrary, however, as I show below, Picard represents a post–Reagan and post–Cold War notion of heroism. On the one hand, this is due to changes in the television industry that affected the ways in which television shows were narrated and characters developed. On the other hand, in its exploration of trauma, torture, and the vulnerabilities of the male hero's body, *TNG* signals a rejection of the tough, overly masculine heroes prominent during the Reagan years.

The Next Generation of Heroes

When *Star Trek: TNG* premiered in 1987, the television industry was going through a period of change. Technological developments, changes in the regulation of the television market, and the decreasing influence of the three major networks gave way to what has alternately been called the "multichannel" or "post-network" era or "convergence culture" (Shimpach 15). TV shows were no longer produced for the All-American mass audiences of the 1950s and 1960s and, instead, were developed for and marketed to "a fragmented collection of niche identities and interests" (18). Together with a heightened emphasis on the style of television productions, or the "televisuality," as John Caldwell calls it (vii), television increasingly presented non-linear, fragmented, and serial narratives and complex characters.

Some of these changes were already manifest in the new *Star Trek* spinoff. Although *TNG*, particularly its first two seasons, is largely modeled on the episodic and procedural narrative structure of *TOS*, it also includes serial narrative elements (Gregory 21). It features multiple-episode story arcs and portrays the core of the *Enterprise* crew as increasingly multi-dimensional characters whose background stories are much more fleshed out than that of *TOS*. With Picard in particular, the serial elements show how his character develops and is marked by the tests and trials he faces during the *Enterprise*'s journeys. There are several episodes which shed light on Picard's origins and family ("Family") and his early life at Starfleet Academy ("Tapestry") or which show him reflecting on or shaped by events that took place in previous episodes. For instance, the effects of his Borg assimilation in "The Best of Both Worlds" reverberate in later episodes,[11] and the events of the fifth-season episode "The Inner Light," in which Picard goes through an entire lifetime, complete with wife, children, and grandchildren, in the duration of some twenty minutes, affect him in the sixth-season episode "Lessons" when he begins a relationship with a crewmember. While Kirk is "not made by his past so much as by his nature and current situation" (Johnstone 59), Picard's character is very much shaped by his past.

Picard is not just more multi-dimensional than Kirk, however. He is also a more vulnerable character that is best seen in *TNG*'s focus on the hero's body. As is true for many hero narratives (cf. Ungaro), heroism in both *TOS* and *TNG* is constructed through the body and the physicality of the protagonist. Yet, while in *TOS* "the gaze" of the camera often lingers on and stylizes Kirk's body—fully clad, with a torn shirt, or naked upper body—to signify both his masculinity and his physical strength when facing the "Other," in *TNG* Picard's body *itself* is constantly under attack and serves as a site of conflict and trauma as he is repeatedly subject to injury, torture, and transmutation over the course of the series. In "Chain of Command," Picard is bound hand and foot and his naked body hangs from the ceiling. In "The Best of Both Worlds," the Borg attempt to assimilate him and change his biological identity by rewriting his DNA. Picard does not (solely) overcome these tests through physical strength or even violence, but rather through mental strength, endurance, and perseverance. In "The Best of Both Worlds," for instance, he conveys to Data vital information on how to defeat the Borg even though he is still Locutus of Borg.

As a much more vulnerable and multi-dimensional hero than Kirk, Picard is actually representative of a new generation of television heroes that emerged in the 1990s. In *Television in Transition*, Shawn Shimpach shows that because of the "fragmentation of audiences" in the multichannel era television culture in the new era was marked by increasing diversity and complexity of cast and characters, a rise in strong female characters, and changing "narrative settings" (30–31). These factors and changing standards challenged the generic action heroes of old, often by showing them caught in a crisis of masculinity and depicted as broken, flawed, and complex characters that went against classical constructions of heroic characters. "The apparently hetero, white, male action hero […] remained a dominant presence on television," Shimpach writes, "if increasingly depicted as under all manner of assault, a conflicted, besieged, unstable subject, facing personal as well as geopolitical crises, transitions, and uncertainty" (31). His body "became the site at which heroics were marked, measured, and performed" (34).

Picard is not yet as complex or flawed—anti-heroic—as the "difficult men" that have come to populate television culture in recent decades: the Don Drapers, Tony Sopranos, and Walter Whites. Yet, he is emblematic of the emerging trends and transitions that Shimpach describes. Picard continuously faces the geopolitical crises of *TNG*'s space-time and his body serves as a site where these crises are solved and fought—his body is under assault, besieged, tortured, injured, and assimilated. In short, his body must endure what the Federation-nation has to endure as a whole in its fights against the technocratic Borg, sadistic terrorists, or corrupt and malicious aliens; by resisting and persisting despite his trauma, the captain exemplifies the values and abilities needed to protect and secure the Federation. As I have shown, his heroism is constructed—marked, measured, and performed—in light of these physical assaults and conflicts. Although he is depicted as vulnerable, suffering, and even aging, and even though he is represented as a less-masculine hero than Kirk, he is still constructed as heroic. He endures every test and crisis; in the end, by overcoming his adversaries and his own physical flaws, he symbolizes the stability and endurance of the Federation and, thereby, reflects *TNG*'s general emphasis on continuity and stability.

The notion of heroism embodied by Picard stands in contrast to the models of heroism prevalent during the Reagan years. In *Hard Bodies: Hollywood Masculinity in the Reagan Era* Susan Jeffords convincingly argues, "Ronald Reagan and his administration […] portray[ed] themselves successfully as […] decisive, tough, aggressive, strong and domineering men" in order to stand apart from the Carter administration that was constructed as soft and effeminate (11). Hollywood productions mirrored this image of tough, heroic masculinity by focusing on the bodily virility of white male action heroes (12). Jeffords posits, however, that beginning with George H.W. Bush's presidency, the "hard bodies" of the Reagan years gave way to "a rearticulation of masculine strength and power through internal, personal, and family-oriented values" (13) and "the creation of a body in which strength is defined internally rather than externally, as a matter of moral rather than muscle fiber" (136). In his comparison of various Arnold Schwarzenegger movies, Rüdiger Heinze identifies a similar change: the next generation of heroes in the 1990s "[we]re physically and mentally vulnerable, occasionally even traumatized" (175). Of course, both Jeffords and Heinze discuss heroes of the big screen, but the depiction of Picard in *TNG* shows that a similar change occurred slightly earlier in television productions of the late 1980s to early 1990s. Picard, then, as a physically vulnerable, traumatized hero with strong family ties—the *Enterprise*—represents a post–Reagan era notion of heroism. He also prefigures a new generation of multidimensional, flawed, and vulnerable male television heroes who are ubiquitous in the television landscape of the 21st century.

Star Trek *Heroism in the Post–Cold War Era*

Interestingly, the four movies which feature the *TNG* cast turn Picard into an (aging) action hero and thereby, retrospectively, into a "hard body"-type hero of the Reagan era. In the movies, Picard no longer inhabits the role of the refined diplomat and paternal authority figure, contently sipping Earl Grey in his quarters. Instead, in *Nemesis*, Picard is happy to take a futuristic ATV out for a spin in the desert of Kolarus III; during a scene on the holodeck in *First Contact*, he goes on a shooting rampage with a machine gun; and in *Insurrection* he saves the day in a martial get-up that is highly reminiscent of the *Die Hard* movies. Rather than talking his way out of dangerous situations, he shoots his way out. And even though he claims that he is getting far too old for physical action (*Insurrection*), he seems to have no difficulty in asserting himself in combat with myriad enemies. His body is also stylized and filmed as an action hero reminiscent of Kirk's body in *TOS*: he often exchanges his Starfleet uniform for short-sleeved or sleeveless shirts to show his muscular arms (*Insurrection; First Contact*); the camera follows him in the action sequences and focuses on his upper body.

Since "Action Picard" seems like a far cry from the role that he performs in *TNG*, many fans have expressed outrage about the movies and argued that they misrepresent Picard's character. On *The Trek BBS* forum, for instance, fans discuss to what extent Picard is a "generic action hero" in the movies and whether or not that is true to his character ("Was Picard"). *First Contact* was a critical and box office success, but attempts to continue the "Action Picard" characterization in *Insurrection* and *Nemesis* led to mixed reviews and disappointing grosses. Turning Picard into a space-version of John McClane may not be true to his television character, but it is true to the medium and, above all, indebted to the media conventions that go along with a translation of the television series to the movie format. *TNG* episodes like "Sarek," for instance, have no any action scenes whatsoever. Here, the main crisis for the *Enterprise* consists of dealing with Sarek's struggle against his Bendii syndrome, a Vulcan version of Alzheimer's that leads to a loss of emotional control—the episode's climax is a Vulcan mind-meld between Picard and Sarek. But to have an entire movie revolve around the mental state of an aging Vulcan leader would probably be tiresome even to the most patient *Star Trek* fan and go against the conventions of mass-marketed movies; the *Star Trek* feature films target a much broader audience than the television show and aim at attracting both knowing audiences, that is, fans of the shows and audiences who are unfamiliar with the source material. Hence, it is not surprising that the movies include more action sequences and cast Picard as a more active leader.[12]

The character development from space diplomat to aging action hero is also already hinted at in some episodes of the later seasons of *TNG*. The episode "Chain of Command," discussed above, not only shows Picard being tortured at the hands of the Cardassians but also going on a strenuous undercover mission that is physically demanding. The sixth-season episode "Starship Mine" serves as a 45-minute version of the *TNG* movies. In the episode, Picard is completely alone on the *Enterprise* when a group of criminals attempts to steal trilithium resin in order to sell the explosive to terrorists. For the remainder of the episode, Picard, almost single-handedly, outsmarts the criminals and, in the end, ruthlessly kills them by secretly removing the control rod from the stolen trilithium container so that their shuttle explodes when they escape. As the episode's title aptly shows, as *pater navis*, Picard quite literally protects his ship at all costs.

Nevertheless, episodes such as "Starship Mine" are the exception, and by the end of the final season of *TNG* Picard still primarily functions as the paternal, diplomatic hero who saves the future of the *Enterprise* and humanity.[13] The rise of "Action Picard" in the feature films, then, illustrates that the heroes of *Star Trek* are as much a product of the medium in which they appear as much as they reflect and articulate larger geo-political and cultural events and trends. As I have shown, both Kirk and Picard are shaped by (changing) conventions in the television industry and (changing) demands of audiences. They also represent very different notions of heroism: to cite Mary Henderson again, Kirk is a hero of the 1960s and Picard a hero of the 1990s—a post–Reagan, post–Cold War hero. In effect, by the turn of the century, Kirk's heroism is obsolete in the world of *Star Trek*, as the 1994 film *Star Trek Generations* underlines.

Premiering six months after *TNG* ended, *Generations* marks the only instance in the diegetic world of *Star Trek* that Kirk and Picard meet, although they only share a few, albeit pivotal, scenes toward the end as they join forces to fight the villain Soran. Throughout the film, the presence of Kirk and other *TOS* characters seem to serve two purposes: first, he is a token character to the fans of *TOS* who have grown older with the franchise, and second, he affirms the franchise's own "legendary" status. As Katja Kanzler shows, since the 1970s, the extra-textual discourse—interviews, autobiographies, commentaries, and guides written and given by producers, writers, and cast members—has helped to construct *Star Trek* not just as a progressive, multicultural project, but also as a "mythical" part of a global popular culture (67–69). The film picks up on this notion as it represents Kirk and the other *TOS* characters as "heroes of myth" (Slotkin 14; also cf. Gregory 23). In the opening scenes, Kirk, Scotty, and Chekov are introduced as living legends who are reduced to performing representative roles. When Soran does not know Kirk's identity, Picard tells him to study the history books in order to learn about the legendary captain of the *Enterprise*.

As a man of legends and history, Kirk is strangely out of place in *Generations*. While he has, of course, aged considerably since the space-time of *TOS*, and the previous feature films already show him as an aging hero, his character has hardly developed or changed since he was first introduced to audiences in the 1960s. When Picard calls on him in the Nexus—an extra-dimensional space where Kirk has been caught for the past 78 years—he finds Kirk chopping wood on his Iowa homestead. Kirk's behavior and his way of speaking have not changed either; he is quick to make jokes and nonchalantly asks Picard to call him "Jim." But while his character is thus easily recognizable to knowing and unknowing audiences alike, next to Picard, he appears even more mono-dimensional and static than in *TOS*. Hence, it is fitting that he dies in the fight against Soran and is ultimately buried by Picard in the symbolic, rugged Western-like terrain of Veridian III (filmed in the "Old West" of Nevada). Having entered history books and cultural memory as a legend, the film suggests there is no longer a place for Kirk in the space-time of the 24th century—or the then-approaching 21st.

I argue that Kirk dies because he represents an outdated model of heroism no longer relevant in the post–Cold War era. Even in the 1960s, his character was modeled on established configurations of heroism as he embodied the attributes and values associated with the heroes of frontier mythology and the Western genre. But in *TOS*'s nods to Kennedy's idea of a New Frontier he also signified a promise for the future; he was brave and daring enough to explore and conquer the final frontier of space. In television's oscillation between similarity and difference, Kirk stood for both, the known and the unknown, the past and the future. In the 1990s, however, Kirk's cowboy and Kennedy heroism only signified the past.

Although the space-time of *TNG* is not necessarily a brave, new world, either, it reflects a different cultural, historical, and also economic context. The representation of Picard harkens back to established models of heroism as well, for instance, to the heroization of George Washington as *pater patriae*, but he also reflects (and goes with) the changing times. A much more vulnerable and even traumatized character, Picard prefigured the next generation of darker, multi-dimensional television heroes who took center stage in popular and television culture of the late 1990s to 2000s. As a whole, then, *TNG* is darker and less optimistic about the future than *TOS*: it deals with trauma, torture, and transmutation, it shows that not even Starfleet command is immune to corruption, and, with the introduction of the Borg, it conveys a degree of technophobia. This development culminates in the later feature films, especially *Nemesis*, which debuted to a post–9/11 audience and begins with a scene of terrorism on Romulus. The rise of "Action Picard" in *First Contact* and the other feature films and the return of "Action Kirk" in the latest *Star Trek* reboot movies, directed by J.J. Abrams and Justin Lin, seems to signify a return to, and need for, the (generic action) heroes of the past. But during the brief window of the 1990s and *The Next Generation*, television and popular culture had no place for the static character of Kirk, the space cowboy with an unbridled optimism about the future.

NOTES

I would like to thank the students who attended my course on *Star Trek* at the University of Tübingen in the summer term 2016. I learned a lot from our discussions of the final frontier, "Ken in space," and utopianism.

1. "The Cage" also differed from Roddenberry's original outline for the series. In his early draft, Roddenberry, for instance, envisioned Spock as a "satanic," red-skinned Martian and the captain was called Robert T. April (Whitfield and Roddenberry 25–27).

2. At the same time, Hollywood movie productions began to undergo a significant change with the emergence of New Hollywood in 1966. New Hollywood films not only went against the classical style but often worked to revise classical genres, such as the Western. Television, in return, filled the void left by New Hollywood and catered to the "classical" audiences, for instance, by reviving the Western or relocating it to space—as in *TOS*.

3. The recent *Star Trek* feature film, *Star Trek Beyond* (2016), satirizes Kirk's proclivity to rip his shirts in *TOS* when Kirk (Chris Pine) remarks that he has ripped his shirt *again*.

4. In an interesting reversal, the *Enterprise* crew does not take up the role of the Earps who were heroized in John Ford's *My Darling Clementine* (1946) but that of the Clantons.

5. Other episodes such as "Arena" or "Errand of Mercy" also highlight this theme of peace before violence.

6. See Justin Ream's and Alexander Lee's essay in this volume.

7. One of these female captains is member of a group of conspirators trying to sabotage Starfleet Command in "Conspiracy" and another meets a quick demise in "Yesterday's Enterprise." La Forge's mother was a captain who also disappears.

8. The series was developed specifically to feature "an 'ensemble' cast" with "eight or nine leading characters" (Gregory 43), yet the sole protagonist is still Picard.

9. See Larry A. Grant's essay in this volume.

10. In fact, several scholars note that Riker performs a similar role to Kirk in *TNG* and Daniel Bernardi has even called Riker "the Kirk-like Casanova of *The Next Generation*" (Bernardi 128; cf. Johnstone 61; Gregory 44). In the episode "Conspiracy," Riker is actually shown in a camera shot that is very similar to *TOS*'s signature shot of Kirk: a close-up of his brooding face, his body leaning to the side.

11. "The Best of Both Worlds, Part I" was the third season finale and thereby marked the first time that a season of a *Star Trek* series ended with a cliffhanger. Picard's trauma, caused by his Borg assimilation, also still plays a significant role in the feature film *Star Trek: First Contact*.

12. To some extent, the same can also be said for Kirk in the feature films which star the *TOS* cast. Yet, Kirk is never depicted as an aging action hero in the same fashion that Picard is, and there is much more continuity between his role in the television series and his role in the feature films.

13. See Alex Burston-Chorowicz's essay in this volume.

WORKS CITED

Allrath, Gaby, Marion Gymnich, and Carola Surkamp. "Introduction: Towards a Narratology of TV Series." *Narrative Strategies in Television Series*. Eds. Gaby Allrath and Marion Gymnich. New York: Palgrave, 2005. Print. 1–45.

Asch, Ronald G., and Michael Butter, ed. *Bewunderer, Verehrer, Zuschauer: Die Helden Und Ihr Publikum*. Würzburg: Ergon, 2016. Print. Helden—Heroisierungen—Heroismen 2.

Bernardi, Daniel. Star Trek and *History: Race-Ing Toward a White Future*. New Brunswick, NJ: Rutgers University Press, 1998. Print.

Butter, Michael. Der *"Washington-Code": Zur Heroisierung Amerikanischer Präsidenten, 1775–1865*. Göttingen: Wallstein, 2016. Print.

"Chain of Command I." *Star Trek: The Next Generation, Season 6*. Writ. Frank Abatemaco. Dir. Robert Scheerer. Paramount Home Video, 2002. DVD.

"Charlie X." *Star Trek: The Original Series, Season 1*. Writ. D.C. Fontana and Gene Roddenberry. Dir. Lawrence Dobkin. Paramount Home Video, 2014. DVD.

"Court Martial." *Star Trek: The Original Series, Season 1*. Writ. Don M. Mankiewicz and Steven W. Carabatsos. Dir. Marc Daniels. Paramount Home Video, 2014. DVD.

Cranny-Francis, Anne. "Sexuality and Sex-Role Stereotyping in *Star Trek*." *Science Fiction Studies* 12.3 (1985): 274–84. Print.

"Encounter at Far Point." *Star Trek: The Next Generation, Season 1*. Writ. D.C. Fontana and Gene Roddenberry. Dir. Corey Allen. Paramount Home Video, 2002. DVD.

"The Enemy Within." *Star Trek: The Original Series, Season 1*. Writ. Richard Matheson. Dir. Leo Penn. Paramount Home Video, 2014. DVD.

"Errand of Mercy." *Star Trek: The Original Series, Season 1*. Writ. Gene L. Coon. Dir. John Newland. Paramount Home Video, 2014. DVD.

"Family." *Star Trek: The Next Generation, Season 4*. Writ. Ronald D. Moore. Dir. Les Landau. Paramount Home Video, 2002. DVD.

Gregory, Chris. Star Trek: *Parallel Narratives*. New York: St. Martin's Press, 2000. Print.

Heinze, Rüdiger. "Conformist Rebels and Popular Outsiders: Arnold Schwarzenegger's Movie Heroes." *Arnold Schwarzenegger: Interdisciplinary Perspectives on Body and Image*. Ed. Michael Butter, Patrick Keller, and Simon Wendt. Heidelberg: Winter, 2011. 169–86. American Studies 198.

Helford, Elyce Rae. "'A part of myself no man should ever see': Reading Captain Kirk's Multiple Masculinities." *Enterprise Zones: Critical Positions on* Star Trek. Ed. Taylor Harrison et al. Boulder, CO: Westview P, 1996. 11–31. Print.

Jeffords, Susan. *Hard Bodies: Hollywood Masculinity in the Reagan Era*. New Brunswick, NJ: Rutgers University Press, 1994. Print.

Jenkins, Henry. "'Infinite Diversity in Infinite Combinations': Genre and Authorship in *Star Trek*." *Science Fiction Audiences: Watching* Doctor Who and Star Trek. Eds. John Tulloch and Henry Jenkins. New York: Routledge, 1995. 175–95. Print.

Johnson-Smith, Jan. *American Science Fiction TV*: Star Trek, Stargate and *Beyond*. London: I.B. Tauris, 2005. Print.

Johnstone, Monica. "Shifting Paradigms for Leadership in *Star Trek* and *Star Trek: The Next Generation*." *Popular Culture Review* 5.2 (1994): 57–66. Print.

Kanzler, Katja. *"Infinite Diversity in Infinite Combinations": The Multicultural Evolution of* Star Trek. Heidelberg: Universitätsverlag Winter, 2004. Print.

Kennedy, John F. "Address of Senator John F. Kennedy Accepting the Democratic Party Nomination for the Presidency of the United States—Memorial Coliseum, Los Angeles." 15 July 1960. *The American Presidency Project*, 2016. Web. 26 Jun. 2016.

Lawrence, John S., and Robert Jewett. *The Myth of the American Superhero*. Grand Rapids, MI: W.B. Eerdmans, 2002. Print.

"Lessons." *Star Trek: The Next Generation, Season 6*. Writ. Ron Wilkerson and Jean Louise Matthias. Dir. Robert Wiemer. Paramount Home Video, 2002. DVD.

Marin, Rick. "Kisses Great!/Less Killing!: Comparing the Captains: Kirk Vs. Picard." *TV Guide* 31 Aug.– 6 Sept. 1991: 5–6. Print.

McVeigh, Stephen. "The Kirk Doctrine: The Care and Repair of Archetypal Heroic Leadership in J.J. Abrams' *Star Trek*." Star Trek *As Myth: Essays on Symbol and Archetype at the Final Frontier*. Ed. Matthew Wilhelm Kapell. Jefferson, NC: McFarland, 2010. 197–212. Print.

Ott, Brian L., and Eric Aoki. "Science Fiction as Social Consciousness: Race, Gender, and Sexuality in *Star Trek: The Next Generation*." The Star Trek *Universe: Franchising the Final Frontier*. Eds. Douglas Brode and Shea T. Brode. New York: Rowman & Littlefield, 2015. 53–63. Print.

Palumbo, Donald. "The Monomyth in *Star Trek* (2009): Kirk & Spock Together Again for the First Time." *Journal of Popular Culture* 46.1 (2013): 143–72. Print.

Pearson, Roberta E., and Máire Messenger Davies. Star Trek *and American Television*. Berkeley: University of California Press, 2014. Print.

Pounds, Micheal C. *Race in Space: The Representation of Ethnicity in* Star Trek *and* Star Trek: The Next Generation. Lanham, MD: Scarecrow, 1999. Print.

Sandefur, Timothy. "The Politics of *Star Trek*." *Claremont Review of Books* 15.3 (2015): 98–103. Print.

Shimpach, Shawn. *Television in Transition: The Life and Afterlife of the Narrative Action Hero*. Hoboken, NJ: Wiley-Blackwell, 2010. Print.

Slotkin, Richard. *Gunfighter Nation: The Myth of the Frontier in Twentieth-Century America*. New York: Atheneum, 1992. Print.

"Spectre of the Gun." *Star Trek: The Original Series, Season 3*. Writ. Lee Cronin. Dir. Vincent McEveety. Paramount Home Video, 2014. DVD.

Star Trek Beyond. Dir. Justin Lin. Perf. Chris Pine, Zachary Quinto, Karl Urban, Simon Pegg, Zoe Saldana, and Idris Elba. Paramount Pictures, 2016. Film.

Star Trek: First Contact. Dir. Jonathan Frakes. Perf. Patrick Stewart, Jonathan Frakes, and Brent Spiner. Paramount Home Video, 1998. DVD.

Star Trek Generations. Dir. David Carson. Perf. William Shatner, Patrick Stewart, Malcolm McDowell, Jonathan Frakes, and Brent Spiner. Paramount, 2000. DVD.

Star Trek: Insurrection. Dir. Jonathan Frakes. Perf. Patrick Stewart, Jonathan Frakes, and Brent Spiner. Paramount Home Video, 1999. DVD.

Star Trek: Nemesis. Dir. Stuart Baird. Perf. Patrick Stewart, Jonathan Frakes, Brent Spiner, and Tom Hardy. Paramount Home Video, 2003. DVD.

"Symbiosis." *Star Trek: The Next Generation, Season 1*. Writ. Robert Lewin et al. Dir. Win Phelps. Paramount Home Video, 2002. DVD.

"Tapestry." *Star Trek: The Next Generation, Season 6*. Writ. Ronald D. Moore. Dir. Les Landau. Paramount Home Video, 2002. DVD.

Ungaro, Jean. *Le corps de cinéma: Le super-héros américain*. Paris: L'Harmattan, 2010. Print.

Vettel-Becker, Patricia. "Space and the Single Girl: *Star Trek*, Aesthetics, and 1960s Femininity." *Frontiers: A Journal of Women's Studies* 35.2 (2014): 143–78. Print.

"Was Picard a Generic Action Hero in the Movies?" *The Trek Bbs*, 27 Jan. 2012. Web. 26 Jun. 2016.

Whitfield, Stephen E., and Gene Roddenberry. *The Making of* Star Trek. New York: Titan Books, 1991. Print.

Worland, Rick. "From the New Frontier to the Final Frontier: *Star Trek* from Kennedy to Gorbachev." *Film and History* 24 (1995): 19–35. Print.

The Queerness of Villainy
in the 24th Century

BRUCE E. DRUSHEL

The relationship between the *Star Trek* franchise and its LGBTQ fans is frequently fraught. On one hand, queers are attracted to the franchise's utopian creed, including its nonjudgmental acceptance of beings regardless of their race, gender, age, or origins. On the other hand, producers responsible for the creation of *Star Trek: The Next Generation* resisted the introduction of identifiably queer crewmembers to the cast in spite of creator Gene Roddenberry's promise to LGBTQ fans to do so.

The series did feature shape-shifters, such as Wesley's first girlfriend in "The Dauphin," and Data's initial androgynous daughter in "The Offspring." However, the majority of characters who could be read as queer are antagonists, including the amoral collector Kivas Fajo (Saul Rubinek) who kidnaps Data in the season three episode "The Most Toys," the gender binary-rejecting J'naii from season five's "The Outcast," and the malevolently mischievous yet unctuous Q (John de Lancie), who appears in several *TNG* episodes, including "Encounter at Farpoint," "Hide and Q," "Q Who," "Déjà Q," "Qpid," "True Q," "Tapestry," and the finale, "All Good Things...."

The villain who can be read as queer is an old trope in the print and motion picture media. Among the first to observe it (and to admit to his role in its furtherance) was author Norman Mailer in a 1955 article in the homophile publication *One*. Film archivist (and openly gay man) Vito Russo wrote extensively of Mailer's article in his book *Celluloid Closet* (1987) and the *New York Times* noted its durability in 1992. In this essay, I argue that *Star Trek: The Next Generation*'s creed of exploration and evidence of its producers' homophobia creates a fissure between its need both to embrace and to reject The Other. This fissure complicates the relationship between the *Star Trek* franchise and its LGBTQ fans and must be resolved if the franchise is to cultivate audiences in a culture that is increasingly accepting of queerness.

A Brief History of Evil Queers

As Gayle Rubin argues, modern Western culture generally, and U.S. culture particularly, tend to privilege individuals whose sexual practices approximate what it considers normal, healthy, safe, and sanctified, while marginalizing those with practices considered abnormal, sick, illegal, and sinful (281). This approach can trace its lineage to ancient laws that were eventually adapted to modern civil codes. Marital, reproductive heterosexuals thus are alone at the top of what might be considered an erotic pyramid. Below them are unmarried monogamous heterosexuals in couples, followed by most other heterosexuals. Near the bottom are homosexuals and prostitutes, who became targets of Victorian-age campaigns against "white slavery," which produced myriad prohibitions against sexual solicitation, lewd behavior, loitering for immoral purposes, age offenses, and brothels and bawdy houses. So woven into the social fabric is this hierarchy, individuals near its bottom are presumed to suffer from mental illness, disreputability, and criminality, and are subject to economic sanctions and the loss of institutional support and of social and physical mobility. As Edward Ingebretsen observes, "gender failure, in commodity culture, is always a significant marker of evil" (25–34).

The equating of villainy and queerness was manifest early on in literature, with roots in the sacred texts of the religions of pre-literate societies, including Christianity, which equated evil with the deviate sexual practices of Sodom and Gomorrah. More recent examples, according to Dyer (72–74) and Storzer (186), are found in the gay literary traditions in France of the 19th and 20th centuries, particularly in the works of Balzac, Gide, du Coglay, and Genet. Connections between lesbianism and male homosexuality on the one hand, and juvenile delinquency and other forms of anti-social behavior on the other, became a persistent theme of so-called pulp paperbacks of the 1940s and 1950s, even as authors such as Radclyffe Hall and Gore Vidal crafted more elaborate and sympathetic queer characters in their novels.

Early film, as author and film archivist Vito Russo notes, featured a surprising number of characters that even the most unsophisticated moviegoer could read as queer. Several scandals in the nascent Hollywood film community, in conjunction with what was considered objectionable content in some films, led to threats of the establishment of local film censorship boards with the power to censor and certify films for exhibition as well as the establishment of a ratings system by the Catholic Legion of Decency. Studios responded with the Production Code Administration (PCA), whose self-censorship apparatus included a prohibition on depiction of what was termed "sexual perversion." Filmmakers soon learned they could continue to represent queerness on screen, so long as the representations were coded in such a way as to evade detection by PCA censors and less sophisticated audiences. Among the tropes to emerge were well-understood gender stereotypes (including effeminate men and masculinized women), the substitution of other stigmatizing conditions (e.g., alcoholism or isolation) for homosexuality, and the suggestion of queerness through criminality. Though the Code disappeared by 1968 with the introduction of the Motion Picture Association of America's (MPAA) rating system, some tropes persisted. Notably, Timon and Pumbaa from Disney's *The Lion King* are stigmatized as a same-sex couple and for breaking into song while on guard duty [Timon] and for excessive odor [Pumbaa] (Sweeney 132).

Thus, as Nico Lang observes, a century's worth of film produced by the U.S. studios includes queer villains who are either explicitly gay or gay-coded. Critic Adam Sandel singles out 21 of those he considers noteworthy for an article in the LGBTQ newsmagazine *The Advocate*, from Prince John in 1938's *The Adventures of Robin Hood* to Silva in the 2012 James Bond film *Skyfall*. Lang notes that Hitchcock's *Psycho*, Huston's *The Maltese Falcon*, and de Palma's *Dressed to Kill* all included villains, and frequently violent ones, who are gay-coded. Occasionally, same-sex attraction could even be cast as the cause of violent perversion. More recently, the gay or transgender villain is "absurdly ubiquitous" in Disney films, from *The Jungle Book* to *Aladdin* to *Hercules*, and is almost always the most memorable character in the film (Lang; Putnam 158).

Like literature and film before it, television has also historically equated queerness and villainy (Barnes-Brus 19). Barnes-Brus adds that even the genres that increase mainstream visibility of queerness tend to exploit social understandings of what it means to be gay (22). This is perhaps not surprising, given that the film studios are major suppliers of filmed television content. In addition, even without a specific self-regulatory prohibition on depicting LGBTQ people and characters, early television emulated film's coding scheme that made villainy and stereotypical gender performance cues to homosexuality it would not otherwise show. Most of the notable veiled gay characters were male, including campy saboteur Dr. Zachary Smith from *Lost in Space* (1964–1967), John Davidson's transgender murderer in *The Streets of San Francisco*'s "Mask of Death" episode (1974), and Mike Barnes, a bisexual man who knowingly infected unsuspecting lovers with HIV in the controversial "After it Happened" episode of *Midnight Caller* (1988).

The Temporal Context of Star Trek: The Next Generation

The sequel to Roddenberry's culturally iconic 1960s television series debuted during an ostensibly dark but ultimately pivotal point in LGBTQ history. By autumn of 1987, knowledge of the HIV/AIDS pandemic, of which the effects on the gay male population were particularly devastating, was more than six years old and a seropositive test result was regarded practically as a death sentence. There was widespread anger in the LGBTQ communities at the failure of then-President Ronald Reagan to make any mention of the health crisis (other than a fleeting one in 1985) until that year ("Against the Odds").

In addition to Reagan's silence, the gay rights movement faced setbacks on many political fronts. Outrage over apparent federal government failure to address HIV/AIDS, the Supreme Court's affirmation of state anti-sodomy laws in *Bowers v. Harwick*, renewed vigor by the U.S. Defense Department to discover and discharge lesbian and gay members of the armed forces, and the support of anti-gay policies by closeted public figures led to the formation of activist groups such as Queer Nation and the AIDS Coalition to Unleash Power (ACTUP), and to the involuntary disclosure of those figures' sexuality to the public, also known as "outing." Lesbians and gays believed they were under siege and felt hard-won progress in social equality from the 1970s, as well as their very lives and livelihoods, lay in the balance.

The Un-Queer Past of Star Trek's *Future*

In addition to the social and political milieu, characters in *Star Trek: The Next Generation* exist in the context of a relationship between the producers of television programs and films in the *Star Trek* franchise and the LGBTQ communities that is historically fraught. While cast members George Takei (Lieutenant Hikaru Sulu in the original series) and Zachary Quinto (Commander Spock in the recent movie "prequels") both self-identify as gay, as have a number of the writers and crew over the franchise's 50 years, no *Star Trek* series or film until 2016 included an openly lesbian or gay character, save for one instance of bisexuality in an "alternative universe" story arc in *Star Trek: Deep Space Nine*. In 2016, the Star Trek franchise "reboot" feature film *Star Trek Beyond* appears to depict Sulu in a same sex relationship, though it is not developed beyond a single scene with no dialogue. Takei expressed displeasure with that depiction, though it was intended as a tribute to his activism on behalf of LGBTQ rights and against anti-queer bullying. Takei called Sulu's revised characterization "unfortunate" and not what creator Gene Roddenberry would have wanted (Abramovitch). In any event, the absence is conspicuous in light of the franchise's pretentions to racial and gender inclusiveness and the generally progressive and utopian philosophical bend of its narratives—and is particularly frustrating to its significant legion of LGBTQ fans and their allies.

As a franchise whose initial television series debuted in 1966 and ended its run just weeks before the uprising at the Stonewall nightclub in Greenwich Village in 1969, which is widely seen as a turning point in the modern gay rights movement, *Star Trek* might be forgiven for its lack of queer characters in its original cast. U.S. commercial television during the late 1960s was largely devoid of openly gay or lesbian characters, save for the infrequent one-off villain in crime dramas or the heavily coded wisecracking male or officious spinster of formulaic situation comedy. But when the positive audience reception to the *Star Trek* feature films in the late 1970s and early 1980s led to rumored plans for a new syndicated television series in 1986, lesbian and gay *Star Trek* fans began forming The Gaylactic Network, a group that would eventually grow to 8 chapters and 500 members, and with a goal to lobby producers for LGBTQ characters in future stories (Aul & Frank 52–53; Altman). Members of the group actually confronted *Star Trek* creator Gene Roddenberry and writer David Gerrold at a fan convention to press their agenda. According to Gerrold, Roddenberry told the group he would consider it, though follow-up letters from the group went unanswered. Another account claims Roddenberry raised the issue at a staff meeting in late 1987, soon after the debut of *Star Trek: The Next Generation*, prompting a homophobic slur from one of his producers (Altman; Kay).

Though characters identified textually as lesbian, gay, bisexual, and transgender became comparatively commonplace on television screens in the U.S. by the late 1980s and early 1990s, audiences hoping to see them in the *Star Trek* films and television shows were deeply disappointed. In response, some fans organized groups of like-minded audience members; some only complained. Still, others adapted time-tested coping mechanisms that previously provided a comparative level of satisfaction for chronically dissatisfied queer viewers for decades: composing and sharing their own fan-fiction. However, fan-fiction was time-consuming and required creative acumen and familiarity with both the conventions of television scriptwriting and fan-fiction writing. Others performed queer readings of textually-straight characters, which can be accomplished in real time while viewing and required only more intuitive talents. But in terms of the series, queer characters were not only villains, they were not members of Starfleet and were not even human. They were the ultimate Other.

Reading Queerness in Villainy

Kivas Fajo

The Zibalian "collector" Kivas Fajo appeared in only one episode as a "villain of the week." But Fajo's appearance and characterization extended the legacy of traditional "queer bad guys" in film and television. While his preoccupation with greed and amoral attitudes toward how valuables are acquired are more evident, Fajo's interest in Data in the episode "The Most Toys" betrays evidence of his queerness. The *Enterprise* encounters Fajo as part of a mission to acquire a volatile compound to fix a colony's contaminated water supply. The compound's instability requires it to be physically shuttled aboard the ship and the android officer Data is selected as the pilot for his meticulous attention to safety protocols and to avoid risk to human life. Data is kidnapped and Fajo's crew rigs his shuttle to explode to make it appear he was destroyed. Fajo reveals to Data he was prompted to kidnap him and add him to his "collection" because of the android's uniqueness. The *Enterprise* crew eventually discover Fajo's ruse and return just in time to transport Data to the ship during his climactic confrontation with Fajo, who subsequently is imprisoned and his collection dispersed.

The principal evidence of Fajo's queerness takes two forms: his transgressive gender behavior and his fetishizing of the android. Character actor Saul Rubinek brought a whimsical attitude, complete with smirks and stifled chuckles, to Fajo that border on the childlike. His camp appearance, including a rotund form, fuchsia outfit, and elaborate hairstyle and cap conjure a parallel to an outsized munchkin from *The Wizard of Oz*, which is perhaps not surprising, given that Rubinek replaced British dwarf actor David Rappaport as Fajo following the latter's suicide (Latchem). Fajo's insistence that Data change from his Starfleet uniform into an outfit of Fajo's choosing is met with resistance from the android, prompting Fajo to admit that, actually, he prefers to see Data naked. While that remark can reflect Fajo's admiration for the technology that Data represents, it also enables a reading of a Fajo interested in the naked male form, albeit a cybernetic representation of it.

Perhaps even more damning in a heteronormative sense is Fajo's ability to "twist" Data's programming. When Fajo kills a woman associate, he taunts Data into executing him for his crime, even though Data claims it is his nature to not take life. Ironically, in the episode, Geordi La Forge deduces Data was not killed in the initial shuttlecraft explosion because the android does things strictly by regulations and Fajo's kidnapping Data prevented him from following Starfleet procedures regarding shuttlecraft operations. However, Data disproves La Forge by subverting his own sanctity-of-life programming. The android changes his mind—and his programming—when he realizes Fajo may kill again. Data attempts to shoot his kidnapper, but the transporter intervenes, saving Fajo. Data then lies to Riker, implying the transporter did something to indicate a weapons discharge. Even though Data supposedly acts righteously in his attempt to execute this thief/murderer/conman, Fajo demonstrates his ability to turn Data "queer": he forces the android to leave his "straight" Starfleet uniform for a purple suit—the same color as Fajo's fuchsia garment—while he internally "rewires" Data to kill and then lie about his actions.

The J'naii

The ability of outsiders to corrupt the straight-and-narrow Starfleet officers extends to the show's ladies-man, William Riker. The fifth-season episode "The Outcast" introduces viewers to the J'naii, a humanoid race that outlaws expressions of gender and considers conventional sexual reproduction, which is not necessary for their procreation, as a form of perversion. In a mission to rescue a J'naii shuttle, Commander Riker is paired with J'naii pilot Soren, who confesses to him that she secretly identifies as female and furtively engages in sexual relationships with members of her race who secretly identify as male. Riker develops feelings for Soren, but a kiss between the two is discovered and reported. Riker learns the J'naii will compel Soren against her will to undergo psychotropic treatments to correct her perceived illness. He and Worf attempt to free her but find she has already been treated and no longer desires a relationship with Riker.

It is necessary to distinguish Soren from two other J'naii since she is a protagonist and demonstrates conventional feminine gender behavior. In essence, Soren is a damsel in distress for Riker (and the warrior Worf) to rescue. The other J'naii, Krite and Noor, are antagonists as they disrupt the nascent romantic relationship between Riker and Soren and, from the perspective of contemporary western culture, are made queer by their rejection of traditional gender binaries. The viewer, approving of Riker's romance with a woman (and not, say, if Soren identified as male), would support the first officer's rescuing of Soren and see the J'Naii as "bad." Even Picard, who lightly warns Riker not to jeopardize his career, ultimately allows him to circumvent the Prime Directive. Ironically, the episode was intended (and is celebrated by LGBTQ fans) as a nod of support to the *Star Trek* franchise's legion of queer fans; however, casting characters who reject conventional definitions of gender as villains would seem to undermine that message.

The J'Naii themselves further underscore American heteronormativity. Concerning Soren and the J'Naii, actor Jonathan Frakes asserted that Soren "should have been more obviously male," but the production crew was not "gusty enough" to move in that direction (Jenkins 288 f49). Producer Rick Berman stated the studio auditioned men and women to play the J'Naii, but opted to make the J'Naii deviant by American gender norms by considering only "non-masculine men or non-feminine women," and selecting women (Jenkins 288 f49). The implication that only "effeminate" men or "butch" women were fit for the part accentuates the J'Naii as "the other."

Q

Appropriately, owing to his popular appearances throughout the run of *Star Trek: The Next Generation*, including its two-part pilot and series finale episodes, the character most amenable to being read queerly is Q, an immortal and non-corporeal being who is equal parts trickster, judge, and mortal threat to the crew of the USS *Enterprise*-D. Ostensibly, his appearance in the two-part pilot episode, "Encounter at Farpoint," is as judge and threat; however, the range of the actor hired to play Q, John de Lancie, was such that he also could appear playful, campy, enraged, and disappointed. His overall function is *agent provocateur*: a character who compels dilemmas and forces confrontations the crew otherwise avoids. At the same time, however, his ability to irk Picard delighted fans and suggests a subversive reading of Q as a queer "hero" who gets under Starfleet's skin.

In "Encounter at Farpoint," the newly commissioned Galaxy-class *Enterprise*-D is dispatched to investigate construction of a new space station in a remote part of the quadrant. *En route*, the *Enterprise* is trapped by Q, who appears to them in medieval judicial garb seated on an ambulatory throne. Q transports key officers to a courtroom where he proposes to try the human race for generalized crimes against the galaxy. The newly-installed captain of the *Enterprise*, Jean-Luc Picard, persuades Q to allow the crew to continue its mission on the premise that by doing so Q's "court" could best judge their worthiness. Ultimately, Q agrees humanity has passed his test but merely suspends the trial's judgment and allows it to continue its mission with the somber caution that he will be watching.

Apart from his evident attraction to theatricality and artifice, de Lancie's embodiment of Q suggests a fondness for multiple costume and identity changes as well as effeteness in language and manner. His judicial robes are red and black velvet material with an elaborate headpiece reminiscent of one worn by David Bowie in his "Ashes to Ashes" video. His gloved hands gesture regally; he initiates changes in location and company by snapping his fingers, as a monarch or lord might summon an underling or a drag diva might punctuate a sentence. His speech is stilted and formalized; his eye contact with those he addresses is direct and imposing. He yawns in disdain at Picard's arguments in favor of humanity. In sum, the character to whom viewers are introduced is regal, but leavened by the campiness of its exaggeration.

Q's behavior bothers Picard, but what really annoys the good captain is Q's ready adoption of human military uniforms. Q appears in various antiquated uniforms, and matching historical attitudes. When he appears as a Cold War general, he demands a "few good men" to battle communism. Picard says Q's rhetoric is outdated and nonsensical, and Q immediately updates his uniform into a World War III, drugged-out, techno-soldier. His final appearance is that of a Starfleet admiral. This one-track line of clothing shows a direct continuity of military corruption, which Q sees leading to the *Enterprise*'s current command crew, whom he places on trial. By donning Starfleet garb, Q brings a queer, flamboyant persona into strict, military decorum. Picard chastises Q, telling the omnipotent being that if he knows what the uniform stands for, he would embrace their mission to explore the unknown. But even though Q lets the crew go on their way to do just that, he knows the *Enterprise*'s crew is less tolerant to those outside their binary gender norms. As a result, when Q subsequently appears, he "queers" them.

Indeed, Q does this in his next appearance in the series, six episodes later. Here, he shifts his attentions from Picard to Commander Will Riker. In "Hide and Q," the *Enterprise* is again halted by Q, who transports the bridge crew (minus Picard) to a hostile world, informing them they are to take part in a game whose only rule is to stay alive. Picard wagers Q that Riker will refuse Q's offer to grant him the near limitless powers of the Q Continuum. During the game, however, Riker is unable to refrain from using his powers to help his shipmates, including saving Worf and Wesley. Riker's desire to continue to use his powers creates a rift with Picard and increases Riker's arrogance. Q and Picard agree that Riker, as a final test, should use his power to give each of the bridge crew what that person most desires—using Q's "queerness" to realize the crew's hidden desires that cannot occur naturally (La Forge has new eyes; Wesley ages instantly; Data becomes human). Each of Riker's shipmates, being good officers, ultimately rejects Riker's gift. When Q attempts to escape the wager, he is recalled to the Q Continuum for punishment.

Q's previous interest in Picard as a verbal sparring partner in "Encounter at Farpoint" prompted creation of slash fan-fiction pairing the two erotically.[1] Now, with his attention turned to Riker and the offer of a potentially priceless gift on the table, the narrative plays out like an extended seduction, with Q and Riker at one point sharing screen space as equals. Once again, Q's attraction to elaborate period military clothing to demonstrate his authority; this time a Napoleonic French field marshal's uniform is on display, as are his effete manner and finger-snapping commands. Interestingly, female cast members are less in evidence: Tasha Yar is placed in a penalty box for refusing to take part in the "game" and Deanna Troi is written out of the episode, which, along with her absence in three others in the first season, led Marina Sirtis to suspect (incorrectly) that her character was about to be eliminated (Nemecek 28).

Q's role in the groundbreaking episode "Q Who" is notable less for Q's histrionics than for its introduction of the Borg, who would prove to be the franchise's most formidable adversary (until the introduction of Species 8472 in *Star Trek: Voyager*.) The episode opens with Picard's kidnapping from the *Enterprise* by Q, who is fresh from his punishment by the Q Continuum and looking for a new adventure. He offers his services as galactic guide to Picard, who, suspicious, rebuffs him, saying his crew prefers to explore the galaxy without his help. Angered by what he sees as the hubris of an inferior species and with the warning that humans are not ready for what they will encounter in space, Q sends the *Enterprise* hurtling across the galaxy and then disappears. Eventually, the crew encounters the Borg, a part-human, part-cybernetic race. The Borg attack and demand the surrender of the *Enterprise* for assimilation. Following an unsuccessful attempt to repel the Borg invaders, Picard calls out for Q's help and Q obliges, returning the ship to where it started.

The Q of "Q Who" is less gender discrepant and less preoccupied with particular members of the crew and, instead, turns more petulant and parental. The episode also portends an evolution in the relationship between Q and the *Enterprise* crew, one in which Q is less a judge and more of a manipulator of characters. The role is no less queer, recalling the machinations of Brandon in Alfred Hitchcock's *Rope* (based upon the real murderous queer couple Nathan Leopold and Richard Loeb). At the same time, the episode's narrative presents an allegory of the would-be suitor who, once spurned and driven mad by desire, seeks to destroy the love that he cannot have—before ultimately relenting. His continuing use of Starfleet uniforms and his ability to trump Picard in his own mission by introducing them to an "unbeatable" foe—one that initially has no gender[2]—signals Q's further intention to "queer" Starfleet. This time, Q uses Starfleet's rhetoric of exploring the unknown and reduces the strong, stalwart Picard to pleading for the lives of the crew. In the end, Q even chastises Picard, telling the flagship captain about the "unknown" and warns him exploration is not for those easily scared or those who refuse to leave their comfort zones. Picard, who had immediately rejected Q's offers, is rebuked for adhering to straight-and-narrow Starfleet standards. The gender-less Borg and Q himself ultimately prove that Picard's inability to fit alternate gender roles within Starfleet's heteronormative outlook will lead to his downfall.

The episode "Déjà Q" returns to the prior device of Q's appearances as the *Enterprise* crew is sent to save a threatened alien world. In this case, Q appears on the bridge naked and stripped of his powers by the Continuum as punishment for spreading chaos through the galaxy. This leaves him vulnerable to attack by members of species whom he has tormented. When Commander Data is nearly destroyed due to his attempts to protect Q from one of the species, Q decides he places the *Enterprise* crew at too much risk and leaves in a shuttlecraft. This comparatively selfless act attracts the attention of the Continuum, which lifts his banishment and restores his powers.

This fourth appearance of Q is distinguished by the campy inflection it brings to Q's malevolence. "Camp" is a literary form frequently associated with LGBTQ subculture, though the exclusivity of that association is subject for debate. Scholars including Moe Meyer argue for its status as a uniquely queer form (1), while Cynthia Morrill goes one step farther, claiming camp is an effect of (and reaction to) homophobia (119). Others, including Susan Sontag, believe there are areas of overlap between straight camp and gay camp, though they are distinct (117). Q's reaction to his powerlessness and consequent experiencing of human discomfort in the form of hunger and pain elicits exaggerated responses that border on hilarity. Most memorable, however, is the over-the-top celebration Q stages when he is accepted back into the Continuum, including a traditional Mariachi band on the bridge (in traditional costume with Q playing trumpet), completely disrupting the military protocol on the bridge. Q also gives a phallic cigar to Picard, and provides Worf and Riker with "fantasy" women.

Q's triumphant finale is reminiscent of scenes from the 1960s television series *Bewitched* involving Paul Lynde's Uncle Arthur, regarded by gay critics as the queerest moments in a queer series. The greatest example of queerness, however, occurs with Data. Like Kivas Fajo from "The Most Toys," Q subverts Data's programming by making him laugh. This perversion of Data's operating system demonstrates a queer reading of Starfleet norms and Data's own masculinity. However, like Q's celebratory band and ephemera in this scene, the show presents Data's "corruption" as a beneficial, even positive moment. Troi smiles, sharing Data's joy in an empathetic sense, and Data laughs even harder when he looks back at the command crew. At the end, Data describes laughter as a wonderful sensation, but it is one he would never have experienced if not for Q. As for Picard, the captain fails to understand the moment's significance. Holding his cigar, he muses that perhaps Q has gained some insight from humanity. Q promptly appears in the phallic cigar's smoke, telling Picard to think otherwise. Indeed, Q's parting gift to Data suggests that the crew benefited more from Q's presence than the other way around.

In his next appearance, Q's emotional manipulation extends to Picard's romantic interests. In "Qpid," Q returns to the *Enterprise* for the stated purpose of repaying his debt to Picard for helping save him in their previous encounter. His visit coincides with the return of Vash, an archeologist with a dubious past with whom Picard has been romantically linked. When Picard declines Q's offer to repay his debt, Q transports Picard and members of his crew to medieval England to reenact scenes from the Robin Hood legend to test Picard's love for Vash. Appropriately for Picard's longtime antagonist, Q takes the role of the Sheriff of Nottingham—again, another authority figure who hunts the outlaw Robin Hood/Picard—and who has imprisoned Vash/Maid Marian. Picard is himself captured after Vash objects to his rescue plan and refuses to leave with him. The crew, disguised as Robin Hood's Merry Men, saves Picard, Vash leaves under Q's protection to explore the galaxy, and Picard considers their debt settled.

As in "Déjà Q," the key marker of queerness in "Qpid" is high camp, in this case, adapting action adventure characters from the 24th century (including a visually-impaired starship engineer and a Klingon) to action adventure characters set in the 13th century. Q's specific artifice is creating for Picard the perfect heroic romance story with what is ostensibly a fairy tale ending, save for the unpredictability of Vash in the role of damsel in distress. While service in Starfleet no doubt carries its own chivalrous code, it is likely less stilted and better suited to 24th century technologies and culture than that of 900 years before. The episode also features a scene with Q at Picard's bedside, which is clearly gender-discrepant behavior and an invitation to queer readings for viewers so inclined. In fact, still photographs from the scene are among the most circulated in cyberspace of Q and Picard.

Fan culture's appropriation of Q's "romance" with Picard demonstrates their acceptance of the queering of Starfleet heteronormative romance. Q claims he wanted to teach Picard a lesson in love, but in the end, it is the omnipotent being who ends up with the captain's love interest. Most notably, Q woos Vash by promising her what the stoic, proper Picard cannot: access to untold riches. To do so, Q disregards Starfleet regulations and "hands-off" policies, much to Picard's outrage and Vash's delight. As with "Q Who," Q gets under Picard's skin, turning the strong captain into a jealous lover as Q trades his Starfleet uniform for beige archeologist garb in the final scene. Q promises to take care of Vash to soothe Picard's anger, but the audience knows that only Q could stir a lack of control in Starfleet decorum in the first place.

Perhaps the episode least available for queer readings of the Q character is "True Q," in which the *Enterprise* plays host to a young biological sciences intern, Amanda Rogers, who unwittingly may be part of the Q Continuum. Q reappears and details of Amanda's past emerge: she is the offspring of two members of the Q Continuum who took human form. Her parents were later killed by the Continuum, who grew to fear them. Under pressure from Captain Picard, Q admits he was sent by the Continuum to encourage her to join the Continuum or to kill her if she refuses. Here, the narrative sides against Q because Amanda lives a heteronormative life: her parents abandon the Q to live as a "traditional" human couple and Amanda wants to live and serve in a Starfleet-approved manner. Of course, the Q Continuum, with its expansive, alternate modes of behavior, sees her as a threat.

In a narrative reminiscent of the choice given Riker in "Hide and Q," Picard persuades Q to give Amanda the option to renounce her powers and live as a human. When the *Enterprise* answers a distress call from a nearby planet, the young woman is compelled to use her powers to save the lives of the inhabitants. Amanda accepts her identity as a "true Q" and leaves with him. Accepting her true nature presumably means an absolute rejection of her gender. She is not human or a woman; she is Q.

Even here, Q can be read queerly by audiences familiar with the functions of film and television characters played by actresses such as Agnes Moorehead. As Patricia White observes, among Moorehead's more enduring roles (including the mother-in-law Endora on *Bewitched*) are those in which she is an acerbic (apparent) spinster who disrupts conventional heterosexual pairings, such as the one between daughter Samantha and son-in-law Darren (108). Since Moorehead herself is now thought to have been a lesbian or bisexual, her work has come to represent its own character type: the witty lesbian whose dialogue drives a wedge between husband and wife, boyfriend and girlfriend.

In "True Q," Q may be thought of similarly as Moorehead's male equivalent, interfering with the burgeoning romance between Amanda and Riker (and between Vash and Picard in "Qpid"). Q unsuccessfully wooed a beardless Riker in "Hide and Q" and, here, comments on how unattractive Riker is with his facial hair in his attempt to dissuade Amanda from romantically pursuing the first officer. When Amanda rescues Riker, Q denies her the possibility of romancing Riker when she decides she is "Q" and not a human woman, and they leave for the Continuum. Like Moorehead, Q interferes with heteronormative romance.

The seventh appearance of the Q character, in "Tapestry," has provided Picard/Q slash fiction fans with their most evocative visual evidence of Q's homoerotic attraction to the *Enterprise* captain. In the episode, Picard apparently dies when his artificial heart is damaged during a diplomatic mission. He awakens in an otherworldly setting to find Q, who offers Picard the chance to re-live his life, including the bar-fight that originally necessitated replacement of his biological heart with a mechanical replacement. He avoids the fight, but then lives life on the *Enterprise* as a lower grade officer with a dreary job. In a resolution that recalls the iconic Frank Capra film *It's a Wonderful Life*, Q reasons that Picard's early near-death experience has taught Picard that life is too precious to squander by playing it "safe." Picard re-awakens in sickbay to discover he, in fact, survived the attack.

The evidence of Q's queerness that sent shockwaves through the *Star Trek: The Next Generation* fan community is a scene in which Picard awakens in bed after what viewers assume was a sexual liaison with Marta, a fellow Starfleet cadet. Instead of Marta, he finds himself in bed with Q, who comments on Picard's re-imagined youth. Fans open to queer readings of Q have wondered aloud with whom Picard really had sex, since none of the acquaintances from his previous life now would exist in the form he remembered. Might he have had sex with Q unwittingly? This supposition is problematic on many levels, since imagined alternative scenarios with fictional characters (including omnipotent ones) would not necessarily adhere to linear timelines or impact reality. But it provided fuel to stoke fan assumptions of a queer Q.

Just as Q's first appearance was in *Star Trek: The Next Generation*'s pilot episode, his last was in the series finale, the two-part "All Good Things...." The episode opens with Captain Picard experiencing temporal discontinuities in which he inexplicably finds himself seven years earlier at the start of his command of the *Enterprise*, in the present, and 25 years in the future as an elderly man. In the past, he finds himself again in Q's courtroom, where he is reminded that humanity's trial never concluded, but is merely suspended. Q admits being the cause of Picard's temporal discontinuities and presents him with a puzzle he must solve in order to save humanity. Picard eventually does so but loses his ship and crew in each timeline. But Q concludes humanity can evolve and thus is worthy of saving.

Scenes involving the robe-bedecked Q recall his earlier campiness, complete with commands initiated with finger-snapping, broad gestures, and elaborate dress and surroundings. The episode also features several instances of Q's classic playfulness (albeit a darker version, given the enormity of the stakes), including his repeated taunting of Picard. At one point in the future timeline, in which the anomaly is so small it is undetectable, the elderly Picard yells at Q, demanding to know where the anomaly is. Q, mimicking the age-related hearing loss and confusion afflicting Picard, replies he has no idea where Picard's mommy is.

Q mocks Picard in this moment, but he also serves as a queer hero in a narrative sense. Picard's former wife, Captain Beverly Picard, tells Picard he may be delusional and imagined the entire plot. For the first time, the elderly former captain, so confident in enlisting his old command crew and taking charge, falters. Q appears and his appearance reassures Picard he is not losing his mind. Q's taunt, that Picard wants his mommy, attacks the captain's masculinity, but Q's very presence bolsters Picard's self-esteem, and points out the aged Starfleet officers (Beverly Picard, Admiral Riker) are wrong. Indeed, shortly before the future timeline ends, Q appears next to Picard, dressed in a Starfleet uniform (not the futuristic version), telling the captain that he had so much potential to expand his mind—not only in interstellar anomalies but also in gender lines, perhaps—but that every good thing ends. Q hinted this idea in "Q Who," but now Picard rises to the occasion; the scene shifts to the courtroom and Picard, back in uniform, realizes Q's lesson to explore human existence, with all of the complexities pertaining to humanity. Q smiles and tells Picard he will see the *Enterprise* crew again.

Considered together, the eight episodes in which Q appears reveal a character whose gender performance frequently transgresses the norms of conventional masculinity. Q employs camp behaviors and artifice. He displays seemingly misogynistic and dismissive attitudes towards female members of the crew (at one point, he briefly turns Beverly Crusher into an Irish setter). He disrupts the heteronormative relationships between Picard and Vash and between Riker and Amanda Rogers. Q is preoccupied with the crew's male members, particularly Picard, Riker, and Data. Furthermore, he regards traditional male displays of aggression and physical prowess as meaningless, and belittles their exemplar, Worf. Though his character is textually asexual, his attempts to seduce Riker into the Q Continuum can be read more broadly and his bedroom scenes with Picard are, at the very least, suggestive.

Queer Unfriendly

Despite the potential for Q to be read as a queer hero, any official recognition of such did not emerge. Instead, the first live-action television sequel of the *Star Trek* franchise reflected an inclination to represent queerness as evil, if it was to be represented at all. Two additional accounts, each verified by multiple witnesses, demonstrate further the toxic environment facing positive queer storylines behind the scenes of *Star Trek: The Next Generation*. In the first, demands by fans for queer characters prompted screenwriter David Gerrold, a self-identified gay man, to write an HIV/AIDS allegory about the rescue of a space vessel infested with deadly plague for *Star Trek: The Next Generation*. The episode, "Fire and Ice," featured a gay male couple as part of the crew, one of whom would sacrifice himself to save the away team (Toth 21). Reaction to the script from the series' creative staff was mixed, with executive producer Rick Berman saying stations airing the series in the afternoon wouldn't run it (Altman) and Roddenberry not wanting an episode with gay crewmen as the primary focus, since by the 24th century sexuality would no longer be controversial (Toth 21). Gerrold was ordered to remove the gay characters from the episode and eventually abandoned it entirely after several re-writes (Clark; Coffren 1-E). Herb Wright, a fellow writer who supported the storyline and had offered to collaborate with Gerrold on re-writes, was fired (Kay). Gerrold, too, left the series soon after (Justman 334). The overall quality of the script has been criticized (Kay) though Gerrold eventually auctioned copies of it online to dispel rumors it was unworkable (Coffren 1-E). However, with the arrival of the Internet in the 1990s and the availability of alternative avenues for distribution, Gerrold revived the project and directed a production of it for *Star Trek: New Voyages* in 2008. CBS, which owns the rights to *Star Trek*, has not contested production of the episode (or the *New Voyages* series) since it was not intended for profits.

For his part, Gerrold has attributed the negative atmosphere toward queer representations to the lessened influence on series production from creator Gene Roddenberry, whose physical health was declining and mental confusion was increasing. Roddenberry died in October 1991, near the start of the fifth season of *The Next Generation*. In his stead, other producers and writers took over, aided by Roddenberry's attorney, Leonard Maizlish, whom, Gerrold recalls, called him "'an AIDS-infected cocksucker. A fucking faggot'" (Kay). However, producer Robert Justman recalled Roddenberry himself "junked" the teleplay for "Fire and Ice" due to its "homosexual content" (Solow and Justman 334). Justman, who regarded "Fire and Ice" much more highly than Gerrold's famed "The Trouble with Tribbles," written for The Original Series, stated he "fought a losing battle to change Gene's mind" (Solow and Justman 334). Regardless of where the fault lies, "Fire and Ice" remains outside the *Star Trek* canon.

The second account concerns production of the third-season episode, "The Offspring," in which Data decides to experience parenthood and constructs an offspring, Lal. Although initially androgynous, Lal chooses a female appearance. In one scene, she is puzzled by the sight of female and male crewmembers kissing in Ten Forward. Guinan, an unofficial ship's counselor, was originally supposed to explain human affection and mating rituals. But according to Richard Arnold, a research consultant for the series, actress Whoopi Goldberg refused to speak her scripted line, "When a man and a woman are in love..." insisting it be changed to, "When two people are in love..." and asserted that a kiss between a same-sex pair be the object of attention.[3] Given Lal's origins, and her choice to become a female, a same-sex kiss would underscore the social construct of gender on- and off-screen. However, producer David Livingston, Arnold claims, personally came on-set to block the change (Kay).

To be fair, one must acknowledge that the failure of the producers of *Star Trek: The Next Generation* to populate the cast with identifiably lesbian or gay characters has many plausible justifications not related to homophobic intent. First, if one assumes the proportion of "Terrans," the science-fiction term for humans from Earth, who are same sex-attracted to be relatively fixed over time (though the notion of sexuality as a social construct suggests queerness would not be), they would be, at best, a minority of the crew, perhaps five to ten percent out of one thousand. Fifty or a hundred lesbian or gay crew, of course, on a vessel with a population of 1,014 could avoid overt notice. Even so, viewers could not be faulted for hoping that, in seven seasons and 178 episodes, they would have seen evidence of at least one queer crewmember. Interestingly, the Centers for Disease Control and Prevention has estimated the number of visually-impaired U.S. citizens to be about five percent of the population, or a number similar to the low end of the estimated number of lesbians and gays. Yet, a prominent member of the *Enterprise-D* main cast for all seven seasons and four feature films, Geordi LaForge, is visually impaired.[4]

It can also be argued that in a quasi-military environment such as Starfleet, sexual and affectionate relationships would not be in the foreground more than, say, professional relationships and friendships. As a result, the failure to address the sexuality of members of the crew would not be unusual. That argument fails, however, when one considers that the sexual and affectionate lives of all of the cast principals are addressed in its episodes, including Picard's attraction to Beverly Crusher and to the infrequent character Vash, Worf's relationship with K'Ehleyr and later with Deanna Troi, Riker's relationship with Troi, LaForge's attraction to the holographic image of the female designer of the *Enterprise*, Data's sexual liaison with Tasha Yar, Wesley Crusher's attraction to Salia in

"The Dauphin" and his involvement with a female engineer in "The Game," and Transporter Chief Miles O'Brien's marriage to Keiko. In addition, background shots in the Enterprise lounge, Ten-Forward, frequently depict evidence of close social ties between opposite-sex couples. The prominence of heteronormativity on the *Enterprise* reduces queer representations to a Starfleet equivalent of a military Don't Ask, Don't Tell policy.

Conclusion

A central tenet of Queer Theory cautions that sexual and gender identities are provisional and contingent; thus, judgments regarding sexuality and gender performance applied to the conventions of one time and place to others are, at best, risky. It follows that readings of Fajo, the J'naii, and Q as queer are based upon a highly subjective and complex system of codes rooted in notions of conventionally appropriate gender performance and behavior and, thus, oppositional readings also have their basis. But though science fiction, by its very nature, transports the audience to contexts other than their own, the fact remains that the objective of such journeys usually is to reveal a truth about contexts closer to home but through means that are far less threatening because of their supposed fictional nature. The creator of the story and the audience, try as they might, carry the baggage of experiences and backgrounds that are common and contemporary. Thus, the standards for behavior conventionally appropriate for one's gender still apply, as do the boundaries that mark deviance from those conventions. According to Meredith Li-Vollmer and Mark E. LaPointe, exhibitions of gender that society defines as unnatural lead both to social stigma and prejudicial evaluation. Such transgressions may also cast doubt on that individual's competence, social acceptability, and morality.

Earlier in this essay, I noted *The Lion King*'s Timon and Pumbaa could be considered queer not just because they are a same-gender couple but also because of transgressive behaviors that were ciphers developed during the Production Code–like Hollywood regarding homosexuality. Cultural critic Mark Simpson has questioned whether sexuality can be a factor in the assessment of queerness for animated Disney characters, given that characters whose sexual behavior is neither witnessed nor alluded to can't be thought of as having sexuality. Like Timon and Pumbaa, he argues, early film comedians Laurel and Hardy weren't gay, but they weren't straight either. Instead, their antics transgressed boundaries of heteronormative masculinity and it was precisely those transgressions that are the source for our pleasure in them (Simpson 274).

My arguments that Q, Kivas Fajo, and the J'naii are both villainous and queer are based upon gender performance and the assumptions mainstream culture traditionally makes about sexuality from gender behavior. While the texts of *Star Trek: The Next Generation* are largely silent concerning the question of these characters' sexual desires, I argue that, from a cultural standpoint, evidence of their sexuality is less a definitive marker of a transgressive, and queer, identity because, as with colorful Disney characters and classic film comedians, transgressions are seldom more than private and assumed for publicly-broadcasted television characters.

Notes

1. Q is queer and specifically polyamorous: his eroticism extends beyond Picard to varied species and sexes. In an episode of *Star Trek: Voyager*, "The Q and the Grey," Q considers Captain Kathryn Janeway as a

potential mate. However, as befitting his non-gendered status, Q considered mating with a Klingon Targ, the Romulan empress, and a Cerelian microbe, among other entities.

2. On the Borg and gender dynamics, see Olaf Meuther's essay in this volume.

3. Perhaps a stronger scene that appeared on screen is "The Host," where Crusher falls in love with a symbiont, Odan, living in a male host. When the male host dies, Crusher implants the symbiont into Riker to keep it alive, which complicates her romantic feelings. When Odan's true replacement host—a woman— arrives, Crusher chooses to end the romance entirely, even though Odan says she still loves Crusher. The ending received mixed reactions from fans as either an affirmation or criticism of heteronormativity.

4. On biopolitics and a further discussion of dis/ability, see Simon Ledder's, Jens Kolata's, and Oonagh Hayes' essay in this volume.

WORKS CITED

Abramovitch, Seth. "George Takei Reacts to Gay Sulu News: 'I think it's really unfortunate.'" *The Hollywood Reporter*, http://www.hollywoodreporter.com/news/george-takei-reacts-gay-sulu-909154, 7 July 2016.

"After It Happened." *Midnight Caller*. Writ. Stephen Zito. Dir. Mimi Leder. NBC. Television Syndication. 13 December 1988.

"Against the Odds: Making a Difference in Global Health." *National Institutes of Health.* 2000, Web. https://apps.nlm.nih.gov/againsttheodds/exhibit/video_transcripts.cfm

"All Good Things…." *Star Trek: The Next Generation*. Writ. Ronald D. Moore and Brannon Braga. Dir. Winrich Kolbe. Television Syndication. Paramount. 23 May 1994.

Altman, Mark A. "Tackling Gay Rights." *Cinefantastique* 23.2/3 (1992). 71–74. Print.

Aul, Billie, and Brian Frank. "Prisoners of Dogma and Prejudice: Why There Are No G/L/B/T Characters in *Star Trek: Deep Space Nine*." *Foundation* vol. 86 (2002): 51–64. Print.

Barnes-Brus, Tori. "The Contradictions of Gay Tele-Visibility: A Reaction to Gamson." *Social Thought & Research* vol. 26, no. 1/2 (2005): 19–23. Print.

"Blood and Fire." *Star Trek: New Voyages*. Writ. and Dir. David Gerrold. YouTubewww. 20 Dec. 2008. Web. https://www.youtube.com/watch?v=PWWR9z71CFI

Bowers V. Hardwick, 478 U.S. 186 (1986). Justia. n.d. Web. https://supreme.justia.com/cases/federal/us/478/186/case.html

Clark, Joe. "Star Trek: The Next Generation—Queer Characters Join the Enterprise Crew." *The Advocate* 27 (1991). Print.

Coffren, John. "Aids Allegory Raises Awareness on 'Enterprise.'" *The Baltimore Sun* 5 February 2003: 1-E. Print.

"The Dauphin." *Star Trek: The Next Generation*. Writ. Scott Rubenstein and Leonard Mlodinow. Dir. Rob Bowman. Television Syndication. Paramount. 20 February 1989.

"Déjà Q." *Star Trek: The Next Generation*. Writ. Richard Danus. Dir. Les Landau. Television Syndication. Paramount. 5 February 1990.

Dyer, Richard. *Now You See It* (rev. ed.). New York: Routledge, 2013. Print.

"Encounter at Farpoint." *Star Trek: The Next Generation*. Writ. D.C. Fontana and Gene Roddenberry. Dir. Corey Allen. Television Syndication. Paramount. 28 Sept. 1987.

"The Game." *Star Trek: The Next Generation*. Writ. Brannon Braga, Susan Sackett, and Fred Bronson. Dir. Corey Allen. Television Syndication. Paramount. 28 October 1991.

"Hide and Q." *Star Trek: The Next Generation*. Writ. C.J. Holland and Gene Roddenberry. Dir. Cliff Bole. Television Syndication. Paramount. 23 November 1987.

"The Host." *Star Trek: The Next Generation*. Writ. Michel Horvet. Dir. Marvin V. Rush. Television Syndication. Paramount. 11 May 1991.

Ingebretsen, Edward J. "Monster-Making: A Politics of Persuasion." *Journal of American Culture* 21.2 (1998): 25–34. Print.

It's a Wonderful Life. Screenplay by Frank Capra, Frances Goodrich, Albert Hackett, Jo Swerling, and Michael Wilson. Dir. Frank Capra. Perf. Jimmy Stewart, Donna Reed, and Lionel Barrymore. Liberty Films, 1947.

Jenkins, Henry. "'Out of the Closet and into the Universe': Queers and *Star Trek*." *Science Fiction Audiences: Watching* Star Trek *and* Doctor Who, edited by John Tulloch and Henry Jenkins. New York: Routledge, 2005, 237–265. Print.

Kay, Jonathan. "Gay 'Trek': After Three Decades and Four Series, the Starship Enterprise Has Never Seen a Gay Ensign. Will 'Star Trek' Ever Cross the Final Frontier? Salonwww. 30 Jun. 2001, Web. http://www.Salon.Com/2001/06/30/Gay_Trek/

Latchem, John. "'Star Trek' Series Soaring on Blu-Ray." *Home Media Magazine*. 4 April 2013. Web. 5 April 2017. http://www.homemediamagazine.com/paramount/star-trek-series-soaring-blu-ray-30088

Li-Vollmer, Meredith, and LaPointe, Mark E. "Gender Transgression and Villainy in Animated Film." *Popular Communication* 1.2 (2003): 89–109. Print.

Mailer, Norman. "The Homosexual Villain." *Advertisements for Myself*. Cambridge, MA: Harvard University Press, 1959. 220–227. Print.

"Mask of Death." *Streets of San Francisco*. Writ. Robert Malcolm Young. Dir. Harry Falk. Television Syndication. ABC Warne Bros. 3 October 1974.

Meyer, Moe. "Introduction: Reclaiming the Discourse of Camp." *The Politics and Poetics of Camp*. Ed. Moe Meyer, London, UK: Routledge, 1994: 1–22. Print.

Morrill, Cynthia. "Revamping the Gay Sensibility." *The Politics and Poetics of Camp*. Ed. Moe Meyer, London, UK: Routledge, 1994: 110–129. Print.

"The Most Toys." *Star Trek: The Next Generation*. Writ. Shari Goodhartz. Dir. Timothy Bond. Television Syndication. Paramount. 7 May 1990.

National Health Interview Survey. Washington, D.C.: Centers for Disease Control and Prevention, 1994–95. Print.

Nemecek, Larry. *Star Trek: The Next Generation Companion* (3rd ed.). New York: Pocket Books, 2003. Print.

Netzley, Sara Baker. "Visibility That Demystifies: Gays, Gender, and Sex on Television." *Journal of Homosexuality* 57.8 (2010): 968–986. Print.

"The Offspring." *Star Trek: The Next Generation*. Writ. René Echevarria. Dir. Jonathan Frakes. Television Syndication. Paramount. 12 March 1990.

"The Outcast." *Star Trek: The Next Generation*. Writ. Jeri Taylor. Dir. Robert Scheerer. Television Syndication. Paramount. 16 Mar. 1992.

Putnam, Amanda. "Mean Ladies: Transgendered Villains in Disney Films." *Diversity in Disney Films: Critical Essays on Race, Ethnicity, Gender, Sexuality and Disability*. Ed. Johnson Cheu, Jefferson, NC: McFarland, 2013. 147–163. Print.

"The Q and the Grey." *Star Trek: Voyager*. Writ. Kenneth Biller. Dir. Cliff Bole. United Paramount Network. 27 November 1996.

"Q Who." *Star Trek: The Next Generation*. Writ. Maurice Hurley. Dir. Rob Bowman. Television Syndication. Paramount. 8 May 1989.

"Qpid." *Star Trek: The Next Generation*. Writ. Randee Russell and Ira Steven Behr. Dir. Cliff Bole. Television Syndication. Paramount. 22 April 1991.

Rope. Screenplay by Arthur Laurents. Dir. Alfred Hitchcock. Perf. John Dall, Farley Granger, Jimmy Stewart, and Joan Chandler. Warner Brothers, 1948.

Rotello, Gabriel. "The Inning of Outing." *The Columbia Reader on Lesbians and Gay Men in Media, Society, and Politics*. Ed. Larry Gross & J.D. Woods. New York: Columbia University Press, 1999. 433–34. Print.

Rubin, Gayle. "Thinking Sex: Notes for a Radical Theory of the Politics of Sexuality." *Pleasure and Danger*. Ed. Carole Vance. New York: Routledge & Kegan Paul, 1984. 267–318. Print.

Russo, Vito. *Celluloid Closet*. New York: Harper & Row, 1987. Print.

Shuster, Fred. "Future 'Trek' from Valley Portal, Space Odyssey Travels Onto the Web." *The Free Library*. 2006. Web. 23 October 2009. https://www.thefreelibrary.com/FUTURE+%60TREK%27+FROM+VALLEY+PORTAL%2c+SPACE+ODYSSEY+TRAVELS+ONTO+THE+WEB.-a0154473678

Simpson, Mark. *Male Impersonation: Men Performing Masculinity*. New York: Routledge, 1994. Print.

Solow, Herbert F. and Robert H. Justman. *Inside Star Trek: The Real Story*. New York: Pocket Books, 1996. Print.

Sonntag, Susan. "Notes on Camp." *A Susan Sonntag Reader*. New York: Vintage Books, 1983: 105–119. Print.

Storzer, Gerald H. "The Homosexual Paradigm in Balzac, Gide and Genet." *Homosexualities and French Literature: Cultural Contexts/Critical Texts*. Eds. G. Stamboulian and E. Marks. Ithaca, NY: Cornell University Press, 1979. 186–209. Print.

Sweeney, Gael. "'What Do You Want Me to Do? Dress in Drag and Do the Hula?': Timon and Pumbaa's Alternative Lifestyle Dilemma in the *Lion King*." *Diversity in Disney Films: Critical Essays on Race, Ethnicity, Gender, Sexuality and Disability*. Ed. Johnson Cheu. Jefferson, NC: McFarland, 2013. 129–146. Print.

"Tapestry." *Star Trek: The Next Generation*. Writ. Ronald D. Moore. Dir. Les Landau. Television Syndication. Paramount. 15 February 1993.

"True Q." *Star Trek: The Next Generation*. Writ. Rene Echevarria. Dir. Robert Scheerer. Television Syndication. Paramount. 26 October 1992.

Toth, Kathleen. "Blood and Fire: The Past Is Prologue." *Doctor Who Bulletin (Dwb)* 107 (1992, November): 21. Print.

Weir, John. "Gay-Bashing, Villainy and the Oscars." *New York Times* 29 March 1992: 22. Print.

White, Patricia. "Supporting Character: The Queer Career of Agnes Moorehead." *Out in Culture: Gay, Lesbian, and Queer Essays on Popular Culture*. Ed. K. Creekmur and A. Doty. Durham: Duke University Press, 1995. 91–114. Print.

Wizard of Oz. Screenplay by Noel Langley, Florence Ryerson, and Edgar Allan Woolf. Dir. Victor Fleming. Perf. Judy Garland, Frank Morgan, Ray Bolger, Bert Lahr, and Jack Haley. MGM, 1939.

Going Where No Woman Had Gone Before

Women's Roles on the Enterprise-D
*as Reflective of Women's Changing Roles
in the American Labor Force*

Erin C. Callahan

When Gene Rodenberry edited the iconic split infinitive in the opening credits of *Star Trek* to eliminate gender-biased language, it signaled that the forthcoming "next generation" of the franchise would provide more open spaces and opportunities for their female characters. In *TOS*, the presence of communications officer Lieutenant Uhura on the bridge spoke to the small successes of the 1964 Equal Employment provision of the Civil Rights Act regarding equal female participation in the workplace. As an officer, she plays a significant role in the successes of the *Enterprise's* mission. To be sure, Uhura is not the only female character, female officer, or female leader on *TOS*, but she is the only featured or primary character presented as such, with other female characters and plot-lines depicting women in roles supportive to their male counterparts or in traditionally female roles.

The debut of *TNG* in the fall of 1987 created expectations that the roles women would play in new series would be expanded beyond *TOS* and reflect 24th century gender equality and relations—a place and time in which expectations of traditional gender performance would be eliminated. However, as Lynne Joyrich explains in her critique of gender performance in *TNG*, to achieve successful ratings, especially because it was launched in syndication rather than on a network, the presentation of gender roles were those that late twentieth century audiences would recognize, accept, and support (62). For this reason, many of the female characters are presented according to traditional patriarchal feminine ideals of women as supportive and receptive to men. Similarly, in her critique of gender portrayals in *TNG*, Victoria Korzeniowska argues that the show more accurately depicts gender relations in the 1980s rather than that of an idealized 24th century. In the eighteen years from the time the final episode of *TOS* aired to the start of *TNG*, efforts of second wave feminists of the 1960s and 1970s shifted part of the dialogue in America to women's equality in the public sphere, in the work force, and in education. Where *TNG* succeeds in creating greater equality between its male and female characters than *TOS* is in its depiction of the women in the Starfleet workforce.

166

Women in the Late–20th Century Workforce

In the decades between the two shows, American women achieved greater participation in the workforce and expanded the types of professions in which they were employed. When *TOS* debuted in 1966, women accounted for 34 percent of the American labor force (Women's Bureau: Department of Labor). They were primarily employed in service-based or supportive occupations, such as clerical or administrative support, retail, nursing, and teaching at the elementary level ("Women at Work"). Female-dominated professions during this era reinforced women's roles as both receptive to and supportive of male professions. The female labor force of *TOS* reflected those standards. Other than Uhura, who was a featured cast member, the only notable female characters in the series were Nurse Christine Chapel and Yeoman Janice Reed. Both of these characters served as secondary mainstays in the films and their career trajectories reflected the changing landscape of the American workforce. Most of this development, particularly in the films, overlapped with *TNG*'s run and parallels female employment as shown in the series. Department of Labor statistics show that "[b]etween 1972 and 2002, the proportion of managerial jobs held by women more than doubled, increasing from 20 to 45 percent" ("Women at Work"). Wooten's research on labor trends between 1970 and 1995 concludes that "[t]he advances of the women's movement, the enactment of laws prohibiting sex discrimination, increases in enrollment in higher education and professional schools, the steady increase in women's labor force participation, and reductions in gender stereotyping in both education and employment all contributed to this trend" (15). Though the featured secondary characters in *TNG* still occupied supporting and low-skill professions like nursing or bartending, women were also seen as scientists, engineers, and command officers. This suggests a stratified female employment structure, a point discussed in detail later in this essay.

However, countering the advances in women's equality during the 1960s and 1970s, the 1980s witnessed a rise in popularity of social conservatism that was deeply rooted in traditional gender roles. Family values were central to this dynamic and focused on heteronormative patriarchy. In discussing the gender roles in American patriarchy, Judith Butler asserts that "[d]iscrete genders are part of what "humanizes" individuals within contemporary cultures; indeed, those who fail to do their gender right are regularly punished (903). Social conservatives sought to challenge progress of the 1960s and 1970s by reinforcing the importance of the nuclear family and the gender roles contained within.[1] They argued that deviations from physical and behavioral norms in gender performance threaten the stasis of the family structure in a heteronormative schema. Additionally, Aaron Devor asserts "[f]eminity, according to this traditional formation, "would result in warm and continued relationships with men, a sense of maternity, interest in caring for children, and the capacity to work productively and continuously in female occupations" (419). Social conservatives highlighted the archetypical role of women as dependent upon male figures, with the dual roles of wife and mother reinforcing the domestic sphere as a safe haven. However, the economic recession during the 1970s that continued into the 1980s demanded that many middle and working-class families maintain two incomes. Women who entered the workforce were expected to "have it all," meaning they could successfully perform in their roles as both professionals and as nurturing and supportive mothers and wives within the American patriarchal schema.

This is the challenge in the representation of women that viewers see among the female *TNG* characters. Creators, writers, and producers worked within this framework of viewers' expectations based on the gender identities of the 1980s, while also attempting to depict the utopian society Gene Roddenberry originally wanted to project among all genders and species. For many scholars, *TNG* falls short of presenting equal and fully developed female characters who accurately reflect this vision of an egalitarian society *Star Trek* idealizes. Indeed, one would imagine that gender would cease to be an issue in the 24th century. Rather, these scholars argue the *TNG* primarily featured depictions of gender performance based on late twentieth century patriarchal stereotypes and archetypes, centering on physical beauty, motherhood, romantic sexual availability, and female characters' reliance on emotions and feelings rather than logic and strength.

However, the primary and featured female characters introduced in the first episode depict a stratification of female gender performance. Two of the main featured female characters, Deanna Troi and Beverly Crusher do, as Korzeniowska and Joyrich argue, reinforce late 1980s gender roles and performance as 24th century norms. Both women wear traditional long hairstyles, accentuate beautification make-up, and wear clothes that deviate from the traditional Starfleet uniform. Deanna Troi, the series' most regularly featured character, creates the ideal of a professional woman valued for both her appearance and her professional acumen.[2] As a mother, Beverly Crusher performs the dual role of mother and worker, most clearly reflective of the majority of the 1980's female work force. However, it is in Chief Security Officer Tasha Yar and the secondary characters that viewers see the most significant deviation from the traditional feminine role. But when *TNG* challenged the social conservative turn of its contemporary period, as in the case of Tasha Yar and these secondary characters, viewers generally resisted these representations, causing the show to revert to more traditional characterizations. Ultimately, the series reinforces the feminine stereotypes and archetypes and female career development of the late twentieth century, but succeeds in forwarding the conversation of workforce equality.

Ambitious Beginnings

The pilot episode, "Encounter at Farpoint," first aired on September 26, 1987, established the foundation of the hierarchy of gender performances and identities that the series developed and reinforced throughout its run. Since it follows a military model, Starfleet is understandably phallocentric and relies on many hypermasculine norms as its organizational model. Most notably, the two highest-ranking officers on the *Enterprise*, Captain Jean-Luc Picard and First Officer William Riker, are male and, in commanding the ship, generally impart a male-oriented perspective for the series' narrative. After the opening epitaph, the first thing viewers hear is Picard giving voice to the ship's mission, with his voiceovers literally providing the framework for the viewers' understanding of the episode's context. Picard's perspective continues to narrate each episode through his Captain's and Personal Logs, with Riker periodically substituting in that role. Through these logs, male viewpoints shape the way viewers mediate the world of the series.

Despite the male-centered narrative, "Encounter at Farpoint" also challenges normalized gender roles of the late twentieth century. After viewers are introduced to Captain Picard and the bridge crew, Deanna Troi senses the presence of a powerful mind just before the antagonist Q appears. When he challenges the crew to prove that humans have evolved beyond being an infantile race, Worf's response that they should fight is stereo-typically aggressive, violent, and masculine, befitting the warrior culture viewers expect of Klingons. However, the women officers offer a rational middle ground. Yar advises that they fight or escape. Troi, sensing they are outmatched by Q, advises they attempt to escape. In this scene, Captain Picard chooses the advice of the female staff, particularly Troi's, over that of the male officer, even if the "man" is a former enemy. As the ship prepares to escape, the show reinforces this reversal in gender construction, in which the woman's advice is accepted over that of a man's, with a shot of a male officer wearing the same mini-dress uniform that Troi wears. This is one of the few times that a man wears this type of uniform, but it signals the producers' attempt to create a more equal environment, where women have authority and men adopt "female" attire.

This female agency extended into blurring social responsibilities. In a poignant scene, Picard and Riker discuss the presence of children on the ship. Picard expresses his discomfort as a "father figure" for children, despite his captaincy, and assigns Riker the official role of helping him interact with the children on the ship with greater sensitivity. Riker takes this in stride, seeing how Picard wants to temper his persona to come across as more tolerant of children, befitting his role as the ship's leader. In this scene, Picard expresses emotional vulnerability traditionally categorized as feminine, which he expresses to Riker, the ship's ladies man. The two men never bring up the notion of having a woman—like the ship's counselor or the ship's chief doctor—assist with the kids. In *TOS*, Kirk did not have this issue, although Kirk, like Riker, was a notorious womanizer. But the 1980s had a different historic context, with a public "crisis" over fatherhood and reports of "missing fathers" in the American family (Haywood and an Ghaill 55). The conservative resurgence in traditional patriarchy required that Picard's crew included family togetherness as a sign of strength. Not only did working mothers, like Beverly Crusher, need living space for their children, Starfleet encouraged having children around—suggesting that men and women should meet, marry, and form families while carrying on with their duties. Picard's sensitivity to children in the first episode (and their responses to him in a later episode featuring "Captain Picard Day") indicates the series immediately set out to establish a progressive gender structure. At the same time, it reflects traditional family values for viewers with a good, albeit reluctant, father figure.

To reinforce this gender construction, the crew's initial interaction with Q defines the series' mission to prove humanity's worth as a species and their evolution from a brutal, violent, and backward race. Implied in Q's challenge for the crew is to prove that antiquated human concepts of gender no longer define identity or performance in the 24th century. Q demands they return to Earth to avoid inflicting their barbarity upon others in the way they did on Earth. This understandably includes sexist gender performance and discrimination.

Despite Q's inclusion of sexism as one of humanity's past crimes, Q himself reinforces these "barbaric" gender performances. When Picard initially surrenders and is placed on trial in a post-apocalyptic 21st century court for humanity's past transgressions, the representative group is gender balanced, including Captain Picard, Troi, Yar, and the masculine android Data, as if men and women shared equal blame for humanity's past behavior (albeit only Picard and Yar are actually human). Demonstrating aggression and physical strength, Yar subdues one of the courtroom guards when he threatens her captain. She also defies feminine stereotypes of passivity by directly defending Starfleet for what it represents and the opportunities it has afforded her. That defense of Starfleet is particularly meaningful when spoken by Yar's character, a female in a traditionally male profession. As a consequence for Yar not following her assigned gender role, Q freezes her, to which the crew responds emotionally. In fact, Picard's response to Q's actions is a request that all of humanity be adjudicated based on his crew's actions during its mission, not just the past roles Q assigns to them. This proposition is the basis for the crew initial mission at Farpoint Station, but also throughout the series' entire run. As seen below, however, Picard never fully convinces Q that humanity outgrew its past.

The Female Characters

Deanna Troi

Critiques of Counselor Deanna Troi as the future's idealized female are based on her hair styles, wardrobe, and sexual availability for men—Riker, in particular—seem at first to be valid because she is placed squarely within a late twentieth century gender schema. She embodies and portrays Devor's assertion that, "[a]s patriarchy has reserved active expressions of power as a masculine attribute, femininity must be expressed through modes of dress, movement, speech, and action which communicate weakness, ineffectualness, availability for sexual or emotional service, and sensitivity to the needs of others" (419). Troi's characterization creates a binary, with her hyper-feminine objectified body highlighted by her clothing. Her physicality is in marked contrast to her professional success and importance among the *Enterprise* crew. Joyrich argues, "Deanna Troi is also the most conventionally feminine of all of Starfleet's female officers, noticeable for her extravagant hairstyles and (at least before the last season) her singular neglect of regulation uniform in favor of low-cut costumes that emphasize her body" (63). The opening sequence of the "Encounter at Farpoint" depicts Troi in a uniform that matches the standard issue uniform in its coloring, but deviates by substituting the pants with a very short mini-dress. Concerning Troi's costumes, *Entertainment Weekly's The Ultimate Guide to Star Trek* noted that though "*TNG* reintroduced the color-coded jumpsuit," the show's "initial spandex uniforms were so uncomfortable that the costumers redesigned them with wool. Deanna Troi, however, kept the cleavage-bearing onesies" (51). Unlike the functional and androgynous uniforms the rest of the crew wears, Troi's form-fitting, low-cut ensembles restrict her movements and signal sexual availability.

However, the argument that her gender is the basis of her professional occupation on the *Enterprise* discredits her importance to the mission and her relationship with the crew. As a half-Betazoid and half-human, Troi is sensitive to and can read people's feelings. To be sure, sensitivity to feelings is a female stereotype, but it is also the foundation to her professional success. Some critics argue that, even here, Troi's role is weak. Rather than serving in an active role in which she begins conversations, Troi is receptive and waits for Captain Picard to include her. Joyrich further claims that "even more noteworthy than Counselor Troi's official function as analyst/advisor is her gender role; indeed, the former seems to emerge from the latter" (63).

Despite these assertions, the focus on Troi's feelings and ability to read emotions are not a weakness, but a path to her success. In her professional role, Troi establishes her importance among the crew and to the mission that counterbalances her stereotypical feminine presentation. Her place on the bridge is on Picard's left, implying she has a position equal to the first officer. She uses her skills to serve as ship's counselor and is often sought by Captain Picard for her advice and assistance, more so, at times, than he consults his Number One. In the early episode, "Code of Honor," it is Troi, not Riker, who accompanies Picard on the mission to rescue Yar from Lutan, and she stays on the surface as a liaison and advisor. Troi's equality is underscored by Picard's observation that people in Lutan's culture have not evolved past their archaic notions of gender as humans have. Indeed, women in this society are valued for the land they own and their ability to transfer land and wealth to the men who claim them. Here, Troi undercuts this sexism by participating as an equal member of the away team. Joyrich notes, "The original *Star Trek* had always had a penchant for engaging with current social issues by project-ing them onto alien cultures and the future, and *Star Trek: The Next Generation* (under [...] Gene Rodenberry) seemed to continue this same strategy" (64). The alien's outdated cultural practices contrasts sharply with the progress humans achieved regarding gender equality. In the professional environment, Troi is equal to men with her bridge position and her importance to missions.

Conversely, in her personal life, Troi is hyperfeminized to balance out her profes-sional power. Her role as a receptive and objectified female parallels the social conser-vative expectations for women in the 1980s. In the ninth episode, "Haven," Troi's career is sidestepped as the episode concentrates on her personal life. She is expected to fulfill the Betazoid custom of an arranged marriage to a man she doesn't know. In doing so, she must also relinquish her position as counselor on the Federation's flagship. In the episode's early scenes, Riker notes that the custom of arranged marriages is strange to him. Though Riker's objections to Troi's arranged marriage may be grounded in self-interest because he is romantically attracted to her, he also voices the difference between human and non-human customs. Similarly, in his personal log, Picard assumes a paternal attitude towards Troi, expressing that his concern for her extends beyond losing a valuable crewmember. Despite recognizing her professional significance, Picard perceives her as someone he must protect. However, Troi submits to her society's expectations, symbolized by her mother, Lwaxana Troi, a woman whose aristocracy and ambassador status make her an apt spokeswoman for her culture. Here, viewers note similarities to the customs of other alien cultures as a stand-in for twentieth-century assumptions about women's roles. They are deliberately outdated and the human characters' critique or objections to them make humans appear more evolved when female characters are treated unequally.

Tasha Yar

If Deanna Troi is presented as the idealized female, Tasha Yar initially challenges that representation. As Chief Security Officer, Yar occupies a position that is defined by protection, strength, strategy, and logical thinking, all of which are traditional masculine attributes. She is also a woman performing a job previously occupied by a man in *TOS*, a non-regular character who appeared in several episodes. Because of this, her character was one of the show's most promising opportunities for equality in both the public and private spheres. For example, in the fourth episode, "The Last Outpost," Yar demonstrates physical strength and acumen when she rescues her ranking male officers from a Ferengi attack in an obvious reversal of gender norms. The Ferengi, who are depicted as greedy, cunning, and deceitful when compared to their human counterparts, draw attention to

Yar's rescue, by calling it abnormal. The Ferengi use this one instance to question the show's vision of social equality, pointing out that Yar's presence proves the inferiority of humanity because men work alongside women and allow women to wear clothes. Until this point, none of the *Enterprise* crew view Yar's role and position as abnormal, signaling their acceptance of Yar's actions. The Ferengi's comments signal their adherence to "backward" patriarchal values, specifically masculine dominance and subordination of women, specifically the objectification and over-sexualization of the female body, which the Federation had long rejected as obsolete. The series, once again, uses an alien culture to highlight human social and cultural evolution, creating the comparison of female bridge officers and the Starfleet crew's response to these less advanced Ferengi ideals.

However, the opportunity to present a fully-developed, independent, and equal female character was quickly undercut as viewers responded more positively to male characters such as Worf, Data, or La Forge. As a result, writers shifted their focus on the male characters with Yar left underdeveloped and often in the background. In addition, Yar's position is consistently challenged and her femininity reinforced. Devor argues that "[p]ersons who perform the activities considered appropriate for another gender will be expected to perform them poorly; if they success adequately, or even well, at their endeavors, they may be rewarded with ridicule for blurring the gender dividing line" (418). The initial negative audience response to Yar signaled that adjustments to the character were warranted. Often dressed in the standard issue, androgynous Starfleet uniform and short two-toned hair, Yar is described as "butch" or not feminine. Her sexuality is also questioned because of her position and appearance. She is placed in a binary opposition to Troi's idealized femininity and the counselor's reliance on female traits for her professional success. In fact, in "The Naked Now," the second episode of the first season, Yar's heterosexuality is confirmed when she seeks Troi's advice on how to dress and style her hair, and she attempts to seduce Data as a result of the intoxication that overwhelms the crew. In this scene, Troi acts as a male-idealized female and the authority on femininity, including what attracts men. The implication is that Yar is not good enough for a man and somehow must improve her appearance to achieve a pre-established ideal of feminine beauty, one that Troi represents, to fulfill a role as lover, and, ultimately, wife and mother.[3]

Similarly, in "Code of Honor," the third episode of the series, Yar is "claimed" or kidnapped and put in the weakened position of needing to be rescued. Her equality is first challenged when Lutan rejects her as Chief Security Officer, putting into question Yar's ability as a woman to perform in a traditionally male profession. Her gender construction is compounded by Lutan's physical attraction to her and her subsequent abduction. When Picard and Troi attempt to rescue her, Yar is further weakened when Troi asks if she is attracted to Lutan, suggesting Yar's desire to be submissive to a dominant and powerful male. Though Yar admits to struggling with those feelings, she refuses to accept Lutan's wife, Yareena's, challenge to fight to the death. Though Yar easily succeeds in the death match, she fights for a worthier cause (the ship needs a life vaccine of which Lutan has sole custody) and, ultimately, convinces Yareena that Lutan, not Yar, is to blame for the disruption in her marriage. Lutan's' obsession with Yar reinforces patriarchal stereotypes in two ways. First, when he questions her ability to perform her duties, he signals to audiences that she may not be competent because of her gender. Second, his attraction to Yar undermines her as an equal, reducing her to a sex object available to men and a damsel in distress. However, despite Lutan's attempts to realign Yar into a gender performance that reflects those of his culture and of the 1980s, her resistance to him and her success in the death match reestablish her as an alternative female identity to Troi's. Summarily, Captain Picard notes the differences between human and alien cultures, saying that people in Lutan's culture have not evolved past their archaic egos as humans have.

After this episode, Yar's appearance and personality are softened, further feminizing her and reinforcing her heterosexuality. She is costumed in a tunic, rather than the standard issue uniform, in episode seven, "Justice," and depicted as physically attractive and attracted to men on Rubicun 3, the Eden-like planet where the crew takes their first shore leave. The episode initially focuses on the crew's reactions to the hypersexualized inhabitants, the skimpily-attired Edo, during the away team's assessment of the planet for shore leave. Upon welcoming the female crewmembers to the planet, their host, Liator, embraces them suggestively. Troi responds tepidly to this advance, while Yar returns the embrace with parallel sensuality. Similarly, in "Hide and Q," after Yar aggressively objects to the equity of Q's game, she is placed in the "penalty box," which relocates her to the *Enterprise* bridge where Picard is waiting. She explains to Picard that if the crew commits one more penalty, she will pay the price and be reduced to a state of nothingness. She expresses her fear by crying, but immediately tries to stifle her overt emotional demonstration. Yar's emotional outburst while at work is perceived as weakness because of its association with female behavior. Her own objection to it and her attempt to suppress it adds to her perceptions of self-weakness. However, Picard's response is a command to allow situational emotional outbursts, thereby legitimizing her tears, while he comforts her in an embrace. Solidifying her feminized identity, Yar alludes that if they were not in a manager and subordinate position, she would pursue him romantically. This short exchange signals to viewers that, despite being in a role historically occupied by men, Yar maintains traditionally feminine qualities. Situations reinforcing Yar's gender occur throughout the first season until her death in "Skin of Evil." This unnecessary feminization of Yar in opposition to her original depiction indicates that her initial performance violated traditional gender roles in a way that defied viewers' expectations.

Though her authority is challenged through masculine dominance or social stereotypes that shaped her characterization, the most significant challenge to Yar's authority and equality is Picard's response to her voicing her opinion and advice, even when he solicits it from her. Picard begins silencing her in the first episode and continues to do so until her death. In contrast to the way that Picard addresses and responds to Troi, Picard is dismissive of Yar's point of view. In "Encounter at Farpoint," after Yar offers her advice that they flee or fight, Picard seeks further advice from Troi, who advises that they flee, advice that he ultimately acts upon even though Yar already offered it. Picard responds similarly to Yar's advice in "Code of Honor." This practice continues throughout the first season to the point that actress Denise Crosby requested that she be released from her contract. In an interview, she expressed her opposition to the character's stagnated development and stereotypically feminine portrayal, saying, "I didn't want to say 'the frequency's open, sir' for five years" (Toepfer, Alexander). As a result, she was written off the show with her character's death.

Ultimately, Yar's characterization illustrates the most promising example of gender equality in the work place that *TNG* provides. She is employed in a historically male position and replaces a male counterpart from *TOS*. She also embodies ambivalence to patriarchal gender roles in both appearance and action until audience reception of her caused writers to change direction with her character early in the series. Her death in

"Skin of Evil" toward the end of the first season signifies the rejection of this type of woman, one who achieves professional success without fulfilling traditional expectations of feminine behaviors. In her final episode, Yar is favored to win the ship's martial arts competition in which the majority of her opponents are male. After her death, Yar delivers a "four-page monologue" as a hologram (Toepfer, Alexander). Of its significance, Crosby noted, "Ironically, I had to die to get the show I wanted" (Toepfer, Alexander). Through it, her character is finally able to express herself, sharing how she felt about her life and those with whom she shared it. The monologue also provides some background details to Yar's life and insight into her character. However, her final address to Troi, stating that she learned so much and especially the idea that she could be feminine and not lose anything, is perhaps the definitive statement on the challenges writers faced in presenting a character like Yar who violates expectations of gender performance ("Skin of Evil"). Being strong or a warrior is clearly at odds with expectations of being classified "feminine."[4] After Yar's death, Picard selects a new Chief of Security. He replaces her with a colleague, the more aggressive colleague Klingon, more popular, and masculine character, Worf.

Beverly Crusher

A featured character in all but the second season, Dr. Beverly Crusher exemplifies the 1980s woman who balances her career with her more traditional role as mother. As a single parent, she supports herself and her son, Wesley, whose role emphasizes her relational identity. Korzeniowska argues that "unlike other mothers in the series, [Crusher] escapes the negative stereotyping which can be associated with that role" (21). Rather, she is treated with the respect someone in her position deserves. Similar to Yar replacing a male officer as Chief Security Officer, Dr. Crusher is *TNG*'s replacement for Leonard "Bones" McCoy, the *Enterprise*'s Chief Medical Officer. Like Yar, Crusher parallels the same trend in the American workforce during this period. However, unlike Troi, whose sensitivity to emotions is central to her occupation and professional success, Crusher's characterization and personality are grounded in logic and the scientific method. She also creates a boundary between her personal and professional lives. She attempts to suppress or mask her emotions, telling Captain Picard in the first episode that her husband's death—Picard's close friend—would not impact how she would perform her duties.

As the Chief Medical Officer of the *Enterprise* and, with a rank of full commander, perhaps the highest ranking female officer on the ship, Crusher is often in the center of the missions, especially when there is an emergency to which she must tend. These episodes focus on her as a logical and strong leader, and extremely competent in her position. In the ninth episode, "Hide and Q," Crusher leads a rescue crew to save survivors of a mining explosion before the bridge crew is overtaken by Q. Once the crew is allowed to proceed to the mine, Crusher leads the effort. Her leadership is accentuated by the confidence the Captain Picard and her fellow crewmembers have for her professional abilities. She is also respected as a senior member of the bridge crew. In later seasons, whether she mentors younger professional women like Amanda Rogers in "True Q," or participates in intelligence operations in "Chain of Command," Crusher demonstrates her worth and commands respect. In "Chain of Command," Crusher works with Captain Picard and Worf in an undercover assignment in which she plays an instrumental role because of her medical knowledge concerning biological warfare. The episode calls for Crusher to scale cliffsides and she is buried under a rockslide, but meets the obstacles with aplomb. Throughout the series, Crusher performs her role with professionalism, while maintaining a strict boundary that balances her responsibilities as a mother.

Beverly Crusher's accomplishments as Chief Medical Officer and, later, the Head of Starfleet Medical are balanced and, at times, overshadowed, by the show's focus on her son Wesley and his potential as a teenage genius. In "Where No One Has Gone Before," Wesley is presented to Captain Picard as a prodigy and, from that point on, is permitted to join the other officers on the bridge. Riker uses Starfleet protocol to appoint Wesley to a field rank of acting ensign, officially making him part of the bridge crew. Before this, Crusher's plot line focused on her demands between balancing her personal and professional lives. Now, with this arrangement, Wesley becomes an intruder into the professional space of his mother, with Crusher managing the impact of his presence as she shifts between performing the two roles. Soon after, Wesley becomes the protégé of both Picard and Riker, even accompanying the crew's away team to assess the location for on their first shore leave in "Justice." In this episode, when Wesley is put on trial for violating the laws of the Edo and sentenced to execution, Dr. Crusher reacts emotionally, causing Data to comment on motherhood as an exceptional category of human behavior. Crusher tells the android to shut up, thereby silencing him, and while her anger is understandable for a mother, it is a rare outburst from the normally-collected doctor.

In season two, Dr. Crusher leaves Wesley and her post on the *Enterprise* to advance her career when she is offered a post as Head of Starfleet Medical. In this position, she works with Lieutenant Commander Noah Hutchinson, most notable for his work with Data. Crusher's return to the series in season three, though mostly unexplained, signals the decision of a mother willing to sacrifice her professional development for the sake of her role as a parent. Upon her return in the first episode of the third season, "Evolution," she is mostly concerned about the effect her return will have on Wesley's developing career and on the distance she perceives between them. She seeks advice from Captain Picard about both issues, asking him to tell her about her son. Picard's response is focused on Wesley's growth within Starfleet. However, Dr. Crusher is more interested in his development from boyhood to manhood, whether he has friends, or if he ever fell in love. Crusher's interest in Wesley's maturation underscores her absence as a mother and her responsibilities for raising him during his formative years. Ironically, Picard, who initially professed reluctance to working with children, stands in as a paternal figure for the crew and for Wesley in particular. However, when she gives up her position with Starfleet Command to return to the *Enterprise* and be with Wesley, she does not see her decision as a step down, but as a completion of the family unit. Crusher exemplifies women in the labor force who balance their careers with motherhood, surrendering one for the other on different occasions, but finding time for both as a source of personal and professional fulfillment. From this point to Wesley's departure in the fourth season, she continues to find equilibrium between her dual roles.

Minor and Recurring Characters

The lead characters Troi, Crusher, and Yar demonstrate the shifting roles of womanhood and women's participation in the workforce during the 1980s. Of the three, Troi has the largest impact, in terms of both screen time and character development. However, her depiction as an idealized woman for traditional gender roles and for feminists underscores the varied feminized pathways to power and participation as part of the crew. Troi serves as a role model for the secondary female characters, through whom viewers can see the stratification of women's occupations in the American workforce. Of the secondary characters, Guinan, the ship's bartender, and Alyssa Ogawa, one of Crusher's staff, are recurring characters who represent women in traditionally feminine supportive or service positions. Their primary functions center on communication, nurturing, and service to others. In particular, as a bartender in the newly constructed Ten Forward in the second season, Guinan serves a similar role as Troi. She counsels crewmembers on both personal and professional matters. She also mirrors Troi in that she is passive and waits to be spoken to or addressed, rather than actively initializing most conversations. Further reinforcing feminine stereotypes, Alyssa Ogawa performs her profession as nurse in a traditionally supportive role catering to patients and assisting other medical staff. Ogawa later becomes pregnant and discusses her romantic life with Dr. Crusher, thereby reinforcing the traditional gender roles of both characters.

However, aside from these major recurring characters, the majority of *TNG*'s secondary characters have occupations more closely reflecting the expansion of women's professional roles: engineers, command officers, mission specialists, attorneys, and scientists. Most significantly, Keiko O'Brien serves as a non-commissioned botanist on the *Enterprise* and characters like Dr. Leah Brahms, a propulsion scientist who served as "Senior Design Engineer of the Theoretical Propulsion Group" that designed the *Enterprise*, indicate that women have earned high ranks in the more traditionally masculine professions in the sciences (Korzeniowska 20). Brahms's and other characters' representation in engineering positions parallels the seven percent increase in female engineers in the American labor force between 1975 and 1995 (Wootton 17). In "Where No One Has Gone," the primary engineer for whom Wesley works is a female. Similarly, the series depicts women engineers like Sonya Gomez, technicians like Robin Lefler, and assorted helm officers who replace Wesley, notably the assertive Ro Laren. Not only do these women fulfill occupations that are not traditionally performed by women, but they are depicted in leadership roles as well. In season two, when Dr. Crusher leaves the *Enterprise*, her replacement is Katherine Pulaski, a crusty, tough doctor who asserts her opinions. Additionally, secondary characters highlighting the growth in women in executive or managerial roles include Captain Rachel Garrett, who commanded the *Enterprise*-C, the direct predecessor to Picard's ship, and Admiral Alynna Nechayev, a direct superior to Captain Picard who first appears in "Chain of Command" with recurring appearances throughout the series, and whose dominating presence even intimidates Picard. Though they function within the hypermasculine patriarchal schema of the military-based Starfleet organization, these women demonstrate expanded female roles within that framework, particularly when compared to *TOS*.

Conclusion

When Q returns in the final episode "All Good Things…" and revisits humanity's trial, he tells Picard that the trial will never really conclude. Although Q does not mention gender roles, the sexism and patriarchy of the twentieth century remain a vital factor in shaping the human adventure. Q's statement shows that, while Picard may have saved the day, humanity still has a long way to go to live up to the captain's claims made in

"Encounter at Farpoint." Indeed, while Picard's opening describing the ship's continuing mission promised gender equality reflective of 24th century progress, *TNG* works within the constraints of both the television industry and the period in which it aired. Viewers' response to Tasha Yar signaled their ambivalence to gender equality by the end of the first season and most notably confirmed the social conservative turn regarding women's work in traditionally masculine positions.

At the same time, the *Enterprise* crew manages to live up to Q's challenge that humans are not a barbarous race prone to violence. In the crew's sociological mission to prove that humans have evolved beyond outdated practices, several characters demonstrate a measure of success. One of the ways *TNG* achieves this is by mirroring and exceeding women's professional development in its contemporary period. The Bureau of Labor Statistics shows women's roles in the labor force expanded in numbers and categories of professions from *TOS*'s end in 1969 to the *TNG*'s beginning in 1987. The three female lead officers exemplify multiple feminine identity performances and pathways to success. The idealized female, Deanna Troi, achieves professional power through traditionally feminine characteristics, and is the most enduring female character in the series. In contrast, Tasha Yar depicts non-traditional pathways for female success, while Beverly Crusher balances single-motherhood and a professional career. Though their professional acumen presents equality in the workplace, some critical objections to the writers' presenting female characters in expected patriarchal depictions are valid. Since the show was released in syndication and relied on ratings for success, it responded to and reflected viewers' expectations. However, the primary female characters, coupled with the assorted secondary characters in executive positions, enable the crew to prevent Q's limiting humanity to Earth, or wiping them out altogether. In the end, the series may not achieve the 24th century utopia that it promises, but the show's women experience more professional equality than their *TOS* predecessors or late twentieth century counterparts. Fittingly, when *The Next Generation* ended in 1994, its successor, *Star Trek: Voyager,* pushed the boundaries further, with a woman who truly went where no woman has gone before, to the captain's chair at the helm of a starship.

NOTES

1. See Peter W. Lee's essay in this volume.
2. See Joul Smith's essay in this volume.
3. Yar ultimately becomes a wife and mother when she travels back in time, is captured by Romulans, becomes a "war prize" of sorts, and gives birth to Sela. Sela later claims that when Yar tries to escape, she was executed, and Sela's human half—including her femininity—died with her mother, leaving only a hardened military officer.
4. On Worf and warrior culture, especially martial arts, see Jared Miracle's essay in this volume.

WORKS CITED

"All Good Things…." *Star Trek: The Next Generation*. 23 May 1994. *Netflix*. Web. 16 Jun. 2017.

Bureau of Labor Statistics. "Women at Work: A Visual Essay." *Monthly Labor Review.* October 2003. 45–50. Web. 6 Mar. 2016.

Butler, Judith. "Performative Acts and Gender Constitution." *Literary Theory: An Anthology.* Second Edition. Ed. Julia Rivkin and Michael Ryan. Malden, MA: Blackwell Publishing, 2004. 900–911. Print.

"Code of Honor." *Star Trek: The Next Generation*. 10 Oct. 1987. *Netflix*. Web. 16 Jan. 2016.

Devor, Aaron. "Becoming Members of Society: Learning the Social Meanings of Gender." *Our America: Cultural Contexts for Critical Thinking and Reading. Sixth Edition.* Eds. Gary Colombo, Robert Cullen, and Bonnie Lisle. Boston: Bedford/St. Martin's, 2001. 415–423. Print.

"Encounter at Farpoint." *Star Trek: The Next Generation*. 26 Sept. 1987. *Netflix*. Web. 16 Jan. 2016.

"Evolution." *Star Trek: The Next Generation*. 23 Sept. 1989. *Netflix*. Web. 10 Mar. 2016.

Franich, Darren. "The Future of Fashion." *Entertainment Weekly: The Ultimate Guide to Star Trek.* 2016. 50–51. Print.

Haywood, Chris, and Máirtín Mac an Ghaill. *Men and Masculinities.* Philadelphia: Open University Press, 2003. Print.

Joyrich, Lynne. "Feminist Enterprise? "Star Trek: The Next Generation" and the Occupation of Femininity." *Cinema Journal* 35.2 (1996): 61–84. Web. 16 Jan. 2016.

"Justice." *Star Trek: The Next Generation.* 7 Nov. 1987. *Netflix.* Web. 17 Jan. 2016.

Korzeniowska, Victoria B. "Engaging with Gender: Star Trek's 'Next Generation.'" *Journal of Gender Studies* 5.1 (1996): 19. *Academic Search Premier.* Web. 9 Mar. 2016.

"The Last Outpost." *Star Trek: The Next Generation.* 17 Oct. 1987. *Netflix.* Web. 17 Jan. 2016.

"Lonely Among Us." *Star Trek: The Next Generation.* 31 Oct. 1987. *Netflix.* Web. 17 Jan. 2016.

"The Naked Now." *Star Trek: The Next Generation.* 3 Oct. 1987. *Netflix.* Web. 17 Jan. 2016.

Roddenberry, Gene, creator. *Star Trek: The Next Generation.* Paramount Pictures, 1987.

"Skin of Evil." *Star Trek: The Next Generation.* 23 April 1988. *Netflix.* Web. 18 Jan. 2016.

Toepfer, Susan, and Michael Alexander. "Denise Crosby, Granddaughter of Bing, Beams Down from *Star Trek* for Some New Enterprise." *People* 29.17 (1988): 57. *Academic Search Premier.* Web. 27 May 2016.

United States Department of Labor. "Women in the Labor Force." Web. 8 Feb. 2016.

"Where No One Has Gone." *Star Trek: The Next Generation.* 24 Oct. 1987. *Netflix.* Web. 17 Jan. 2016.

Wootton, Barbara H. "Gender Differences in Occupational Employment." *Monthly Labor Review.* April 1997. 15–24. Web. 16 Jan 2016.

I Sensed It

Deanna Troi's Cognitively Restructured Trek *and the Futurism of* The Next Generation

JOUL SMITH

In 1987, Deanna Troi immediately gave critics plenty of fuel for analyzing *TNG* along cultural and gender lines when her character debuted in the series' first episode. Her half-human status stood in stark contrast to the infamous half-human of *TOS*, Spock. As the ship's therapist, possessing psionic empathy from her Betazoid half (a telepathic and passionate humanoid species), Deanna validated the emotional reactions to space exploration; Spock, the ship's science officer, had notoriously repressed them. Moreover, for more than five seasons of *TNG*, audiences watched her nontraditional uniforms vary until, in the middle of the sixth season, she adopted the standard Starfleet issued uniform. Spock, and most of the characters from both shows, underwent only the slightest uniform changes, if any. Wardrobes, emotions, and subordinated comparisons to male counterparts all smack of gender-biased stereotyping, ripe for the critics' picking. For the viewer, a mental re-orientation to *Trek* and the future it presented was in the making.

Amid these drastic changes, Troi also represented a strong professional psychologist and a Starfleet officer with a healthy body image. Her unapologetic personality regularly manifested itself professionally and socially through unabashed femininity. As a character on *TNG*, Deanna Troi makes us think. She forces us to re-conceive some of the ways that *Trek* represents the future of humanity, and she established a significant tone for *TNG* as it took the torch of *TOS* to usher in a fresh look at the vision creator Gene Roddenberry offered. In this essay, I examine *TNG* as a literary unit, an organic whole, of which Deanna Troi serves as a lens that viewers can use to examine humanity's future as depicted in the *TNG* series. Based on her description above, I believe it is vital for critics to give Counselor Troi some richer consideration within the scope of the series' entire impact. Understanding Counselor Troi can help us understand Roddenberry's vision of the future that he hoped would proceed from *TOS* to *TNG*.

I argue that the stereotyped criticisms of her character attest to the powerful effect she has on the audience, an effect requiring viewers to uncomfortably confront their gender-based prejudices that they may not have even recognized. As a result, the tension generated by Troi's presence onboard the *Enterprise* (whether it's sexual, professional, or personal) eventually serves as a defamiliarizing agent that allows viewers to reconceptualize the hopeful future that is crucial to *Trek*'s role as an American epic. I outline Troi's supposed "flaws," and then showcase how Troi's specific role as a therapist allows her empathic abilities and half-human status to project a "futurism" onto viewers, a perception that *TNG* is a believable future because it values and destigmatizes mental health, even for its epically heroic Starfleet crew. By cognitively restructuring "the future" through Deanna's liminal and uncomfortable role onboard the *Enterprise*, *TNG* achieves a cohesive message about humanity's indelible spirit of progress and improvement.

The sense of a better tomorrow, of an improved humanity, undergirds the idea behind *Trek*. Gene Roddenberry regularly made this point in his own philosophical musings alongside his reflections on the meaning of *Star Trek*. As critics reflect on *Star Trek*'s fifty years as a cultural and historical artifact of American popular culture, understanding how *TNG*'s (now thirty years since its debut) Counselor Troi fits into the "better future" motif of *Trek* can and should come in a variety of analyses. Critics, fans, and philosophers all have a stake in exploring *TNG*'s representation of an American mythos, and, indeed, many have offered important critiques of the show's success as both entertainment media and a humanistic message.

Deanna's Flaws: Attractive, Feeling, Vital

Throughout the series, fans, critics, writers, directors, and even Marina Sirtis struggled to comfortably label Troi's role on the ship. Reticence about validating Troi posed a problem for *TNG* because it might undermine *Trek*'s progressive messaging. She represents so much of the diversity that *Trek* celebrates as improvements to humanity: a professional with authority (psychologist, bridge officer, and eventual commander), a woman with a special super-skill (psionic empathy from her Betazoid side, the ability to sense emotions and telepathically communicate), and a racially diverse make-up (half-human/half-Betazoid). Denying this major character a serious contribution to the conversations on diversity and sexism only serves to place *TNG* out of any culturally significant commentary on modern society. Yet, the fuel for critics began before the pilot episode even aired. According to the *Writers/Directors Guides*, this is where her role(s) start, and this is where the critical flaws in her character are found:

COUNSELOR DEANNA TROI (played by Marina Sirtis): An attractive and very witty Starfleet professional, she is the ship's Counselor, a position of vital importance on space vessels of the 24th century; the success of a starship's mission depends as much on efficiently functioning human relationships as on the vessel's mechanisms and circuitry. Troi is a master in human and alien psychology, also Starfleet-trained as a bridge officer. Her mother was a Betazed alien that allows her to "feel" the emotions of others.

Troi and Riker are old friends who had a tempestuous relationship sometime in the past. Somehow it didn't work and, with both on the same vessel, now that fire is only embers, a warm and comfortable friendship [Roddenberry 1987, 6].

Deanna Troi comes across as a dire necessity for the ship and the entire message of *Trek*. Yet her description strikingly contradicts that necessity when compared to a description like that of the lead character:

CAPTAIN JEAN-LUC PICARD (played by Patrick Stewart): Already a 24th century Starfleet legend, Picard is an extraordinary man, much revered by his crew. He deserves the description "distinguished" despite being only in his youthful fifties. He has an unspoken but deep father-son relationship with [Commander William Riker ("Number One")] [Roddenberry, 1987, 5].

The show presents Deanna as someone who, from the start, must prove herself. Her description reads, in some places, like a desperate rationalization for her existence on the ship, a struggle that the male Captain Picard does not have to face. She has to live up to the expectations embedded in the terms "attractive," "feel," and "vital," which suggest that Troi may reinforce gender stereotypes more than she deconstructs them, in direct contrast to the vision of *Trek* progressivism. Critics have primarily fixated on these three qualities when examining *TNG* and Troi's role in its success, so I will offer a brief overview of the way they are used to scrutinize the counselor.

First, "attractive" limits her character to the sexualized desires of heterosexual male perceptions. This type is well known in science-fiction (SF) media, which is infamous for establishing expectations about sexually aesthetic female tropes. Indeed, SF programs often thrive on strong space cowgirls with sex appeal and superpowers. *TOS* was replete with them (Uhura, Yeoman Rand, Orion slave girls), but other examples, pre–*TNG*, abound: Barbarella (Jane Fonda), Princess Leia (Carrie Fischer), and Ellen Ripley (Sigourney Weaver) to name a few. So *TNG*'s version of that stock female character seems to develop in the form of an empathic counselor who serves as the hot romance interest, custom made to science-fiction's futuristic male-gaze.

For Troi, that gaze could land upon stereotypical "damsel" or "dame" narratives, or, more problematically, manifests in overt dismissals of sexual violence perpetrated on her character. In season one's "Skin of Evil," where *TNG* takes one of its biggest risks by allowing a major bridge-crewmember to die (Chief of Security Tasha Yar), Deanna spends the entire episode trapped inside a wrecked shuttle, yearning for rescue, eventually declaring her desire to be a sacrifice for her fellow officers outside the wreckage. Troi's distress, foregrounding Yar's death, positions Troi and *TNG* to serve as reminders that space is hard, especially for women.[1]

Even the more light-hearted moments for Troi, like the frequent reminders about her love for chocolate, reinforces a gender stereotype about women and eating. Emotion-induced junk food binges of any kind are reserved solely for this one female character. In "The Game," for instance, Troi mentions she never encountered a chocolate she did not enjoy, and in this and other episodes, she is often depicted eating chocolate. This is often in contrast to male characters, like Riker, who expressed a distaste for chocolate ("The Game") and Q, who, despite ordering ten chocolate sundaes in Ten-Forward (on the suggestion that Deanna Troi eats sundaes when she is depressed), fails to indulge in even one after losing his appetite ("Déjà Q").

Critics have regularly found fault with Troi's attire and general appearance. Feminist theorist Lynne Joyrich suggests that Troi is only "noticeable" as a character because of "her extravagant hairstyles and … her singular neglect of regulation uniform in favor of low-cut costumes that emphasize her body" (63). Critics further echo negative tones about Troi's clothing, sometimes as outright condemnations. Steven Scott's essay on cultural awareness in *Star Trek* insists Troi's clothing choices "counterbalance the female agency of the show" (26). Reserved criticisms like these found in scholarship pale in comparison to the tone of popular reactions to Troi's attire. Just six hits into a simple Google search for "Deanna Troi" produces "Seven Bizarre Facts About Deanna Troi's Cleavage" (thegeektwins.com). Critics from various backgrounds converged with contention for Deanna's "attractive" wardrobes.

But the most troubling, sexually charged gender-biases for Troi come from the expectations that she must accept certain forms of sexual assault. The episodes "The

Child" and "Violations," along with the movie *Nemesis*, feature moments in which outside, predatory "male" types violate Troi's body. In "The Child" a non-corporeal entity impregnates Troi while she sleeps. That scene features heavily coded, graphic, rape-like imagery that is only permissible for production because it uses computer graphics to represent a non-humanoid "attacker." The intrusion follows the glowing entity as it invades Troi's quarters, "creeps" up to her bed by floating slowly, slides under her sheets, and slowly moves along the outline of her lower body until it "enters," what one could only presume is, her sexual organ. In slumber up to that moment, Troi reacts to the "entrance" with groans that evince both discomfort and pleasure. Had the intruder been a humanoid, this scene could not have aired on syndicated network television.

The resultant child produces strong maternal tendencies in Troi while the rest of the episode essentially brushes aside the issue of her alien seeder. Though Troi finds some validation through the apparent option of termination during her consultation with mostly male officers, the entity is given a pass for using Troi's body non-consensually. After birth, it is determined that the entity, now residing within the child, is harming the ship, so it chooses to terminate the child's corporeal exterior and return to its energy form. This action, perceived as noble by Deanna and the *Enterprise* crew, allows the entity to earn the respect of the crew because they equate its actions to nothing more than mere curiosity about human life; rather than a violent abuser, the entity is an explorer just like them. Deanna, after losing her child and enduring the trauma any parent would experience in that circumstance, smiles with approval as the "father" arrogates the rights for termination that once resided with Deanna and leaves, all without accounting for its behavior.

In "Violations" and *Nemesis*, telepathic species force the experience of a sexual encounter into Troi's mind. Though the show condemns the actions as criminal, Troi is clearly selected as a character who is especially susceptible to unwelcome sexual activity, which is born out even in non-violent attractions like Riva's in "Loud as a Whisper" and Captain Okona's in "The Outrageous Okona." In each instance, gifted and extraordinary men immediately express attraction to Troi upon first seeing her, even though she initially approaches both of them as a professional Federation officer. No other character receives as much unsolicited romantic attraction as Troi, whether that action is predatory or not. It is as if her attractiveness gives her a vulnerability that other characters, particularly male characters, do not have.

Feminist criticism gravitates toward the overt shaming inherent in these representations that are reserved solely for a female character. Troi serves, in these instances, as an object for the male perspective to explore within the safety of its status. Such invasions are all too common within the limitless options available to the SF imagination, as in the film *Demon Seed*. Based on Dean Koontz's novel, the film graphically depicts Julie Christie's character raped by a super computer. This scene is perhaps the inspiration for an episode like "The Child," a reminder of the predatory gaze in SF that futuristically blames female characters for being caught up in a hetero-patriarchal exploration setting. Troi often becomes the needless and hapless victim within those parameters when they are adopted by *TNG*.

Troi's empathic abilities intensify this vulnerability, amplifying the "hysterical" stereotype of an overly emotional female who "feels" her way through circumstances. SF is also infamous for embedding extra-sensory (Psi) activity into stories as a narrative convenience, often sidestepping explanations of the mechanics of Psi. The impression that SF critics garner from Psi is that it wildly exaggerates typical human activity. Critics often equate Deanna's Psi abilities as an emotional plethora. As Scott puts it, "further complicating any view of the series as progressive in gender terms is the fact that the Counselor [sic], an 'empath,' is (of course) female, since she is emotional, nurturing, caring, empathetic" (26). Scott's argument draws on a dilemma that the audience faces, that *TNG* loses an advanced sense of the future that is endemic to *Trek* because it finds ways to utilize the future as a form of gender discrimination. *TOS* had the problem of being "associated with the *sexism* of its era" (Greven 9), and it is a loss for *TNG*'s vision if Troi's character continues that pattern by stereotyping feminine emotions.

Deanna's emotionally charged Psi also challenges the premise of *TNG* that everything has a rational explanation. Picard regularly asks Troi if she senses anything from the aliens they encounter, and in those instances, her Psi usually serves as factual proof of a reality. The ability to sense emotions is usually celebrated as a special talent, whether it is Psi-based or not. But having that talent legitimized as empirically indisputable evidence from the somatic function of a Betazed comes across as too abrupt for many critics. Troi's acute attention to emotions, especially through her Psi, represents irresponsible irrationalities in a future that has scientific explanations for everything.

Critics rightfully challenge the "magic" of telepathy. Deanna Troi's specific Psi, which the series mostly relegates to empathic reception, too often serves as a simple, stereotypical plot device. *TNG* all but admits this in "The Survivors," when Troi's Psi is blocked by a super-being who appears as a human named Kevin. Kevin's blocking Troi from sensing his presence reduces her role throughout the episode to experiencing internal anguish while all the other crewmembers can only wonder about her erratic behavior. Her first major lapse actually takes place during a conference with other senior officers, as Riker looks on protectively. It reaches a critical point at which the empathic obstruction completely consumes Troi and renders her comatose. Kevin finally reveals himself as a powerful entity and explains that blocking Troi was the only way to conceal his identity. It just so happens that discovering his true identity is the main conflict of the plot. Had Troi not been blocked, the episode would have lost its driving action. The Psi is problematic for the integrity of the show and the rendering of gender on *TNG*.

These factors lead to the third category of criticism: is Deanna "vital" to *TNG*'s *Enterprise*? What is her role aboard the ship? Did she get the job because of the obvious advantage that her Psi offers the crew? Most of the characters have descriptions that solidify their roles and require almost no explanation: Captain, Tactical Officer, Chief Medical Officer, for instance. Though those descriptions come with some personality traits, they maintain a close and specific alignment with the characters' places onboard the *Enterprise*. For *Trek*, a professional counselor was new. That her role as counselor onboard the ship was as vital to the *Enterprise* as "the vessel's mechanisms and circuitry" was even newer (Roddenberry, 1987, 6). Trying to understand the legitimacy of this role came in many forms.

According to *The Star Trek: The Next Generation Companion*, the writer-producer staff struggled to label Troi and find acceptable parts for her after the success of the pilot episode. She certainly established herself as a vital crewmember in "Encounter at Farpoint." Without her empathic powers, it is likely the mission would have failed. But, through the rest of the first season, the writers apparently labeled her character "loose," unquestionably a double-entendre (Nemecek 27). It seems that being "attractive" and "feeling" converge upon the ultimate question of her vitality. Most commonly, the question boils down to "Is she sexy or is she serious?" After the series ended, fan/critic Phillip Ferrand, in an attempt to mock the show, questioned Troi's taste, professionalism, and sex appeal: "Why does Troi get to wear the skin-tight bunny suit? ... Why would Troi want to wear the bunny suit? ... How would you react to a psychologist dressed like this?" (241). Unsurprisingly then, the news media, *Trek* companions and handbooks, and brief critical explorations of Troi, often obsessed with her breasts, questioned her role on the show and her purpose as a character. Unfortunately, this question serves as a barrier to most critical literary analyses of the crew's sophisticated and feeling therapist.

The Troi Effect: A Response to Her Flaws

Counselor Troi's role as a therapist and a strong female presence provides a way to rethink her place on *TNG* and the show's cultural influence. She has flaws as a character, which I have outlined through the three major categories above ("Attractive," "Feeling" and "Vital"), and a thoughtful critic must bear those in mind and react to them when they offer legitimate openings for criticizing the gender biases rooted in Troi's character. But why shouldn't a crew, even one of near super-humans, have access to a mental health care professional? Wouldn't that be a source of their successes, as Roddenberry described her? Why is Troi's professionalism and emotive tendencies considered to be at odds with the *Enterprise*'s mission? Can't a feminine presence provide emotional support, even on a scientific expedition? Could her attire be a representation of a body-healthy mindset rather than a producer's male-gaze? The true degree to which Troi is sexualized, used as a plot device, or given a meaningless function on the ship, though problematic, really is minimal, and perhaps mistaken, when compared to the number of times she proves herself invaluable as a therapist and a positive representation of feminine confidence and leadership. I propose that Troi's "job" onboard the ship, as counselor, serves as the starting point for considering the extent to which Troi actually reinforces gender stereotypes. From that vantage point, a different Troi emerges, one whose critical reception may be a projection of biases from the audience as they confront their own aversions to her non-traditional role onboard the *Enterprise*.

Feminist criticism has certainly taught us that aggressions are often embedded and subtle, stemming from ignorance just as much as they stem from overt sexism. These aggressions are most likely to surface when preconceived notions about traditional gender roles are challenged and a sense of patriarchal order comes under the threat of deconstruction, especially when the source of that deconstruction is an underrepresented identity.

Critic Dale Palmer most accurately, though unwittingly, represents this kind of aggressive sexism in his analysis of Troi. He has trouble accepting that Troi is sometimes referred to as "commander" and sometimes as "counselor" while being an officer on the *Enterprise* (never-mind the label "Number One" for Riker). For Palmer, this warrants placing Troi within the category of an "arbitrary authoritarian [position]" (102). Then he extends his assessment of her value to the *Enterprise* based mainly on her appearance (attire), which he believes diminishes her status. Palmer explains that "tight body suits" means that her importance is based more on "[her] 'to-be-looked-at-ness' and less as [a metaphor] in social criticism" (104). In other words, Palmer perceives Troi as a useless addition to the cohesive message of *TNG*, primarily because she has a non-traditional rapport with the crew and she wears clothes that he deems inappropriate for accentuating "her breasts, legs, and buttocks" (104). Certainly, it is possible to rely on Troi's flaws for criticizing *TNG*, but Palmer demonstrates that those flaws can be misinterpretations born out of the audience's distaste for a disruption in patriarchal control and leadership styles.[2] Troi's unconventional, highly talented feminine contribution, along with her unabashed body-confidence, makes the audience uncomfortable more than it makes the show's progressive message unacceptable.

I will label the discomfort and defamiliarization that we see in Palmer's analysis as the Troi Effect (TE). It is very much like the effect therapy has on a client: an uncomfortable realization that may or may not lead to insight and epiphany. The flaws we perceive in Troi very well may represent the cultural biases and stigmas associated with mental health and the separate problem that American culture has with women serving in professional roles. Deanna Troi represents a coming-to-terms with our aggression toward these issues. Whether the viewer knows it or not, Troi becomes *TNG*'s conduit for conceptualizing an American culture that Gene Roddenberry envisioned for humanity, one where even traditional femininity could co-exist with professionalism, authority, and personal skill.

The TE, therefore, must be understood in relation to Troi's duties as ship's counselor. That she is a therapist caused considerable problems for fans' reception and, sadly, this is seemingly based solely on stigmas associated with mental health care. Rightfully so, I found no academic study that made a mockery of Troi based on her profession. But I would be remiss to discount the common refrain from fans and popular media that the *Enterprise* crew is above mental health concerns because they are "the best of the best." Consider this reaction from *TNG* writer Joe Menosky:

> I had a love/hate relationship with Troi. Loved the actress, but hated the character. I used to say that having a full-time therapist on board the *Enterprise*—in a command position no less—would date our series more than any other story element.... In the 1980s, America was the "Therapeutic Culture." Therapy-speak and thinking infected pretty much everything. Unfortunately, Gene Roddenberry felt the need to include it as something essential in terms of updating the "new" *Star Trek*. But look around now [in 2012]. All that stuff is gone. Drugs took over, things like Prozac, which is not necessarily an improvement [238].

Menosky's reticence to legitimize Troi's professional role stems primarily from his concern about the show's lasting effect. But his issue with "Therapeutic Culture" is also a major issue for a sect of fans, who don't seem to think that the stress of interstellar travel can possibly affect highly trained professionals like Picard or Riker. Below, I discuss the importance of having a counselor on the *Enterprise*, but for now, suffice it to say that much of the stigma surrounding mental health care is, by any critical account, discounted as prejudice. Our culture, though often more interested in pharmaceutical remedies, does value mental health care in the form of therapeutic procedures, and openly mocking it is more regularly deemed a form of narrow-mindedness or bigotry. Placing Troi on the *Enterprise* regularizes mental health care.

In a glaring oversight, virtually no critics discuss the regular therapy sessions that Troi conducts on-screen. Those sessions validate Troi's role, as I discuss below, and they often provide the means for the *Enterprise* to resolve conflict. They primarily make the TE function because through these sessions the audience observes the difficult psychological transformations and breakthroughs necessary for healthy functioning in a high-stress environment.

Apart from integrating Troi's profession into the cohesion of the show, the TE also allows *TNG*'s audience and characters to account for Troi's Psi. Most importantly, her Psi emphasizes the importance and skills of a therapist. Professional counselors are highly sought-after, heavily-trained, mental health care providers in the 21st century. Based on their practice described above, they often seem to have an extrasensory ability to read and react to clients' emotions. Deanna's Psi serves a simple allegorical function in this regard. That Psi in counseling is associated with a female stereotype eventually fails to resonate, and audiences have to carefully reconsider how they judge Troi's face as it is intensely wrenched by the effects of her Psi. In that judgment (unless approaching it as an acting strategy), the audience makes a decision about how it wants to receive a female character and ascribe her merit.

Troi's empathic abilities are also commonly crucial to the success of the ship's missions, which are always associated with a quest to "seek out" the unknown. Though *TNG* episodes usually end with rational explanations for improbable phenomena, Troi's Psi gives the TE a balance between the unknown and the known, a link to some mysteries that science hasn't been able to explain. The unique empathic emphasis on her Psi contrasts with the emotionless Spock of *TOS*, and allows the show to draw on Psi tropes from classic print SF without overt plot take-overs. Explanations are always needed for Psi to function, but Troi's role as counselor and the limited capacity of her Psi help *TNG* avoid some of the problems of Psi-overcompensation.

Based on what can be gathered from the series, telepathy is the result of a highly-evolved mind. But we never get a satisfying explanation for the machinations of Psi, with perhaps the exception of Troi's mother, Lwaxana's, conversation in the first season episode "Haven." She doesn't quite suggest a Jungian collective consciousness, but instead indicates that consciousness has rationally explainable tracks upon which minds can infinitely make connections. Lwaxana attributes the ability to understand a universally bound consciousness to species with higher functioning brains, which excludes humans. In this regard, Psi represents recognition of the unknown, a link to twentieth-century humans who may view the future's scientific advances as too intrusive upon the universe's mysteries. Psi also ascribes a special quality to the diverse crew onboard the *Enterprise*. Whatever induces feelings and an adventurous spirit within humans is felt internally. That "spirit" has the potential to undermine the *Trek* message of humanity's improving evolution. To further the Vulcan-Betazoid parallel, a device like Psi reminds the audience of the universe's "infinite diversity in infinite combinations," leaving them with a believable amount of unexplored territory that may not lend itself to our preconceived notions about humanity. Psi becomes, what C.S. Spinks suggests about science-fiction in general, "a voice for some kind of values clarification for the issues that surround technological discovery" (100). Where something seems disconnected or unexplainable, Troi's Psi adds a unifying quality to the TE, which then realigns binary tensions to the larger *Trek* themes. Ina Rae Hark, in her analytical guide to the various *Trek* series, successfully captures the counselor's function as a nucleus to the polar stability in *TNG*'s conflict denouements:

> The bifurcation of the command structure between Picard and Riker divides the cast into two contrasting but parallel groups along an intuitive/empirical axis, which mimics the chief ontological questions of *Star Trek*. Neither captain nor "Number One" represents a synthesis of the two problem-solving methods in the way that Captain Kirk did. Decisions are always a matter of negotiation and complementarity between them and their surrogates [61].
>
> To have the captain of the ship on one side of such a set of binary oppositions presents a practical

problem in regard to the command decisions he makes. A lack of "people skills" is not the best quali-
fication for a leadership position. *TNG* resolves this dilemma by having Troi serve as a link between
Picard's intellectual and scientific advisers and the more passionate field operatives. She even has a
seat on the bridge so that she can read the emotional nuances of potential adversaries for her emotionally tone-deaf captain [63].

We often neglect "links" because they "[resolve] the dilemma" of our disconnectedness;
they are too often invisible. In this case, Troi plays a hidden but vital role. Her outward
qualities seem amplified, while her underlying effects work therapeutically upon the
other characters, the unity of the series, and the viewer. By re-examining Counselor Troi
through the TE, we will also see how truly extensive the reach of *Trek*'s mythic quality
can be, how *TNG* improved upon the great American epic that Roddenberry instituted
with *TOS*, and how powerfully Troi's character impacted viewers' perception of mental
health awareness and female leadership.

Trek *as an American Epic*

As I contend with Troi's flaws, I ascribe a great power to her, the Troi Effect, which
directly affects the audience and characters of *Trek*. That kind of ability elevates Troi to
a heroic status, which is, in one way, the point of this essay. To validate Troi's presence
on the *Enterprise*, I label Troi as an epic hero within an American epic. For *TNG*, Troi
embodies the ethos (a combination of myth and utopia) that the audience associates with
its society. But to continue this, I offer some groundwork for understanding *Trek* as an
American Epic so that we can rightfully place Troi within the roster of its heroes.

Much of the literature associates *Trek* with "mythos" and "utopianisms," which are
terms that work synonymously with "epic." However, there are a few subtle distinctions
that align *Trek*, and *TNG* more specifically, with the epic genre. Epics are not required
to look to the past, like myth, or construct a perfect society, like utopias. Epics tell us
about the ideal journey, one that a hero takes, bringing along his or her "origins" and
"utopian" mentality, but not fully bound by them because of the difficulty of the journey.
The epic's heroes bear admirable traits limited by the epic's consumers. If America is to
have an epic, it can't look to the past, and this is at the heart of *Trek*'s vision. The heroes
of America's epic must serve as heralds and representatives of American ideals, primarily
those of a better tomorrow for a diverse society.

Myth, as a literary genre, typically looks to the past and to superstitions, as this definition suggests: "A kind of story or rudimentary narrative sequence, normally traditional
and anonymous, through which a given culture ratifies its social customs or accounts for
the origins of human and natural phenomena, usually in supernatural or boldly imagi-
native terms" (Baldick 143). Many of these traits easily contribute to an understanding
of *Trek* as an American epic, as long as those traits are extracted from the "rudimentary"
and "supernatural" labels.

Works like William Wilhelm Kapell's *Star Trek as Myth: Essays on Symbol and Archetype in the Final Frontier* and John Shelton Lawrence's "*Star Trek as American Monomyth*,"
attempt to correlate *Trek* themes with mythic motifs. Kapell's argument suggests that
Roddenberry successfully projected "an American mythological system into the New
Frontier headiness of an American of the 1960s" (10).[3] Lawrence sees that "projection" in the way *Trek*, overall, "celebrates the freeing of the human spirit from both

superstition and narrow-mindedness. It wears the cloak of empirical science" (98). *Trek* is myth, but only as far as it "ratifies its social customs" within the larger epic setting of the scientifically-improved future. In *Trek*, an epic journey motif captures the frontier-ism of space without enshrining a "golden past" fraught with imperialism and supersti-tion.

Utopian literature, on the other hand, typically envisions a future, which satisfies the problems of "the past" that myth presents. But utopianisms also need to be extracted from a definition in order for us to understand the distinction of *Trek* as an epic as opposed to a utopia. The *Oxford Guide to Critical Theory* defines utopia as a "deliberately construct[ed]... world that was better than the existing world out of which it was pro-duced" (Buchanan). *TNG*'s advanced Federation and Starfleet clearly adhere to that defi-nition, with lifestyle improvements like replicators, artificial hearts, and readily available professional counselors. Deanna Troi summarizes these improvements to Samuel Clemens in "Time's Arrow Part II" by explaining that suffering is eliminated by the 24th century.[4] Clemens, a social critic pulled out of the nineteenth century, unsurprisingly reacts with skepticism toward her perception of what suffering might entail. But the notion of a society where all needs are met and strife has ended is a refrain in *Trek*, and is heightened in *TNG*. Its heroes consciously reflect upon humanity's improved condition, like Troi does with Clemens.

Deanna Troi gives us a glimpse into the inherent problems of both myth and utopia labels in the episode "Samaritan Snare." The *Enterprise* encounters a ship that appears damaged and the crew onboard, a species called the Pakleds, seems incapable of repairing their ship because of their ignorance about the "origin" of the problem. The *Enterprise* crew, in typical "utopian" fashion, is trusting, technologically sophisticated, and eager to help. The mythos of *Trek*, knowledge originated from scientific exploration, demands that the *Enterprise* beam their smart engineer over to the Pakleds. Throughout their interaction, Troi senses that the Pakleds are untrustworthy and tries to bring LaForge back before they take him captive. Riker rejects her suggestion, no doubt driven by his utopian impulse and his scientific identification of the problem. But Troi transcends both of those issues. She knows the source of another problem, a real problem, one that is nei-ther "mythic" and is certainly not pleasantly utopian. Her intuition and passionate plead-ing, juxtaposed against the crew's inattention (outright rejection on Riker's part) to her "knowledge," suggests a completely different kind of situation, neither "myth" or "utopian," though elements of both are present.

Trek also bears more resemblance to an epic than it does to a myth or a utopia because myth and utopia are embedded generic features of the epic. *Trek* presents a voyage where representatives of a utopian society must exist in a chaotic space outside of the utopia's social prescriptions. To survive that chaos, the heroes rely on the knowledge of their mythos (science and rationality) and the message of hope from their "perfect" home. An epic was "originally a lengthy poem recounting in elevated style the exploits of a legendary hero or heroes, especially in battles or voyages" (Birch and Katy 344). In addition, according to *The Oxford Companion to World Mythology*, a hero is "culturally analogous" to its society's values (Leeming 181). So if *Trek* is an American epic, its heroes, the bridge officers, must appeal to the audience's American ethos. It accomplishes this by showcasing the "American Dream's" future in a highly diverse setting. Roddenberry claimed *Star Trek* "speaks to some basic human needs: that there is a tomorrow, it's not all going to be over with a big splash and a bomb, that the human race is improving, that we have things to be proud of as humans" (Adler). Troi's heroic identity espouses this kind of positive view of humanity through her therapeutic practice.

As the ship's counselor, Troi makes possible the self-efficacy of the characters, who, in turn, function with heightened confidence and awareness. Due to Troi's intervention, or the knowledge of her potential intervention, the *Enterprise* (as metaphor for civilization), whose crew heroically embodies the diverse American ethos in civil terms (leader, medical professional, security officers, scientists, mental health professional), functions. The view naturally absorbs this effect of interconnectedness, and cognitively realigns the positive messaging in *Trek* based on the knowledge and assumption of resolved complications.

In "Chain of Command, Part 2," Troi's role is minimal, but she serves as a great healer when Picard seeks her counsel at the end of the show. He has just returned from imprisonment and torture by the Cardassians, with whom the Federation is reconciling after a long war. This episode is replete with epic battle adventures and survival narratives. Picard's interrogator is bent on breaking him psychologically through physical abuse, sleep and food deprivation, and, most prominently, attempting to force him to admit that he sees five lights in the room when, in fact, there are only four. In her brief therapeutic role at the end, Troi's presence gives the reader an insight into Picard. She uses a simple reflection technique whereby a counselor's brief statement paraphrases a client's experience, leading to more insight, and in that moment, Picard admits to actually seeing five lights even though he knew one was a hallucination. Picard's vulnerability is exposed, as is his strength of will. Troi's presence on the ship establishes an access to her empathy and healing processes that are available to the crew and the audience. This is the bright, epic future that she offers *TNG*.

Counselor Troi as a Heroic Futurism

But it is worth considering whether or not the Troi Effect represents a believable future. So far I have shown that Troi's role is a valid one onboard the *Enterprise* and within the scope of the *TNG* universe. Troi overcomes the flaws of gender stereotypes that she sometimes presents. She also functions as a kind of epic hero because she contributes to *TNG*'s representation of the American ethos. But aside from being a valid crewmember, is a mental health care professional likely to serve such a prominent role on a human spacecraft in the future? *TNG* introduces us to touchscreens, artificial hearts, unisex clothing, and unapologetic tolerance. These futurisms are the philosophies and technologies that an audience can easily accept because they are not so far outside of humanity's grasp, even though they obviously require a great deal of progress and innovation. Arguably, all of the items in the list above are (or are aspiring to be) realities today. So a futurism represents the plausibility of progression. An American/human future is only believable if it represents a change that might happen in the future, even if it is unlikely or too progressive today.

We can better understand this concept by understanding modernisms, not to be confused with the aesthetic movement in art and literature. In film or television, a modernism is an attempt to make an image, like wardrobes or hairstyles, appealing to contemporary viewers' sensibilities when the film or television program is set in the past or future. An extreme example may be a movie like *A Knight's Tale* (2001), where the characters all wear clothing and hairstyles that are reminiscent of the middle ages but so contempized that they can just as easily be seen in a suburban American mall, a motif extended to their "We will rock you" chants at jousting tournaments. *Star Trek* also uses modernisms. Consider the women's dress-uniforms in *TOS* (late sixties styles) or the civilian's vests in *TNG* (late-eighties styles).

In a like vein, a futurism attempts to mimic what might be plausibly passed off as a future image without losing the audience in the effort. Sometimes it works on *TNG*. Uniforms, for example, generally found acceptance, with a few exceptions like the short-lived unisex dresses (Of course, Troi's uniforms may contribute to her inability to garner "futurism" status). Sometimes, the metallic-colored bed sheets are a bit much. But the most important futurisms in *Trek* are the ideational ones that the show has us take for granted. Of course there is a Klingon officer on-board; it's the tolerant future, no questions asked. Of course there is a female doctor; it's the non-sexist future and Crusher's presence makes sense. Of course the *Enterprise* crew needs a mental health professional; it's the trauma-inducing future, just as natural as a bald Bolian hairstylist.

Troi's empathic abilities place her in a unique position to represent the future. Sensing emotions is a believable trait and a part of human evolutionary functions. That emotional reception is enhanced in the future therefore seems believable. Troi relies on this ability regularly throughout the series, usually in attempts to save or help others.

Perhaps the most pointed exploration of this futurism comes in the episode "The Loss." Due to an encounter with a two-dimensional life form, Troi's empathic ability disappears. She has to cope and does so admirably with the help of her crew, who have to take on the role of therapists themselves, mimicking Troi's techniques. The episode emphasizes just how advantageous this ability is and just how important such a progression in mental health care is to a crew of frontier-explorers. Though her shipmates help her cope, no one on board suggests that her job will remain as effective with the loss because that futurism is clearly an improvement.

More importantly, "The Loss" emphasizes another futurism that Deanna Troi brings to *TNG*: mental health awareness. In the episode's opening scene, before she loses her ability, Troi conducts a therapy session with a Starfleet officer (Ensign Brooks, whose husband died five months prior) by employing actual therapeutic methods and psychological knowledge. Specifically, Kubler-Ross's "five stages of grief" serves as the theoretical basis for her session. Troi herself, coping with "normal" empathic abilities, goes through the same stages: (1) denial, (2) anger, (3) bargaining, (4) depression, (5) acceptance (Block, Erdmann and Moore 185).

Mental health awareness is one of those issues we still mull over and stigmatize. Aversions to mental health were more intensified during the original airing of *TNG* than they are today, but the stigmas persist. One doesn't have to do too much research to discover that medical and psychology journals like *The Lancet* or *The American Journal of Public Health* or *Psychiatry Research* regularly provide studies demonstrating the necessity of routine mental healthcare. These studies also show that the public regularly dismisses or avoids this care because of unwarranted stigmas associated with it (Bockting et al.; Xavier et al.; Corrigan et al.). So normalizing mental health serves as a futurism; it showcases something that humanity has overcome. But *TNG*'s counselor actually goes a step further in securing mental health awareness as a futurism. Deanna Troi not only forces a positive rethinking of mental health, her character is unprecedented in light of media depictions of the mental health profession.[5]

Almost any profession represented on television tends to be sensationalized for dramatic effect. Although that is typically acceptable for the purpose of entertainment, we should consider some of the ethical dilemmas that come with that because these dilemmas can reinforce stereotypes and create stigmas that might even prevent someone from seeking needed care. A recent study in the *Journal of Behavioural Sciences* demonstrates that the popularity of accurate mental health services posted to YouTube is insignificant next to the popularity of distorted portrayals of mental healthcare services on television. The study also finds that well over half of these television portrayals are inaccurate, which is due to a desired dramatic effect (Furlonger et al.). I doubt any of us consider this surprising, if we contemplate the various depictions of psychiatric professionals on television. Consider this non-exhaustive, but representative, list of television and movie characters who are therapists: Sidney Freedman (*M*A*S*H**, 1972–1983), Bob Hartley (*The Bob Newhart Show*, 1972–1978), Frasier Crane (*Cheers*, 1982–1993 and *Frasier*, 1993–2004), Leo Marvin (*What About Bob?*, 1991), Sean Maguire (*Good Will Hunting*, 1997), Malcolm Crowe (*The Sixth Sense*, 1999), Ben Sobel (*Analyze This*, 2000), Jennifer Melfi (*The Sopranos*, 1999–2007), Tobias Funke (*Arrested Development*, 2003–2006 and 2013), and Barbara Hofstadter (*The Big Bang Theory*, 2007–present). All of these characters are therapists who are either stereotyped or caricatured, or their patients are. I would also be remiss to leave out Harley Quinn, the psychiatrist-turned-sidekick who serves the Joker in *Batman: The Animated Series* (also featured in the 2016 motion picture *Suicide Squad*). It is worth noting that Quinn and Melfi, the only women on this list, are highly sexualized in their portrayal (Melfi is raped in one graphic scene during an episode of *The Sopranos*; the rape plays virtually no role in the overall plot of the show).

Though my list is not exhaustive, viewers seem to prefer drama over reality, which is understandable if the implications aren't so dangerous. In another study, "The Influence of Television on Willingness to Seek Therapy," three Iowa State University psychologists examine the correlations between an exposure to television programs and perceptions of therapy. The study reveals that television exposure increases the perception of stigma and risks and minimizes the perception of benefits and positive attitudes towards therapy. As a result, the intention to seek therapy diminishes. According to Vogel:

> Generally, it seems like therapists are portrayed unethically—like sleeping with the client, or implanting false memories, or talking about their clients outside the session…. These are things that almost never happen with real therapists, but on a show—because they're probably more exciting—they happen more frequently [Interview].

Based on Vogel's expertise, this also applies to potential patients: "If you examine the portrayal of the clients, it's probably as bad or worse…. So why would you seek therapy if you believe you're going to be perceived negatively and you're going to see someone who's incompetent and not able to help you" (Vogel, Gentile, and Kaplan 278).

In nearly categorical terms, television programs purposely de-normalize the therapeutic process. As a result, viewers tend to develop negative perceptions of mental health care and mental health-care professionals. Even the few "positive" portrayals in the list above, like Sean Maguire (*Good Will Hunting*, 1997) or Malcolm Crowe (*The Sixth Sense*, 1999), don't give mental health processes, like therapeutic sessions, much credence because the professionals cross boundaries or the patients represent extreme (even paranormal) cases. Audiences then absorb a distorted and frightening perception of the mental health care profession, which becomes their expectation for on-screen depictions and causes their hesitations about real psychiatric care.

Though Troi's intense sensing of emotions may fit the drama-induced mold for onscreen depictions of therapists early on in the series, her character evolves away from that. Eventually, she came to represent the only non-caricatured, de-stigmatized television therapist before and during *TNG*'s airing. Troi's character does have the advantage of an already fantastical backdrop, space, to serve as a balancing mechanism. But even within the outer space setting, which almost any other program would have exploited, Troi resists drama-lust. Typically, Troi maintains her professionalism to the point that her lines seem mundane. This is especially true during the last two seasons when her empathic abilities are used less frequently. Troi transcends all of the evidence that American culture harbors biases toward mental care, and as a result, she renders *TNG*'s future as an advanced society.

Table 1 shows the extent to which Troi's abilities are employed, and can be considered somewhat representative of the entire series because it offers a picture of Troi's role in the first and final seasons. The number of times Troi serves as an empath or counselor decreases as the series ends, and this progression functions in two important ways. First, it represents the realistic nature of Counselor Troi serving as a futurism. In the first season, she may have played too prominent a role, especially in relation to her Psi abilities, but that role finds equilibrium by the final season as a safe representative of the future. But, secondly, it also mimics a successful therapeutic process, whereby the therapist's role is diminished in proportion to the client's health. It is as if the series itself benefited from years of counseling, another microcosm of *Trek*'s epic progress into a better future.

Table 1. Frequency of Counselor Troi's Psi and Mental Health Interventions in Seasons 1 and 7 of *TNG*

	1	7
TNG *Season*	1	7
Number of Episodes	26	26
Number of episodes where Troi employs her Psi abilities	19	4
Number of episodes where Troi conducts therapeutic counseling sessions	16	14
Number of episodes where Troi's therapeutic counseling sessions or Psi abilities contribute to a resolution of the main conflict	9	4

Whether using her version of telepathy or her counseling techniques, Troi is never portrayed as a "shrink" or a cartoonish psychologist bent on manipulation. Rather, her variety of techniques and abilities serve to amplify the audience's perception of *TNG*'s commitment to diversity in the future. When in a session with a client, Counselor Troi asks questions that any typical therapist might ask and behaves professionally even in the most difficult of circumstances. A serious mental health professional is a futurism that allows *TNG* to carry on the plausibility of *Trek* as the American epic. It also helps to transform viewers' perceptions about mental health professionals.

In an episode like "The Dauphin," Troi senses something odd about the changeling who has just boarded the ship, but she establishes therapeutic boundaries and refuses to pry. In "Hero Worship" Troi's trauma therapy helps a youth recognize the underlying causes of his obsession with Data. She is depicted in several counseling scenes with the boy, and the episode illustrates a process of psychological healing. In "Cost of Living," she operates as a family therapist and develops a sensible plan for Worf and his son, Alexander, to work out their issues of respect. She even serves as Riker's career counselor in "The Best of Both Worlds, Part 1," when he has to come to grips with his professional aspirations in Starfleet. In "Lower Decks," her personnel evaluations of the entire ship determine which crewmembers are fit for promotion. These examples, in which the audience copes with the psychological toll that space-travel can take on anyone, are representative of Troi's futurism. Regardless of status, denizens of the future need not worry about seeking mental health care. It is common and normalized through Troi, even for the other heroes onboard the *Enterprise*.

Though the show often draws from pop-psychology and allusions to Freud, Troi essentially hosts what viewers perceive of as a modern professional psychotherapeutic practice. She regularly conducts therapeutic sessions with characters to maintain a healthy and functioning community. Her role is to apply, as Oxford's *Dictionary of Psychology* would suggest of counseling in general, "psychological theories and communication skills to clients' personal problems, concerns, or aspirations…" in an environment where the "dominant ethos is one of providing facilitation without directive guidance" (Colman 176). Set on a ship, a highly trained counselor must use her expertise to help crewmates process the trauma and the social dynamics of space travel and away missions. Cognitive psychology, a major psychotherapeutic theory contemporary to the airing of *TNG* (and still prominent today), predominates Troi's counseling methodology on the show. It was and is the most dominant form of therapy practiced by counselors and embedded in the American public consciousness.[6] Troi is modeled on the perceived necessity and capabilities of mental health therapists.

A brief overview of cognitive therapy will help us understand what makes the TE so substantial to *TNG* and the larger cultural impact that the show has on its audience. Most basically, one of the primary goals of cognitive therapy, "cognitive restructuring," comes from encouraging and helping clients to "adopt more rational or constructive ways of thinking about their problems" (Colman 146). Processing through thoughts and experiences initiates "cognitive restructuring," which, through guided professional counseling, progressively and positively leads to enhanced "cognitive reflection" (reflective deliberation toward a correct behavior) and increased "self-efficacy" (assurance in handling circumstances that would otherwise be intimidating [Bandura 194]). The process, in a sense, bolsters confidence in one's perceptions and behaviors. Beneficiaries of cognitive therapies can use their newly constructed patterns of thought to make a claim to "agency" ("a sense of competent action" [Anderson and Goolishian 372]) within their environments. Though cognitive psychotherapy has far more applications, this definition matches a general understanding of its manifestation on *TNG*. Troi regularly guides characters through psychological construction activities, and the viewer experiences, albeit through the limited and fantastical scope of popular SF television, "cognitive reconstruction" and "agency" alongside the *Enterprise* crew. The audience believes the mental health of the crew and takes that reality for granted when experiencing the organic unity of *TNG*.

In one of the most significant counseling scenes in the series, Troi helps Data (an unfeeling android) trace his thoughts to the source of an emerging neurosis in "Phantasms." She encourages further sessions and suggests his visits with a holographic Sigmund Freud were a mistake. In this moment, she reflects contemporary counseling knowledge and discounts older psychotherapies that have fallen out of favor. As a result, the characters and the audience participate in trustworthy techniques for developing cognitive awareness that leads to healthily restructured thoughts about reality.

The outcome of her onboard practice is the believability of self-efficacious crewmembers who are regularly challenged with extreme psychological trauma. The audience benefits from this because the cognitive realignment that she facilitates for the crew of the *Enterprise* results in a trusting ship staff. The expectation that everyone onboard will exhibit heightened cognitive reflection because of the healthy atmosphere available to them allows the audience to rest assured in that procedure and affirms the harmony of the show as a textual unity.

Through Troi's counseling service, the TE functions in much the same way as when counselors establish therapeutic rapport and foster agency within treatment groups. In "Lower Decks" and "Man of the People," among other episodes, Troi is established as the officer who helps Commander Riker conduct crew evaluations, and in both of these episodes, her capacity for this duty stems from her high rank, her duty as counselor, and her rapport with the crew. She is both evaluator and advocate. John Walter and Jane Peller explain this kind of diversity as the key to rapport in *Becoming Solution-Focused in Brief Therapy* (a text which may best demonstrate therapeutic processes concurrent with TNG's airing): "The way to maintain rapport with different clients is to match and pace their unique way of thinking and feeling ... to use their language ... to reflect their ... emotional response to their situation" (43). Troi regularly exhibits this kind of behavior, interacting with the diversity experienced by space travel. In "Eye of the Beholder," Troi helps solve a mysterious death by interacting with and sensing the psychological conditions of multiple alien races involved in the death's circumstances. In this and many other episodes, Troi's perceivable receptivity of emotions makes her the conduit for transferring and translating the psychological diversity of alien species that the *Enterprise* encounters. All of these episodes expose a variation on this function of the TE; Troi gives us a glimpse into emotional complexity and satisfies the dramatic tension we have with her and the crew.

Her rapport even extends to group counseling sessions that represent her expertise for leading crewmembers to workable solutions in difficult situations. Throughout most of "Schisms," Troi helps four characters reconstruct a shared experience by counseling them through it. As they gain confidence by recreating their experience, they turn their "learning and discovery" into, as David G. Martin's *Counseling and Therapy Skills* puts it, "experiential change" (50). Martin, a long-time counseling educator, explains that therapeutic processes aim for "conceptual analysis" that direct clients to change (50). The conflict is resolved because the characters voluntarily and willingly trust in Troi's professional capacity to lead them to an actionable transformation. That trust derives from the importance of community health that Troi's presence and actions imply. Once the psychological barrier is surpassed, the group and the ship can transition into a solution-oriented action to the conflict of the episode. Counseling techniques contemporary with *TNG*'s airing and still practiced today urge the audience to participate in the necessity of a counselor onboard the ship.

As a final example of the TE and its epic futurism, let's examine Troi's therapeutic technique with Chief Engineer Geordi La Forge in "Interface." Aside from Data, La Forge may be the most emotionally inaccessible character on *TNG*. When he begins to see visions of his deceased mother in a dangerous environment, he irrationally returns to that environment for the sake, as Counselor Troi helps him understand, of fulfilling his desire to come to terms with his mother's death. La Forge's behavior is highly dangerous, yet he continues it despite orders and despite the self-harm it would inflict. Troi employs a typical confrontational intervention for cognitive processing, which therapist often use when clients are a danger to themselves or others. In this technique, a therapist uses a series of leading questions, which directs the client to open up about the various unresolved problems inherent in his circumstance. At this point, the therapist can interject a diagnosis that the client must confront. La Forge is often portrayed on the show as an out-of-touch tech geek who is overly self-assured because of his technical knowledge. So he ignores Troi and still attempts his dangerous behavior. But the therapeutic effect is on the audience, who can contrast their likely behavior with La Forge's. Near death, the chief engineer does experience some insightful cognitive restructuring, and the viewer has a frame of reference for understanding why he finally corrects his behavior, which is the underlying mental strength produced during the confrontation session with Troi.

Conclusion

To sum up, Deanna Troi's character ascribes an epic quality to *TNG* by affecting viewers' perceptions of her role onboard the *Enterprise*. That the well-trained, super-human crew onboard the utopian Federation's flagship requires the presence of a mental-health care professional speaks volumes about Gene Rodenberry's forward-thinking vision. Deanna Troi realizes and transcends that vision by instituting a unique effect on viewers whereby they can glimpse into the process of an improved American ethos (the Troi Effect). When Counselor Troi senses emotions, we sense a better future.

NOTES

1. See Erin C. Callahan's and Peter W. Lee's essays in this volume. That "space is hard" has become a refrain for SF critics to reflect upon the overarching theme of tragic difficulties and human drama inherent in space travel. It's often associated with Tom Godwin's "Cold Equations" (1954), a story in which a sympathetic stowaway on a spaceship must be jettisoned as a punishment.

2. On patriarchy, see Olaf Meuther's and Simon Ledder's, Jens Kolata's, and Oonagh Hayes' essays in this volume.

3. See Katharina Thulmann's essay in this volume.

4. Troi reiterates the end of social ills in the twenty-first century in *Star Trek: First Contact*.

5. Though anecdotal, the TE is also regularly invoked as a call to mental health professions. My own spouse, Becca Smith, a therapist at a psychiatric hospital, identifies Troi as a positive view of the future and a partial inspiration for her career. Becca also deserves acknowledgement for guiding me to most of the definitions I provide for psychological terminology.

6. A 1999 study by Robins, Gosling, and Craik suggests that, within the last fifty years, cognitive psychology has become, by far, "the most prominent school" of psychotherapeutic practice because of its popularity among professional psychologists (117). To date, cognitive psychology is regularly adapted and utilized by mental health professionals (See chapters 1 and 4 of Braisby and Gellatly for a rationale of cognitive psychology's prominence) and major universities, including Yale, the University of California Los Angeles, Rutgers, and Stanford, have divisions of cognitive psychology for research and counseling activities.

WORKS CITED

Adler, Margot. "Present at the Creation: *Star Trek*." *NPR*. National Public Radio, 20 May 2002. Web. 18 Sept. 2016. http://www.npr.org/templates/story/story.php?storyId=1143643

Anderson, Harlene, and Harold Goolishian. "Human Systems as Linguistic Systems: Preliminary and Evolving Ideas About the Implications of Clinical Theory. *Family Process*. 27.4 (1988): 371–394. Print.

Baldick, Chris. *The Oxford Dictionary of Literary Terms*. Oxford: Oxford University Press, 2015. Print.

Bandura, Albert. "Self-Efficacy: Toward a Unifying Theory of Behvioral Change." *Psychological Review* 84.2 (1977): 191–215. Print.

Birch, Dinah, and Hooper Katy. *The Oxford Companion to English Literature*. Oxford: Oxford University Press, 2012. Print.

Block, Paula M., Terry J. Erdmann, and Roanald D. Moore. *Star Trek: The Next Generation 365*. New York: Abrams, 2012. Print.

Bockting, Walter O., et al. "Stigma, Mental Health, and Resilience in an Online Sample of the US Transgender Population." *American Journal of Public Health* 103.5 (2013): 943–51. Print.

Braisby, Nick, and Angus Gellatly. *Cognitive Psychology.* 2nd ed. Oxford: Oxford University Press, 2014. Print.

Buchanan, Ian. "Utopia." *A Dictionary of Critical Theory.* Oxford: Oxford University Press, 2010. *Oxford Reference.* 2010. Web. 01 April. 2016.

Christie, Julie, actress. *Demon Seed.* Metro Goldwyn Mayeer, United Artists, 1977.

Colman, Andrew M. *A Dictionary of Psychology.* Oxford: Oxford University Press, 2015, Print.

Corrigan, Patrick W., et al. "Mental Health Stigma and Primary Health Care Decisions." *Psychiatry Research* 218.1–2 (2014): 35–38. Print.

Editorial. "The Health Crisis of Mental Health Stigma." *The Lancet* 387.10023 (2016): 1027–27. Print.

Engel, Joel. *Gene Roddenberry: The Myth and the Man Behind* Star Trek. 1st ed. New York: Hyperion, 1994. Print.

Farrand, Phil. "Trek Silliness: The Top Ten Oddities of *Star Trek: The Next Generation.*" *The Nitpicker's Guide for Next Generation Trekkers.* New York: Dell, 1993. Print.

Furlonger, Brett, et al. "The Portrayal of Counselling on Television and Youtube: Implications for Professional Counsellors." *Journal of Behavioural Sciences* 25.2 (2015): 1. Print.

Greven, David. *Gender and Sexuality in* Star Trek: *Allegories of Desire in the Television Series and Films.* Jefferson, NC: McFarland. Print.

Hark, Ina Rae. *Star Trek.* BFI TV Classics. London: Palgrave Macmillan, 2008. Print.

Hastie, Amelie. "A Fabricated Space: Assimilating the Individual on *Star Trek: The Next Generation.*" *Enterprise Zones: Critical Positions on* Star Trek. Ed. Harrison, Taylor. Boulder, CO: Westview Press, 1996. 115–136. Print.

Isaacs, Bruce. "A Vision of Time and Place: Spiritual Humanism and the Utopian Impulse." Star Trek *as Myth: Essays on Symbol and Archetype at the Final Frontier.* Ed. Kapell, Matthew. Jefferson, NC: McFarland, 2010. 182–96. Print.

Jerry, Buck. "Marina Sirtis Fought to Join the Enterprise Crew." *Worcester Telegram & Gazette (Ma)* 1989 Dec 24 1989: 12. Print.

Joyrich, Lynne. "Feminist Enterprise? 'Star Trek: The Next Generation' and the Occupation of Femininity." *Cinema Journal* 35.2 (1996): 61–84. Print.

Lawrence, John Shelton. "*Star Trek* as American Monomyth." Star Trek *as Myth: Essays on Symbol and Archetype at the Final Frontier.* Ed. Kapell, Matthew. Jefferson, NC: McFarland, 2010. 93–111. Print.

Leeming, David. "Heroic Monomyth." *The Oxford Companion to World Mythology.* Oxford: Oxford University Press, 2005, 2006. Print.

Martin, David G. *Counseling and Therapy Skills.* 3rd ed. Long Grove, IL: Waveland Press, 2011. Print.

Nemecek, Larry. *The* Star Trek: The Next Generation *Companion.* New York: Pocket Books, 1992. Print.

Ott, Brian L., and Eric Aoki. "Popular Imagination and Identity Politics: Reading the Future in *Star Trek: The Next Generation.*" *Western Journal of Communication* 65.4 (2001): 392–415. Print.

Palmer, Dale. "Redefining the Masculine Hegemony: Gender and Sexual Politics in *Star Trek.*" *Electric Sheep Slouching Towards Bethlehem: Speculative Fiction in a Post Modern World.* Ed. Harry Edwin Eiss. Newcastle upon Tyne: Cambridge Scholars Press, 2014. 99–110. Print.

Robins, Richard W., Samuel D. Gosling, and Kenneth H. Craik. "An Empirical Analysis of Trends in Psychology." *American Psychologist.* 54. 2 (1999): 117–128. Print.

Roddenberry, Gene. "Mission Logs: Year Five, a Tribute to Gene Roddenberry." *Star Trek: The Next Generation.* Season 5, Disc 7. Paramount, 2002, DVD.

_____. *Star Trek the Next Generation: Writers/Directors Guide.* 2nd season rev. Hollywood, CA: Paramount Pictures, 1988. Print.

_____. *Star Trek: The Next Generation: Writers/Directors Guide.* 3rd season rev. Hollywood, CA: Paramount Pictures, 1990. Print.

Scott, Steven. "Making It So: *Star Trek* and Ideology." *The Everyday Fantastic: Essays on Science Fiction and Human Being.* Cambridge: Cambridge Scholars Press, 2008. 20–30. Print.

"7 Bizarre Facts About Deanna Troi's Cleavage." *Geek Twins,* 7 June 2016, Web. 18 Sept. 2016. http://www.the geektwins.com/2014/06/7-bizarre-facts-about-deanna-trois.html.

Spinks, C.W. "Motifs in Science Fiction as Archetypes of Science." *Extrapolation* 27.2 (1986): 93–108. Print.

Star Trek: First Contact. Dir. Jonathan Frakes. Perf. Patrick Stewart, Jonathan Frakes, Brent Spiner, LeVar Burton, and Michael Dorn. Paramount, 1996. DVD.

Star Trek: Nemesis. Dir. Stuart Baird. Perf. Patrick Stewart, Jonathan Frakes, Brent Spiner, LeVar Burton, and Michael Dorn. Paramount, 2002. DVD.

Vogel, David. Interview by Mike Ferlazzo. *Iowa State University News Service.* 21 Apr. 2008. Web. 7 Jun. 2016.

Vogel, David L., Douglas A. Gentile, and Scott A. Kaplan. "The Influence of Television on Willingness to Seek Therapy." *Journal of Clinical Psychology* 64.3 (2008): 276–95. Print.

Walter, John L., and Jane E. Peller. *Becoming Solution-Focused in Brief Therapy.* New York: Brunner/Mazel Press, 1992. Print.

Xavier, Salomé, et al. "Mental Health Stigma: Where Do We Stand?" *PsiLogos* 11.2 (2014): 10–21. Print.

TNG *Episodes*

"Chain of Command, Part II." *Star Trek: The Next Generation.* Writ. Frank Abatemarco. Dir. Les Landau. *Netflix.* Web. 7 Jun. 2016.

"The Child." *Star Trek: The Next Generation.* Writ. Jaron Summers, Jon Povill, and Maurice Hurley. Dir. Rob Bowman *Netflix.* Web. 7 Jun. 2016.

"The Dauphin." *Star Trek: The Next Generation.* Writ. Scott Rubenstein and Leonard Mlodinow. Dir. Rob Bowman. *Netflix.* Web. 7 Jun. 2016.

"Déjà Q." *Star Trek: The Next Generation.* Writ. Richard Danus. Dir. Les Landau. *Netflix.* Web. 7 Jun. 2016.

"Encounter at Farpoint, Parts 1 and 2." *Star Trek: The Next Generation.* Writ. D.C. Fontana and Gene Roddenberry. Dir. Corey Allen. *Netflix.* Web. 7 Jun. 2016.

"Eye of the Beholder." *Star Trek: The Next Generation.* Writ. Rene Echevarria. Dir. Cliff Bole. *Netflix.* Web. 7 Jun. 2016.

"The Game." *Star Trek: The Next Generation.* Writ. Brannon Braga. Dir. Crorey Allen *Netflix.* Web. 7 Jun. 2016.

"Haven." *Star Trek: The Next Generation.* Writ. Tracy Tormé. Dir. Richard Compton. *Netflix.* Web. 7 Jun. 2016.

"Hero Worship." *Star Trek: The Next Generation.* Writ. Joe Menosky. Dir. Patrick Stewart. *Netflix.* Web. 7 Jun. 2016.

"The Loss." *Star Trek: The Next Generation.* Writ. Hilary J. Bader, Alan J. Adler and Vanessa Greene. Dir. Chip Chalmers. *Netflix.* Web. 7 Jun. 2016.

"Lower Decks." *Star Trek: The Next Generation.* Writ. Rene Echevarria. Dir. Gabrielle Beaumont. *Netflix.* Web. 7 Jun. 2016.

"Man of the People." *Star Trek: The Next Generation.* Writ. Frank Abatemarco. Dir. Winrich Kolbe. *Netflix.* Web. 7 Jun. 2016.

"The Outrageous Okona." *Star Trek: The Next Generation.* Writ. Burton Armus. Dir. Robert Becker. *Netflix.* Web. 7 Jun. 2016.

"Samaritan Snare." *Star Trek: The Next Generation.* Writ. Robert L. McCullough. Dir. Les Landau. *Netflix.* Web. 7 Jun. 2016.

"Schisms." *Star Trek: The Next Generation.* Writ. Brannon Braga. Shearer. Dir. Robert Wiemer. *Netflix.* Web. 7 Jun. 2016.

"Skin of Evil." *Star Trek: The Next Generation.* Writ. Joseph Stefano and Hannah Louise Shearer. Dir. Joseph L. Scanlan. *Netflix.* Web. 7 Jun. 2016.

"The Survivors." *Star Trek: The Next Generation.* Writ. Michael Wagner. Dir. Les Landau. *Netflix.* Web. 7 Jun. 2016.

"Time's Arrow, Part Ii." *Star Trek: The Next Generation.* Writ. Jeri Taylor. Dir. Les Landau. *Netflix.* Web. 7 Jun. 2016.

"Violations." *Star Trek: The Next Generation.* Writ. Pamela Gray and Jeri Taylor. Dir. Robert Wiemer. *Netflix.* Web. 7 Jun. 2016.

Out of Order

Tasha Yar's Downfall in the Age of Reagan

Peter W. Lee

On stardate 41601.3, the 24th century joined the 1980s. In the first season episode "Skin of Evil," the *Starship Enterprise*'s security chief, Natasha Yar, dies in the line of duty. Yar was not the first *Star Trek* regular to meet a grisly fate. In 1982, Spock saved the ship and crew from a wrathful superman, but at great cost, namely, himself (*Star Trek II: The Wrath of Kahn*). But Yar's demise, delivered on prime time to television audiences, conveyed a different outlook and tone. Her end comes swiftly, without warning, and contributes nothing to resolve the episode's storyline. Creator and producer Gene Roddenberry insisted the security chief have a "meaningless death," a fate so common in Yar's profession and one that dozens of "red shirts" could attest to from the franchise's history (Willey 6–7, Reeves-Stevens 61).

But the Great Bird of the Galaxy laid a figurative egg with his claim. Yar's fate was not merely an incidental, misfortunate plot twist. Rather, actress Denise Crosby's exit symbolized a larger cultural and political shift concerning women, specifically, a backlash against the gains made by second wave feminism and the marginalization of disadvantaged groups in American society, especially the poor. In "Skin of Evil," Yar's death came from Armus, a "living" puddle of blackened Metamucil (Nemecek 55). According to Data, this pool was the cast-off remnants of "bad" emotions from a supposedly enlightened species of Titans several centuries earlier. The episode never identifies the former inhabitants of Vagra II, although their grandiose name from Greek mythology suggests a superior species of sorts. However, a historical and cultural perspective pinpoints Armus's origins coming from the people of planet Earth.

Namely, Americans in the age of Reagan.

Frequencies Open

Gene Roddenberry attributed the original *Star Trek*'s eventual success to the show's portrayal of an optimistic future highlighting racial and sexual equality. In the 1960s and 1970s, the counterculture and youth activists celebrated the show's diversity, the positive presence of minority groups, and the women's movement. *Star Trek*'s strong progressive appeal even took actress Nichelle Nichols by surprise when feminists criticized Starfleet's female miniskirt uniforms as sexist—even though Nichols asserted her attire was far more comfortable than Kirk's bell bottoms (Nichols 169). Still, feminists wondered, with all the advancements in the 23rd century, why women explorers bared their legs at all. Even in the *Star Trek* movies, with their more militarized look and tone, Uhura wears a skirt and nylon stockings.

By the 1970s and into the 1980s, American media started to respond to these feminist critiques. Television programs, such as *Maude* (1972) and *One Day at a Time* (1975), feature matriarchs and divorced women making their ways through the televisual settings of "liberated" America (Douglas and Michaels 75–79). In addition, women expanded their roles on television. From superheroines *Wonder Woman* (1975–1979) and *The Bionic Woman* (1976–1978) to peace officers *Cagney & Lacey* (1982–1988), female characters demonstrated their street smarts, aptly juggled their careers and homemaking skills, and kept up their traditional physical attributes. Confident, radiant, and powerful, these women challenged decades of sexism in film and television. Even Uhura has an opportunity to shine in *Star Trek III: The Search for Spock* (1983) when the communications officer intimidates a young male adventurer into submission.

Within this context, Gene Roddenberry's plans for *Star Trek: The Next Generation* incorporated societal shifts regarding womanhood on television. The Chief Medical Officer, Beverly Crusher, for instance, is a single mother and holds the rank of commander. The expansion of actors of color in American media also mirrored the next generation of space explorers. The creation of an android and a last-minute Klingon addition to the cast indicated a level of diversity among the ship's crew—prosthetics notwithstanding— greater than that of the original *Enterprise*. Notably, the producers added a Latina-sounding name to one character in the ship's command structure. The role of the original Chief of Security was twenty-six-year-old Macha Hernandez, whom Roddenberry described with "a fire in her eyes and muscularity well developed and a very female body, [although] much of her strength comes from attitude" (Nemecek 13). With her muscularity, attitude, and "fire," Hernandez embodied both the strengths of the feminist movement and racial inclusivity.

The producers and actress Denise Crosby later linked Captain Picard's new security chief to a larger context concerning sexual equality, where women joined men in the combat zone, rather than stay on the sidelines as passive spectators. They openly compared Hernandez/Yar to cinematic space marines such as Jennette Goldstein's "Vasquez" character in the sci-fi shoot-'em-up *Aliens* (1986) (Nemecek 15). Crosby herself identified directly with *Aliens*'s main heroine, Ellen Ripley: "You would almost expect Ripley to wind up in the position she's in. In the case of Tasha, it's like a street kid who has finally made it good" (Shapiro "Security Chief," 49–51). Roddenberry's concept of Macha Hernandez blended "hard" masculinity with femininity. As the Federation flagship's top security officer, Hernandez would presumably man the front lines to protect her captain. Roddenberry emphasized this relationship; Hernandez has an "obsessive devotion to protecting the ship […] and treats Capt. Picard and Number One as if they were saints" (Nemecek 13). Despite her tough exterior, Hernandez's "obsession" with Picard indicated a need for approval from a father figure.

The dearth of father figures—especially among minorities—was not incidental in Hernandez's description in Roddenberry's character bible. The Civil Rights Movement made impressive strides in the latter twentieth century, but stark reminders of racial inequalities remained. Government experts and the media circulated reports about class differences between whites and minorities, particularly African and Latino-Americans, centered on the family unit. In 1965, Daniel Patrick Moynihan reported to President Lyndon Johnson, claiming the black nuclear family was in a state of fragmentation due to missing fathers and overly-fertile mothers. According to Moynihan, this "pathology" among minority groups supposedly led to juvenile delinquency, underemployment, and a burden on the welfare system (Greenbaum 10). Twenty years later, critics still blamed African American underperformance in the classroom and the workforce on its "innate" (i.e., non-white) familial structure. Journalist Bill Moyer's 1986 television documentary, *The Vanishing Family: The Crisis in Black America* centered on teenage mothers, absent fathers, and social malfeasance. The result: poverty, crime, and government incompetence in addressing the crisis (Douglas and Michaels 193).

For science-fiction television programs, this background played into Macha Hernandez's character bible and her desire for a strong father figure. The character trait remained when Roddenberry cast Denise Crosby in the role. The tale is well known in *Star Trek* lore; Marina Sirtis and Denise Crosby originally auditioned for the parts of Hernandez and Deanna Troi, respectively, and came close to winning the parts. But Roddenberry thought Crosby's audition for Troi recalled Grace Kelly, the American "Golden Girl" who lingered in public memory as the 1950s regal screen queen, matched by her subsequent royalty ("Selected Crew Analysis"). Given the changing female characterizations reflecting second wave feminism, this image of domestic femininity was obsolete in modern 1980s television. As a morbid cultural marker of sorts, Grace Kelly died in a tragic car accident in 1982. Roddenberry preferred to toughen Crosby's performance by channeling Macha Hernandez through Crosby. He switched the two actresses, thrusting Sirtis into a role based on psychic empathy and condemning Crosby to an early death as the renamed Tasha Yar.

Yar's background reflected the grim and grittier side of minorities situated among the urban poor. According to the revised character bible, Yar came from a failed colony, Turkana IV, in the Federation's hinterland. The colony dissolved into political and social chaos, including feuding factions, rape gangs, and drug addiction due to "environmental disasters and fanatical leaders" (Nemecek 15). The planet is such an embarrassment on the Federation's spotless record of optimism and progress, the august Council actually cut off ties rather than devote resources to fix it. After having washed its hands of Turkana IV, the Federation simply lists the planet on its verboten list.[1] While *The Next Generation* later reveals that many of the *Enterprise*'s command crew also have troubled backgrounds (Riker's paternal neglect,[2] Data's and Worf's orphaned status, Troi's domineering mother, and the lack of two-parent households all around), Yar is the only character who grew up on the streets. When the *Enterprise* returns to Turkana IV in the fourth season, the crew learns nothing changed; open warfare remains prevalent in this dark corner of the Federation ("Legacy").

When the show debuted, Crosby and critics applauded Yar as a representative of female strength for surviving, and surmounting, her origins. The *Los Angeles Times* called Crosby's presence "especially good casting against type," describing the security chief not as a typical red shirt who succumbs on Away Teams, but a woman who is "visible in areas of command" (Martin E16). Crosby also explained her role had no counterpart in the original *Star Trek* series because Kirk's security officers "usually wound up dead by the second commercial" (Shapiro "Security Chief," 52). In early interviews, the actress stressed how relevant Yar was to the series. Her character suffered from "low self-esteem and low self-worth." These rough edges made Yar unique; she was not a "perfect Starfleet graduate" nor did Crosby want her that way ("Denise Crosby" 14). In a broader context, Gates McFadden, prepping for her role as Beverly Crusher, confirmed the new series would reflect societal shifts in gender relations. "This is the '80s," she told *Starlog* magazine, and the "series will explore stronger, more relevant relationships and attitudes" (Shapiro "Star Trek," 49). McFadden's statements indicated the next generation of *Star Trek*'s female leads offered viewers more than the original series' minimalist costumes designed by costume designer William Ware Thesis. Indeed, McFadden called James T. Kirk's one-night-stands with female guest stars obsolete. Instead, Picard's crew would feature extended story lines and "the very real possibility of evolving sexual and romantic relationships" centered on emotional commitments (Shapiro "Star Trek," 49). The title, *The Next Generation*, referred to the development of sexual equality—truly, where no one has gone before.[3]

Tasha Yar's short life illustrated these broader social changes. In the pilot episode, she rebels against the malevolent Q's putting humanity on trial—even to the point of death when Q freezes her. In "The Arsenal of Freedom," Yar takes charge of the Away Team, informing Commander Riker she will not permit a secondary team to follow until she surveys the landing point and deems it safe. When quaint special effects later incapacitate Riker, she orders her superior, Lieutenant Commander Data, around as if he is a mere robot. Yar's strong demeanor stems from her checkered background on a troubled planet, and Crosby saw Yar's outspokenness as the character's distinguishing trait. "There was something troubling about her, something rough around the edges. She wasn't so polished and slick in that world where everything seemed so antiseptic to me. Everybody seemed so perfect" (Spelling "Like," 52).

Such glossy "perfection" finds a home in the show's early take on childhood, personified in Wesley Crusher. Wesley, named after Roddenberry, represents the idealized boy hero. The adolescent genius saves the ship and crew on several occasions, but at the endangerment to himself among more "adult" sci-fi fans who hated kid/cadet sidekicks. However, as a child of the utopian Federation, Wesley is ignorant of twentieth century social diseases. Yar, the most "imperfect" of the adult characters, voices the unfavorable aspects of the future the other crewmembers cannot.

In "Symbiosis," a drug-addicted species feud with their suppliers for a planetary fix. While Picard and Dr. Crusher debate the philosophical applications of the Prime Directive,[4] Wesley Crusher remains in the dark about the causes of drug addiction. Data offers bland and meaningless statistics about the universal problem of narcotics, but the emotionless android cannot contextualize the human toll. On cue, the Chief of Security steps in and gives young Crusher the facts of life. She uses her childhood and upbringing as an example about how poverty and social uncertainties drive desperate people to drugs and embrace their intoxicating effects as an escape from real-life hardships.

Yar's testimony taps into the contemporary War on Drugs under President Ronald Reagan. The Commander in Chief assigned the job to First Lady Nancy Reagan, who basically dared kids to "just say no" and walk away (Robinson and Scherlen 29). But this vocal refusal and retreat do not explore the greater, underlying causes of drug abuse. Kids were not just susceptible to peer pressure; they faced burdens from poverty, social and racial inequalities, and the hopelessness that comes with the judgmental name-calling and finger-pointing as critics and reformers assign blame. Drugs, Yar states, give a euphoric release from those pressures and a sense of power and control. She understands this phenomenon because she lived it and is the only regular cast member who can explain it to the acting ensign. One of the episode's writers confirmed he intended the scene to address kids in the audience, even against the objections of the actors and production crew who thought it too preachy: if the message "bothers some adults but it hits home with a couple of the kids, then, by God, we're going to do it" (Gross and Altman 166). As for Wesley, the naïve teenager still doesn't get it and Yar lets the topic go, but her dialogue gives an earthly context the episode's premise otherwise lacks. Viewers can witness the aliens' withdrawal symptoms and sympathize, but the episode's plot, about an abstract planetary plague and rare miracle cures, are the stuff of science-fiction. For television viewers, like the innocent youths onboard the ship, Yar's presence gives a real-life reminder of *The Next Generation*'s relevancy affecting Americans on Main Streets.

This relevancy ends when the *Enterprise* dashes to Vargas II to rescue a crash-landed Counselor Troi and Yar's subsequent death in the attempt. However, even before "Skin of Evil," Yar's character was already in decline. Denise Crosby later stated she left the show due to a lack of presence for her character. Daunted by a strong and complex ensemble cast, the writers gave most of the screen time to Picard, Riker, and Data. However, from a cultural perspective, Yar's diminished status was apparent near the beginning and originated from a larger backlash against feminism during the 1980s.

Security Alert

Gene Roddenberry described Lieutenant Macha Hernandez in the character bible as a tough woman. But even as Roddenberry listed her hard-body characteristics, he explicitly observed the character's fierceness, "attitude," and muscularity were balanced by "a very female body" (Nemecek 13). Even when "Macha Hernandez" became "Tasha Yar," this blend of masculine/feminine attributes remained consistent. The bible also treated the other female characters with similar references to femininity; Beverly Crusher had "a natural walk of a striptease queen" while the exotic Deanna Troi was "quite beautiful" and "romantically involved" with Number One (Nemecek 13). In one early interview, Crosby noted Yar remained very much a woman, regardless of her duties: Yar "*does* have a tender side to her. But make no mistake, she is *more* than capable of doing her job." Crosby laughed, noting Yar "will even use her body as a weapon if she has to" (Shapiro 18).

As the first season developed, Yar's limited presence beyond the communications console was no laughing matter. As scholars note, the "backlash" against women grew as the Reagan administration centered a renewed masculinity against communism abroad and social problems at home (Faludi 50, 232). The New Right's idealization of traditional gender roles under a patriarchal hierarchy came at the expense of feminist gains, such as child day care programs and public education funds. Socially conservative women, notably Phyllis Schlafly, insisted on separate gender spheres and led the movement to shoot down the Equal Rights Amendment in the 1970s and 80s (Critchlow 219). First Lady Nancy Reagan, criticized for her lavish spending and redecorating the White House in 1981 during an economic recession, did not refute the derogatory title of "Queen Nancy"—a label reflecting her prioritizing homemaking over the homeless (Loizeau 93). Instead, the First Lady declared "women libbers" seeking careers outside traditional gender roles should rethink their lot: "I think a woman gets more if she acts feminine" (Kelly

193). Despite the gains for women on television, in 1983, media scholar Diana M. Meehan noted the "boob tube" still reflected "muddied versions of boyhood adolescence" with women cast as "witches, bitches, mothers, and imps" (131). Writing after the Reagan Administration ended, cultural critic Darrell Y. Hamamoto observed television sitcoms projected career women who find fulfillment by pining away for steady male companionship (132–134).

The conflict about the nature of womanhood impacted the development of Tasha Yar. Theorist Robin Roberts points out Starfleet reflects a hetero masculine-centered organization that subordinates female and feminine characters. According to Roberts, *The Next Generation* marginalizes feminism by casting women as racial and sexual "others," such as various alien species, machines, or guest stars and secondary players. Roberts goes so far to label Yar's gender as ambiguous; her short hair, aggressive demeanor, and position as security chief render her a masculine character (95). While critics later denounced the series for lacking a homosexual protagonist, for Roberts, Yar veered uncomfortably close to the taboo topic of lesbianism.

In American culture, the 1980s was a nadir for the LGBT community. The explosion of AIDS reinforced the stigma of homosexuality as a direct sin against God, who was supposedly punishing homosexuals with a "plague" (Feldman and Miller 148). Roddenberry admitted he himself was not above gay-bashing, although he explicitly denied being homophobic. He also claimed he wanted a gay character on *The Next Generation* but the idea never materialized (Robb 184). The one episode that touched upon sexual orientation, "The Outcast," met with critical praise for its gutsy move, and condemnation for not going far enough (Roberts 123–124).[5]

Even in the enlightened 24th century, the producers realized they needed to soften their security chief's aggressive behavior. Anticipating fanboy reactions before the 1987 debut, Crosby told *Starlog* her character was "not being a butch little tank" (Shapiro "Star Trek," 48). Rejecting the implicit lesbian stereotype of a security officer with short hair, a lack of make-up, and who fires "the big guns" during battle, Crosby explained her character's tough exterior belied an inner vulnerability. Yar was not "a fighting machine." Rather, she was "brought up on a ghetto planet in a very aggressive society" which made her "an insecure person" (Shapiro "Star Trek," 49). Growing up, Yar uses her survival skills to blend in, but secretly yearns to be like a "normal" woman. As the series progressed, Crosby reiterated she did not want to see Yar "start doing her nails" in an attempt to display femininity, but she did want to see the softer side of the character develop so she would not seem like a "butch, stone-faced soldier" (Shapiro "The Security Chief," 53).

One way to feminize Yar was to isolate and marginalize her skills. In action-intensive episodes like "Heart of Glory," Yar surrounds herself with armed men. More pointedly, Yar herself has limited agency in performing her job. In the pilot "Encounter at Farpoint," Yar stands up for Starfleet's ideology before Q's recreation of a 21st century Earth dystopia, where governments keep their soldiers in line through drugs. All too familiar with the concept of sham courts, Yar defends her captain. In response, Q freezes her, possibly to death, until her captain intercedes on her behalf. In Q's next appearance, "Hide and Q," the omnipotent alien casts the bridge crew as soldiers in a war game. When Yar again defies Q by wanting to change the rules—as she herself did when she "made good" and escaped her home planet—Q sends her to a penalty box. By refusing to play Q's game, Yar's rejection of her assigned role makes her a non-player, a concept the self-appointed

"God" cannot tolerate. In the penalty box, Yar complains to Picard and breaks out in tears over her newfound helplessness. She knows if she acts up again, Q will eliminate her entirely. The inability to save herself reinforces her emotional breakdown. Picard, the father figure she never had, offers comfort, but she never again confronts Q.

The episode ends with a Q-powered Riker giving presents to the crew and fulfilling their greatest desires. La Forge receives the sense of sight, Worf gets a Klingon harlot to throw around, and Wesley ages ten years—except for his fourteen-year-old voice. However, Riker does not offer anything to Yar. Like Data, who declines the gift of becoming human, Yar cannot attain her wish to become "feminine" without negating her core characterization. Nevertheless, La Forge's brief vision allows him to compliment Yar, telling her she is lovelier than he imagined. La Forge's dialog confirms the security chief was "not a butch tank" and this angle of beautification gave the writers, producers, and Yar herself the means to align the security chief with the re-emergence of traditional femininity during the 1980s.

Twenty-fourth century motifs had a hand in Yar's feminization, especially fashion. For exploring the unknown, Starfleet provided the crew with "skant" uniforms, an update of Uhura's miniskirt. The producers intended the garment as a unisex outfit, fulfilling Roddenberry's vision of a non-sexist crew; after all, the men on Kirk's *Enterprise* never wore dresses.[6] Despite Roddenberry's intentions, however, *The Next Generation*'s female crewmembers seemed to favor the outfit much more than males, perhaps because the women's knee-high boots reveal less of their legs than the men's shoes. Roddenberry's vision notwithstanding, the audience might have been wary of seeing men run around the ship in skirts. Indeed, of the command crew, none of the males ever wore the skant. In comparison, Yar briefly dons the garment in the closing shot of "Encounter at Farpoint" and Troi wears the miniskirt in the timeframe of their Farpoint mission (in television time, the first and last episodes).

For Yar, her job as the ship's security chief rendered the skant counterproductive. Aside from freedom of movement, the exposed arms and legs hardly made for an impressive display of force. While some security officers wear the skant, including a female relief officer at tactical in "Home Soil" and a male officer standing as a ceremonial bouncer for Lwaxana Troi's party in "Haven," these are in non-combatant roles. Certainly, no security officer wears a miniskirt when charging into combat; while waging limited wars in Latin America, the Reagan Administration projected an image of "hard" anti-communism, mandating security men not don dresses, either in the military or on television (Jeffords 77–78). This masculine image manifested in other cultural facets. For instance, the proliferation of toy guns and war cartoons for boys (along with "action figures"—the male counterpart of girlie Barbie dolls) taught American youngsters to recognize war as a manly art (Douglas and Michaels 283–290). While Yar's security team includes women, including one called upon to confront Q in the first episode, no female security personnel do any actual fighting during Yar's stint other than the security chief herself. Yar's lone gunwoman role on the *Starship Enterprise* is an anomaly, but the show soon rectifies this with her death and the big, burly Klingon warrior who takes her place.

For Troi, the skant connoted too much sexuality, leading to its discontinuation, but its elimination did nothing to diminish the counselor's attire. In her debut, Troi appears as "too 'loose' and cheerleader-like in her skant," a concept and a costume that actress Marina Sirtis expressed discomfort with (Nemecek 27).[7] Although the creators opted to emphasize Troi's physical beauty for most of the series via the outfits she wears, this merely followed a trend for women Starfleet had long upheld. Dr. Crusher wears a lab coat over her uniform and her replacement, Kate Pulaski, whom actress Diana Muldar described as a "strong woman who was feminine *and* had authority," favors a modified skant and pants (Garcia 13).[8] As for Troi herself, the show's first season tags her as an exotic of sorts who hails from a sexually permissive culture and an aristocratic family. Although the creators confine Troi to a drab gray jumpsuit and constrain her hair in a bun throughout the first season, viewers recognized the counselor offered more to the show besides her emotional psychobabble.

In the second episode, "The Naked Now," the drunken crew lowers their inhibitions. For Yar, the security chief loses her guarded poise and displays her yearning for femininity. Yar sashays around Engineering, making out with unnamed extras before heading into Troi's quarters. There, she ransacks the counselor's clothes, wrapping herself in makeshift sarongs while voicing her desire to be more like Troi. For her part, Troi immediately senses something is wrong. Yar's sudden femininity contrasts sharply with her exterior, as displayed in the pilot where she stood up to Q's sham court and froze to death in the process. Clearly, the counselor realizes, Yar is not herself.

Troi alerts the captain to Yar's mischaracterization, but does little except succumb to the virus herself. For her, it's a rather short fall; the sensual Troi was visually tagged as the sexiest crewmember, signified with her trademarked plunging neckline. Yar rummages through Troi's belongings and selects a backless, bare midriff ensemble; ironically, despite Troi's garments throughout the show, the counselor herself never wears anything so scanty. But that the counselor has a wide range of seductive attire comes as no surprise to Yar, who comments on how pretty Troi always looks.

In later interviews, Denise Crosby looked back on her time in *The Next Generation* and lamented Yar never had a "woman-to-woman" talk with Troi or Crusher. The actress recalled her initial reading for Yar featured a scene that never made it on film, in which the security chief is insecure in her position as a woman. In this scene, Yar asks Troi for professional advice and the counselor asks her when she last had sex. According to Crosby, Troi tells her, "Go and get laid for a few days, then come back and tell me how you feel" (Spelling "Like," 54). For Crosby, this intimacy displayed a form of camaraderie as the female officers bonded. But in a wider context, Yar's sexlessness and unfeminine demeanor indicate a psychological breakdown common among 1980s television career women. She is unable to be traditionally "feminine," which, in turn, makes her unable to perform adequately in her job. Fittingly, Troi recommends Yar to re-establish her identity by bedding down, presumably with a man.

The scene in "The Naked Now" echoes this cultural construct surrounding Yar's gender identity. Sharing some banter with the ship's counselor while intoxicated was probably not what Crosby had in mind for a woman-to-woman chat, but the outcome is the same; whether drunk or under mental stress, Yar needs male companionship. As a result, her father figure, Captain Picard, sends Data down to her. Robin Roberts argues Yar's "unfeminine" portrayal in the series requires her to dominate a "feminized" character, Data, whose drunken behavior turns him into a "giddy girl" (94). However, aside from Data's "android" designation identifying him as a male ("gynoid" is the term for a "female" robot), Yar's cultural context in the twentieth century demands she herself take on a feminine role. Yar's "nakedness," as the episode's title indicates, points to her immediate desires to reacquaint herself with a lost feminine ideal. As a novice to dressing up (or down) in feminine attire, Yar's inauguration into traditional American womanhood requires a step-by-step instructional tutor, i.e., Data. The second officer assures her he is fully programmed and functional to perform sexually, to which Yar hisses in delighted heat. At the end of the episode, she insists this interlude never happened. Unfortunately for her, Data's positronic neural net never forgets. For an android, the moment of intimacy lasts an eternity.[9]

Once exposed to traditional gender roles, Yar never escapes it. In the next episode, "Code of Honor," she has another suitor. This time, Lutan, the ruler of an all African-esque alien race, becomes smitten with Yar's physical prowess after she defeats one of his men in mock combat, and he kidnaps her. Since Lutan also controls a vitally needed vaccine, Picard must toe a narrow path between rescuing his security chief and not endangering the treaty negotiations for this miracle cure. Lutan tells the captain the three are linked; should Starfleet interfere, the Federation will not only have no treaty or vaccine, but no Lieutenant Yar. The *Enterprise* prevails, of course, but only by having Yar fight Lutan's mate … over the loutish Lutan. The prospects of a catfight over a man does not entirely repel Yar; Troi tricks Yar into admitting she enjoys Lutan's machismo to a degree, despite his treatment of women, his abducting her, and possibly even his raping her. Apparently, her dalliance with Data in the previous episode awakened such passions. Perhaps the creators thought the suggestion of an interracial romance was a sign of progress, but any such attempt backfired, even among the staff and actors. Series writer Tracy Tormé called the "1940s tribal Africa" view of blacks embarrassing, especially the stereotype of African Americans lusting over white women (Nemecek 34).

Unfortunately for Yar, she never has a chance to develop, either as an affirmation of traditional feminine resurgence during the 1980s or as a symbol of the accomplishments of the woman's movement. Yar dies quickly and in the line of duty. Crosby recalled fans were struck hard, simply because Yar represented relevant contemporary tensions over the meaning of womanhood. Fans felt "this was a character who needed to be expressed. Tasha was a woman of the future who could stand her own ground" (McDonnell "Survivor," 48). Crosby understood this perspective; she saw in Yar a self-reflection of her own background in a "very confused, very violent atmosphere in Hollywood," in which she struggled to emerge from the shadow of her estranged grandfather, movie legend Bing Crosby (McDonnell "Survivor," 64). But she insisted Yar's story was one of optimism and a success story to inspire other "ghetto kids" to not only survive their hardships, but to succeed.

Yar's death created a vacuum the show's other women could not fill. Marina Sirtis later commented she wished both Troi and Dr. Crusher developed more during the original run. Indeed, despite some dramatic moments and character growth, Troi- and Crusher-centered episodes usually focused on tragic romances. Appropriately, as a psychologist and doctor, Troi and Crusher were in a position to mend their broken hearts. But even their skills had limits in this regard. "Crusher and Troi were both in the healing profession," recalled Sirtis. "There were certain things that, quite rightly, the producers said, 'Now hang on. A psychologist and a doctor would *not* do what you're suggesting'" (Spelling "Sweet," 23). Sirtis's admission that the producers "quite rightly" prevented the actresses from broadening their characters beyond the medical profession affirmed the limited roles afforded them, Crusher's and Troi's ranks as commanders notwithstanding. Indeed, outside for emergencies placing them in charge of the ship, Troi and Crusher remain outside the ship's command structure, unlike Yar who served as chief of security. Some scholars even saw Troi's and Crusher's roles as healers as signs of strength. Diana M.A. Relke argues Troi, Crusher, and Guinan (a "listener" who often undercut Troi's job), excelled as nurturers and caretakers. She singles out Crusher as the "superwoman of popular feminism" because of her role as a single mom, professional career woman, a scientist and a face like "goddess Greta Garbo" (283).

Despite this curtailment of female strength, Yar's presence never leaves the show. Later episodes, including "The Bonding" and "Ethics," reference her death in passing. In the third season, Yar re-appears via an alternate timeline in "Yesterday's Enterprise," but the episode makes clear Yar can only thrive in an unsavory reality based on continuous war (and even then, she finds romance). Crosby wanted to use the episode as a springboard to re-introduce her character via Yar's daughter, Sela. In her proposal, Sela becomes a peace-maker of sorts, a human-Romulan hybrid who fulfills her heritage by bringing the Federation and the Romulans together. Rather than a nemesis undermining Ambassador Spock's attempts at reunification, Sela would become instrumental in bridging rifts. "It would have been in the spirit of the show," Crosby recalls (Spelling "Like," 54). Roddenberry, who died in 1991, might have approved of Sela who, like her mother, exceeds societal expectations and "makes good." Yar emerged from a failed colony as a success story; her daughter, in building a more perfect galaxy, had the potential to do the same.

But this scenario never happened. Sela became a hardened military officer whose alien heritage allows her to defy traditional American womanhood in a police state.[10] She comes across as a cunning schemer bent on universal conquest—and meets defeat every time. Another character, Ensign Ro Laren, who debuted in the Yar-esque mold of survivor from a planet devastated by war and oppression, existed mainly to set the premise of another *Star Trek* spinoff, one set in a deep space hinterland far from the utopia of the human-oriented Federation. One of *The Next Generation*'s successors, *Star Trek: Voyager*, features a strong female lead, but Captain Janeway also couldn't bump up the show's sagging ratings without Seven of Nine's skin-tight sex appeal for the fans (Robb).

Conclusion: Skinned-Off Evil?

In 1990, Denise Crosby reminisced about Tasha Yar, even while preparing for her indirect return involving "yesterday's" *Enterprise*. Yar, Crosby noted, "had dreams of great success in Starfleet [...] She did it all her own, relying on her talents, her strengths, her perseverance. The whole point to her was that she came from nowhere—with all odds against her—and Tasha Yar made a mark in life" (McDonnell "Yesterday's," 25). She reiterated fans remained attached to the "insecure Security Chief" because Yar differed from the rest of the 24th century.

Tasha Yar was a character who defied the show's premise of human perfection. She was a relevant reflection of the cultural, political, and social shifts regarding American gender norms in the 1980s. Although Roddenberry envisioned a utopia, the series largely mirrored the reaffirmation of heteromasculine patriarchy in American culture. Even after the 1994 film *Star Trek Generations* bumped off Cold Warrior James T. Kirk to make way for the *Enterprise*-E, critic Larry Letich claimed nothing really changed in terms of a masculine-dominated hierarchy. The female characters, Letich asserted, were "total wimps" with Troi meriting "all the respect of your typical vice president of human resources" and who "has no authority over anyone or anything." Doctor Crusher distinguishes herself with a lab coat, but was plagued by "overwork, depression, and low self-esteem" (Letich C3). In contrast, Yar, "who broke the mold by being chief of security," is forgotten in the movie and the unfortunate Dr. Pulaski, described as "just like a real woman doctor" with the crusty attitude, disappeared altogether after the second season—not even appearing in the celebratory final episode (Letich C3; Garcia 13).[11] Appropriately, neither Denise Crosby nor Diana Muldar attended Riker's and Troi's wedding in *Star Trek: Nemesis*. The wedding, immaterial to the plot but created for the fans to celebrate the show's legacy, had no room for characters who no longer had any cultural relevancy as the "generation's final journey"—the movie's tagline—unfolded and ended.

Despite Yar's applicability as a twentieth-century woman whose background bespoke of violence and social diseases, her story arc and characterization jarred sharply with the utopian outlook. Roddenberry famously insisted the 24th century had no hunger, poverty, disease, or strife. These concepts not only inspired Trekkies, but also enabled the franchise's history to start; in *Star Trek: First Contact*, Zefram Cochrane, the inventor of warp drive, survives a post-apocalyptic nuclear horror and finds strength from a sovereign class of humanism when he meets Picard's time-travelling crew. Cochrane himself later imparts these ideals to Captain Jonathan Archer and the first chronological crew of the *Starship Enterprise* ("Broken Bow"). Set against this history of a developing, progressive future, Tasha Yar's short-lived presence from an anarchic, distant planet contradicted the narrative of this fictional universe.

More importantly, the backlash against feminism in the twentieth century glorified traditional womanhood of feminine beauty and sexuality. A serious, hard-hitting career woman performing in a "man's" job, Yar had little to do, prompting Crosby to leave the show. Yar *did* experience the beginnings of a "softening" of her personality. From a narrative standpoint, this feminization violated Yar's character, just as many feminists bemoaned the contraction of gains made by the feminist movement during the 1980s. Her 24th century death reflected the closing of channels towards women in contemporary America.

NOTES

1. Given the association between minority groups with crime and poverty in the twentieth century American consciousness, it is ironic when the *Enterprise* revisits Turkana IV in "Legacy," the majority of the colonists are white. One can read a subversive message in the casting choices as a commentary on stereotypes, but it is likely a reflection of the dearth of positive minority characters on television programs during the 1990s.

2. See Jared Miracle's essay in this volume.

3. See Erin C. Callahan's essay in this volume.

4. See Larry A. Grant's essay in this volume.

5. See Bruce E. Drushel's essay in this volume.

6. See Katharina Thalmann's essay in this volume.

7. See Joul Smith's essay in this volume.

8. The issue of gendered uniforms continued throughout the series. During the third season, the male cast received two-piece uniforms, that were more comfortable to wear (and which introduced the Picard Maneuver). In contrast, the female crew remained dressed in form-fitting, one-piece jumpsuits, although Troi's various outfits and Crusher's medical robe often hid this distinction.

9. In "The Measure of a Man," Data proves his manhood, and the rights associated with masculinity, by confessing in court he had sexual relations with Yar. The use of sex to demonstrate sentience is, according to Picard, a legacy Yar does not mind.

10. See Anh T. Tran's and Alex Burston-Chorowicz's essays in this volume.

11. Pulaski appears in the novelization of the final episode, sharing page space with Lwaxana Troi (Friedman 119–121).

WORKS CITED

Anonymous. "Denise Crosby." Star Trek: *The Magazine*. Westport, CT: Midsummer Books, Ltd, 1999: 14–22.

"The Arsenal of Freedom." *Star Trek: The Next Generation—The Complete First Season*. Writ. Richard Manning and Hans Beimler. Dir. Les Landau. Paramount Home Video, 2002. DVD.

"The Bonding." *Star Trek: The Next Generation—The Complete Third Season.* Writ. Ronald D. Moore. Dir. Winrich Kolbe. Paramount Home Video, 2002. DVD.

"Broken Bow." *Star Trek: Enterprise—The Complete First Season.* Writ. Rick Berman and Brannon Braga. Dir. James. Conway. Paramount Home Video, 2005. DVD.

"Code of Honor." *Star Trek: The Next Generation—The Complete First Season.* Writ. Katharyn Powers and Michael Baron. Dir. Russ Mayberry and Les Landau. Paramount Home Video, 2002. DVD.

Critchlow, Donald T. *Phyllis Schlafly and Grassroots Conservatism: A Woman's Crusade.* Princeton: Princeton University Press, 2005. Print.

Douglas, Susan J., and Meredith W. Michaels. *The Mommy Myth: The Idealization of Motherhood and How It Has Undermined Women.* New York: Free Press, 2004. Print.

"Encounter at Farpoint." *Star Trek: The Next Generation—The Complete First Season.* Writ. D.C. Fontana and Gene Roddenberry. Dir. Corey Allen. Paramount Home Video, 2002. DVD.

"Ethics." *Star Trek: The Next Generation—The Complete Fifth Season.* Writ. Ronald D. Moore. Dir. Chip Chalmers. Paramount Home Video, 2002, DVD.

Feldman, Douglas A., and Julia Wang Miller (eds.). *The Aids Crisis: A Documentary History.* New York: Greenwood Publishing Group, 1998. Print.

Friedman, Michael Jan. *All Good Things....* New York: Simon and Shuster, 1995. Print.

Garcia, Frank. "Diana Muldar—Dr. Katherine Pulaski." *The Official* Star Trek: The Next Generation *Magazine* #8. New York: Starlog Communications, 1989. 13–15. Print.

Greenbaum, Susan D. *Blaming the Poor: The Long Shadow of the Monyihan Report on Cruel Images About Poverty.* New Brunswick, NJ: Rutgers University Press, 2015. Print.

Gross, Edward, and Mark A. Altman. *Captains' Logs: The Unauthorized Complete Trek Voyages.* Boston: Little, Brown and Company, 1995. Print.

Hamamoto, Darrell Y. *Nervous Laughter: Television Situation Comedy and Liberal Democratic Ideology.* Westport, CN: Praeger, 1989. Print.

"Haven." *Star Trek: The Next Generation—The Complete First Season.* Writ. Tracy Tormé. Dir. Richard Compton. Paramount Home Video, 2002. DVD.

"Hide and Q." *Star Trek: The Next Generation—The Complete First Season.* Writ. C.J. Holland and Gene Roddenberry. Dir. Cliff Bole. Paramount Home Video, 2002. DVD.

"Home Soil." *Star Trek: The Next Generation—The Complete First Season.* Writ. Robert Sabaroff. Dir. Corey Allen. Paramount Home Video, 2002. DVD.

Jeffords, Susan. *Hard Bodies: Hollywood Masculinity in the Reagan Era.* New Brunswick, NJ: Rutgers University Press, 1994. Print.

Kelley, Kitty. *Nancy Reagan: The Unauthorized Biography.* New York: Simon and Shuster, 2011. Print.

"Legacy." *Star Trek: The Next Generation—The Complete Fourth Season.* Writ. Joe Menosky. Dir. Robert Scheerer. Paramount Home Video, 2002. DVD.

Letich, Larry. "Don't Bother Beaming Me Up." *Washington Post,* December 11, 1994, C3. Print.

Loizeau Pierre-Marie. *Nancy Reagan in Perspective.* New York: Nova Publishers, 2005. Print.

Martin, Sue. "An Enterprising *Star Trek* Series Warps Back to TV." *Los Angeles Times,* December 24, 1987, E16. Print.

McDonnell, David. "Survivor." *Starlog* #151. New York: Starlog Communications International. February 1990. 46–48, 64. Print.

_____. "Yesterday's Heroine." *The Official* Star Trek: The Next Generation *Magazine* #12. May 1990. New York: Starlog Communications. 25. Print.

Meehan, Diana M. *Ladies of the Evening: Women Characters of Prime-Time Television.* Lanham, MD: Scarecrow, 1983. Print.

"The Naked Now." *Star Trek: The Next Generation—The Complete First Season.* Writ. J. Michael Bingham. Dir. Paul Lynch. Paramount Home Video, 2002. DVD.

Nemecek, Larry. *The* Star Trek: The Next Generation *Companion.* New York: Pocket Books, 1992. Print.

Nichols, Nichelle. *Beyond Uhura:* Star Trek and *Other Memories.* New York: G.P. Putnam's Sons, 1994. Print.

Reeves-Stevens, Judith, and Garfield Reeves-Stevens. Star Trek: The Next Generation—*The Continuing Mission.* New York: Simon & Shuster, 1997. Print.

Relkie, Diana M.A. "Gender, the Final Frontier: Revisiting *Star Trek: The Next Generation.*" *Homer Simpson Marches on Washington: Dissent Through American Popular Culture.* Eds. Timothy M. Dale and Joseph J. Foy. Lexington: University Press of Kentucky, 2010. 277–293. Print.

Robb, Brian J. *A Brief Guide to* Star Trek: *The Essential History of the Classic TV Series and the Movies.* Philadelphia: Running Press, 2012. Print.

Robinson, Matthew B., and Renee G. Scherlen. *Lies, Damned Lies, and Drug War Statistics: A Critical Analysis of Claims Made by the Office of National Drug Control Policy,* second edition. Albany: State University of New York Press, 2014. Print.

"Selected Crew Analysis—Casting." *Star Trek: The Next Generation—The Complete First Season.* Paramount Home Video, 2002. DVD.

Shapiro, Marc. "Denise Crosby." *The Official* Star Trek: The Next Generation *Magazine.* #1. New York: O'Quinn Studios, 1987: 18–19. Print.

_____. "The Security Chief Who Got Away." *Starlog* #130. New York: O'Quinn Studios, 1988: 49–53. Print.

_____. "Star Trek: The Next Generation." *Starlog* #247. New York: O'Quinn Studios, 1987: 46–50. Print.

"Skin of Evil." *Star Trek: The Next Generation—The Complete First Season.* Writ. Joseph Stefano and Hannah Louise Shearer. Dir. Joseph L. Scanlan. Paramount Home Video, 2002. DVD.

Spelling, Ian. "Like a Phoenix." *Starlog* #218. New York: Starlog Group, 1995. 52–55, 66. Print.

_____. "Sweet Imzadi." *Starlog* #259. New York: Starlog Group, 1999. 20–23.

Star Trek: First Contact. Dir. Jonathan Frakes. Perf. Patrick Stewart, Jonathan Frakes, and Brent Spiner. Paramount Home Video, 1998. DVD.

Star Trek II: The Wrath of Kahn—The Director's Edition. Dir. Nicholas Meyer. Perf. William Shatner, Leonard Nimoy, and DeForest Kelly. Paramount Home Video, 2002. DVD.

Weinstein, Steve. "Newest *Star Trek* Zooms at Warp Speed." *Los Angeles Times*, May 3, 1988, H1. Print.

Willey, André. "Star Trek: The Next Generation." *TV Zone: The Monthly Magazine of Cult Television.* #5. London: TV Zone, Visual Imagination Limited. 1988: 6–7.

"Yesterday's Enterprise." *Star Trek: The Next Generation—The Complete Third Season.* Writ. Ira Steven Behr, Richard Manning, Hans Beimler, and Ronald D. Moore. Dir. David Carson. Paramount Home Video, 2005. DVD. 2002.

Klingon Kung Fu

Martial Arts in Future History

JARED MIRACLE

Martial arts are a significant—if often understated—part of all human cultures. From the neighborhood karate club to ancient Maori stick fighting, these embodied means of expression have served as vessels for transmitting human traditions and ideas since before recorded history. It is therefore reasonable to question how and to what end combative disciplines are represented in *Star Trek: The Next Generation (TNG)* as an important popular culture influence, as well as a reflection of contemporary society. Specific instances of martial arts appearing throughout the series display certain conceptualizations of not only fighting arts, but also Orientalism, exotification, political zeitgeist, and our own vision of the future. The mere presence of physical combat not mediated by future technology like starships and phasers holds implications for the creators' and fans' understanding of human nature and society.

Martial arts are best seen as elements of folklore, which is to say they are often subject to vernacular interpretation and transmission, change with the times, and take on variations depending on context. This is quite well established in the literature, with perhaps the most cogent summation of their cultural significance manifested in the idea of "weapons of the weak" or tools for those who are marginalized by the powerful members of society. Beyond simple means of combat, martial arts take on stylization relevant to the setting and people involved. In many cases, they are not genuinely functional as life-or-death combat methods at all, but, rather, depend entirely on arbitrary rules upon which participants choose to agree. This tends to be the more important aspect of the martial arts employed for storytelling in *TNG* since the technology available would make interpersonal combat without futuristic weaponry an absurd notion otherwise. Instead, it is best to consider how the narrative unfolds contextually vis-à-vis the martial arts as yet another means of conveying information. The physical proximity factor and ability for characters to express relationships by physical rather than verbal means is likely the best starting point for this line of inquiry (Green 9). In addition, we may consider *TNG* as a cypher to view social and cultural developments during the late 1980s and early 1990s. In particular, radical changes in public masculinity are reflected through the numerous appearances of martial arts and Orientalism during the show's run.

Social Context

One of the legacies handed down to all subsequent franchises from *The Original Series*, and one that has entered into everyday parlance, is the legendary Vulcan nerve pinch. This maneuver, first introduced by Mr. Spock, is typically used as a source of amusement as it is also frequently a *deus ex machina* when physical odds are overwhelming. At the same time, the nerve pinch is an apropos way to have sophisticated, nonviolent characters succeed in fistic struggles. This is why it is associated with the otherwise non-belligerent Spock, who would be very much out of place should he execute one of the more bombastic techniques of the *Star Trek* universe, such as the signature two-handed blow that shows up in every series. It comes as something of a surprise, then, to discover that the Vulcan nerve pinch appears in only two episodes of *TNG*: once in "Starship Mine" (1993) and several times in "Unification II" (1991). The latter is a baton-passing episode in which Spock clashes with Picard over the matter of Romulan-Vulcan peace relations. At one point, when escaping from their erstwhile captors, Spock employs the nerve pinch to one opponent while Picard punches out another. Near the end of the episode, Data executes a nerve pinch of his own, eliciting an impressed response from Spock as a subtle way of handing over the series' torch. "Starship Mine," airing two years later, includes a scene in which Picard applies the nerve pinch. Although unstated, one may go so far as to speculate that Data and Picard learned the technique directly from Spock. It is worth noting that these two characters have arguably less violent tendencies and certainly are less traditionally masculine than other officers, such as Worf and Riker. With Spock representing an alternative lifestyle to the militarism of Vietnam-era America, it makes sense to associate the new generation with the Vulcan holdover from the first series.

In terms of characterization, an underappreciated point of discussion among action designers is suitability of technique. It simply doesn't make sense for a peaceful character to act out in violent fashion without introducing some story element to explain away the incongruity. Naturally, this mirrors real life martial arts practice (or lack thereof) as action design's first order of concern tends to be realism and believability. With a science fantasy program as extreme as *TNG*, it is necessary to make fight sequences as believable as possible or risk taking the viewing audience out of the story. In the history of martial arts in America, too, innate preferences for one method of combat over another can be seen quite explicitly. The concept of gentlemanly behavior espoused during the nineteenth century, for instance, called for violent action to be properly stylized and made to adhere to a particular cultivated aesthetic. Unlike the "rough-and-tumble" of rural bouts in which any means of overcoming one's opponent could be employed (including biting and eye-gouging), gentle society mediated physical conflicts by publishing clear rules for the conduct of belligerents (Gorn 18–22). This was true of unarmed contests such as boxing (which famously employed the use of gloved hands and a referee for the first time in European combat sports) and lethal armed trials. Those same rules led to the deaths of many well-known historic figures, most notably Alexander Hamilton. Hamilton's killer, Aaron Burr, was a man of class and social standing; it would have been anathema to his personality to engage in a wrestling match with his opponent. In this way, *TNG*'s production team made excellent use of action design to fit characters and situations. At the same time, the action design choices point to a greater change in American culture that took place over the course of the show's run. That change revolves heavily around exotification of East Asia and a crisis of masculine identity.

The year 1993 was an important one for martial arts in the United States as, in many ways, the social and historic strands leading the modern state of public consumption and engagement came to a head. The same year in which *TNG*'s audience was privy to in-depth treatments of Klingon combat styles also brought with it the inaugural *Ultimate Fighting Championship* (*UFC*), which popularized mixed martial arts in the Western world. Briefly, the goal of the *UFC*, as advertised, was to bring together exponents of several fighting styles from around the world and pit them against each other in a cage-arena under minimal rules. This way—so went the televised rhetoric—the most effective martial art would be determined. While the reality of the situation was somewhat different, the fact that a violent enterprise of this kind appealed to viewers, such that they were willing to shell out for Pay-Per-View, underlines the social climate of the time (Gerbasi 11–13).

The *UFC*'s popularity grew out of a masculinity crisis in which American men found themselves as the 1980s drew to a close. That crisis, in turn, was the result of a larger post–World War II narrative in which women and ethnic minorities achieved greater levels of independence and access to the highest reaches of business, government, and culture. As returning soldiers and sailors faced confrontation with the elimination of their traditional roles, it was necessary to look elsewhere to construct a masculine identity that did not rely on being a household's bread winner or sitting in a superior social position to others. Before the watershed moment of the Second World War, one of the primary acceptable outlets for traditional masculinity was boxing. In post-war America, though, boxing was maligned in the media as a form of brutality and, in addition, was dominated by ethnic minorities in the absence of White champions. For the men in this position, the East Asian martial arts held a great appeal (Woodward 2004, 9–11). Considering that their children were raised in such a radically different America of the Cold War, it was natural for them—young and middle-aged adults during *TNG*'s initial airing—to see East Asian fighting styles as the de facto aesthetic for all such activities, even in the spacefaring future.

Soldiers and sailors returning from the Pacific war were frequently exposed to East Asian fighting styles, especially those of Japanese origin. During the United States' occupation of that country, a multi-year ban was issued by the General Headquarters on all martial arts practice except those conducted under the supervision and direct participation of occupying forces (Svinth 2002). This is how a wave of American men came to acquire arts such as karate and judo without fully grasping their cultural context as the language, history, and other cultural aspects were necessarily divorced from the arts themselves due to simple lack of communication. Returning to the U.S., then, these same men taught those portions that they understood and invented a new culture to fill in the rest. Grafting American concepts of masculinity onto ostensibly East Asian practices, it became possible for participants to realize their shared innate desire for masculine identity by embodying it in a socially acceptable pursuit. East Asian martial arts, "exotic" and "foreign" as they were, did not have to conform to the same pressures as Western traditional combat sports like boxing.

Having been raised in a time period wherein the once unusual martial arts were more accessible in popular culture, the descendants of those same returning soldiers anticipated East Asian motion aesthetics in film and television. This was also due in no small part to martial arts cinema produced in Hong Kong during the 1960s and 1970s, and the counterculture during those decades that explored facets of various Asian cultures.

The 1980s brought these exotic disciplines into popular discourse through films, television, and graphic novels featuring domestic stars and locations so that, by 1993, activities like karate were no longer the escape for tough masculinity that they once were. A more intense type of endeavor was necessary to achieve the same end, and that activity proved to be mixed martial arts (Miracle 18).

Just as men in the real world were digging deeper to seek greater extremes of controlled violence, *TNG* came to feature Klingon martial arts more and more heavily while minimizing the appearance of human styles, especially those from Earth. Casting the exotic Asian styles with a thin veneer of Klingon makeup, it is apparent that the discourse surrounding masculinity and Orientalism in 1980s and 1990s America is directly found within the walls of the *Enterprise*. Over time, Worf becomes more traditionally masculine, adhering closer to the Klingon warrior ideal which, stripped of its alien accouterments, is plainly nothing more than an extreme version of Western masculinity.

This was the atmosphere in which *Star Trek* producers made a place for depictions of alien fighting styles. On one hand, they had the advantage of an influx of martial arts systems facilitated by a growing American fascination with all things traditional, Asian, and violent brought about by the flow of popular culture. On the other, creating something unique to escape the trap of a preexisting cultural association proved difficult. As an experienced science fiction visual effects producer, Dan Curry was the best possible candidate for crafting a unique martial system for the Klingon race. The weapons, in particular, were troublesome for the property department and Curry had to intervene with his own designs. During the course of preproduction on "Reunion," the original design brought in for the bat'leth was a kind of sword that resembled a pirate's cutlass. Deeming this design unsuitable for a genuinely alien culture, Curry took inspiration from an unusual category of Chinese hooked swords, which he then reimagined as being two-handed while still practical for real combat (Rose). Utilizing martial arts as an extension and expression of masculinity is not limited to personal characterization, however, and pervades interpersonal relationships among both Klingons and human vis-à-vis father-son dynamics and student-mentor relationships.

Fathers, Sons and Fisticuffs

Among the series' most memorable and explicit uses of a martial art is "Anbo-jyutsu" as displayed in "The Icarus Factor." In this episode, Riker reunites with his father and the two work through their troubled past via this combat sport. The B-story of this episode is an external parallel of Riker's internal conflict and centers on the ten-year memorial of Worf's coming-of-age ceremony. The Klingon ritual calls for the application of pain-inducing torture devices as a means of affecting personal growth by displaying the subject's true feelings, which is apparently only effected through extreme physical endurance. Meanwhile, Riker and his father come to blows in a literal sense by mutual challenge to an Anbo-jyutsu match. The combat sport is supposed to be of Japanese origin, with each competitor donning motocross armor, and, eyes covered, make blind strikes at each other using long, padded staffs.

One of the episode's underlying themes is the use of interpersonal violence as a means of socially mediating aggression. Even though neither the Rite of Ascension nor Anbo-jyutsu are real-world activities, they are clear stand-ins for actual endeavors.

Human cultures have, until very recently, revolved around rites of passage. As Joseph Campbell and other mythologists brought to public attention during the two decades from the mid-seventies through the mid-nineties, modern American (and, indeed, much of Western) culture displaced and eliminated most semblances of universally recognized transitional moments from childhood to maturity. In so doing, Campbell and his ilk influenced an entire generation of Hollywood productions that grew to a near national obsession with depth psychology and rites of passage (Campbell 1972:111). It is difficult to argue that the *Star Wars* films are not the most famous example of this movement, but *TNG* was perfectly timed to approach this matter as well. Many of the individual episodes, particularly during the early seasons, are focused on growth, adulthood, and moments of liminality—no doubt due in large part to the presence of Wesley Crusher, the ship's under-aged cadet and Starfleet fanboy. One of the ways in which Americans at large sought to reestablish a sense of formal adulthood transition was through participation in the martial arts. Films (most notably *The Karate Kid* franchise), television, and graphic novels influenced the general population's perception that martial arts (and those of Asian derivation especially) provided an avenue for curing the psychosocial ills brought about when rites of passage are no longer available (Mandich, et al. 583–585; Svinth 2010, 1–5).

Curiously, that same drive to legitimize adulthood through participation in Asian martial arts was at once caused by and resulted in the exotification of the "mysterious East." The Rikers could just as easily have faced off in a boxing or wrestling match. That the production team chose to employ quasi-Japanese imagery and wording is quite telling. What Americans interested in Asian martial arts during the late 1980s and early 1990s wanted was not legitimate, thoroughly researched fighting systems represented on-screen. Rather, audiences prized the veneer of a generic and nonexistent Orient (Miracle 163). The Anbo-jyutsu scene contains several elements pointing to this fact. The Chinese character written on the arena means "star." The armor is obviously designed for motocross. The sticks do not come from any actual Japanese martial art, but do bare resemblance to those utilized on the set of the then-popular television show *American Gladiators*, where the combatants use these sticks for safe jousting.

Why, too, should a martial art of a future in which everyone speaks English require non–English terminology? If Anbo-jyutsu is the "ultimate evolution in martial arts," why does it not include the same amalgam of cultural traits found in other aspects of the series? The moment when Riker overcomes his father-complex and realizes that the man is fallible comes after being struck with an illegal strike ("hachidan kiritsu," which is essentially meaningless in Japanese, was perhaps intended to convey something like "eighth-level stance"). As with other ways in which Americans interacted with East Asian martial culture, it was, in fact, a simply guised manifestation of traditional Western values acted out with a thin façade of Asian origin. In this way, Orientalism was on full display in *TNG*. "The Icarus Factor" was an early example of this, having aired in 1989. The series' treatment of martial arts went through a number of changes that reflected the zeitgeist in other areas, including taking into account which martial arts were then-current "fads," and how characters chose to interact through various combat systems.

Eventually, conventional Earth fighting styles were eclipsed by the exoticism of Klingon combat systems. The Klingon unarmed style called "mok'bara" makes its first appearance in the 1991 episode "Clues." Although not given much screen time during the series' run, mok'bara shows how East Asian martial arts came to have a strong influence on the way Americans chose to see unarmed combat. Visual effects artist Dan Curry designed almost all on-screen items in the Klingon combat arsenal, and mok'bara is no exception. Curry traveled extensively throughout the world prior to his work on *TNG* and, as such, brought a bevy of visual styles to the production. Curry is also a lifelong martial artist and spent a great deal of time in Thailand, as his wife is Thai. Given his extensive background, it is interesting to see how Curry—who certainly understood the differences between East Asian martial arts in both the American and native contexts—chose to adapt real-world ephemera in order to flesh out Klingon culture. This is nowhere more pronounced than with mok'bara (Rose).

The Klingons' unarmed fighting style strikes one as quite distinct because it is essentially Chinese *taiji* (or *taichi*), a sequence of slow, soft movements said to cultivate internal energy and wellbeing. This is not the sort of kinesthetic palette usually associated with Klingons, who are hard, loud, aggressive, and inclined to favor points and sharp angles in their design elements. Curry may have chosen to base mok'bara on *taiji* for that very reason. It is commonly only seen when Worf is teaching it to his crewmates. It almost never appears in scenes focused on more typical Klingons. In this way, it serves to distinguish the more understated portions of Klingon culture, which audiences tend not to associate when they see this "warrior race" in any given episode. We know, for instance, that there are artists and poets on the Klingon home world, but they have almost no apparent interaction with the *Enterprise* crew. Worf, in particular, requires distinction from other members of his race because of his unusual position between what may be called "full" Klingons and the Federation. He resides somewhere at the halfway point and it is important from a storytelling standpoint to demonstrate his softer side on occasion (Rose).

On a societal level, *taiji* didn't really enter the American consciousness en masse until the 1980s and 1990s. It isn't a terribly exciting form to watch, nor is it believable as a viable means of self-defense, so its appearance in films and television did not take place until it became an exercise fad like yoga and Pilates. Yoga makes for an excellent comparison, too, because of the mode in which Americans adopted the practice. In its Indian Hindu context, yoga refers to a wide range of ascetic spiritual practices, is highly religious, and represents a way of life often constructed around personal privation. When Siddhartha Gautama (alias Buddha) was fasting, meditating, and generally suffering in solitude to achieve enlightenment, he is said to have been occupied with yoga. The word is short, however, and easy for advertisers to use as a label for certain practices, so it was quickly snatched up by Americans looking to monetize Orientalism. Yoga in the American context came to mean a set of light calisthenics and stretching, possibly accompanied by basic meditation and a bit of relaxation. As with *taiji*, one could take a short course to become an instructor and even practice at home thanks to mail-order videos. And just like yoga, *taiji* pointed to the comfortably exotic; its contents were nonthreatening, made easily digestible for the masses, and yet carried a pastiche of the mysterious East— never mind that the most commonly known form of *taiji* was packaged by the Chinese government in recent memory as a means of gentle exercise for the general public (Lau 11–15).

Worf's practice of mok'bara is most frequently shown as something he teaches to his crewmates in organized group sessions on the holodeck. This is also how *taiji* and most other East Asian martial arts were presented to the American public. While older, more legitimately traditional martial practices were—to paint with a broad brush—taught to individuals and small groups in personalized ways, passed on from mentor to student, mass-market martial arts reconstituted for American consumer interest have usually been transmitted in quasi-militaristic group settings wherein participants move together in uniform sequence. The East Asian combat arts in an American consumer context were rendered into a shape reminiscent of high school gym class, or at least health club aerobics sessions (Lau 124). Even Dan Curry, familiar as he was with the classical means of *taiji* instruction, realized that the visual reference to the art most readily understood by Americans was the more familiar fitness class conceptualization (Prooth).

One of the more curious manifestations of cultural appropriation of East Asian martial culture by Americans is seen in what can be termed the "Mr. Miyagi Effect," named after the Japanese martial arts instructor from movie *The Karate Kid* (1984) and its sequels. The film uses Miyagi as a "life coach" who uses martial arts like *taiji* and karate as a rite of passage for angry youths, albeit only after the martial arts were sufficiently reconstituted to suit American tastes (Miyagi's instructions of "wax on, wax off" to describe karate moves became a cliché). In the episode "Lower Decks" (1994), which focuses on the competition for a promotion between two junior officers, Worf uses mok'bara to fulfill this role. One of the officers, Sito Jaxa, is a regular of the Klingon's classes. She is the stronger candidate, but she lacks assertive self-confidence. Worf informs her that she cannot move on to his advanced class unless she passes a special test called the gik'tal challenge. Forced to spar with him blindfolded, Sito is repeatedly abused and eventually refuses to continue because the test is unfair. Worf imparts that this level of assertion should be employed in all cases of unfair treatment, a clear lesson for her ongoing evaluation by the captain. The Mr. Miyagi Effect is an interesting phenomenon as it grafts new levels of meaning onto systems of physical culture. As may be supposed, despite the guise of Asian-ness, the deep life lessons culled from training with a master teacher are more indicative of American cultural values than those of, say, *taiji*'s native setting (Miracle 15–16). Worf and Mr. Miyagi could just as easily coach a basketball team and impart the same lessons. After all, the inspirational sports film, notably *The Mighty Ducks* series that started in 1992, is a thoroughly established genre for self-discipline and individual growth.

Another 1994 episode, "Sub Rosa," is notable for two further examples of Orientalism. Throughout the season it is made apparent that Beverly Crusher and Deanna Troi are regular attendees of Worf's mok'bara class. The art is introduced to *Enterprise* social life by manifesting the mold of an Americanized martial arts class. It then becomes a routine plot device to move characters from one setting to another. Once again manifesting the real-world dynamics of the time, Worf's cherished Klingon (e.g., Asian) martial art that he employs for both personal development and combat becomes a plaything among the human (e.g., Western) crew. In this case, when Troi needs an excuse to visit the Crusher residence, it is with the excuse of asking if the doctor will be attending Worf's class that evening. Crusher replies that she will not, since she is distracted with the mystery at center in this episode. At this point we can see that the crew does not take mok'bara any more seriously than they would other hobbies, like Riker's musical efforts or Data's pursuit of art. As real-world martial arts were adapted to fit an American context, their portrayal on-screen started to reflect a societal shift, in which the public developed a casual relationship with the fighting arts. The change over time is palpable in the history of popular culture. For instance, in the 1970s, one of television's highest rated programs was *Kung Fu*, about a wandering Shaolin monk. Here, the Chinese martial arts are treated with absolute seriousness and their valued ideologies are primary features of the narrative.

However, 1984 saw the first martial arts themed birthday party, followed soon after by the release of the *Teenage Mutant Ninja Turtles*, at which point most gestures toward solemn treatment of martial arts in the popular media were more or less abandoned (Miracle 127–129).

In addition to Crusher's casual approach to mok'bara, it is worth noting "Sub Rosa's" employment of a one-off character named Ronin. Ronin turns out to be an extraterrestrial entity that enjoyed a parasitic relationship with members of the Crusher family for generations. The name was ostensibly chosen for its resemblance to traditional Scottish monikers, as the episode takes place on a colony styled after nineteenth century Scotland to reflect the undertones of Crusher's heritage. *Ronin* is, in fact, a Japanese word literally meaning "wave person" and applied in history to homeless traveling warriors who were without a clan to serve and sat rather low on the honor hierarchy. Because the alien parasite is both dishonorably feeding off the Crusher women and exists only as a wandering entity, the name is quite apt, if a bit misplaced. Historically speaking, the association of Japan with the samurai class is, at best, myopic. Japan was only home to a professional warrior class for a very short period and, even then, at no time could more than five percent of the population claim samurai status (Yamamura 68–72). As a simple caricature of a much more complex situation, the American desire to equate Japan with the samurai is more fantasy than reality, and reflects American values more so than Japanese. Indeed, this projected image of Western values placed on a veneer of Japanese culture can also be seen in works like James Clavell's *Shogun*. In addition, the modern usage of *ronin* denotes not soldiers, but university graduates who are unable to find work (Takeuchi 183–190).

Fighting Fans

Klingons are, of course, not as closely associated with mok'bara as they are with one of the most iconic weapons in the *Star Trek* universe: the bat'leth. As the iconic warrior race, it was necessary for producers to craft an iconic tool that also seemed plausible as an implement of combat. Dan Curry was charged with this task as well, and the bat'leth, unlike mok'bara, had frequent appearances in every subsequent *Star Trek* series. The bat'leth was so well designed that a Korea-based global martial arts association actually honored it as the only newly-invented blade weapon formulated in the past century to be practical in nature (Prooth). Curry, the consummate martial artist, is quite proud of this fact. When asked how he came to fabricate the design (rather than the art or prop departments), Curry explained:

> My studies of martial arts lead to the development of the Klingon weapons such as the bat'leth and the mek'leth. We had an episode in which Worf was to inherit an ancestral bladed weapon. The art department came up with something that resembled a pirate's cutlass. I felt that the Klingons should have something unique and original and I wanted to create something ergonomically sound. I have never liked movie weapons that just look cool but can't be used [Prooth].

Drawing on his experiences traveling Asia and studying East Asian martial arts, Curry also noted that the initial inspiration for the bat'leth came from the design of curved Chinese hook-shaped blades. Once again, in order to generate an image for the show that would strike the audience as sufficiently alien and exotic, the production team drew on East Asian aesthetics. Nor was this the first time that Curry made use of his knowledge of Chinese culture. In the episode "Arsenal of Freedom" the script called for scenes in which the model robot levitates. The visual effects producer noted that he did so manually; rather than using special effects, he performed *taiji* movements while manipulating the model by hand (Prooth).

The bat'leth's first appearance is in the 1990 episode "Reunion." This is one of the most important installments for the Klingons in general and Worf's character development, especially. The main story focuses on a political dispute within the Klingon Empire between two rival factions. Meanwhile, Worf meets his son, Alexander, for the first time. Worf's attempts to bond with his son by teaching him the basics of bat'leth usage fall short, as Alexander is established as markedly different from his father in a single phrase: he has no desire to be a warrior like his dad. Considering the episode's timing alongside the real-world changes in American popular culture's regard for the martial arts, Worf's failed attempt to pass a combative legacy on to his offspring is eerily prescient.

Among the most important moments for martial arts in *TNG* is the two-part episode "Birthright" (1993). In the first installment, Worf learns that his father may be alive. This runs contrary to what he and everyone else believed previously and, if true, would cause Worf's entire family (including Alexander) to suffer the humiliation of dishonor. A Klingon warrior is expected to die in battle rather than be captured. Should the latter happen despite his best efforts, he is expected to commit suicide. The revelation sends Worf into a rage, whereupon he calms himself by practicing mok'bara. After settling his emotions, Worf investigates the rumors. This takes him to a Romulan prison camp, where he joins the prisoners. Worf is disheartened to learn the Klingon prisoners—now aged—not only live peaceably among the Romulans, but they have not passed down their Klingon heritage to their children. Worf takes it upon himself to teach the younger Klingons what it means to be a warrior. He practices mok'bara and introduces techniques to hone their hunting skills. Spurred on by seeing this, the young Klingons begin to follow his example until Worf agrees to instruct them. This then inspires the young Klingons into revolt against their captors in what appears to be a nod to classic Akira Kurosawa plots like *Seven Samurai*. The martial arts' social plasticity is on full display here as they fulfill multiple roles simultaneously. The application of the *taiji*-based martial art to achieve a state of tranquility draws somewhat candidly on Dan Curry's influence and personal credentials; in a rare role shift, Curry served not only as visual effects supervisor, but he also directed this episode. This is almost certainly because he had a strong influence on the Klingon culture developed during the show's run. This two-part feature elucidates more components of the warrior civilization than almost any other, so Curry made for a natural choice as the foremost on-set expert on both Klingons and fighting arts.

In a case of life-imitating-art-imitating-life, fans immediately latched on to the bat'leth and began dreaming up their own ideas about its possible use. *Star Trek* fans are known for their frequent and well-attended conventions, which tend to include a fair amount of costumed participation. This is even the case at more general popular culture conventions, where *Star Trek* actors tend to make appearances. Organizations for enthusiasts of all things Klingon are exceptionally active even by *Star Trek* fan standards. Not limiting themselves to costuming alone, there are several groups focused on building, choreographing, and even competing with bat'leths. They are known to sometimes perform at conventions or in other public venues. For instance, a club called IKV Melota (after the naming convention of Klingon war ships) makes its rules for bat'leth combat sports available online, and they have since become relatively popular among Klingon groups as a result. The Melota's membership is dedicated to pursuing bat'leth training as any other form of martial arts training. In their own estimation:

> We have had a solid weekly Batleth practice for 5 years.... We have had only minor injuries because we remember Rule #1. The object is to HAVE FUN, but in a manner that everyone will return next week for a rematch for the fun of it. Thus we must remember to always be Honorable, always courteous, and always careful about the combat. Likewise, we have had various police units and EMT units come and observe us; but since we are running a structured, fun, safe event, there is nothing present to attract their official attention [Batleth Basic Concepts].

The same handbook offers detailed guides for manufacturing weapons safe enough to use against an unarmored opponent. The author then explains some of the common injuries in the course of bat'leth combat, such as bruises and dislocated fingers. In all cases, the competitive sport is taken as a legitimate endeavor in the vein of any other martial art or combat sport.

In keeping with the straightforwardly serious manner in which fan communities approach Klingon fighting arts in real life, a most interesting volume was published by a now defunct company, Pacific Warriors, Inc. No longer in print, *Secret Fighting Arts of the Warrior Race, Volume 1* was meant to be the first installment in a series on Klingon armed fighting methods. The pseudonymous author, HetaQ, is presented as an actual Klingon martial arts master, complete with impressively full makeup and battle armor. The illustrated volume covers all aspects of bat'leth usage, from stances to swings, tactics, and practice methods (apparently culled from the Chinese martial arts, appropriately enough). Conveniently enough, the company responsible for the book seems to have done much more business in weapons sales than publishing. The paperback's catalog description concludes with a fitting appeal to the potential customer: "*Secret Fighting Arts of the Warrior Race* is presented seriously, even though it is intended for fandom fantasy. You won't have to search for a betleH [Klingon word for "bat'leth] forged in the Klingon Empire you can order one from the publisher of this book." Unfortunately for anyone looking to study the ostensible masterwork on the topic, Pacific Warriors closed up shop after running afoul of Paramount Entertainment's licensing division by printing *Secret Fighting Arts* without the explicit permission. Consequently, all unsold copies were ordered destroyed, making the book difficult to obtain at a reasonable price (Pacificwarriors.com).

Conclusion

Given the history of East Asian martial arts in the United States, the case of Klingon combat is seen as the fantasy-to-reality complex running full circle. Cultural objects like judo and karate were exoticized by Americans when they were first made available. They took on the patina of something rare, unusual, inscrutable, and, therefore, powerful. Without a native recourse for men in the midst of a masculinity crisis, these arts became the target of their psycho-social needs. As the same arts became widely available in the national consciousness, their exotic appeal disappeared. The same adherents who first used them to differentiate themselves from the general population by asserting their masculinity reacted by introducing new concepts, such as other foreign styles and the *Ultimate Fighting Championship*, the latter an "ultimate" contest to determine masculinity. The exotification process was reflected on-screen in *TNG* as Klingon combat methods were designed to reflect Asian exoticism. Fans, in order to better act out and embody their fantasies, then took the fictional combat seen in the series and made it manifest in the real world, even going so far as to print a high quality handbook apparently ripped straight from the Klingon Empire itself.

This dynamic negotiation of cultural and gendered identity is most prevalent in the first season episode "Code of Honor" (1987). Security Chief Tasha Yar is the focus, forced to fight in a gladiatorial tournament by an alien race that holds women as the inferior sex. Her aikido training receives much attention, pointing to both the American perceptions of women and East Asian martial arts in the late 1980s. Aikido is a Japanese system explicitly meant for passivity. That is, in an ideal application, aikido techniques are meant to neutralize violence without harm to either participant. Unlike a more violent method that may be more suitable for a military security officer, aikido is used here as a physical expression of Yar's strong, independent feminine characterization. True to form, she overcomes her adversary in the climactic scene without killing, thereby showing an underlying assumption about gender identity in American society. At the same time, the episode is an obvious criticism of supposed traditional Western attitudes toward women. The alien diplomat dismisses Yar as an effective security professional until proven wrong.[1] In this way, *TNG* shows the range of how American society interacted with itself throughout its production. From this early example of gendered empowerment to the exotification exhibited in Klingon martial arts and the Orientalism of *anbo-jyutsu*, *TNG*'s reflection of the 1980s American mode of masculine identity marks it as among the most socially relevant television shows in recent memory. Or, more poignantly, in recent Memory Alpha.

Notes

1. See Erin C. Callahan's and Peter W. Lee's essays in this volume.

Works Cited

"Batleth Basic Concepts." Janissaries.net. N.p., 2016. Web. 1 June 2016.
"Birthright, Part I." *Star Trek: The Next Generation*. Writ. Brannon Braga. Dir. Winrich Kolbe. *Netflix*. Web. 28 May 2016.
"Birthright, Part II." *Star Trek: The Next Generation*. Writ. Rene Echevarria. Dir. Dan Curry. *Netflix*. Web. 28 May 2016.
Campbell, Joseph. *The Hero with a Thousand Faces*. Princeton: Princeton University Press, 1972. Print.
"Catalog of Books—Pacific Warriors, Inc." Pacificwarriorswww. N.p., 2016. Web. 1 June 2016.
"Clues." *Star Trek: The Next Generation*. Writ. Bruce D. Arthurs and Joe Menosky. Dir. Les Landou. *Netflix*. Web. 28 May 2016.
"Code of Honor." *Star Trek: The Next Generation*. Writ. Katharyn Powers and Michael Baron. Dir. Russ Mayberry. *Netflix*. Web. 28 May 2016.
Gerbasi, Thomas. *UFC Encyclopedia*. Indianapolis: DK/BradyGames, 2011. Print.
Gorn, Elliot J. "Gouge and Bite, Pull Hair and Scratch." *The American Historical Review* 90 (1985), 18–43.
Green, Thomas A. "Sense in Nonsense: The Role of Folk History in the Martial Arts." In *Martial Arts in the Modern World*, edited by Thomas A. Green and Joseph R. Svinth, 1–12. Westport, CT: Praeger. 2003. Print.
"The Icarus Factor." *Star Trek: The Next Generation*. Writ. David Assael and Robert McCullough. Dir. Robert Iscove. *Netflix*. Web. 28 May 2016.
Lau, Kimberly J. *New Age Capitalism*. Philadelphia: University of Pennsylvania Press, 2000. Print.
Mandich, A.D., H.J. Polatajko, and S. Rodger. "Rites of Passage: Understanding Participation of Children with Developmental Coordination Disorder." *Human Movement Science* 22.4 (2003): 583–595. Print.
Miracle, Jared. *Now With Kung Fu Grip! How Bodybuilders, Soldiers and a Hairdresser Reinvented Martial Arts for America*. Jefferson, NC: McFarland, 2016. Print.
Prooth, Sebastian. "Star Trek *TNG*, DS9, YOY and ENT's Dan Curry Speaks to SebRT.com!" *Seb's Web Archive*. N.p., 2006. Web. 1 June 2016.

Rose, Rebecca. "Hollywood Jobs: Dan Curry, Visual Effects Supervisor." *Crushable.* N.p., 2011. Web. 1 June 2016.

"Starship Mine." *Star Trek: The Next Generation.* Writ. Morgan Gendel. Dir. Cliff Bole. *Netflix.* Web. 28 May 2016.

"Sub Rosa." *Star Trek: The Next Generation.* Writ. Brannon Braga, Jeri Taylor, and Jeanna F. Gallo. Dir. Jonathan Frakes. *Netflix.* Web. 28 May 2016.

Svinth, Joseph. "Documentation Regarding the Budo Ban in Japan, 1945–1950." *Journal of Combative Sport.* http://www.ejmas.com/jcs/jcsframe.htm (accessed 4 February 2017) (2002).

_____. "Social Uses of the Martial Arts." In *Martial Arts of the World,* edited by Thomas A. Green and Joseph R. Svinth, 1–12. Santa Barbara: ABC-CLIO. 2010. Print.

Takeuchi, Yo. "The Self-Activating Entrance Examination System–Its Hidden Agenda and Its Correspondence with the Japanese 'Salary Man.'" *Higher Education* 34.2 (1997): 183–198. Print.

"Unification II." *Star Trek: The Next Generation.* Writ. Michael Piller and Rick Berman. Dir. Cliff Bole. *Netflix.* Web. 28 May 2016.

Woodward, Kath. "Rumbles in the Jungle: Boxing, Racialization and the Performance of Masculinity." *Leisure Studies* 23.1 (2004): 5–17. Print.

Yamamura, Kozo. "Samurai Income and Demographic Change: The Genealogies of Tokugawa Bannermen." *Family and Population in East Asian History* (1985): 62–80.

Listening to the 24th Century
*Music and Musicians Heard Throughout
the Voyages of the* Enterprise-D
(and Some of the Enterprise-E)

Tom Zlabinger

Music has always been a large part of the *Star Trek* universe. Alexander Courage's theme for the original television series (1966–1969) is iconic. Jerry Goldsmith's, James Horner's, and other composers' scores for the first 10 *Star Trek* movies (1979–2002) and the *Star Trek: The Next Generation* (1987–1994) television series are unforgettable. The music of *Star Trek* was even performed live by an orchestra accompanied by video footage on a 100-city concert tour across North America in 2016 to mark the 50th anniversary of the franchise. As part of the celebration of *ST: TNG*'s 30th anniversary, we should boldly go beyond the soundtrack of the show and take a closer look and listen to the musicians of *ST: TNG* by observing the characters' use of music in their lives in addition to their own roles as musicians within 24th century society.

We witness members of the crew of the *Enterprise-D* (and later the *Enterprise-E*) make music or engage with music several times over the course of the voyages within the television series and in the *ST: TNG* films (1994–2002). William Riker often plays his trombone. Worf is knowledgeable in singing Klingon opera. Ro Laren has memories of her father playing the belaklavion, a traditional Bajoran instrument. Data repeatedly attempts to hone his musical abilities on various instruments. And Jean-Luc Picard learns to play flute after coming in contact with an alien probe, and he continues to play the instrument after the experience. These are only a few examples.

This essay examines the musicians and their music making in *ST: TNG*. What is the role of the musician in the show's fictional future? What is the function of music making? When and where is music made? This essay tackles these questions, arguing that an exploration of musicians and music making in the fictional world of *ST: TNG* allows us to better understand the role of musicians and our own use of music here and now.

In the William Shatner-directed documentary *Chaos on the Bridge* (2014), writer and producer Ron Moore pointed out an important shift early in *ST: TNG*'s storytelling focus that not only ensured the survival of the new television series, but possibly the future of the entire *Star Trek* franchise:

223

If we'd not shifted from plot to character in the third season, the show would have continued, but I don't think it would've broken through [to success] the way it did. I think [*ST: TNG*] would have been "that other series they have done of *Star Trek*." And I get the feeling that *Star Trek* would have kinda stopped there. That there would not have been a *Deep Space Nine,* would have not been a *Voyager,* and so on. And certainly not more movies.

This shift is quite relevant to the role of musicians and music making in the series. In *ST: TNG,* the act of making music is usually related to someone's identity. Music making also allows some characters to transform themselves. The new emphasis on character (as opposed to plot) affords us the opportunity to learn more about the characters and music making is a perfect opportunity to easily explore a character's identity more deeply. This essay first looks at more traditional music making by William Riker, Worf, Miles O'Brien, Ro Laren, and Dr. Zefram Cochrane, all of whom perform or refer to music in the expected contexts of entertainment, ritual, or identity construction. Later, the essay focuses on the special musical roles of Wesley Crusher, Data, and Jean-Luc Picard, who all pursue extra-musical goals. Rather than look at an all-encompassing field of music making, this analysis will look at the particular roles of musicians and their music making in the *ST: TNG* universe.

Riker, Worf, O'Brien, Ro and Cochrane: More Traditional Music Making in ST: TNG

On several occasions throughout *ST: TNG,* we see musicians performing in expected situations like social functions, concerts, ceremonies, rituals, and elsewhere, both within and outside Federation space. In addition to onboard the *Enterprise,* music making is practiced among many civilizations across the universe. For instance, in "Haven," the Betazoid ritual of "giving thanks" for food consists of ringing a gong at regular intervals—much to Counselor Troi's annoyance. A few musicians on and near the *Enterprise* are seen performing or making reference to music making several times. The ship's crew also listens to music to relax or set the mood when entertaining.

William Riker is possibly the most frequently visible musician throughout *ST: TNG.* Riker identifies as a jazz musician in multiple episodes. His love of the "archaic music form" of jazz is displayed several times across the series. Riker is first seen performing trombone on the holodeck in the episode "11001001," where he recreates an intimate New Orleans style jazz club circa 1958. Playing jazz is simply a recreational outlet for Riker. Unfortunately, his music making is not taken very seriously by others, as it is often the source of humor for some of his shipmates. In "Future Imperfect," Riker performs the jazz standard "Misty" (1954) at his own birthday party, but when he makes a mistake while performing the melody, everyone laughs. Riker comically wishes for music lessons after he blows out the candles on his birthday cake. In the later episode "Second Chances," Deanna Troi dares Riker to attempt the fictional jazz tune "Nightbird" at his own gig in Ten Forward. Riker has been practicing the difficult tune for years, but luckily avoids the challenge when he is suddenly called to the bridge. Riker's trombone playing is a continued source of folly between him and Troi, as seen when he jokingly "talks" to her with his trombone in the episode "Thine Own Self." We even see him play piano in the two-part episode "Unification," where he jams with a seven-armed alien woman in a club as an exchange for vital information about a Ferengi arms dealer. Although Riker never pretends to be a serious musician, he also performs at Geordi La Forge's and Ensign Ro's premature memorial in the episode "The Next Phase." All the while, Riker continues to love jazz above any other form of music, once stating to Worf in "Phantasms" that an annoying music program he gave Worf's son, Alexander, is "better" than music simply because it's jazz. Performing and loving jazz is an important part of Riker's identity, as jazz parallels Riker's tendencies to take chances, break the rules, and improvise, while maintaining a relatively cool demeanor.

For Worf, music is also an important part of his identity. Though we do not see Worf make music nearly as often as Riker, two of the times that Worf sings in *ST: TNG* are moments that express his Klingon identity. In "Unification," Riker jams with an alien woman at the bar and Worf takes a page from his senior officer, albeit as a means of relaxation. Worf requests a theme from the Klingon opera *Aktuh and Maylota*. He and the pianist then sing a short excerpt together. Even though he is supposed to be on the lookout for a Ferengi arms dealer and is usually a stickler for the divide between luxury and duty, Worf does not see a conflict between relaxing with Klingon opera and keeping an eye out for his target. Indeed, when the Ferengi barges in and demands they stop playing the "noise," Worf is visibly annoyed at this insult to his heritage. When Riker later violently humiliates the Ferengi, Worf watches with satisfaction. Later, in the episode "Firstborn," both Worf and his son Alexander participate in a Klingon street opera during the festival of Kot'baval. Like the opera, their singing propels the storytelling of a Klingon epic that also includes staged combat. Repeatedly, Worf attempts to teach Alexander an appreciation for Klingon traditions and urges him to maintain a connection to his Klingon heritage (which Alexander later rejects). For Worf, his music making is integrated into an expression of his Klingon identity. As an orphan raised by humans, Worf often struggles with the expression and maintenance of his Klingon identity. Performing Klingon opera allows Worf to refer to his Klingon heritage in a less violent manner than seen elsewhere in *ST: TNG*.[1]

Just as Klingon opera serves as a way for Worf to keep ties with his heritage while serving as the only Klingon in Starfleet, other crewmembers use music to remind themselves of their identities. In the episode "The Wounded," Miles O'Brien sings the traditional Irish song "The Minstrel Boy" (ca. 1798) after reuniting with his former captain, Benjamin Maxwell. First, O'Brien's wife Keiko hears him singing the song in their quarters, which is a patriotic Irish tune that tells the story of a boy who has gone to war. Later in the episode, O'Brien sings the first lines of the song with Maxwell:

> The minstrel boy to the war has gone
> In the ranks of death you will find him
> His father's sword he hath girded on
> And his wild harp slung behind him
> "Land of song!" said the warrior bard
> "Tho' all the world betrays thee
> One sword, at least, thy rights shall guard
> One faithful harp shall praise thee!"

After singing the tune, Maxwell realizes that his obsession to continue to fight the Cardassians is based on past prejudices and is now misguided, given the improved political climate. Maxwell's rebellion is in line with the patriotic pride found within the tune. Because of his shared experiences with Maxwell, O'Brien continues to distrust the Cardassians in *Deep Space Nine*. Though O'Brien's singing of the folk tune is not an explicit expression of identity like Riker's and Worf's music making, O'Brien's Irish identity is accentuated by his singing the traditional Irish song. "The Minstrel Boy" also serves as a reminder of the atrocities of war and thus also accentuates the universality of warfare and loss.

Though Ro Laren does not perform like Riker, Worf, and O'Brien, her references to music making are clearly an extension of her Bajoran identity, especially in light of the Cardassian occupation of her homeworld. Like O'Brien, she uses music to assert a form of resistance to the memory of the Cardassian atrocities she witnessed. At times, the trauma of the occupation makes her bitter, even about her own culture. In the episode "The Next Phase," for instance, Ro hopes that Data decides against performing the over two-hour long Bajoran death chant at her premature memorial. Still, music serves as a backbone for her identity as a Bajoran, which she places above her duties as a Starfleet officer. In "Preemptive Strike," Ro infiltrates the Maquis, an anti–Cardassian resistance group that rejects the peace the Federation made with the Cardassians. Ro connects with Maquis leader Macias over hasperat (a Bajoran delicacy) and the belaklavion (a Bajoran musical instrument). Macias befriends her and their Bajoran commonality draws Macias and Ro closer together. Ro tells them a story about how her father scared away "monsters" when she was a child by playing the belaklavion. But, after her father died in the Cardassian occupation, she realizes that her father could not scare all the monsters—the Cardassians—away. Though Ro does not make music, music making is part of her identity and past. Ultimately, her bonding with Macias leads her to abandon Starfleet and join the Maquis.

Finally, in the movie *First Contact* (1996), music is very important to warp drive inventor Dr. Zefram Cochrane. Although not a musician, Cochrane is included here as his use of music is not too distant from a musician making music. Cochrane uses recorded music as his medium, rather than a trombone, singing, or memories of a belaklavion. While drinking with Troi at the post-apocalyptic Montana settlement, Cochrane is seen dancing as Roy Orbison's rockabilly hit "Ooby Dooby" (1956) blasts on the jukebox. Rock music is again important to Cochrane as he madly searches for a cassette tape of Steppenwolf's classic rock hit "Magic Carpet Ride" (1968) to play during the maiden voyage of his ship, the *Phoenix*. Cochrane would again play "Ooby Dooby" on the jukebox after the first contact meeting with the Vulcans, as a gesture of friendship (though it may not have been received as such by the Vulcans). Granted, Cochrane does not perform any of the music himself, but his love of rock and roll is obviously a part of who he is.

All five characters (Riker, Worf, O'Brien, Ro, and Cochrane) use music to express, reference, or accentuate their identities. Each one of them performs, refers to, or uses music in a way that is not unlike the way most people on Earth in the 21st century perform, refer to, or use music. Music making is never expressed as a universal language in *ST: TNG*. Rather, music making is depicted as a common social practice across space and time.

Wesley Crusher: Apprenticeship as Metaphor for Music Making

Before continuing the discussion of music and musicians in the *ST: TNG* universe, there is an unlikely character that must be examined: Wesley Crusher. Granted, Wesley is not a musician. He never makes music. But Wesley's story is the classic coming-of-age story of a musician, not unlike Charlie Parker, Elvis Presley, Sting, Cyndi Lauper, or others who heeded the call of becoming a professional musician at the price of leaving a more traditional or expected life path behind.

Wesley has a unique place on the *Enterprise* as the son of Beverly Crusher. He is eager to impress and always interested in the workings of the ship and other scientific phenomenon. Over time, Wesley becomes a fine young officer who gains valuable experience on the *Enterprise* and later goes to study at Starfleet Academy. But his story does not end as expected, as he eventually decides to leave his studies. When examined carefully, Wesley is an exceptional person beyond description who eventually listens to his heart and veers from his expected course.

In the early episode "Where No One Has Gone Before," we are first introduced to The Traveler, who, over the course of the series, has a tremendous impact on Wesley's life. In a conversation with Picard, The Traveler refers to the intricacies of music and genius. He further remarks that Wesley is as gifted as someone like Mozart. But instead of having the command of music, Wesley has a gift to understand time and energy. We see evidence of Wesley's atypical abilities in the episode "Ménage à Troi," where Wesley hears a complex music-based rhythm in Riker's coded message that no one else can recognize. In addition, in "Remember Me," The Traveler coaches Wesley on how to think beyond mathematics to save his mother who is stuck in an alternate dimension.

The episode "Journey's End" is the climax of Wesley's story. The inhabitants of Dorvan V are being forced to leave their world, as the Federation must relinquish control of the planet to the Cardassians. Wesley is on vacation from Starfleet Academy and revisits the *Enterprise* during the mission. While on the planet, he is guided on a vision quest by one of the colonists. During the vision quest, Wesley envisions his deceased father who informs Wesley that he is destined to go down a non-traditional path. As a result of the vision and the conflict over the relocation of the Dorvan V inhabitants, Wesley decides to leave Starfleet. The inhabitant that guided Wesley reveals himself as The Traveler. Wesley decides to apprentice with The Traveler in order to develop his abilities to understand the intricacies of time and energy.[2]

There is some confusion as to whether Wesley continues to apprentice with The Traveler or returns to Starfleet. Wesley appears in a formal Starfleet uniform at the wedding of Riker and Troi in *Nemesis*. (There is also a deleted scene from the film in which Picard and Wesley discuss his assignment on the *Titan* under Riker's command.) Wesley's story is extended in the *Star Trek* novels, although they are not canon. According to Keith DeCandido's novel *A Time for War, A Time for Peace* (2004), Wesley mistakenly arrives on Earth naked and needs to be clothed. He assumes that Troi's wedding ceremony, as per Betazoid custom, would be conducted in the nude. And in Davis Mack's *Cold Equations* (2012) books, Wesley is confirmed as a full-time Traveler for some time. Though there are other books and a short film as part of the traveling exhibit *Star Trek: The Exhibition* (2012) that depict Wesley's return to Starfleet, his choice to veer from his expected path is still relevant.

Wesley's story is analogous to numerous musicians who left traditional lives in order to apprentice with a master musician or join a group of musicians to learn and perfect their musical craft. Many musicians are drawn to both the musical possibilities and life style of being a musician. And many non-musicians (or musicians who did not commit to a life in music) may not understand or support someone's choice to change course.

Wesley's decision to follow his vision and desires beyond his expected path thus outline the dangers and the risks involved in choosing a less traditional and possibly less stable way of life, similar to many musicians.

Data: Music Making as Transcendence

In *ST: TNG*, music making is not exclusively a human endeavor, as we have seen Ro, Worf, and other species also make music. Although the android Data repeatedly states that his attempts to make music and pursue other art forms (like acting, dance, painting, sculpture, and poetry) are means of becoming more human, he is, in fact, hoping to attain something other than humanity. Rather, Data aims to evolve beyond his positronic brain and the technology that created him to eventually transcend his artificialness.[3] His entire story arc begins and ends with references to Data's music making, from the very first episode "Encounter at Farpoint" to the final movie *Nemesis*, with several moments of music making throughout. By exploring Data's music making, we can better understand the character of Data, plus a greater *ST: TNG* aesthetic.

In the very first *ST: TNG* episode, Riker first meets Data on the holodeck as Data attempts to whistle the 19th century English nursery rhyme "Pop Goes the Weasel." Data has trouble finishing the melody and marvels at Riker's ease in completing it. Data continues to have problems whistling throughout the series. In the episode "Brothers," Data meets his inventor and "father," Dr. Noonian Soong, who asks him to whistle. Soong is disappointed that Data still cannot whistle well. Interestingly, later in the same episode, Data's evil "brother" Lore awakes singing after Soong mistakenly installs the emotion chip intended for Data into Lore. Is this a possible commentary on the differences between Data and Lore? Is the emotion chip necessary to allow Data to transcend his artificialness? The juxtaposition of Data's whistling and Lore's singing cannot be completely coincidental. Data later becomes proficient on violin, oboe, classical guitar, and could also sing. But despite his proficiency, Data continues to struggle with music making and, therefore, the endeavor (along with his other creative endeavors) remains a manifestation of his efforts to transcend his artificialness throughout *ST: TNG*.

In the episode "Elementary, Dear Data," Data emulates the fictional private detective Sherlock Holmes on the holodeck. La Forge is amazed at how well Data can play violin as part of the character. Data simply explains that playing violin is part of emulating Holmes, suggesting he cannot "feel" his music. In "The Ensigns of Command," Data criticizes his own violin playing as simply an amalgamation of many violinists, including Jascha Heifetz and Trenka Bron-Ken. Picard challenges Data, stating the android is actually choosing elements of Heifetz and Bron-Ken and, therefore, may be transcending his programming. Data ponders the idea and declares such selection and combination as innovation. This signals the beginning of Data stepping away from his artificialness.

In the episode "Sarek," Data performs violin as part of a Mozart string quartet for Ambassador Sarek, the father of Spock. At a key moment in the episode, Sarek is seen shedding a tear during Data's performance. The moment is already unusual, as Vulcans are not known to cry. But in the context of Data's musical pursuits, the moment can also be seen as unusual for Data, who has honestly moved someone with his music making. However, despite this breakthrough, Data is first and foremost a machine and he regards music as a technical performance more than an emotional one.

For instance, Data uses his superhuman listening abilities to approach music, but he does it in a way that no human would. In the episode "A Matter of Time," Data listens to four classical pieces simultaneously: Bach's Brandenburg Concerto No. 3 (1721), Mozart's Symphony No. 41 "Jupiter" (1788), Beethoven's Symphony No. 9 (1824), and "La Donna è Mobile" from Verdi's *Rigoletto* (1851). In the episode, Data explains that he can listen to up to one hundred and fifty simultaneous compositions at once. But in order to accomplish his task of analyzing the aesthetics of the pieces, he can only listen to ten or fewer at the same time. Data's continued attempts to analyze and understand music is further evidence that his attempt to transcend his artificialness is an ongoing process, but an uneven one.

In the episode "Inheritance," Data meets the scientist Juliana Tainer, who is in fact the former wife of Data's creator, Dr. Soong, and whom the episode presents as Data's "mother." Over the course of the episode, Data learns that Tainer plays the viola and they later perform together. While performing with Tainer, Data deduces that Tainer is an android because she performs the same music passages exactly the same every time. Data later learns that his android "mother" is in fact a duplicate of the original human Tainer, but the android copy is not aware that she is an android. Data decides not to reveal to his "mother" that she is an android, for doing so would rob her of her humanity. While making the decision not to reveal the truth to Tainer, Data is reminded of his own artificialness. But in this context, Trainer is more artificial than Data since her humanity comes at the cost of her not knowing the truth. Keeping that fact in mind, Data possibly becomes more self-aware as a result of the experience and may better continue his journey to transcend his artificialness.

Data's experience in "Inheritance" is not unlike his discussion with Ambassador Spock in "Unification II," when Spock comments on both Data's and Picard's dispassionate analytical abilities. In response, Data remarks on Spock's half-human heritage, which Spock has abandoned by choosing a Vulcan way of life. Data is obviously "saddened" that Spock has rejected the very humanity Data pursues. But the conversation concludes with Spock stating that he has no regrets. Data quickly points out to Spock that he used a human expression, which Spock simply acknowledges and finds fascinating. Though no music is performed or referenced in the scene between them, the conversation is an earlier counterpart to Data's decision to not tell his "mother" the truth that she is an android. This conversation with Spock informs Data's outlook on what it means to be human and the presence of a vital component: the ability to choose a non-logical solution or outcome and transcend its incongruity. In the moment that Data decides to conceal the lie of his "mother's" artificialness, he arguably becomes a bit more human and less artificial. One can draw a parallel between the differences between the strict true/false nature of Boolean logic and the ambiguity allowed in fuzzy logic, which is based on degrees of truth. Data is able to step away from the limits of a Boolean logic and step closer to a more fuzzy, nuanced, and (dare we say) organic approach to situations. Truth becomes a little less absolute and thus more contextual, particular, and possibly malleable. This new awareness ties back to Data's original critiques and observations of his "mother's" repeatedly perfect viola performance. The subtle differences and flexibility in performance or in thinking allow Data to begin to transcend his artificialness. The very subjectivity of music and its purpose (and even enjoyment) is quite similar to the ambiguity found in fuzzy logic. Thus, Data is using his experiences with music to begin to attain his extra-musical goal to transcend his artificialness.

In the movie *Generations*, Data finally has Soong's emotion chip installed. (We can argue that nothing can be more artificial for Data than having his emotions installed via a chip, but let us suspend our disbelief and see this irony in the spirit of the above discussion on Boolean vs. fuzzy logic.) It is notable that Data now has no problems singing: when Riker asks him to scan for life forms, the android creates his own composition in an impromptu ditty, using his console as an instrument, while singing about his assignment. This is matched later in the subsequent movie *Insurrection*, where the emotion chip's effects are more noticeable, even though Data does not take the chip with him on assignment. After Data's neural net is injured and he commandeers a shuttle, Picard captures Data by distracting him while singing the Gilbert & Sullivan song "A British Tar" from the operetta *H.M.S. Pinafore* (1878). Data was rehearsing music from the operetta before the incident and his eagerness to join Picard in the refrain (and thus be distracted) could be seen as a product of Data's emotion chip's effect, even when it is removed. Prior to having the chip installed, Data could not take such pleasure in singing, since pleasure is an emotion, and therefore could not have been distracted.

Later in *Insurrection*, Data displays more emotional growth while on the Ba'ku planet. During his time on the planet, Data befriends the boy Artim, who asks Data if androids ever play. Data answers that he plays violin and chess. The boy is unsatisfied with Data's answer and attempts to play a game of tag with Data, which Data does not quite understand, as Data is much faster than Artim. The boy explains that one plays tag because it is fun. Data responds that androids do not have fun. But before Data and the *Enterprise* crew leave the planet, we see Data in a haystack obviously having fun with Artim. Though Data only refers to his violin as a tool and does not make any music, the idea of play and having fun is made obviously clear to Data (as will be seen in *Nemesis*). Data's emotion chip allows him to experience the pleasure of non-logical activities. Thinking back to the episode "Déjà Q," where Q makes Data laugh as a gesture of thanks for saving his life, we are reminded how far Data has come to be able to experience and value such playful moments and activities. Early on in the series, Data can only begin to fathom what it was like to be human and less artificial. But through his experiences meeting and later playing with Artim, Data obviously can now truthfully experience and value moments of play beyond simply replicating them, as he does with his music.

In the final *ST: TNG* movie, *Nemesis*, we are given a rather large piece of the puzzle regarding Data's attempt to fully transcend his artificialness. Music is performed and referred to throughout these final moments of the filmed *ST: TNG* universe. After the assassination of the members of the Romulan Senate in the opening scene, we witness Picard's toast at the reception following the wedding of Riker and Troi. For a wedding gift, Data enthusiastically sings Irving Berlin's "Blue Skies" (1926) with a jazz band. Data is obviously enjoying himself and the senior officers of the *Enterprise* are quite entertained. Data's performance is further evidence that he has either transcended, or is at least in the process of transcending, his artificialness—perhaps even without his emotion chip (in a deleted scene from the film's ending, La Forge takes Data's emotion chip as a memento of their friendship). Nevertheless, gone is his inability to carry a tune and he performs with abandon. Data now fully embraces the concepts of fun and play first introduced and explained by Artim. Later in the film, Data downloads his knowledge and memories into the recently discovered Soong prototype B-4. After Data is killed, the senior officers of the *Enterprise* hold a memorial for Data, where Riker remembers Data struggling to whistle "Pop Goes the Weasel" years ago—perhaps a metaphor for the android's growth from humming child songs to singing Irving Berlin. The film ends with a private conversation between Picard and B-4, in which B-4 sings a segment of "Blue Skies" as Picard begins to leave. Though unsaid, Picard obviously believes some portion of Data lives on in B-4, as music making was one of Data's greatest pursuits to understand humanity. Somewhere within B-4 is the product of Data's efforts to transcend his artificialness via music, evidenced by B-4's singing.

Unfortunately, Data does not speak directly about his music making after the emotion chip is installed in *Generations*. The assumption that the emotion chip allows Data to transcend his artificialness can only be deduced from a few scenes in the final two *ST: TNG* films. But Data paradoxically achieves his transcendence of artificialness through the artificial means of a hardware upgrade. The obvious difference in Data's behavior after the chip's installation is his playfulness with others. He makes others laugh. He is seen enjoying himself in front of people and immerses himself in music making. He also no longer questions the validity and value of his actions. The transcendence that the emotion chip provides is ultimately found in Data's ability to share himself with others while enjoying what he is doing: a more-outward journey rather than an inward journey. No longer are his music making and other creative endeavors solely for his achievement and betterment. Music making is no longer an exercise or a challenge to solve, but rather an activity that he enjoys and shares with others. He finds his transcendence after no longer needing to look for it.

Jean-Luc Picard: Music Making as Connection

Jean-Luc Picard is not portrayed as a musician initially. *Nemesis* reveals that, as a child, Picard suffered from a rare genetic disease known as Shalaft's syndrome, which makes him hypersensitive to sound. Although Picard is cured of this disease, the experience explains his latent musical skills that do not manifest themselves until much later in his adult life. Indeed, in the episode "The Perfect Mate," we learn Picard had piano lessons as a child and dreaded performing in recitals. Throughout the first half of the television series, Picard is very much a reluctant musician.

However, as an adult, Picard obviously loves music, as he is seen often listening to music. We do not see Picard make music until the second half of the television series. In fact, one of the signs that a doppelganger took Picard's place in the episode "Allegiance" is that he breaks character and asks his shipmates to sing with him in Ten Forward. But we later do see the real Picard sing while drunk with his brother in the episode "Family." In "Disaster," Picard even sings the French nursery rhyme "Frère Jacques" (ca. 18th century) to soothe some scared children as they attempt to climb a turbolift shaft during a ship-wide power outage. So, there is a reluctant musician within Picard that emerges over the course of the second half of the television series and the films. In fact, his diplomatic abilities to listen and understand others are related to his musical abilities. As the musician remerges from within Picard, we see that his music making serves as an additional way he can connect with other people and other cultures.

In the episode "First Contact," Picard and Troi explain to the alien scientist Mirasta that they first learn as much as possible about an alien civilization through broadcast signals, journalism, popular music, and humor. Mirasta is visibly worried that someone would attempt to learn about a civilization through its popular music and entertainment.

Picard quickly agrees with her that it is an incomplete picture and therefore more reconnaissance is done. But Picard's initial sensitivity is a testament to his attention to detail and nuance and his ability to listen to others deeply and accurately. Even though over time Picard becomes comfortable with music making as an important part of his own identity, the captain also understands that a civilization's music might not be a complete or even accurate depiction of a civilization's ideals and beliefs. Picard's statement demonstrates his sensitivity as he assures Mirasta they use music as a gateway to examining their complete society.[4]

Picard's music making emerges in "The Inner Light." In this episode, Picard is stunned by an alien probe from an extinct civilization and becomes unconscious. In a matter of minutes, he lives more than half a lifetime, where he has children and becomes quite proficient on an alien flute. Though these are only memories from an alien civilization, Picard remembers the experiences after he regains consciousness. At the end of the episode, Riker gives Picard the flute that is discovered within the alien probe and Picard retains the ability to play it. Because Picard is forced to learn the flute against his will after having the memories and experiences implanted in his brain, we cannot see the experience as Picard's chosen endeavor. But the experience does lead Picard to overcome his reluctance to make music. After the alien probe invades his mind, he is able to instantly connect to a wealth of knowledge and abilities that allow him to make music in a new way. No longer is music making connected to the memory of being forced to play piano in front of audiences at a recital as a child. Rather, music making emerges as an activity he voluntarily engages in for his own enjoyment. Like Data, music becomes more about personal enjoyment. The alien probe transforms Picard's approach to making music. Music is no longer an activity of re-creation (by playing a previously composed piece of music), but is now an activity of recreation (where one enjoys the process).

After learning to play the alien flute, Picard is later seen making music as part of his life. In "A Fistful of Datas," Picard rehearses a piece of music with computer playback that he wrote himself called the "Mozart Trio." In "Lessons," Picard forms a deep relationship with new crewmember and stellar cartographist Nella Daren, who also plays piano. The two perform several times and Daren even inspires Picard to improvise. Unfortunately, the relationship between Daren and Picard does not last. But over the course of the episode, music enables Picard to connect with Daren in a way he has never connected with another person before. Originally an extension of the alien probe experience, music making for Picard transforms from a private recreational activity to a social activity. Though Picard's journey as a musician is no longer elaborated upon after "Lessons," several moments in two films, *First Contact* and *Insurrection*, link Picard's childhood experience and his musical journey as an adult.

Throughout *First Contact*, Picard hears the Borg Collective in his head. He anticipates their arrival and he is haunted by their sounds. It is never determined whether these noises are real or imagined. But after his experience of being assimilated by the Borg in "The Best of Both Worlds," Picard is forever marked by the traumatic experience. When he meets the Borg Queen onboard the *Enterprise*, she even alludes to the fact that he may still hear their Borg "song." After Picard's rediscovery of the power and joy of music making, the haunting nature of the Borg's sounds and music is an unwanted connection. These sounds are an invasion and, magnified by Picard's experience with Shalaft's syndrome as a child and his assimilation with the Borg, the sounds of the Borg become a deep violation that he cannot expunge. This violation heightens the drama when Picard is almost reassimilated into the Borg collective. Thankfully, Picard and *Enterprise* are saved by Data. But the sonic invasion-turned-violation cannot be forgotten. Picard's reconnection to the Borg is the antithesis of his adult musical journey. Where music making allows him to awaken his creativity and social activity, the Borg sounds almost paralyze him via the channels that made the awakening possible. Though Picard never speaks of the experience as such, we cannot help but wonder if his faith in music and music making is possibly shaken because of his reunion with the Borg.

Finally, in *Insurrection*, Picard's ability to hear and listen well is extended to an unnamed and unexplained ability to slow down time. If music making is seen as an activity that happens within time, the ability to make music can be extended to manipulating time or, at least, the perception of time. While on the Ba'ku planet, Picard befriends the Ba'ku woman Anij. She explains to Picard that because of the Ba'ku's longevity, part of their way of life involves artisans apprenticing for thirty to forty years. Picard is obviously mesmerized by the possibilities. Though it is never quite explained, the Ba'ku are able to slow down time. For example, when Picard and Anij kiss, time slows down as Picard sees the wings of a humming bird flap slowly. A similar experience happens when Picard miraculously saves Anij's life in a blink of an eye by slowing down time. Anij jokes with Picard that he thought it would take centuries for him to learn the ability. But Picard somehow acquires it quickly. When Picard's ability to hear well—in *Insurrection*, he can detect the ship's misaligned sensors—is coupled with his openness and sensitivity to others, it comes as no surprise that he understands and can execute Ba'ku abilities. Earlier, Anij comments on Picard's ability to engender trust with others. All of these abilities are a testament to Picard's character. He connects to others very easily, first as a diplomat, then as a musician, and now ever greater through the mystical powers from the Ba'ku planet.

As mentioned earlier, at the end of *Nemesis* Picard hears the echo of Data through B-4's singing of "Blue Skies." Keeping in mind his Shalaft's syndrome, his adult musical journey, his reunion with the Borg, and his mystical experiences on the Ba'ku planet, the last moments of the last *ST: TNG* film take on new meaning. On the surface, Picard is listening to an android's attempt to sing a song. But on a deeper level, Picard may be able to hear the triumph and convergence of a multitude of unique voices across time and space. Dr. Soong invented the B-4 prototype, Lore, and Data as attempts to recreate (and possibly improve) the human experience. Picard is reawakened creatively and socially thanks to the music making of an extinct alien culture. Having his senses heightened after his experience on the Ba'ku planet, Picard can connect deeply to that impulse to understand and improve the human experience within the universe. Thus, Soong's impulse to create life is transformed by that life's (Data's) desire to transcend its own artificialness via creative endeavors (like music making), which is then heard by Picard transmitted as an echo via B-4 (a precursor to the life created). This quickly becomes a seemingly paradoxical chain of events analogous to a Möbius strip, a single-sided surface existing in three-dimensional space that seems to fold into itself. But Picard is well aware of the intertwined chain of events and, thus, can hear beyond this confusion. As he leaves the room, he smiles knowing that nothing is lost. Soong's impulse to create is similar to the *Enterprise*'s mission to explore. By creating and exploring, we ultimately return to ourselves. By connecting beyond ourselves through others, we begin to truly perceive who we are and thus begin to understand ourselves. Contrary to the film's tagline that a generation's final journey begins, Picard knows the *Enterprise* begins a new chapter with a new crew. Thus, *Nemesis* is better understood as an open road to another continuing mission, rather than *ST: TNG*'s swansong.

For Picard, music making is a manifestation of the above process of creation and exploration. Music making allows us to apply technology to connect to the past via a tradition of music making. But this musical connection to the past informs the present and connects people to possible futures. Picard's aural sensitivity, combined with his unbiased analytical abilities (which even Spock comments upon in "Unification"), allows him to not only make music, but also perceive time and space (and the people and objects within time and space) deeply. Always fascinated with the abilities and accomplishments of humans and other species, Picard owes his appreciation and ability to deeply perceive such wonders to his highly-developed capacity to hear and understand.

Conclusion

Several crewmembers of the *Enterprise-D* and *Enterprise-E* enjoy or make music. Many use music as a means to express or reinforce their identity. But three specific crewmembers use music as a means to achieve extra-musical goals. First, although Wesley may not be a musician, his chosen life path mirrors that of a musician who fully dedicates his or her life to music making. His choice to apprentice with The Traveler goes against the expectation of a life in Starfleet. He simply cannot ignore the calling or the opportunity to pursue such a life. Second, Data is able to explore music and other arts to transcend his artificialness. Later, via his emotion chip, Data thoroughly integrates his music making in his life as an outlet for pleasure and entertainment. Finally, Picard uses music to connect with other people on a deeper level. His aural sensitivity allows him to be a better diplomat and to better understand aspects of the role of humans and other species within the universe. The character development for all three would not have progressed as it did if they had not chosen to explore the possibilities related to music making or a non-traditional life similar to a musician. Wesley, Data, and Picard are profoundly transformed by taking risks, making tough choices, and going on a creative journey. Nothing could be more in line with boldly going where no one has gone before.

NOTES

1. On Worf's warrior culture, see Jared Miracle's essay in this volume.
2. On Wesley Crusher's departure from Starfleet, see Justin Ream's and Alexander Lee's essay in this volume.
3. On Data's sentience within Starfleet norms, see Olaf Meuther's essay in this volume.
4. On Picard as a diplomat, see Alex Burston-Chorowicz's essay in this volume.

WORKS CITED

"Allegiance." *Star Trek: The Next Generation.* Writ. Richard Manning and Hans Beimler. Dir. Winrich Kolbe. *Netflix.* Web. 12 Sept. 2016.
"The Best of Both Worlds, Part 1." *Star Trek: The Next Generation.* Writ. Michael Piller. Dir. Cliff Bole. *Netflix.* Web. 12 Sept. 2016.
"The Best of Both Words, Part 2." *Star Trek: The Next Generation.* Writ. Michael Piller. Dir. Cliff Bole. *Netflix.* Web. 12 Sept. 2016.
"Brothers." *Star Trek: The Next Generation.* Writ. Rick Berman. Dir. Rob Bowman. *Netflix.* Web. 12 Sept. 2016.
Chaos on the Bridge. Dir. William Shatner. Vision Films, 2014. Film.
DeCandido, Keith. *Star Trek: A Time for War, a Time for Peace.* New York: Pocket Books, 2004. Print.
"Déjà Q." *Star Trek: The Next Generation.* Writ. Richard Danus. Dir. Les Landau. *Netflix.* Web. 12 Sept. 2016.
"Disaster." *Star Trek: The Next Generation.* Writ. Ronald D. Moore. Dir. Gabrielle Beaumont. *Netflix.* Web. 12 Sept. 2016.

"Elementary, Dear Data." *Star Trek: The Next Generation*. Writ. Brian Alan Lane. Dir. Rob Bowman. *Netflix*. Web. 12 Sept. 2016.

"Encounter at Farpoint, Part 1." *Star Trek: The Next Generation*. Writ. D.C. Fontana and Gene Roddenberry. Dir. Corey Allen. *Netflix*. Web. 12 Sept. 2016.

"Encounter at Farpoint, Part 2." *Star Trek: The Next Generation*. Writ. D.C. Fontana and Gene Roddenberry. Dir. Corey Allen. *Netflix*. Web. 12 Sept. 2016.

"The Ensigns of Command." *Star Trek: The Next Generation*. Writ. Melinda M. Snodgrass. Dir. Cliff Bole. *Netflix*. Web. 12 Sept. 2016.

"Family." *Star Trek: The Next Generation*. Writ. Ronald D. Moore. Dir. Les Landau. *Netflix*. Web. 12 Sept. 2016.

"First Contact." *Star Trek: The Next Generation*. Writ. Dennis Russell Bailey, David Bischoff, Joe Menosky, Ronald D. Moore, and Michael Piller. Dir. Cliff Bole. *Netflix*. Web. 12 Sept. 2016.

"A Fistful of Datas." *Star Trek: The Next Generation*. Writ. Robert Hewitt Wolfe and Brannon Braga. Dir. Patrick Stewart. *Netflix*. Web. 12 Sept. 2016.

"Future Imperfect." *Star Trek: The Next Generation*. Writ. J. Larry Carroll and David Bennett Carren. Dir. Les Landau. *Netflix*. Web. 12 Sept. 2016.

"Haven." *Star Trek: The Next Generation*. Writ. Tracy Tormé. Dir. Richard Compton. *Netflix*. Web. 12 Sept. 2016.

"Inheritance." *Star Trek: The Next Generation*. Writ. Dan Koeppel and René Echevarria. Dir. Robert Scheerer. *Netflix*. Web. 12 Sept. 2016.

"The Inner Light." *Star Trek: The Next Generation*. Writ. Morgan Gendel and Peter Allan Fields. Dir. Peter Lauritson. *Netflix*. Web. 12 Sept. 2016.

"Journey's End." *Star Trek: The Next Generation*. Writ. Ronald D. Moore. Dir. Corey Allen. *Netflix*. Web. 12 Sept. 2016.

"Lessons." *Star Trek: The Next Generation*. Writ. Ron Wilkerson and Jean Louise Matthias. Dir. Robert Wiemer. *Netflix*. Web. 12 Sept. 2016.

Mack, Davis. *Star Trek: The Next Generation—Cold Equations. Book I: The Persistence of Memory*. New York: Pocket Books, 2012. Print.

_____. *Star Trek: The Next Generation—Cold Equations. Book II: Silent Weapons*. New York: Pocket Books, 2012. Print.

_____. *Star Trek: The Next Generation—Cold Equations. Book III: The Body Electric*. New York: Pocket Books, 2012. Print.

"A Matter of Time." *Star Trek: The Next Generation*. Writ. Rick Berman. Dir. Paul Lynch. *Netflix*. Web. 12 Sept. 2016.

"Ménage à Troi." *Star Trek: The Next Generation*. Writ. Fred Bronson and Susan Sackett. Dir. Robert Legato. *Netflix*. Web. 12 Sept. 2016.

"The Next Phase." *Star Trek: The Next Generation*. Writ. Ronald D. Moore. Dir. David Carson. *Netflix*. Web. 12 Sept. 2016.

"11001001." *Star Trek: The Next Generation*. Writ. Maurice Hurley and Robert Lewin. Dir. Paul Lynch. *Netflix*. Web. 12 Sept. 2016.

Orbison, Roy. "Ooby Dooby / Go! Go! Go!." Sun Records, 1956. 7" single.

"The Perfect Mate." *Star Trek: The Next Generation*. Writ. Reuben Leder and Michael Piller. Dir. Cliff Bole. *Netflix*. Web. 12 Sept. 2016.

"Phantasms." *Star Trek: The Next Generation*. Writ. Brannon Braga. Dir. Patrick Stewart. *Netflix*. Web. 12 Sept. 2016.

"Preemptive Strike." *Star Trek: The Next Generation*. Writ. René Echevarria. Dir. Patrick Stewart. *Netflix*. Web. 12 Sept. 2016.

"Remember Me." *Star Trek: The Next Generation*. Writ. Lee Sheldon. Dir. Cliff Bole. *Netflix*. Web. 12 Sept. 2016.

"Sarek." *Star Trek: The Next Generation*. Writ. Peter S. Beagle. Dir. Les Landau. *Netflix*. Web. 12 Sept. 2016.

"Second Chances." *Star Trek: The Next Generation*. Writ. René Echevarria. Dir. LeVar Burton. *Netflix*. Web. 12 Sept. 2016.

Star Trek: First Contact. Dir. Jonathan Frakes. Perf. Patrick Stewart, Jonathan Frakes, and Brent Spiner. Paramount, 1996. *Netflix*. Web. 29 Jun. 2016.

Star Trek Generations. Dir. David Carson. Perf. Patrick Stewart, Jonathan Frakes, and Brent Spiner. Paramount, 1994. *Netflix*. Web. 29 Jun. 2016.

Star Trek: Insurrection. Dir. Jonathan Frakes. Perf. Patrick Stewart, Jonathan Frakes, and Brent Spiner. Paramount, 1998. *Netflix*. Web. 30 Jun. 2016.

Star Trek: Nemesis. Dir. Stuart Baird. Perf. Patrick Stewart, Jonathan Frakes, and Brent Spiner. Paramount, 2002. *Netflix*. Web. 9 Jul. 2016.

Steppenwolf. "Magic Carpet Ride." *The Second*. ABC / Dunhill Records, 1968. LP.

"Sub Rosa." *Star Trek: The Next Generation*. Writ. Brannon Braga. Dir. Jonathan Frakes. *Netflix*. Web. 12 Sept. 2016.

"Thine Own Self." *Star Trek: The Next Generation*. Writ. Ronald D. Moore. Dir. Winrich Kolbe. *Netflix*. Web. 12 Sept. 2016.

"Unification I." *Star Trek: The Next Generation*. Writ. Jeri Taylor. Dir. Les Landau. *Netflix*. Web. 12 Sept. 2016.

"Unification II." *Star Trek: The Next Generation*. Writ. Michael Piller. Dir. Cliff Bole. *Netflix*. Web. 12 Sept. 2016.

"Where No One Has Gone Before." *Star Trek: The Next Generation*. Writ. Diane Duane and Michael Reeves. Dir. Rob Bowman. *Netflix*. Web. 12 Sept. 2016.

"Where Silence Has Lease." *Star Trek: The Next Generation*. Writ. Jack S. Sowards. Dir. Winrich Kolbe. *Netflix*. Web. 12 Sept. 2016.

"The Wounded." *Star Trek: The Next Generation*. Writ. Jeri Taylor. Dir. Chip Chalmers. *Netflix*. Web. 12 Sept. 2016.

The Future Past

Reflections on the Role of History

ALEXANDER SIMMETH

For a historian, popular culture is an immensely rich source. As a mass cultural expression, it conspicuously mirrors societies and societal change, cultural evolution, and the political zeitgeist. Cultural artifacts, as well as tastes and preferences of audiences, mark the twentieth century as an era of transcending borders between sometimes centuries-old notions of gender, class, and ethnicity. This is especially true for the *Star Trek* universe, a science fiction classic and one of the 20th and 21st centuries' most popular franchises to date. Audiences of *TOS* will never forget Uhura, bending racial conventions of her time; or Chekov, the Russian, whose presence, as part of the main cast on the bridge, made a clear statement in the middle of the Cold War. *TNG*, on the other hand, might be read as a reflection of societies in times of transition between the end of the Cold War and a new world order. Earlier essays in this book describe some of the contemporary concerns addressed in *TNG* during its initial broadcasts and subsequent film series; in this essay, we explore the role of the past in its imagined future. Why did history play such a central role in writing *TNG*? How did the creators depict the future past? Finally, considering the sweeping success of *TNG* worldwide, what can the answers to those questions tell us?

The first question might be relatively easy to address. Science fiction, as in *Star Trek*, is based on the authors' present age. *Star Trek* turns "today" into history: It speculates about a possible future not as an "unrealistic" fantasy, but rooted in the empirical environment of the creator. Speculative thinking on empirical grounds, one might say, rather than genres such as fantasy or science fantasy, drives the narrative. As a result, *TNG* episodes oftentimes directly reflect public discourses taking place during its time of production, in this case the late 1980s and early 1990s.[1] However, even though the boundaries between genres are surely blurred, it is safe to say that *Star Trek* embodies the "classic" approach to science fiction. Its empirical groundings in the present inform the imagined future, and that, in turn, makes the present its reference point. How could phenomena of the present possibly develop within the next few hundred years? And how is our present going to be viewed in the future? This kind of "what if when" question, with its direct link to the present, is at the core of writing and producing *Star Trek*. And this is the main reason why in *TNG*, the future past plays such a central role.

The concept of history is the basic grounding of *TNG*, with the seven seasons arched by the future past. As early as in the pilot, "Encounter at Farpoint," mankind is put on a show trial for its *history*: its history of wars, cruelty and suppression. The prosecutor and judge is Q, an entity from a Continuum with seemingly boundless power and potency. At first, Q appears on the bridge in different historic clothing from mankind's history, mimicking their respective habitus and language.[2] Charging humanity with being a cruel and infantile race, the being warns the crew not to travel any further into space and return home—or they shall die. After changing the stage into a World War III style courtroom, which appears entirely real to the crew, Q eventually agrees on Picard's proposal: To test the crew of the *Enterprise* if the cruelty and savagery of the past is presently true of humans. As the overarching story unfolds, the stage for the upcoming seven years of *TNG* is set.

There are many possible ways to explore the fundamental role of history in the production of *TNG*. On the following pages, we will focus on the question how history is appropriated for the show. How it is "used"? What function does it have? Does it appear as something "good" or "bad"? We start off by looking at the concept of capitalism, recurring in multifaceted ways throughout the show. Then we focus on an example concerning history that seemingly repeats itself. Next, we take a closer look into the "intermediate time," the centuries between the audiences present of the late twentieth, and *TNG*'s present of the 24th century. From there, we look at history as personal experience in the 24th century. The episode "A Matter of Time," in which a future historian visits the *Enterprise*, shows the limits of history as an ideological lesson for the future.

The Concept of Capitalism

In human societies, and the Federation at large, capitalism in the 24th century is an ambiguous concept—at best.[3] The Federation's official ideology renders capitalism a relic from the past, long overcome. All people are considered equal, hunger and poverty are eliminated, and life is a journey of exploration and self-betterment instead of an endless struggle to survive. The drive for personal gain is considered at least awkward, often primitive, and backwards. Capitalist alien societies are usually portrayed as being on a stage of earlier development, less advanced morally and technologically than the Federation and human societies. Capitalism, no doubt, is a "bad" thing.

It is always worth looking at the exemptions from the rule, and there are some here as well. Think, for example, about Picard's romantic encounters with the archeologist Vash ("Captain's Holiday," "Qpid"). Vash's sense for profit, linked to a strong self-independence and self-reliance, are major parts of her appeal to the Starfleet captain. However, those qualities also render her outside Starfleet norms—eve bordering on criminality. Beyond that, capitalism does have its practical uses. In "The Neutral Zone," the *Enterprise* finds three frozen twentieth century humans in an ancient, largely defunct, capsule floating in space. After the crew revives them from their cryogenic stasis, the three humans turn out to display all too familiar—to the present viewer—characteristics by having a fondness for money, gambling, smoking, and drinking alcohol. Those habits are, rather unsurprising, depicted as primitive and from a distant past. But, Picard has to admit, the twentieth century instinct and seemingly backwards attitude can also be of help four hundred years in the future. When the Romulans show up in the Neutral Zone on an alleged mission that coincides with the *Enterprise*'s assignment, one of the twentieth century humans, based on his experience of negotiating business, senses Romulan wiliness to cooperate—and Picard concedes. As the audience learns, these "imperfect" humans from the past are better equipped for encounters with certain alien species than an experienced captain from the shiny Federation with its idealistic principles.

Despite Picard's romantic encounters with the profit-driven character Vash or his dealing with canny capitalists from the twentieth century, however, greed and the hunt for profit are clearly marked as backwards and savage throughout the show. It is stunning to see how, especially in *TNG*'s early seasons, capitalism appears as primitive and crude when compared to the "superior" Federation. Capitalism usually surfaces as a reference point, either among other races or as negative example of humanity's darker past. As a prominent example for the former, the Federation is contrasted with the Ferengi, a race of sharp-toothed, large-eared aliens who literally embody capitalism and greed. The first encounter with Ferengi ("The Last Outpost") portrays the species as profit-driven savages who are dishonest and devious. They appear clothed in fur and armed with long whips— features that supposedly underscore their backwardness, but disappear in later episodes— and close ups showing their stylized, long and voracious fingers. Sure enough, the crew links the aliens with the human past. In this first encounter, Data compares Ferengi with Yankee traders of eighteenth and nineteenth century United States. As a computer, Data's description affirms the Federation's official history, tying the Ferengi to a past epoch when mankind was also savage, backwards, and profit-driven. The Ferengi are construed as a mirror of human history, a past that humanity has long rendered obsolete.

One of the most prominent meetings with the future past, again intrinsically linked to capitalism, is the senior staff's time travel into nineteenth century San Francisco in order to investigate an alien presence ("Time's Arrow"). These aliens, the Devidians, travel to the past and kill by literally sucking the life out of their human victims, draining their neural energy. In nineteenth century San Francisco, the deaths are linked to a Cholera outbreak—as so often, this mistaken belief reinforces the backwardness of humanity's past and simply not "knowing any better." The *Enterprise* crew, of course, manages to solve the puzzle and keep the Devidians not only from killing humans, but from intervening with Earth's history. An especially interesting character appearing in this episode is Samuel L. Clemens, alias Mark Twain. Initially, Twain considers the crew as part of an invasion force from the future, but he helps their mission after he finds out that the *Enterprise*'s staff arrived in his present time to save mankind.

Links to capitalism in this double episode are manifold. At first, one can think of possible connotations between the life-draining aliens and similar qualities oftentimes ascribed to capitalism. Even stronger are the associations viewers might have with the character of Mark Twain. The "real" Twain of the nineteenth century was a notorious critic of capitalism (Foner 233), and this is strongly reflected in the episode. At one point, Clemens appears on board of the *Enterprise*; as he walks down the corridor with Counselor Troi, he expresses disappointment with the future as it presents itself on the starship. With all its technology, he states, simple pleasures, like gentlemen opening doors for ladies, are lost. This humorous quip underscores a deeper conviction; he is convinced the *Enterprise* must have terrible weapons and be on a mission of military conquest— themes that he will later exploit in *A Connecticut Yankee in King Arthur's Court*. When he and Troi passes aliens in the corridor, he suspects they are actually slaves or some kind of underprivileged servants.

Troi responds by explaining the ideals of the peaceful United Federation of Planets, emphasizing the equality among the thousands of species they have encountered—Betazoids among them. She adds that poverty has long been eliminated on Earth, along with other ills of human civilization—implicitly, of course, one of them is the ideology of capitalism. She paints a teleological picture of mankind's historical development from a dark past into a better future, in the process creating a society marked by the ideals of equality and equal opportunity. Clemens, then, reflects on "his" nineteenth century, the rampant inequality and prejudice, and the widespread and ruthless pursuit of power and wealth. He eventually admits that, perhaps, humanity's future might be better after all. And again, this time with nobody less than Mark Twain's personal absolution, the picture of a superior Federation prevails. At the end, he leaves his gold watch behind for 24th century archaeologists to find. This suggests he wants a tangible part of him to "exist" in the future, aside from his books … and shows he, too, can leave materialism behind.

In *TNG*, capitalism is one of the major themes that serves as lynchpin for uses of history, for appropriating the future past. But *what* uses and functions it has, is not as easy to answer as it might seem on first sight. We clearly see capitalism used as a negative reference to a backwards, unjust, even dangerous past that humanity has outgrown. But we also see the crew's fascination for that same past, and their eagerness to learn from it. We even occasionally witness capitalist instincts as superior to Federation idealism when it comes to dealing with wily or greedy aliens.

History Repeating Itself?

In *Star Trek*, encounters with human artifacts in space are frequent, and they are all intrinsically connected to the future past. Such relics include the 21st century NASA debris the *Enterprise* finds in a distant system ("The Royale"), or descendants of human settlers or adventurers. The latter is used in several episodes: The crew meets descendants of 22nd century naturalists ("Up the Long Ladder"), descendants of former emigrants from Earth on another planet who have to be resettled ("The Ensigns of Command"), or descendants of Native Americans who are once more driven off land they consider theirs ("Journey's End"). Many of these plots center on forced displacement, evoking mankind's past in multiple ways.

The plot of "Journey's End," for instance, is directly linked to Picard's family history. Ironically, for all of Picard's posturing about the barbaric human past, his own family is not immune to this charge, and this brings a darker tone to the bright future audiences expect and typically see in the series. As the story goes, the *Enterprise* is called to resettle descendants of Native American settlers from a planet that, after fierce and long negotiations, is given to the hostile Cardassian Empire.[4] Reluctantly, Picard tries to carry out his orders. In doing so, he is confronted with the tribe's strong resistance, who point out that one of his ancestors participated in a forced Native American relocation scheme on Earth 700 years ago. This tribe holds Picard liable for the actions of his distant ancestor, and their beliefs prohibit the tribe from leaving. Their new home is "sacred" to them, and settling on another planet out of the question. In the end they are allowed to stay on the planet under Cardassian rule, with Picard receiving an absolution from his dark family history by the tribe's spiritual leader. The sins of the past are redeemed.[5]

The use of history in this episode is again multi-layered. On the one hand, we are reminded of human atrocities in Earth's history in the form of forced displacements of

Native Americans by Europeans and their descendants. This is an example of "bad" history, and is in sharp contrast to the Federation's ethical principles in the 24th century. But, as we learn in this episode, Federation politics can have very similar results, and the plot intertwines the 24th century with a seeming repetition of Picard's family history. On the other hand, holding Picard liable for atrocities some distant ancestor committed 700 years ago—some kind of clan liability or *Sippenhaft*—and religious practices and beliefs, such as the promised redemption of the whole biological line after Picard seemingly "makes up" for it, seem almost evenly backwards and dark. In this case, history constitutes a negative backdrop that shapes current events for the *Enterprise* crew, and even sets the stage for the alleged "redemption" of Picard's family. However, that the humans are left under Cardassian rule (with unforeseeable consequences), leaves a stale aftertaste, especially since the episode does not have a resolution. As it seems, the future is not always "better" than its past.

Between the Viewer's Future and the Future Past: The "Intermediate Time"

Notions of "good" and "bad" history also inform the time-span between the viewer's and the *Enterprise*'s presents: the 21st to 23rd centuries constituting *TNG*'s past and the audience's future. In *TNG*, the 21st through 22nd centuries generally play important roles as this kind of "intermediate time," with epic world conflicts such as the Eugenic Wars mentioned in *The Original Series*, climate change and eco-disasters (e.g., "When the Bough Breaks," "A Matter of Time"), or World War III bringing humanity on the brink of extinction (e.g., "Encounter at Farpoint," "A Matter of Time," "Up the Long Ladder"). The past actually appears especially gloomy when set in the audience's immediate future— all things are still to come from the perspective of the viewer, but long past by *TNG*'s present. The audience has the impression that the worst is yet to come, but the distant future will be bright for having survived and thrived; among many classic science-fiction works, the film *Star Trek: First Contact* is based on this premise. The "intermediate" centuries, however, also stand for early space travel and first alien contacts, for technological and societal progress. Looking deeper into some of those and other aspects, and replacing the topical with a chronological focus, the central question in this subessay stays the same. How is the history of this "intermediate time" appropriated for a fictional future past?

The "bad" history of the "intermediate" centuries, for instance, is repeatedly exercised by playing with possibilities and dangers of biotechnology and human genetic engineering.[6] Several episodes in *TNG* are concerned with that topic, although they are, by far, not the only aspects underscoring the progressive character and timeliness of the show: In the late 1980s and early 1990s, the public discourse about the possibilities and dangers concerning those new scientific developments only began to unfold. In *TNG*, the highly complex field of biotechnology is usually broken down into easily digestible plots and narratives. Genetically engineered humans generally appear healthy and somehow superior, but in the end all turn out to have serious flaws: some carry and spread sicknesses that may be deadly for non-engineered humans ("Unnatural Selection"), others misuse genetic engineering for creating soldiers ("The Hunted"), and, again, others realize that their "perfectly engineered" society falls apart with the tiniest change ("The Masterpiece Society").

The latter example is of particular interest here, since it is concerned with the future past of the "intermediate" time mentioned above. The *Enterprise* encounters a human biosphere, founded sometime between the audience's and the *Enterprise*'s present, and endangered by a stellar core fragment. Confronting the human population with a possible evacuation, the crew finds out that its leaders do not want to leave. In fact, according to them, remaining in the biosphere is of vital importance to their entire society. The colony is a genetically engineered, fully integrated masterpiece, a "perfect society," and any kind of distortion or separation would cause irreparable damage. The damage is done at the end of the episode. Even though the technical problems are resolved and the colony is able to survive, a large part of its population decides to leave with the *Enterprise*. Interaction with the crew makes them curious about the outside, and some build personal relationships during the rescue mission. When the leaders of the colony plead for their colony to be left as-is, Picard refuses to leave the discontented colonists behind; but, as an outspoken opponent of genetic engineering, he admits that the *Enterprise*'s presence turned out just as destructive to the colony as the core fragment was.

In this example, the future past of the "intermediate" time serves as a negative reference point in human development, as "bad" history. First of all, the captain, as moral authority of the show, clearly and unmistakably repudiates genetic engineering as a grave error from the human past. Moreover, as the story unfolds, it becomes clear that the "masterpiece society" is also doomed to fail in the 24th century, solely by having contact with the outside galaxy. As relationships between the inhabitants and the strangers from the *Enterprise* develop, curiosity and affection makes the genetically engineered humans question their seemingly "perfect" world, while their leaders get increasingly caught up in a web of contradictions. At the end of the show, viewers do not know if the remainder of the colony will survive and adapt, if the remaining inhabitants can recalibrate its social integrity; according to the statements throughout the episode, the chances seem slim. In any case, there is no doubt that genetic engineering as a human practice from the "intermediate time" between the audience's and *TNG*'s present appears as a tragic failure. History, in this case, is not only a "bad" example; it is a warning to the present audience. More than that, it has tangible consequences in the 24th century, signifying that the dark chapter from the past is not yet closed.

The Future Past as Personal Experience

After looking at examples for topical and chronological approaches to the uses of history in *TNG*, the individual, respectively the personal level of appropriating history, is another fruitful approach. Jean-Luc Picard, to pick a prominent example, fancies himself an amateur archaeologist, and he is literally enamored with history as an explorer of the human—and alien—condition.[7] These passions occasionally even clash with his sense of duty and his responsibility for the well being of the crew (e.g., "Booby Trap"; "The Chase"; "Gambit, Part I")—unthinkable otherwise. Picard also repeatedly advises his "Number One" officer, William Riker, and the other senior staff to read and learn history in order to understand the 24th century. From this perspective, no matter if history is "good" or "bad" per se, the outcome of exploring the past turns up to be instructive—hence positive. History gives good examples and bad examples, and one can learn from both.

In "The Inner Light," one of the episodes with the highest critical acclaim, Picard lives half a life as humanoid on a distant planet, while, for the rest of the crew, this lifetime takes just twenty minutes. By setting up an invisible and inseparable connection, an alien probe controls Picard's mind; through this link, the captain experiences several decades of the end of the alien civilization annihilated by an ecological disaster. In that fictional, though for him very real, life, he has a family, raises children, makes friends, tries to save this already-dead world, and learns to play the flute. He lives a life so real that his existence as Starfleet officer almost vanishes from his mind, thinking it is a vision or fantasy. As it turns out, the probe was built by the extinct race itself, in order to tell others of their existence and culture. In fact, Picard's virtual life ends with the launch of that probe from the dying planet. When he comes back to his "real" world on the *Enterprise* after (in his experience) several decades, he has to cope with the fact that his experience of the "alien" life span was, in fact, just twenty minutes.

From this point onwards, Picard actually lives two life-spans—an aspect unfortunately never directly picked up again throughout the remainder of the show. As a matter of fact, we learn with this episode that the present and the personal experience of the 24th century are not only informed by the human, but also alien history. At this point Picard's personal history transcends the human experience, and the future past obtains a hybrid character that, in turn, also informs the 24th century's present. Indeed, in other episodes, such as "Lessons," Picard hints at his experience from the probe by practicing his flute.[8] Although the show does not reference "The Inner Light," long-time viewers recognize that the captain keeps this dead civilization alive—even if no one else on his ship can identify with this experience.

For Data, on the other hand, it is human history that plays an essential role in his ongoing quest for understanding mankind. Fittingly, and also because of his naiveté and innocence, Riker calls Data "Pinocchio" ("Encounter at Farpoint")—a reference to the wooden puppet from the famous and ingenious nineteenth century Italian novel who longed to become a real boy.[9] Data accepts people at face value just as he looks to the goodness of the human condition, and he does so especially in the human past. In order to understand humanity and to finally become, just as his fellow Pinocchio, "more human," Data regularly recreates aspects of human history using the holodeck, the ship's virtual reality center. In the holodeck, Data likes to recreate human fiction from the past, such as Arthur Conan Doyle's Sherlock Holmes universe (e.g., "Elementary, Dear Data"; "Ship in a Bottle"). Taking the role of Holmes, he is not only fascinated by Holmes's criminological methods, but by interacting with "bad" (or at least ambiguous) characters such as the fictional mastermind Professor Moriarty. Next to fictional characters, Data also recreates virtual alter egos of "real" historical figures such as Sigmund Freud, Stephen Hawking, Isaac Newton, and Albert Einstein, asking them for advice ("Phantasms"; "Descent, Part I"). As heroes who advanced human civilization, they are most certainly considered "good" actors on the historic stage. Whether "good," or "bad" or ambiguous, fictional or "real," Data uses the virtual human past to help him grow, to enable him to understand humanity, to become "more human."

Data is not the only character to use the holodeck to recreate a fictional future past. Even the captain engages in this behavior. Picard's favorite means of escapism on the holodeck is the world of private investigator Dixon Hill, a fictional gumshoe from the twentieth century. Hill is set in San Francisco's 1930s, and this time period of the Great Depression is portrayed as extremely crude and violent. For Picard, this backwardness and violence of the past seems to have a recreational quality; for him there even seems a melancholic aspect to the simplified plots of good and bad, black and white heroes. In the viewer's first encounter with Dixon Hill ("The Big Goodbye"), for example, Picard tries to involve other members of the crew into the exciting, seemingly harmless adventure: Dr. Crusher, Data, and a future twentieth century historian named Whalen join in. Something goes wrong with safety protocols of the holodeck, and the four get caught up in a fatal confrontation with the holodeck gangsters armed with weapons now deadly "real." Whalen almost dies when this fictional, dangerous, and savage past literally "backfires."

These examples show an ambiguity in the crew's personal experiences with the past. The past may appear as cruel, savage, or backwards; but cruelty and savagery obviously evoke a certain fascination for fantasy, even though for different reasons. History appears as less as a question of "good" or "bad," but as provider of personal *learning* experiences. Picard and Data may combat criminal masterminds and undesirable traits of greed and evil in the holodeck, but they do this as a form of "slumming." Once they leave the holodeck, they embrace the real, pristine environment of the Federation. The past, which helped to construct their present, primarily stays in the past.[10]

This sort of living history plays the decisive role in shaping the future. Recreations of fictional and "real" worlds from the future past facilitate personal growth as much as it is to have fun, as Troi, Worf, and Alexander do in the Wild West ("A Fistful of Datas"). However, history also contains a subversive critique of the future. Crewmembers who lack confidence or do not fit in, such as Reginald Barclay, use the holodeck as escapism. Barclay becomes a masculine hero—a fantasy that the rigid, uniform structures of Starfleet renders impossible for officers who lack Picard's leadership abilities ("Hollow Pursuits"). For Barclay (and possibly other crewmen), the anonymity and polished environment of the Federation may be too confining. The holodeck seduces them with opportunities to travel back into history, allowing Barclay to assert himself through the "barbaric" behavior that humans thought they left behind. The episode title suggests that Picard and company regard Barclay's pursuits as "hollow," but Barclay's addiction to the historical roleplay is an extension of their own fascination with Dixon Hill, Sherlock Holmes, and gunslinging cowboys. In addition to fantasies, we learn that in the 24th century, human history is increasingly intertwined with cybernetics and non-human experiences, underscoring the complexity of the future past from the crew's point of view. Most of all, history is the pivotal reference point for evolution, even beyond the human experience.

A Historian in the Future Past: Rasmussen

Actual historiography is part of a rather unusual episode, "A Matter of Time." The plot centers around a human time traveler named Rasmussen. He seemingly arrives from the 26th century in a futuristic spacecraft to witness the *Enterprise*'s current mission, where the crew must fix a planet's atmosphere or the entire population will die. According to Rasmussen, the captain is in the future's history books; he claims he cannot wait to witness the things to unfold in "real life," right in front of his eyes. The crew becomes increasingly excited about a future time traveler among them. In the course of the episode, however, Rasmussen turns out to be a thief from the past, not a scholar from the future. After different bits of technology disappear from the *Enterprise*, the crew becomes increasingly suspicious and they eventually learn that the future "historian" stole a time-travel pod in the 22nd century.

Rasmussen's lies show the limits of history as a tool in this future. Rasmussen gains the respect of almost the entire crew because of his venerated status as an explorer and a historian. Troi suspects Rasmussen is hiding something, but the crew generally believe him and his presence on this mission validates their efforts as humanitarians and explorers. Indeed, Picard, as an amateur archaeologist, believes Rasmussen is a kindred scholar. The captain actually violates the Prime Directive to ask Rasmussen for help when the mission starts to go wrong. The captain firmly believes in historical "truths," and as we have seen in the light of examples above, the past—as "good" or "bad" examples—has guided him straight in many of his previous missions.

When Rasmussen refuses to help (as a historian from the past, he certainly doesn't know the outcome), Picard's faith in history is challenged. Although the captain doesn't yet know the historian's true origins, Rasmussen makes a mockery of the show's concept of history. As a 22nd century historian, he has more in common with the thawed-out, flawed humans of the twentieth century from "The Neutral Zone," especially the desire for material gain. Indeed, Rasmussen's 22nd century origins may even predate the Federation.[11] The humans from "The Neutral Zone" prove useful when dealing with the wily Romulans, but here, Picard faces his own doubts and uncertainty. When the captain turns to Rasmussen for help, he tosses aside Starfleet regulations and also violates his own sense of history.

As a result, Picard must reclaim "history" as a means for personal growth and learning. He tells Rasmussen he will act on his gut instinct and justifies this decision by claiming he never plays it safe. While the episode "Tapestry" supports this assertion, in which Picard learns that taking risks contributed to his success as a captain, many previous episodes show the captain as a calm, rational officer, thus complicating his statement. In the end, Picard reinforces history's purpose by refusing to let Rasmussen return to the past; Picard violates the Prime Directive again, in a chronological sense, by keeping Rasmussen in the future. But he does so in order to restore the status of history as a tool for education and personal growth. Since Rasmussen perverts that ideology with the "antiquated" traits of avarice and material capitalism—with the gullible crew hanging on to his every word—Picard must revalidate history's purpose. He says the Federation's own historians (and amateur ones like himself) will benefit by learning about the past and Rasmussen will "learn" his lesson about trying to shape the future. In Picard's eyes, the purpose and meaning of historical inquiry is restored, even if the timeline now records a scholar who "disappeared" from the 22nd century. Showing the broad diversity of narratives in *TNG*, the show about historiography and a time-travelling historian show history's potential to disrupt the unfolding future in rather unexpected ways.

Conclusion

There is no doubt that the future past and the appropriation of history for the future present play decisive roles in *TNG*. History and its impact on the future's present are basic groundings of the show. As laid out in the pilot "Encounter at Farpoint," and partially concluded in "All Good Things…" seven years later, the crew's overarching mission is to prove that mankind has learned and progressed from its dark and gloomy past. As we have seen in the pilot, mankind is put on trial by the Q, which sets the stage for the next seven years; "All Good Things…" closes the narrative arc.

This time Picard travels through his past, present, and future to solve a mystery that threatens human existence; as it turns out, Picard himself is to blame for the near extinction of humanity, but he again manages to master the situation. It also appears as the final test by the Q. In the very same apocalyptic courtroom from seven years earlier, Q exonerates Picard. The Q Continuum agrees that Picard and his staff convincingly demonstrate that mankind, after all, has progressed. Taking even a glimpse into the vast possibilities of the future, humanity has proven worthy for the next stages of evolution to come. For the time being, the circle opened at the beginning of the show comes to a close as Q anticipates seeing Picard in future voyages. In this sense, the past in *TNG* introduces a better future; the future actually becomes a promised land of united humanity, freedom, and betterment for everyone. At the same time, space exploration, encounters with other species, and seemingly endless possibilities awaited humanity. This is at the very core of *TNG*: visions of a better future, grounded in the future past. This is its main appeal to audiences worldwide.

History as backdrop of a brighter and more advanced future, though, is not the whole story in *TNG*. As the examples show, the appropriations and "uses" of history have multiple functions, and the picture of a bright future that develops out of a savage past is only one of them. It is true that the future past is used as an ever-present threat to the high ideals the Federation stands for. Even though the Federation is at the threshold of an evolutionary process, which Q even acknowledges, the potential to backslide to a less civilized age remains. Thankfully, Picard and his crew *learn* from this very same, savage past. And they not only learn by simply using history as a negative counterpoint, they are fascinated by it and gain positive and helpful inspiration from even the "bad" parts of the human experience. History in *TNG*, "good" *or* "bad," turns out to be a crucial part in humanity's evolutionary progression. As we have seen, sometimes relics and characters from the past even seem superior in mastering the problems of the future; and sometimes the 24th century is not better than its past at all.

As stated in the beginning, the core questions of "classic" science fiction strongly link our present to the imagined future. The creators of *TNG* clearly intended the show to reflect societies in times of transition. The depictions of capitalism, for example, indicate an ideological quest during and after the disappearance of the Soviet Union and the end of the bipolar world around 1990. Despite the triumphant narratives heralding the "End of History" (Fukuyama xi–xxiii), with the U.S. "winning" the Cold War, the producers of *TNG* were obviously not convinced that capitalist democracies would be the final stage of human development. On the contrary, the "intermediate time" between the audience's and *TNG*'s present is construed as a long and stony path into a better future, ideologically embodied by the United Federation of Planets and its sublime principles. Thinking about *TNG*'s references to ecological disasters or the dangers of genetic engineering (amongst many other concerns in the 1990s), one can read *TNG*'s message as a warning to its then-present audiences. Still, the bright future of the 24th century evokes hope, and it provides audiences with role models, a paradigm to follow, even though, or exactly because, the imagined future is not always better than its past.

Notes

1. One might think of gender aspects ("The Outcast"), or the recurring references to smoking tobacco products, to name just two.

2. For a queer reading of Q, see Bruce E. Drushel's essay in this volume.

3. For a construction of Federation technocracy, see Justin Ream's and Alexander Lee's essay in this volume.

4. See Alex Burston-Chorowicz's essay in this volume.

5. On the applicability of the Prime Directive in this episode, see Larry A. Grant's essay in this volume.

6. On biopolitics and dis/ability, see Simon Ledder's, Jens Kolata's and Oonagh Hayes's essay in this volume.

7. Picard's esteem for history extends to Shakespeare; he keeps an antiquated hardbound book in his ready room.

8. On music, see Tom Zlabinger's essay in this volume.

9. On Data's (and artificial life's) relationship with Starfleet, see Olaf Meuther's essay in this volume.

10. Even Moriarty learns to appreciate the future in "Ship in a Bottle," where he leaves the nineteenth century behind to become an explorer.

11. The signing of the Federation Charter took place in 2161, as established in the series finale of *Enterprise*. This show also reinforces the idea of history as a means of human progression and moral development. Under Troi's urging, Riker uses the holodeck to revisit the past (the future past of Captain Jonathan Archer's *Starship Enterprise*) to reach a moral decision about whether to uphold Starfleet values when a superior officer subverts a signed treaty.

Works Cited

"All Good Things…." *Star Trek: The Next Generation—The Complete Seventh Season*. Writ. Ronald D. Moore and Brannon Braga. Dir. Winrich Kolbe. Paramount Home Video, 2002, DVD.

"The Big Goodbye." *Star Trek: The Next Generation—The Complete First Season*. Writ. Tracy Tormé. Dir. Joseph L. Scanlan. Paramount Home Video, 2002, DVD.

"Booby Trap." *Star Trek: The Next Generation—The Complete Third Season*. Writ. Michael Wagner & Ron Roman. Dir. Gabrielle Beaumont. Paramount Home Video, 2002, DVD.

"Captain's Holiday." *Star Trek: The Next Generation—The Complete Third Season*. Writ. Melinda M. Snodgrass. Dir. Winrich Kolbe. Paramount Home Video, 2002, DVD.

"The Chase." *Star Trek: The Next Generation—The Complete Sixth Season*. Writ. Ronald D. Moore and Joe Menosky. Dir. Jonathan Frakes. Paramount Home Video, 2002, DVD.

"Descent." *Star Trek: The Next Generation—The Complete Sixth Season*. Writ. Jeri Taylor. Dir. Alexander Singer. Paramount Home Video, 2002, DVD.

"Elementary, Dear Data." *Star Trek: The Next Generation—The Complete Second Season*. Writ. Brian Alan Lane. Dir. Rob Bowman. Paramount Home Video, 2002, DVD.

"Encounter at Farpoint." *Star Trek: The Next Generation—The Complete First Season*. Writ. D.C. Fontana and Gene Roddenberry. Dir. Corey Allen. Paramount Home Video, 2002, DVD.

"The Ensigns of Command." *Star Trek: The Next Generation—The Complete Third Season*. Writ. Melinda M. Snodgrass. Dir. Cliff Bole. Paramount Home Video, 2002, DVD.

"A Fistful of Datas." *Trek: The Next Generation—The Complete Sixth Season*. Writ. Robert Hewitt Wolfe and Brannon Braga. Dir. Patrick Stewart. Paramount Home Video, 2002, DVD.

Foner, Philip Sheldon. *Mark Twain: Social Critic*. New York: International Publishers, 1958. Print.

Fukuyama, Francis. *The End of History and the Last Man*. New York: Free Press, 1992. Print.

"Gambit, Part 1." *Star Trek: The Next Generation—The Complete Seventh Season*. Writ. Christopher Hatton and Naren Shankar. Dir. Peter Lauritson. Paramount Home Video, 2002, DVD.

"Hollow Pursuits." *Star Trek: The Next Generation—The Complete Third Season*. Writ. Sally Caves. Dir. Cliff Bole. Paramount Home Video, 2002, DVD.

"The Hunted." *Star Trek: The Next Generation—The Complete Third Season*. Writ. Robin Bernheim. Dir. Cliff Bole. Paramount Home Video, 2002, DVD.

"The Inner Light." *Star Trek: The Next Generation—The Complete Fifth Season*. Writ. Morgan Gendel. Dir. Peter Lauritson. Paramount Home Video, 2002, DVD.

"Journey's End." *Star Trek: The Next Generation—The Complete Seventh Season*. Writ. Ronald D. Moore. Dir. Corey Allen. Paramount Home Video, 2002, DVD.

"The Last Outpost." *Star Trek: The Next Generation—The Complete First Season*. Writ. Richard Krzemien. Dir. Richard Colla. Paramount Home Video, 2002, DVD.

"The Masterpiece Society." *Star Trek: The Next Generation—The Complete Fifth Season*. Writ. James Kahn and Adam Belanoff. Dir. Winrich Kolbe. Paramount Home Video, 2002, DVD.

"A Matter of Time." *Star Trek: The Next Generation—The Complete Fifth Season*. Writ. Rick Berman. Dir. Paul Lynch. Paramount Home Video, 2002, DVD.

"The Neutral Zone." *Star Trek: The Next Generation—The Complete First Season*. Writ. Deborah McIntyre and Mona Clee. Dir. James L. Conway. Paramount Home Video, 2002, DVD.

"Qpid." *Star Trek: The Next Generation—The Complete Fourth Season*. Writ. Randee Russell and Ira Steven Behr. Dir. Cliff Bole. Paramount Home Video, 2002, DVD.

"The Royale." *Star Trek: The Next Generation—The Complete Second Season*. Writ. Keith Mills. Dir. Cliff Bole. Paramount Home Video, 2002, DVD.

"Ship in a Bottle." *Star Trek: The Next Generation—The Complete Sixth Season*. Writ. René Echevarria. Dir. Alexander Singer. Paramount Home Video, 2002, DVD.

"These Are the Voyages…." *Star Trek: Enterprise—The Complete Fourth Season*. Writ. Rick Berman and Brannon Braga. Dir. Allan Kroeker. Paramount Home Video, 2005, DVD.

"Time's Arrow." *Star Trek: The Next Generation—The Complete Fifth Season*. Writ. Joe Menosky. Dir. Les Landau. Paramount Home Video, 2002, DVD.

"Time's Arrow, Part 2." *Star Trek: The Next Generation—The Complete Sixth Season*. Writ. Joe Menosky. Dir. Les Landau. Paramount Home Video, 2002, DVD.

"Unnatural Selection." *Star Trek: The Next Generation—The Complete Second Season*. Writ. John Mason and Mike Gray. Dir. Paul Lynch. Paramount Home Video, 2002, DVD.

"Up the Long Ladder." *Star Trek: The Next Generation—The Complete Second Season*. Writ. Melinda M. Snodgrass. Dir. Winrich Kolbe. Paramount Home Video, 2002, DVD.

"When the Bough Breaks." *Star Trek: The Next Generation—The Complete First Season*. Writ. Hannah Louise Shearer. Dir. Kim Manners. Paramount Home Video, 2002, DVD.

About the Contributors

Mehdi **Achouche** is an associate professor of American studies and English at Jean Moulin University, Lyon, France. His research focuses on representations of progress in popular culture in science fiction cinema and television, technological utopianism and transhumanism.

Alex **Burston-Chorowicz** completed his master's degree at the University of Melbourne and teaches history and political science at the University of Melbourne and RMIT University. His interests include 20th century political, economic and Jewish history. He has published on labor history and Australia/Israel relations, and lectured on post-war global history and late Soviet history.

Erin C. **Callahan** is a professor of English at San Jacinto College in Houston. She earned her Ph.D. in modern history and literature from Drew University. She researches identity construction focusing on gender and the intersection between popular culture and identity. Her next major project focuses on Don Robey and the history of blues music in Houston, Texas.

Bruce E. **Drushel** is an associate professor of media, journalism, and film at Miami University. He is the editor of *Fan Phenomenon* and coeditor of *Queer Identities/Political Realities, Ethics of Emerging Media* and *Sontag and the Camp Aesthetic*. He is the founding coeditor of *Queer Studies in Media & Popular Culture*. His work appears in several journals and anthologies.

Larry A. **Grant** earned degrees in European and U.S. history at the University of California, San Diego, and then served as a U.S. Navy officer for 23 years. He writes military history full time when not teaching or volunteering.

Oonagh **Hayes** studied history and romance philology at the Universities of Tübingen in Germany and Aix-en-Provence in France. Her research focuses on the 20th century, comparative history and the history of medicine.

Jens **Kolata** studied history and sociology at the Universities of Tübingen in Germany and Groningen, Netherlands. He is the scientific assistant of the Geschichtswerkstatt Tübingen (history association). His research interests include the history of medicine during National Socialism, eugenics in Germany, and National Socialist perpetrators.

Simon **Ledder** majored in media studies and sociology at the universities of Göttingen, Germany, and Sevilla, Spain, and later earned his Ph.D. His research interests include gender and dis/ability, biopolitics, and the sociology of technology. He specializes in popular culture, science fiction movies, television and digital games.

Alexander **Lee** is a practicing ADA building inspector, real estate broker, mortgage loan originator and programmer for web and mobile applications. He has worked in venture capitalism, avant-garde publishing, house flipping, eCommerce, and online/print marketing. His interests include the social justifications by which humans self-organize and determine what is acceptable reasoning.

Peter W. **Lee** is a doctoral candidate in the history and culture program at Drew University in New Jersey, focusing on American Cold War culture and youth culture. He is the editor of *A Galaxy Here and Now*. Other publications include articles in *Boyhood Studies* and *The Ages of the Justice League of America*.

Olaf **Meuther** studied history and philosophy at the Heinrich-Heine-University in Duesseldorf, Germany. He works in the IT department of a German insurance company and has looked after the parish archives in his pastoral area for 10 years.

Jared **Miracle** is an anthropologist and folklorist who specializes in the scholarly study of martial arts. His book *Now with Kung Fu Grip!* explores East Asian martial arts and Western culture over the course of the last century. He is also the world's leading Pokémon researcher and a sci-fi enthusiast.

Justin **Ream** works in technology with a specialization in computer networks and content workloads. In addition to his professional practice, he enjoys science fiction in its various media forms.

Alexander **Simmeth** earned his Ph.D. from the University of Hamburg in Germany. He is a cultural historian and a research associate at the European University Viadrina in Frankfurt (Oder), Germany. His interests are European and transatlantic history, intellectual history, and popular culture.

Joul **Smith** is a fellow researcher at the University of Texas at Arlington and has taught rhetoric and literature at various colleges and universities in Texas. His research interests include cultural analysis, early modern literature and American rhetoric, and religious studies.

Katharina **Thalmann** is an assistant professor of American studies at the University of Tübingen in Germany. She studied language and translation at the University of Mainz and earned an MA in American cultural studies from the University of Freiburg, also in Germany. She teaches and researches Cold War culture, conspiracy theory, and American popular culture.

Anh T. **Tran** is pursuing a Ph.D. in political science at the City University of New York (CUNY). Her published and forthcoming works include "Terror as State-Builder," "ISIS's Forbidden Fruit" and "Democracy Managed." She lectures at Baruch College and is a union leader in PSC Local 2334.

Tom **Zlabinger** earned his Ph.D. from the City University of New York (CUNY) and is an assistant professor of music at York College. He has written about music in *The Big Lebowski*, Neil Gaiman's *Sandman*, *The Simpsons*, and *Star Wars* as well as decolonization in jazz. Other research interests include the pedagogy of improvisation and the music industry.

Index

abortion 101
AIDS 152, 161, 203
"All Good Things…" 85, 150, 160–161, 176, 245–246
"Allegiance" 231
"American Century" 9
"Angel One" 95
Archer, Jonathan 208; *see also Star Trek: Enterprise*
"The Arsenal of Freedom" 201, 219
Artim 230; *see also Star Trek: Insurrection*
Aster, Jeremy 100; *see also* "The Bonding"
"Attached" 99

B-4 128, 230, 233; *see also Star Trek: Nemesis*
Bajorans 17, 82, 87, 226
"Balance of Terror" 47, 137
Barclay, Reginald 5, 244
Bates, Hannah 104; *see also* biopolitics; "The Masterpiece Society"
Bat'leth 214, 219–220
"The Battle" 33
Berman, Rick 18, 155, 161
"The Best of Both Worlds" 27, 65, 66, 67, 68, 118, 143
"The Big Goodbye" 244
biopolitics 91, 92, 97–99; and eugenics 101–105, 241–242; and the Federation 93–95, 108, 144, 168; and sexuality 99–101, 107; *see also* cloning; disability
"Birthright" 219
Black Panther Party 44, 50–52, 53; *see also* COunterINTELligence PROgram
"Bloodlines" 101
"Blue Skies" 230, 231, 233
"The Bonding" 2, 100, 207
"Booby Trap" 99, 242
Borg 3, 11, 27, 34, 37, 60 74, 118, 119, 126, 130, 144, 147, 157, 232–233; and assimilation 67–68, 81–82, 87; and matriarchy 124–125, 127; and multiculturalism 61, 63, 64–66, 69–70; *see also* Borg Queen; Locutus of Borg
Borg Queen 65, 66–67, 87, 119, 124–125, 126, 127, 131, 232; *see also* Borg; Locutus of Borg; *Star Trek: First Contact*
Brahams, Leah 176
Bringloidi 106–108; *see also* "Up the Long Ladder"
"Broken Bow" 208
"Brothers" 121–122, 228
Bush, George H.W. 13, 62, 100, 140, 144
Bush, George W. 55–56, 69
"The Cage" 135

capitalism 11, 13, 31, 43, 75–76, 80, 81, 86, 238–240, 245
"Captain's Holiday" 99, 238
Cardassian Union 2, 12–13, 17–20, 26, 81, 82, 84, 87, 140, 189, 226, 240–241
"Chain of Command" 36, 83, 120, 143, 144, 146, 174, 176, 189
Chapel, Christine 167
"Charlie X" 137
"The Chase" 102, 242
Chekov, Pavel 146, 237
"The Child" 101, 120, 182
Clarke, Arthur C. 30, 37
cloning 105–108
"Clues" 215
Cochrane, Zefram 27, 34, 74, 208, 224, 226; *see also Star Trek: First Contact*
"Code of Honor" 95, 171, 172, 173, 206, 221
COINTELPRO *see* COunterINTELligence PROgram
Cold War 1, 2, 4, 8, 9, 13–14, 43, 46, 54, 55, 237, 246; "cowboy" parallel 3, 20*n*1, 76, 80, 135, 137–138, 142, 147; *see also* COunterINTELligence PROgram; National Security Council 68
Communist Party-USA 44, 47, 49; *see also* COunterINTELligence PROgram
"Conspiracy" 120
COunterINTELligence PROgram 3, 43–44, 45, 47, 49–56; design 48; *see also* Black Panther Party; Federal Bureau of Investigation; New Left; Socialist Workers Party
Courage, Alexander 223

Crosby, Denise 198, 199, 200, 203, 205, 206, 207, 208; *see also* Yar, Tasha
Crusher, Beverly 4, 20, 65, 95, 97, 99, 100, 120, 126, 128, 142, 161, 162, 168, 177, 201, 202, 207, 217–218, 227, 244; as professional 174–175, 190, 199, 206, 207
Crusher, Jack 84, 100, 227
Crusher, Wesley 3, 4, 24, 25, 93, 100, 141, 142, 150, 156, 162, 201–202; and music 224, 226–228, 234; as Starfleet officer 83–84, 174, 227
Crystalline Entity 118, 122
Curry, Dan 214, 216, 217, 218–219; *see also* martial arts

Data 3, 4, 12, 14, 30, 37, 51, 64, 67, 68, 77, 105, 106, 128, 150, 157, 158, 161, 174, 193, 198, 200, 201, 205–206, 212, 217, 232, 239, 243, 244; and family 118, 121–122, 129, 162, 194, 228; and music 223, 224, 228–231, 234; and sentience/rights 120–121, 122–124, 155; *see also* Lal; Lore; Soong, Nonnian/Noonien
"Datalore" 121
"Data's Day" 36, 50, 100
"The Dauphin" 150, 162–163
"Déjà Q" 150, 157–158
de Lancie, John 155–156, 160; *see also* Q
de las Casas, Bartolomé 27–28
"Descent" 68–69, 82, 119, 125, 126, 127
"The Devil in the Dark" 121
disability studies 96–99, 104; *see also* biopolitics
"Disaster" 78
"Divergence" 56
Doctor (holographic) 130; *see also Star Trek: Voyager*
Dominion 47
Dougherty, Admiral 33; *see also Star Trek: Insurrection*
Drake, Frank 35
drug use 24, 32, 201–202; *see also* "Symbiosis"
Dukat, Gul 78
Duras, House of 13, 46, 52; *see also* Gowron, House of; Klingon

"The Drumhead" 2, 37, 50 78; *see also* Satie, Norah; Tarses, Simon

Ehman, Jerry R. 35
"Elementary, Dear Data" 228, 243
"Encounter at Farpoint" 7, 8, 27, 100, 142, 150, 155–156, 168, 173, 177, 183, 203, 228, 238, 241, 243, 245–246
"The Enemy" 91, 98
"The Enemy Within" 136
"Ensign Ro" 2, 11, 17
"The Ensigns of Command" 122, 228, 240
"Errand of Mercy" 10, 141
"Ethics" 97, 118, 128, 207
eugenics 1, 2, 91, 102–; *see also* biopolitics; disability; "The Masterpiece Society"; "Unnatural Selection"
"Evolution" 102
"Eye of the Beholder" 194

"Face of the Enemy" 44, 49; *see also* Tal Shiar
Fajo, Kivas 4, 150, 154, 163; *see also* homosexuality; "The Most Toys"; queerness
"Family" 143, 232
Federal Bureau of Investigation (FBI) 43, 44, 47, 48, 49, 51, 53–54; *see also* Black Panther Party; COunterINTELligence PROgram; New Left; Socialist Workers Party
Federation *see* United Federation of Planets
feminism 95, 120, 130, 199, 200, 202, 204, 221; and Borg 124–125; and television 134–136, 137, 143–145, 150–152, 199, 203, 204, 237; *see also* feminism
"Hollow Pursuit" 244
"Home Soil" 204
"Homeward" 36, 94
homosexuality 4, 94–95 99, 203; *see also* J'Naii; "The Outcast"; queerness; Soren
Horner, James 223
"The Host" 99
Hugh 3, 66, 119, 126, 127, 130, 131; *see also* Borg; "I, Borg"
"The Hunted" 2, 241

"I, Borg" 65, 66, 119
"I, Mudd" 124
"The Icarus Factor" 100, 214
"Imaginary Friend" 2, 100
information embargo 3, 29, 33–38; *see also* history; Prime Directive; United Federation of Planets
"Inheritance" 124, 229
"The Inner Light" 142, 143, 223, 232, 243
"Interface" 100, 194–195

Janeway, Kathryn 87, 131, 177, 207; *see also* Star Trek Voyager
J'Naii 94–95, 108, 150, 155, 163; *see also* homosexuality; "The Outcast"; queerness; Soren
"Journey's End" 19, 27, 84, 227, 240–241
"Justice" 24, 32, 141, 173

Kahless 105; *see also* cloning; Klingon Empire; "Rightful Heir"
K'Ehleyr 162
Kennedy, John F. 134, 135–136, 137, 138, 143
Kingsley, Sara 103
Kirk, James T. 2, 3, 10, 12, 61, 100, 126, 134–140, 199, 200, 201, 204, 207; as "Kirok" 138–140; and Picard, Jean-Luc 146–147, 169
Klingon Empire 7, 10, 12, 14, 50, 52, 60, 67, 77, 81, 87, 97–98, 105–106, 138; Klingon Civil War 15, 17, 46, 47; *see also* Duras, House of; Gowron, House of; martial arts; Worf
kung fu *see* martial arts

La Forge, Geordi 27, 33, 46, 67, 82, 91, 100, 108, 126, 127, 154, 172, 188, 194–195, 225, 230; and

VISOR 96–97, 98, 104–105, 118, 128
La Forge, Silva 194
Lal 3, 101, 123–124, 150, 162
Laren, Ro *see* Ro Laren
"The Last Outpost" 95, 171, 238
Lefler, Robin 163, 176
"Legacy" 200
"Lessons" 100, 143, 232, 243
Locutus of Borg 65, 66, 67–68, 82, 118, 125, 144; *see also* "The Best of Both Worlds"; Borg; Borg Queen; Picard, Jean Luc
Lore 68–69, 119, 122, 125, 126, 129, 131, 228; *see also* Data; Soong, Noonian/Noonien
"The Loss" 97, 190
"Loud as a Whisper" 98, 182
"Lower Decks" 93, 194, 217
Luce, Henry R. 9
Lutan 171, 172–173, 206

machine life 3, 124, 130; *see also* Data; "The Measure of a Man"
Madred, Gul 83; *see also* "Chain of Command"; Picard, Jean-Luc
"Man of the People" 99, 121, 194
Manhattan Project 36
Maquis 19, 20, 226; *see also* Cardassian Union; "Journey's End"
Mariposa 106–108, 122; *see also* "Up the Long Ladder"
martial arts 211–221; Asian 213, 215, 216, 218, 220–221; fans 219–220; and Klingon "mok'bara" 215, 216–217, 218
"The Masterpiece Society" 2, 92, 97, 98, 102, 103, 104, 108, 241–242
"A Matter of Honor" 35, 77–78, 79
"A Matter of Time" 5, 229, 238, 241, 244–245
Maxwell, Benjamin 225–226; *see also* "The Wounded"
McCoy, Leonard 136, 137, 174
McFadden, Gates 201; *see also* Crusher, Beverly
"The Measure of a Man" 2, 12, 121, 122–123; *see also* Data; machine life
"Ménage à Troi" 84, 227
"The Mind's Eye" 46
"The Minstrel Boy" 225–226; *see also* Maxwell, Benjamin; O'Brien, Miles; "The Wounded"
Moore, Ronald D. 223–224
Moorehead, Agnes 159–160; *see also* homosexuality
"The Most Toys" 150; *see also* Fajo, Kivas
Mozart, Amadeus 227; works 228, 229, 232
Muldar, Diana 208
multiculturalism 3, 69–71; history 61–64, 68; *see also* Borg
music 4, 217, 223–234

Naglium 77; *see also* "Where Silence Has Leased"

Hernandez, Macha 199–200, 202; *see also* Yar, Tasha
"Hero Worship" 101
"Hide and Q" 30, 85, 150, 156–157, 159, 173, 174, 203–204
Hill, Dixon 244–245; *see also* history; Picard, Jean-Luc
history 4, 13–14, 28–29, 75–76, 208, 237–246; and COINTELPRO 46–56; and martial arts 213–214; and multiculturalism 62–64; and television 134–136,

"Final Mission" 84, 93
"Fire and Ice" 161
"First Contact" 231–232
"Firstborn" 225
"A Fistful of Datas" 232, 244
"Future Imperfect" 101, 224
"future past" 4, 241–245, 246

"Gambit" 32, 36, 242
Garrett, Rachel 176; *see also* "Yesterday's Enterprise"
Gerrold, David 153, 161, 162
Goldsmith, Jerry 223
Gomez, Sonya 81–82, 176
Gorbachev, Mikhail 10, 13
Gowron, House of 47, 52; *see also* Duras, House of; Klingon Empire
Guinan 67, 118, 162, 176, 207

"Half a Life" 98
Hampton, Fred 52; *see also* Black Panther Party; COunterINTELligence PROgram
"Haven" 95, 100, 171, 204
"Heart of Glory" 67, 203

Ferengi 4, 26, 80–81, 87, 95, 140, 171–172, 224, 225, 238

"The Naked Now" 99, 172, 205–206; *see also* Troi, Deanna; Yar, Tasha
National Security Council Report 68 44, 45
Nazi Germany 17, 19, 36
Nechayev, Alynna 176
"The Neutral Zone" 2, 11, 14, 15, 31, 93, 95, 100, 238–239, 245
New Left 52–53; *see also* COunter-INTELligence PROgram
"The Next Phase" 225, 226
Nichols, Nichelle 198–199; *see also* Uhura
"Night Terrors" 97
Nimoy, Leonard 1, 16; *see also* Spock
NSC (National Security Council) 68

O'Brien, Keiko 95, 100, 163, 176, 225
O'Brien, Miles 78, 100, 163, 224, 225–226
Obsidian Order 47, 48; *see also* Cardassian Union
Odan 99; *see also* "The Host"
Odell, Brenna 106–107; *see also* "Up the Long Ladder"
"The Offspring" 101, 123, 150, 162
Ogawa, Alyssa 176
"11001001" 2, 94, 224
"Ooby Dooby" 226
"The Outcast" 2, 94–95, 109, 150, 155; *see also* homosexuality; queerness
"The Outrageous Okona" 182

Palestine 13, 18, 20
"The Paradise Syndrome" 10, 138
"The Pegasus" 15, 31–32, 37, 54
"The Perfect Mate" 93, 100, 231
"Phantasms" 93, 193, 243
Picard, Jean-Luc 2, 3, 4, 5, 23, 27, 30, 32, 34, 36, 50, 77, 78, 93, 97, 103, 105, 106, 107, 118, 119, 122, 123, 126, 131, 143, 162, 168, 173, 174, 181, 183, 185, 187, 199, 206, 212, 227, 228, 239, 242, 246; as "Action Picard" 145–147; and Cardassians 17–20, 83, 84, 189, 240–241; and father figure 83–84, 100, 101, 134, 142, 169, 204, 205; as historian 243–244, 245; and internationalism 7, 8, 11, 12, 14, 20, 64; and Kirk, James T. 76–77, 100, 134, 140–143, 143–144, 169; and music 223, 224, 230, 231–234; and Prime Directive 24–25, 32–33, 38, 98; and Q 82, 85–86, 156–158, 160–161, 177; and Romulans 15–17, 51; *see also* Borg Queen; Hill, Dixon; Locutus of Borg
Pine, Chris 2
"Pop Goes the Weasal" 228, 230
Posthumanism 128
"Power Play" 35
"Preemptive Strike" 19, 226

Pressman, Admiral 15–16, 31–32; *see also* "The Pegasus"
Prime Directive 1, 2, 3, 12, 18, 23–25, 32–33, 38, 75, 98, 141–142; and grand strategy 25–27, and history 27–29; and machine life 122, 126, 129, 130; *see also* information embargo; *Star Trek: Insurrection*
Pulaski, Katherine 95, 100, 103, 106–107, 205, 208

Q 3, 4, 5, 7, 27, 30, 81, 82, 84–87, 118, 126, 131, 140, 168–170, 173, 176–177, 181, 203–204, 237, 245–246; and queerness 150, 155–161, 163
"Q Who" 2, 5, 64, 81–82, 85, 94, 118, 131, 150, 157, 161
"QPid" 150, 158–159, 238
"The Quality of Life" 102
queerness 150–162; in media 150–152
Quinto, Zachary 153

Rakal, Major 49, 55; *see also* "Face of the Enemy"
Rand, Janice 141, 167
Rasmussen 5, 244–245; *see also* history; "A Matter of Time"
Reagan, Nancy 201, 202
Reagan, Ronald 4, 13, 16, 100, 140, 143, 201–202, 204
"Redemption" 15, 46
"Remember Me" 227
"Requiem for Methusaleh" 124
"Reunion" 214, 219
"Rightful Heir" 91, 105–106
Riker, Kyle 95, 214–215
Riker, Thomas 79; *see also* cloning; "Second Chances"
Riker, William 27, 30, 32, 35, 36, 77–78, 79, 85, 99, 100, 107, 108, 122, 141, 142, 143, 168, 169, 181, 185, 188, 194, 200, 201, 204, 212, 228, 230, 232, 242, 243; and music 217 223, 224–225, 226; and Q 155, 156–157, 158, 159, 161; and Riker, Kyle 214–215
Riva 98, 108, 182; *see also* biopolitics; "Loud as a Whisper"
Ro Laren 11, 18, 19–20, 95, 176, 207; and music 223, 224, 225–226
Roddenberry, Gene 1, 5, 7, 8, 35, 56, 70, 75, 76, 135, 137, 152, 153, 161, 162, 166, 168, 179, 180, 184, 185, 187, 188, 195, 198, 200, 204
Rogers, Amanda 159–160, 161, 174; *see also* "True Q"
Romulan Star Empire 2, 3, 12, 14–17, 20, 26, 32, 44 47, 54, 60, 80, 81, 98, 106, 138, 147, 207, 219, 230; *see also* Tal-Shiar
"The Royale" 240
Rozhenko, Alexander 81, 100, 219, 225, 244

Russell, Toby 97–98, 128; *see also* biopolitcs; "Ethics"
Rwandan genocide 18, 29

"Samaritan Snare" 188
"Sarek" 27, 145, 228
Satie, Norah 50, 78, 79; *see also* "The Drumhead"
"Schisms" 194
"The Schizoid Man" 120, 128
Scott, Montgomery 146
"Second Chances" 79, 105, 224
Section 31 56
Sela 45, 52, 55, 81, 207; *see also* Crosby, Denise; Tal-Shiar; Yar, Tasha
Seven of Nine 130, 207; *see also* *Star Trek: Voyager*
Shatner, William 1, 2, 223; *see also* Kirk, James T.
Shinzon 91, 95, 106; *see also* *Star Trek: Nemesis*
"Ship in a Bottle" 243
Sirtis, Marina 157, 180, 200, 204, 206; *see also* Troi, Deanna
Sisko, Benjamin 87; *see also* *Star Trek: Deep Space Nine*
Sito Jaxa 217; *see also* "Lower Decks"
"Skin of Evil" 173–174, 181, 198, 202
Socialist Workers Party 44, 47, 49–50, 53; *see also* COunterIN-TELligence PROgram
Soong, Noonian/Noonien 38, 120, 121–122, 124, 128, 228, 229, 233; *see also* Data; "Datalore"; Lore; Tainer, Juliana
Soran 147; *see also* *Star Trek: Nemesis*
Soren 94–95, 155; *see also* homosexuality; "The Outcast"; queerness
Species 8472 157; *see also* *Star Trek: Voyager*
"Spectre of the Gun" 137–138
Spock 1, 16, 43, 44, 51–52, 55, 76, 135, 136, 179, 198, 212, 228, 229, 234; *see also* "Unification"
Star Trek Beyond 153
Star Trek: Deep Space Nine 2, 5, 17, 19, 64, 67, 78, 83, 87, 153, 224, 225
Star Trek: Enterprise 2, 5, 56
Star Trek: First Contact 5, 27, 34, 65, 66–67, 74, 75, 82, 87, 93, 119, 147, 208, 226, 232, 241
Star Trek Generations 94, 100, 146–147, 207, 230, 231
Star Trek: Insurrection 5, 30, 32–33, 94, 128, 230, 232, 233
Star Trek: Nemesis 5, 91, 94, 106, 128, 147, 182, 208, 227, 228, 230, 231, 233–234
Star Trek: New Voyages 161
Star Trek: The Motion Picture 127
Star Trek (*The Original Series*) 1, 8, 16, 47, 60, 75, 94, 103, 173, 179, 212, 241; and Cold War 9–10, 76

Star Trek: Voyager 2, 4, 5, 19, 64, 67, 87, 125, 130, 157, 177, 207
Star Trek II: The Wrath of Khan 198
Star Trek III: The Search for Spock 199
Star Trek IV: The Voyage Home 1, 34, 121
Star Trek VI: The Undiscovered Country 10, 16, 121
"Starship Mine" 146, 212
Students for a Democratic Society 53
"Sub Rosa" 217–218
"Suddenly Human" 35, 101
Sulu, Hikaru 153
"The Survivors" 31, 183
"Symbiosis" 24, 201

Tainer, Juliana 124, 229; *see also* Data; "Inheritance"; Soong, Noonian/Noonien
Takei, George 152, 153
Tal Shiar 3, 14, 43, 44–45, 47, 48, 55; *see also* Romulan Star Empire; Sela; "Unification"; Vulcan
"Tapestry" 31, 85, 118, 142, 150
Tarses, Simon 50, 53, 56, 78
technostructure 3, 75; Borg 82; Cardassians 82–83; Federation 77–80; Ferengi 80–81; history 75–76; Klingons 81; Romulans 81, 83
"Thine Own Self" 224
The Thing from Another World 36
"Time's Arrow" 36, 93, 188, 239–240; *see also* Twain, Mark
Toleth, Captain 44, 49, 55
"Transfigurations" 102

Transhumanism 3, 119, 127–130
The Traveler 83–84, 227
Treaty of Algeron 15–16, 37; *see also* "The Pegasus"; Romulan Star Empire
Troi, Lwaxana 98, 171, 186, 204
Troi, Deanna 4, 27, 44, 49, 55, 64, 77, 95, 99, 100, 101, 105, 108, 118, 120, 121, 123, 143, 157, 158, 162, 168, 172, 177, 200, 217, 224, 230, 232, 239–240, 244, 245; and "American Epic" 187–189; and empathic psi 97, 98, 170, 182–183, 186, 190; as professional 170–171, 179, 190, 192–195, 206, 207; sexualization 181–182, 183–184, 190, 202, 204–205; "Troi Effect" 184–187
"True Q" 150, 159–160, 174; *see also* Rogers, Amanda
Truman, Harry 26, 45, 47, 48
Twain, Mark 93, 94, 188, 239–240; *see also* "Time's Arrow"

Uhura 199, 204, 237
"The Ultimate Computer" 126
"Unification" 14, 16, 31, 36, 51–52, 55, 76, 212, 224, 229, 230, 234
"Unimatrix Zero" 125
United Federation of Planets 93–96, 100, 102–105; and biopolitics 93–95, 108, 144, 168; and "federationism" 7, 10–12; and grand strategy 26–27; and multiculturalism 68; *see also* Prime Directive; Section 31
"Unnatural Selection" 91, 102, 103–104, 241
"Up the Long Ladder" 91, 94, 102, 105, 106–108, 122, 239

Vash 32, 158, 159, 162, 238
V'ger 127
"Violations" 120, 121, 182
Vulcan 11, 16, 32, 36, 45, 51, 55, 74, 82, 145, 226; *see also* Romulan Star Empire; "Unification"

War on Terror 55–56, 69, 147
Washington, George 134, 142, 147
"What Are Little Girls Made Of?" 124
"When the Bough Breaks" 100, 241
"Where No Man Has Gone Before" 137
"Where No One Has Gone Before" 83, 174, 176, 227
"Where Silence Has Leased" 77
"Who Watches the Watchers" 29, 36, 141–142
Wilson, Woodrow 12
Worf 7, 30, 35, 50, 53, 64, 67, 68, 77, 79, 95, 100, 101, 118, 155, 156, 158, 161, 162, 169, 174, 200, 204, 212, 244; and Klingon heritage 81, 97, 98, 105–106, 214, 216–217, 219; music 223, 224, 225, 226
"The Wounded" 33, 78, 95, 225–226

Yar, Tasha 4, 81, 95, 120, 121, 157, 162, 168, 169, 170, 177, 181, 198, 199, 221; as professional 171–174, 200–202, 207–208; sexualization 202, 203–206; *see also* Sela
Yareena 172, 206; *see also* "Code of Honor"; Lutan
"Yesterday's Enterprise" 207

Zubrin, Robert 35–36